MAN AGAINST THE SALT

Harvey Shapiro

MINERVA PRESS

LONDON

MONTREUX   LOS ANGELES   SYDNEY

MAN AGAINST THE SALT
Copyright © Harvey Shapiro 1997

All Rights Reserved

ISBN 1 85863 898 4

First Published 1997 by
MINERVA PRESS
195 Knightsbridge
London SW7 1RE

2nd Impression 1997

Printed and bound in Great Britain by
Antony Rowe Ltd, Chippenham, Wiltshire

MAN AGAINST THE SALT

In 1964, Betty Skelton drove Art Arfons' jet dragster, Cyclops, to a new women's land speed record. A year later, she and her husband produced a prize-winning documentary about the racing legend. The following is the dedication.

On this earth, there is a special breed of men...

Men who believe challenge is the greatest gift of life.

They measure life in terms of accomplishment, not years...

They know fear, yet are not afraid.

They welcome challenge with each new morning light...

They believe it is more important to even die, if one must,

Trying to meet the challenge of the unknown, the impossible

Than never to have tried at all.

From the award-winning documentary film

CHALLENGE

written, directed and produced by
Betty Skelton and Don Frankman,
Winner of the Silver Award of Excellence
New York International Film Festival, 1965.

In October 1990, *Man Against the Salt* author Harvey Shapiro, returned to Bonneville to see his old friend, Art Arfons, try for a fourth land speed record. While there, Shapiro was interviewed by film makers shooting a full-length documentary about Arfons. Shapiro subsequently wrote a song (words and music) for the film, and even did the vocals.

ARFONS AND HIS MONSTER

Words and Music by Harvey Shapiro
© 1991

There's this kinda quiet guy I know, might say he's even shy
He's got a warm and friendly smile and a twinkle in his eye

Looks like everybody's Grandpa, mild-mannered you might say
You'd never guess there's a demon that just won't go away

That demon is the lust for speed, a deadly sort of game
Riding on that ragged edge, a beast too tough to tame

Just hold your breath and go like hell, no time to say a prayer
He's cheated death, he knows not why, but he will not live in fear

Arfons and his Monster
Streaking down the salt
Three records in the sixties
Now he's poised for the assault

A last hurrah, he knows it
There's time enough to rest
Now Monster do your special thing
On this glorious, noble quest

He's strapped inside the cockpit, the missile poised for flight
Soon the engine shrieks at max, the old man's outta sight

A brilliant orange hall of fire trails the streaking jet
Each second seems a lifetime when you play this kind of bet

Arfons and his Monster
Streaking down the salt
Three records in the sixties
Now he's poised for the assault

A last hurrah, he knows it
There's time enough to rest
Now Monster do your special thing
On this glorious, noble quest

Acknowledgements

Words cannot adequately express a 'Thank You' to all those who have contributed to *Man Against The Salt*. My gratitude to Richard Noble, Craig Breedlove, Bob and Bill Summers, Al Teague, Don and Rick Vesco, Walt Arfons, Waldo Stakes, Pete Farnsworth, Roger Gustin, Bob Motz, Betty Skelton, Don 'Big Daddy' Garlits, Thomas Palm, Dick Keller.

H.A. 'Humpy' Wheeler (general manager, Charlotte Motor Speedway), Donald Davidson (historian, United States Auto Club), David Petrali (chief timer, USAC), Don Naman (executive director, International Motorsports Hall of Fame), Ron Watson (executive director, Motorsports Hall of Fame), Don Richetti (director, Automotive Hall of Fame), Bob Thomas Associates, George Long Photography, Indianapolis Motor Speedway, American Gas Association, Gregg Morgan (Bureau of Land Management), Southern California Timing Association.

Bob Russo, Ed Snyder, Tim, Ron and Dusty Arfons, June Arfons, Mrs. Lou (Arfons) Wolfe, Ken Squier, Alan Woll, Eric Duckleberger, Franklin Ratliff, Deke Houlgate.

Daily Express (London, England), *Indianapolis Star* (Indiana), *New York Times, Los Angeles Times, Tampa Tribune* (Florida), *Sebring News* (Florida), Dallas Public Library (Texas), *Salt Lake City Tribune* (Utah), *Miami Herald* (Florida).

Hot Rod, Sports Illustrated, Cars, Racecar, Mechanix Illustrated, Sport, Autoweek, Car & Driver, Popular Science, Motor Trend, National Motor Museum, Beaulieu, England.

My 'super amigo', Alberto White.

And most especially, Arthur Eugene Arfons. I'm glad I got to know ya.

If I've forgotten anyone, please forgive me.

About one week before he set his land speed record of 622.407 mph in October 1970, I called Gary Gabelich at his Wendover motel in Utah. He did not know me. I was then in the beginning stages of my first book, *Faster Than Sound*, man's quest of the world land speed record.

It was a very friendly phone interview. Gary predicted he'd set the record within a week and he was right. However, it wouldn't be until 1980 that we would finally meet face to face.

We kept in touch through the years. I sent him a copy of his chapter and he sent back corrections. I later sent him a copy of the completed manuscript, and likewise, he was quite helpful in pointing out factual mistakes.

We met at Michigan International Speedway. Gary was there to compete in a celebrity race. When we said goodbye, we hugged. It would be the first and final time I would see him. Gary 'Rocket Man' Gabelich was killed in a highway accident in January, 1984.

In the course of writing that first book, I also interviewed Tom Green and Dr. Nathan Ostich. They both left their own mark on land speed racing.

Green, driving Walt Arfons' jet-powered Wingfoot Express, set a record of 413 mph in 1964. The record lasted seventy-two hours, or until Art Arfons took the salt with his fire-breathing Green Monster.

Ostich, a Los Angeles baby doctor with a penchant for speed, was the first to introduce jet power to the sport. That was in 1960. However, Ostich failed to set a record in his Flying Caduceus.

Both men were very gracious. They too have since passed away.

Whenever Gary Gabelich would autograph a picture or sign a letter, he would inscribe this beautiful sentiment: "Have A Happy Forever."

Same to you Gary, Tom Green, Doc Ostich.

About the Author

For more than twenty years, Harvey Shapiro was a full-time, national award-winning journalist, primarily a sportswriter with a passion for motorsports in general and land speed racing in particular. He now freelances, as he puts it 'to keep my sanity', not only as a racing writer but as a songwriter as well. But that's another story.

He covered his first race in 1961, a champ car event on the one mile dirt oval at Springfield, Illinois. Rodger Ward beat the likes of A.J. Foyt, Parnelli Jones, Jim Hurtubise.

He covered his first of 12 Indianapolis 500s in 1965. The late Jimmy Clark of Scotland, driving a revolutionary rear-engine machine, won in record time.

During a distinguished career in newspapers, wire service and his own national award-winning monthly motorsports tabloid, *World of Speed*, Shapiro covered virtually the full gamut of motorized competition, from drag boats and unlimited hydroplanes, to Can-Am sports cars, drags, motorcycles, etc.

He met the Arfons Brothers in 1964 as a sportswriter in Akron, Ohio. He was at Bonneville in November 1966 when Art Arfons miraculously survived his 610 mph crash. Twenty-four years later, Shapiro returned to Utah to see his old friend try again in Green Monster No. 27.

His first book, *Faster Than Sound*, was published in 1975, both in the United States and England. It chronicled man's quest for the land speed record. *Man Against The Salt* is Shapiro's fourth book. His book about the legendary sprint car driver, Jan Opperman, was published in August 1996. Opperman was paralyzed in a crash in 1981.

Shapiro and his wife, Eileen, live in Springfield, New Jersey.

Foreword

by Art Arfons

It's a strange thing about Bonneville, something I'll never understand. When I'm there, I can't wait to get the hell out and go home. But as soon as I get home, I can't wait to go back.

The feeling is always the same, in 1960, 1962, 1964, 1965, 1966, 1989, 1990 and 1991. Maybe it's the setting. It's an unforgettable place, with the salt, the mountains, the long black line.

Funny, despite my crashes there, I never considered Bonneville as my enemy, as a place I feared. To me it was kinda like 'Man Against The Salt'. To me it's always been the ultimate challenge. This tiny, delicate creature known as Man and his tiny machine in this vast, eerie environment.

When I started out on my land speed adventure in 1960, it never dawned on me that I'd become a part of its history, someone that people would read about and hopefully admire.

It's as you get older and can't quite wrestle the bear like you once could that you come to realize you're a part of this never-ending story. I'm glad to have played my small part in that story.

ART ARFONS

Foreword

by Richard Noble

Hold the World's Land Speed Record for even twenty-four hours and you have joined an elite band of thirty-five drivers who have at one time or another driven faster than anyone else in the world. Interestingly, they have only been British, American, French or Belgian – and as far as I can tell only four of us are alive today.

Like flying a fighter aircraft, it is totally addictive and I can still remember every second of my best LSR run, driving in relaxed style, holding the wheel between fingers and thumbs.

The speedo read 650 mph and the airflow over most of the car was supersonic – we had difficulties with the supersonic airflow under the car, the engine JPT was reading 1100°C, which meant we were overcooking the engine by 250°C whilst the big turbines were running at over 8000 rpm alongside my left elbow.

Above 550 mph, the engine seemed to come on song, with a tremendous roar, and from the cockpit, I could see the condensation trails caused by the pressure changes across the shock waves.

On a cold morning run, this took the form of a very fierce fog, caused by the shock waves standing on the wheel arches. The Black Rock Desert course marker flags appeared to be on a conveyor – popping up over the horizon two miles away and then flashing past. Although they were six feet square, I could never read them!

There's no doubt it was a high risk experience; the Avon engine could have destructed at any time under this kind of treatment and the car was within 7 mph of an involuntary take-off.

There was a time when a good circuit car could hold the Land Speed Record – but it was a long time ago, for the circuit car speed has been limited by rules in order to increase safety and reduce capital cost. The Land Speed Record by contrast is unlimited and here we can have sensible cars with 30,000 or more horsepower.

Whilst it was a tremendous experience in teamwork and driving, it's also important to understand that in this half world of low-risk, manufactured film and television effects – it was real! The risk is extreme, the measurements in time and distance are definitive and many drivers have been killed.

As you will see from *Man Against The Salt*, most of the successful drivers want to repeat the experience; it's difficult to come to terms with the fact that the pinnacle of your life's achievement may have just passed and from now on it's downhill all the way!

So, we all want to get back, particularly Art Arfons, whom I was lucky enough to meet at Bonneville in 1990. I will be proud indeed if I am still driving on the salt at sixty-four, as he was in 1990.

I also had the privilege to meet Harvey Shapiro at Bonneville during that three day holiday. We had corresponded since 1981, and it was indeed nice to meet this well-respected land speed historian.

Harvey's chief forte is as a 'people person', not as a technical expert, and for more than two decades he has had the privilege of knowing and studying Art Arfons, as you Americans say, 'Up Close And Personal'.

Faster Than Sound was his first book, published back in 1975. This latest effort not only zeroes in on the life and times of one of our sport's legendary figures, but covers Land Speed Racing from just about every conceivable angle.

The real heroes in all this are Art Arfons, Craig Breedlove and George Eyston, who not only designed, built and financed their cars, but drove them to new world record speeds. After them come the greatest drivers – Gabelich, Cobb, Campbell, Segrave, who set milestone records.

RICHARD NOBLE, OBE
Holder World Land Speed Record 633.468 mph, 1983

Contents

Introduction

Way back in the spring of 1964, as the story goes, a young reporter was given a routine assignment.

"Go to Pickle Road and talk to Walt Arfons," said the sports editor. "Here's his phone number."

So I called Arfons, chatting for a few minutes, and with instructions, headed off to Pickle Road. I was then a seven year news veteran on dailies in Colorado and Illinois before joining the *Akron Beacon Journal* (Ohio). A salary increase of $31 per week to $136 to start, was big stuff way back then.

Arfons, then in his early fifties, was friendly, personable. He had built a jet car, Wingfoot Express, which failed in its 1963 attempt to break the world land speed record. But 1964 would be different, he vowed.

I had never seen a land speed car until then. What guy born in Brooklyn and raised on the Brooklyn Dodgers, New York Giants, New York Yankees, had ever heard of land speed racing? Back in 1961, I covered my first auto race at the Illinois State Fairgrounds in Springfield, a one mile dirt layout. That was exciting. Rodger Ward, A.J. Foyt, Parnelli Jones. Legends in their time.

Starting in 1965, I would cover my first of twelve Indianapolis 500s; later I published my own monthly motorsports tabloid, *World of Speed*.

After the interview, I returned to my office and wrote the seemingly routine story. A day later, I received a phone call at work. The man identified himself as Art Arfons.

"I'd like to clear up a few things in your story," he said.

So, I returned to Pickle Road. The Arfons Brothers had workshops about one hundred yards apart.

Art was the youngest of three brothers. Walt was ten years older. Once partners in building drag cars, they were now rivals. We headed to Art's office. Pictures adorned the paneled walls. Trophies of all sizes filled one portion of the room.

It was a cordial meeting. All Arfons wanted to do was correct a few errors that had appeared in the story.

"As long as you're here," he said, "why don't you look at my baby?"

We walked from the office to that adjacent work area. Taking up almost all the space was Arfons' 17,500 horsepower Green Monster, still in the building stage.

Dual cockpits, that massive J–79 engine, the tail fin. An awesome-looking sight, even in the raw, unpainted stage.

"What's the speed potential?" I asked.

"The way she looks now, conservatively, about five hundred," said Arfons. "But with the changes I have in mind, I'd say six hundred to six hundred and fifty."

The land speed record at the time was 407 mph, set in 1963 by Californian Craig Breedlove in his three-wheeled, jet-propelled Spirit of America.

From that point, I was hooked. I made regular trips to Pickle Road, to capture in words and photos the birth of a land speed car. I was there when Art Arfons chained his Green Monster between two trees, squeezed into the cockpit and unleashed the fiery afterburner. The whine was ear-piercing.

Two years and three land speed records later, I was at the Bonneville Salt Flats when Art's 'baby' made its final ride, a 610 mph horror trip that should have ended in death. While the car was destroyed, Art suffered only cuts and bruises. Not one broken bone. The next day he flew home, thinking of a faster Green Monster.

We all thought that Art would get the record that day (Thursday, November 17, 1966). Nothing had gone right the previous three days. It was a fantastic blast-off. He hit burner and that huge orange flame fired out the back end. When Art started, Jim (Firestone racing PR and Jim Cook) gunned his rental car down the salt.

I was seated in the back left side, my two hands holding an 8 mm camera out of the rolled-down window. It took only a few moments for Jim Cook to realize something was wrong. I guess it was the dust, the salt on the horizon. He pushed the car to about 110 mph.

About a half-mile before we came to the car, the Monster's nose cone was lying there by itself. It was an eerie, sickening kind of feeling. Huge chunks had been ripped out of the salt. We know the car hit at least twice, the wheels flying off, then it rolled for quite a distance before coming to rest.

I was the first newsman on the scene. The rescue workers were just pulling Art out of the battered left-side cockpit. His face was covered with blood. His hands were covering his face. I thought he was dead.

Within a matter of minutes, a private plane flew Arfons to a Salt Lake City hospital, some 125 miles away. I remained at the Flats until an engineer from Firestone (Art's main sponsor) told me that the company had chartered a Cessna that would take me to Salt Lake City.

Veteran ambulance driver, Ted Gillette, told me Arfons would be okay. By then the charter pilot had picked me up, and we drove eleven miles to my motel where I hastily checked out.

In a short time we were airborne. The trip to Salt Lake City seemed an eternity, hitting speeds of 125 miles an hour at a height of 7000 feet. Flying over the seemingly endless Great Salt Lake was spectacular.

From the airport, I took a taxi to the hospital and a short while later spoke with Art's doctor. I told him I was a friend and the doctor said I could visit him that evening.

I checked into a nearby hotel, called my newspaper and started writing the crash story on a yellow pad by longhand. That night I visited Art Arfons. He was under sedation. His face was swollen and discolored. But he hadn't lost his sense of humor.

"I hear you got lost."

Starting in 1964, I had given Art my two dollar bill for good luck.

"Guess my two dollar bill didn't bring you much luck," I said.

Art tried to crack a smile. "You gotta be kiddin'. I'm still here, ain't I?"

We chatted for a few minutes.

"If you want to keep the bill, it's yours."

"No," replied Arfons. "When we get back to Akron, I'll give it to you back."

He did.

Walt Arfons had flown to Salt Lake City from Akron when he heard about the crash. When the doctor said that Art would be flying home the next day, I tried to book a return on the same flight. All booked.

"Let me take you to the airport," said Walt, "and maybe you can get out tonight."

I accepted the offer. We talked on the way. Walt Arfons hoped his younger brother would quit the chase, but he knew better.

I was able to book a flight to Cleveland, with a change of planes in Denver. Once airborne, I put my attaché case on my lap and continued to write the story. Between flights in Denver I called the newspaper office and dictated what I could.

The continuation flight landed at Hopkins Airport in Cleveland at 5 a.m. I rented a car and drove directly to the *Akron Beacon Journal* and finished the story. It was 7 o'clock. I had been up for some twenty-seven hours.

Considering the circumstances, it's probably the best news story I've written. For the record, I won about two dozen state and national writing awards in a career than spanned more than twenty years.

The next day, I headed back to Pickle Road, talked a while with Art about the crash, his plans. A man of his word, he returned my 'lucky' two dollar bill, which I still keep in my wallet.

A week or so later, Art Arfons was floating his 'Green Submarine', as his wife dubbed it, on a chemical pond at a Firestone plant. It was actually his 8,000 horsepower jet dragster, Cyclops, fitted with two pontoons filled with Styrofoam.

He had converted the car into a hybrid jet boat in quest of Donald Campbell's world water speed record. A jet boat with four Firestone tires. His strategy was simple. When the boat hit speeds of 80–100 mph, the front end would lift and the boat would ride comfortably on the tires.

But when Campbell was killed, Arfons abandoned his quest. However, he did take the 'Green Submarine' out on a small Akron lake and reached speeds of 20–30 miles an hour. The 'boat' handled flawlessly.

Between 1964 and 1965, the land speed record was increased by almost 200 miles an hour. Breedlove and Arfons set records during that short span. And even when I left Akron in the Fall of 1967, I kept in touch with Arfons. In the winter of 1969, while Ohio UPI Sports Editor, I began work on my first book, *Faster Than Sound*, man's quest of the land speed record. Despite completion of the book, followed by a complete re-write, the book was not published until the summer of 1975. By then, Californian Gary Gabelich and his rocket-powered Blue Flame had held the record (622.407) for almost five years.

Art Arfons had turned to tractor pulling in the 1970s, but his heart still belonged in the cockpit of a jet-powered Green Monster. In 1988, my freelance article detailing Arfons' 1800 pound two-wheeler appeared in *Hot Bike* magazine.

Two years later, in October 1990, I flew from New York to Bonneville to once again see an old friend attempt to defy Father Time. After a 350 mph crash in 1989, Arfons had converted the Monster to a four-wheeler. He was sixty-four years old! No one his age had ever attempted to set a land speed record. He is still trying at the age of seventy-one!

This is the story of an American treasure.

Designer/Builder/Driver/Dreamer.

Chapter One
The Fire Still Burns

The fire within! A drive, a passion, an obsession that cannot be exorcised. Not by a 610 mile an hour crash in 1966... Not by a life-saving triple bypass operation more than a decade ago... Not by the relentless march of 'Father Time'.

At the age of seventy-one, Art Arfons still yearns for one more ride in the fast lane. One more burst of adrenaline surging through his body. One more land speed record.

A perfect and most fitting way to finally bring to a close a storybook career that began innocently enough on a Sunday afternoon in the early 1950s, amidst the roar of engines at a local drag strip.

By no means a wealthy man, no longer a saleable commodity, Arfons put his money into his 'dream machine', despite the protests of his family, of friends.

He poured $100,000 of his own money into a six year project, Green Monster No. 27, a 650 mile an hour missile weighing less than 2000 pounds.

No logical reason to spend all that money; there would certainly be little or no financial return from this investment.

The hell with logic! Not for this man. The ultimate pay-off – a fourth land speed record – would be worth all the blood, sweat and tears.

Sometimes dreams and past history just aren't enough. He failed in his attempts in 1989, 1990 and 1991. He tried to return to his beloved Bonneville Salt Flats in 1994, 1995 and 1996, but poor weather and other factors beyond his control kayoed Art Arfons.

He had hoped to sneak in 'under cover of darkness', so to speak, push his car to the limit, knowing it would only be a matter of time until more powerful machines would take center stage and push the record far beyond his reach.

As long as there was a window of opportunity he would seek the record (Arfons would have to average 640 miles an hour), even if it would fall within an hour, a day, a week. That would not really matter.

His last opportunity for the 1996 season would be the World Finals in October. Art Arfons was ready, his car was packed in its trailer for the cross-country trip. But the meet was canceled due to a lack of entries.

Arthur Eugene Arfons was bitterly disappointed.

Now all he could do was watch helplessly.

The awesome shadows of bigger and better loomed even more ominously:

– Craig Breedlove's 48,000 horsepower Spirit of America – Sonic Arrow.

– Richard Noble's awesome 106,000 horsepower Thrust SSC.

Breedlove and Arfons had started the most exciting jet duel in land speed history, a titanic battle between the Californian hot rodder and the legendary Ohio drag racer. During that heart-pounding two year period (1964–65), the record had soared from 407 to 600 miles an hour.

But at fifty-nine (he would be sixty in March 1997), Craig Breedlove still sought a sixth speed record in a car he designed, a five-wheeler with 850 mile an hour potential.

"It's an extension of my personality," he said proudly. "It's a synergy between a machine and a man. You know the car better than you know your wife or girlfriend. I love this machine because it's very beautiful. I'm infatuated with it. I'm in the part of the relationship where I'm in lust."

By September 1996 Breedlove's machine appeared at Bonneville for three days of testing. What he hoped was that the long deteriorating conditions would not prevent him from setting the record in Utah. After all, his five records were set there. Bonneville held a special place in Breedlove's heart.

It had been more than thirty years since Craig Breedlove had squeezed himself into the cockpit. But once you've traveled in that fast lane you just don't forget.

Despite a pencil-thin crust, Breedlove clocked an easy 400 plus during a shakedown run. But it was apparent he had to shift to Plan B

– move the operation to Black Rock Desert in Nevada, some seventy miles from Reno.

Noble had tried unsuccessfully to set a speed record at Bonneville (1981–82) in his jet-powered Thrust 2. The salt did not suit his big car with its metal wheels, so Noble moved to Black Rock in 1983.

The rest is history. The softer surface was perfect. The gritty Englishman finally fulfilled his nine year quest, averaging 633.4 mph. He was the fastest man on wheels.

Overcoming the resistance of environmentalists, as was the case with Noble a decade previous, Breedlove clocked an effortless 448 on Wednesday. The car was stable. No afterburner, no drag chutes. Just an application of brakes to halt the four ton beast.

Breedlove was pleased. "It was a good run. Just about right."

Rain, however, would curtail any further speed activity until Sunday, October 27. Breedlove averaged 563 miles an hour, completing the required two runs – in opposite directions – through the measured mile.

The stage was set for Monday, October 28, 1996!

Winter closes in quickly in Nevada. A sudden cloudburst can easily turn Black Rock Desert into a lake. It was clearly a race against 'Mother Nature'.

Breedlove clocked a 'warm-up' run of 475. All systems were 'GO'!

With a crowd of four to five hundred on hand, it was time to get down to business. But conditions were far from ideal. He would be running into a strong headwind.

Spirit of America accelerated across four miles of desert. So far so good. Breedlove hit afterburner. As the car reached the six mile marker, all hell broke loose.

At an estimated 675 miles an hour, Breedlove was in jeopardy – another life-and-death runaway ride.

By the time this 'cool cat' would safely bring the forty-four foot long car under control, some two miles off course, Spirit would make two ninety-degree turns and barely miss smashing into a parked camper.

Craig Breedlove was not hurt, but the car suffered damage to a rear right wheel and part of its aluminum skin. It would end his 1996 record bid.

His original 'battle plan' was to shatter Noble's record in 1996, push his car to about 700 miles an hour, then shoot for the sound barrier in 1997.

But that plan could be subject to change, depending on the performance of his 'dream machine'.

Now all he could do was keep abreast of developments taking place thousands of miles away, at Al Jafr Desert in Jordan.

The British Are Coming! The British Are Coming!

Craig Breedlove must have felt like a salmon trying to swim upstream. Every step of the way resulted in resistance. It did not go 'according to Hoyle'.

His biggest setback however did not come on the desert. It came in the courts... and resulted in a six week delay in first testing and then finally running Spirit of America – Sonic Arrow.

Back in 1983, Richard Noble faced strong resistance from the Sierra Club, an environmental power group. Running his massive jet would hurt the environment, they claimed.

Finally, Noble prevailed and set a land speed record that has survived for thirteen years.

Craig Breedlove faced the same opposition in 1996.

In his words:

"Certainly, the biggest problem that happened to us was this environmental coalition filing a complaint against our permit, which began a pre-determined process where our permit has to go before a board of Land Appeals at Arlington, Virginia. It's a very lengthy process.

"I think it became apparent to me that this was intentional on their part. For whatever their political agenda is they wanted to prevent us from running.

"They had a ten page complaint that was totally unfounded in its facts. For instance, they said my car would create a seismic disturbance. That's utter nonsense.

"When I requested a face-to-face meeting so that I could alleviate their fears or objections they refused to meet with me.

"They were really after the BLM (Bureau of Land Management). They believe BLM doesn't run Black Rock properly. They had a whole laundry list about the things they didn't like. They said that was their agenda.

"They said as a permittee I had the right to run anyway. Of course, I talked to the BLM and the BLM said, 'That's not correct'. The BLM had issued us a permit to run, but while the objection was still pending we would have been cited for going out there. Then we would have been in trouble. The environmentalists lied to us. They were very, very unethical.

"I'm talking about a gal in Reno named Susan Lynn, who is sort of an environmental activist for the Black Rock area. She got the Sierra Club and another group for the Preservation of the Lassen Trail. They formed the High Point Black Rock coalition. And for a thirty-two cent stamp and a ten page letter they put a halt to a multi-million dollar project.

"Because of all the legal stuff we were stuck. We couldn't get to Black Rock. We had to present our appeal to Judge Harris and the Bureau of Land Appeals, appealing for him to give us preferential treatment for an expedited ruling, because he had 1200 other cases on his calendar that were ahead of us."

A positive thinker, Craig Breedlove was optimistic that the judge would expedite the matter. In the meantime, plans were changed and the team headed for the Bonneville Salt Flats for early testing.

"We had to go to Bonneville," says Breedlove. "We had no choice. But Bonneville was extremely problematic. The salt condition was poor. It packed into our wheel-well openings.

"We destroyed our data acquisition system on the very first rolling test. We damaged the vehicle every run we made there."

Judge Harris ruled in Breedlove's favor.

"The BLM said that we had prepared such an excellent letter to the judge, and that was the key to getting our appeal expedited."

The team could not lay down a black oil line at Black Rock. It would be environmentally damaging.

"We had to invent a way to mark the desert," points out the five-time speed king. "We had to survey and lay a track out there. It's not like going to Bonneville where everything is laid out for you.

"We had to go through the whole thing, and it's not salt. We had to make the dozen to two dozen lanes fifteen miles in length in such a way that it was environmentally sound. We had to come up with biodegradable markings that would not make a permanent mark out there.

"We ended up using a carbon compound that was suspended in water. It was like a black dye. We used a spraying machine similar to what they mark highways with. It's not only a time-consuming process, but it's awfully expensive."

Craig Breedlove had been leery about running at Black Rock. But he found his fears unfounded.

"For one thing we had fifteen miles. It was relatively smooth and pretty consistent in hardness. I liked it. For another thing the townspeople at nearby Gerlach were very supportive, cooperative and friendly."

Craig Breedlove made a total of seven runs at Bonneville (three) and Black Rock (four). Certainly not enough time spent in the cockpit to really learn about his latest toy. That added up to three minutes 'on the job'.

What should have been a gradual build-up in speed as per usual for this very meticulous man, turned out to be a race against the weather.

"Everything was really problematic," he points out. "The fact of the weather closing in and a limited time to get the record were against us from the start.

"I had promised Shell I would take the car to a marketing meeting in Las Vegas. That was an important event for them. But because of the long delay in getting out to Black Rock they agreed on the mock-up instead. Certainly, it would have been a nice gift for them to have the record. It didn't work out that way.

"I thought we were home free. I thought we'd have the record in plenty of time for the show. I didn't count on the environmentalists filing their protest and dragging it out for weeks. They waited until the last minute to file it. It was right before we were scheduled to go out there. They knew every trick in the book.

"But running on the desert that late in the season is very iffy. The sun could be shining one minute and a few minutes later you're hit with a storm. We had several such episodes and had to shut down activity for a few days."

A series of problems continued to plague Breedlove on his last day – Monday, October 28 – at Black Rock. It somehow seemed a fitting climax.

"If we could have had the car ready very early in the morning we would have had time to get the record.

"The night before we literally had a hurricane-force storm out there and it blew away our awning or canopy where the guys worked on the car. It literally destroyed a $25,000 awning and did some damage to the car.

"They tried to hold it down but the storm just blew the whole thing away. They stayed up all night long to work on a problem we had with the parachute.

"The parachute canopy was very unstable with the amount of ribbon density that there was. The guys stayed up all night to get the car ready. They were cutting every other ribbon out of the parachute with scissors.

"That was an all-night deal. It's quite a lengthy process.

"By 7:30 in the morning the chutes weren't ready. Then our tow dolly, that we pull the car out to the starting line with, the winch cable broke on that. We had to jerryrig that. It was just a series of things.

"They worked all night in that sub-zero weather. It was very, very difficult work. To try to work under these conditions, especially to work on a very precision piece of machinery designed to go that fast, is difficult and it just caused us a lot of problems.

"You're out in the elements. You're freezing cold. The wind's blowing. There's dust and dirt all over the place. It's a very adverse situation to do what you need to do.

"It was really nice by 7:30. By the time we got out to run the course it was like eleven o'clock. We made a run (470 mph). We tested the parachutes and the chutes worked fine.

"But by the time we got the car turned around they had a problem with the timing lights. That was about a thirty minute delay. When we fired the engine I had a compressor-shake. I had to shut it down and restart it.

"By then it was getting late. The weather was starting to move in on us again. We had only a small window of opportunity.

"When I was initially ready to run I was given a wind reading of 1.5 knots headwind at the far end of the course which is very acceptable. As I was sitting in the car while they were working on the timing it was becoming very dark and overcast. The wind was starting to pick up.

"When I talked to Charlie Liefer in the airplane he reported that the wind was one–five. That was my mistake. I interpreted it as 1.5 because I had had the previous report of 1.5 knots. When he said,

'1–5', my mind just said, 'Okay, great'. Had I realized I would be running into a headwind of fifteen knots I certainly would have aborted the run.

"And even if I had made the final run without any problem I would not have run back because of the wind. A record would not have been possible. The only thing that would have been possible was to get in one run.

"One of the problems that happens at Black Rock is that the dirt is a sort of dark tan color. We used black marking lines which when the sun is out the desert reflects light from the tan part and then the black lines don't reflect light. So, you have a very adequate contrasting course to run by.

"However, it began to get very dark and the desert no longer reflects. It's difficult to see the first line. That was problematic in the sense that I couldn't see the course well because it was getting dark."

With fifteen miles of running room Craig Breedlove decided on a four mile approach entering the measured mile. That, in hindsight, he says, was a mistake.

"We used a four mile approach to the mile. It was five miles under power. At the end of the first mile I realized we had way too long an approach distance. The car had gone from zero to five hundred miles an hour in the first mile. At that rate it was going to be an eight hundred mile an hour run.

"I had to back off, take it out of burner, then cruise along for a while, and then light burner again. Then it was building up too much speed. I had to pull back again, cruise along and hit burner again.

"As I entered the measured mile I was going 677 miles an hour. Just as I went into the first timing trap all hell broke loose. My first reaction was, 'Oh, shit'."

Fortunately, Craig Breedlove was finally to bring the car under control. He had made the fastest U-turn in land speed history. This cat does indeed have nine lives!

Back at his Rio Vista workshop (California), Breedlove still isn't sure what turned Spirit of America every which way but loose.

The 677 peak was set with only first-stage burner. The J–79 is equipped with a four-stage afterburner.

"This is a fast car. It hasn't any problem going fast. It's basically a thousand mile an hour car. I can show you the tapes that will show you.

"The acceleration is going straight up. There's no break-off in the speed acceleration at all. At 670 it's accelerating just as hard as it was at 100 miles an hour.

"I felt very secure in the car. It felt very good. It has blinding speed potential. There's absolutely no reason under God's earth to build a twin-engine car. [Laughing]

"What I mean is that there were some suggestions. Richard [Noble] told me I needed to build a twin-engine car to go supersonic.

"We have enormous speed potential. The problem always has been to control the speed and be able to harness it. It's stability and control. You've gotta keep it on the ground and you've gotta be able to control it. The car has potential. It's fun to drive.

"[The final run at Black Rock] was way faster than our planned procedure. It would have put me supersonic. I don't have any data yet. I was too premature in the speed build-up.

"It's very distracting trying to watch a speedometer and then get on and off the power. I didn't have a choice. Also my breathing system didn't work."

Instead of bitter disappointment, Craig Breedlove views the experience/wild ride in a positive way.

"Maybe it's a blessing in disguise.

"I feel very positive, very confident about the record program. We're getting ready to go back out. Hopefully we'll be out early next year. Optimistically, the earliest we can get out may be May/June.

"We'll have a whole different set-up. I would expect we'll have the record early in the summer. Our budget to go run in 1997 is over 2.1 million dollars.

"While Shell continues to be our primary sponsor, Shell isn't going to foot the entire bill. I'm gonna have to go to the other sponsors and try to see what they can contribute. Money is always a problem, or should I say lack of it. I've got to face the reality that we may not be able to raise enough money to go back.

"It's a great car. It really works very well. It handles very well. The steering works really good. The engine works wonderful. The air ducts work well. The fuel system works fine. Everything on the car works well.

"We really don't know why the rear end lifted. It's pretty definite that it came up. I can't say with any certainty it was caused by any one particular thing because we don't have any data on the loading on the back of the car.

"Like they say it could have been a gust of wind that did it. Certainly coming in and out of burner like that is very destabilizing. That may have had an effect on it.

"It's possible that we were at 0.9 Mach [just under the speed of sound] and it's possible that the lifting in the back was due to supersonic flow and that's one of the reasons why I'm going to make a major change on the car.

"We have to build a new rear frame section on the car. There's a lot of work to do. We've got a lot of sheet metal damage, a lot of carbon fiber damage. We're in the process of changing the airfoil on the rear axle and bringing in more downforce.

"We're gonna change the ventral fin off the car, put up a slightly larger vertical fin and take the lower fin off. The ventral fin tends to divide the body of the car into two separate chambers because it divides the right side from the left side.

"There was a tendency to lift one side and then lift the other side, which is an indication to me that the tunnels are acting independently.

"So I'm gonna take the ventral fin out from underneath the car and make it like one chamber because I think the pressure will be able to distribute itself more equally.

"Unfortunately, in a way I'm reluctant to do it because I hate to make that big a change with something that's working very well. But anyway it's my call. I have to make it and I've decided I'm gonna change the foil."

On October 28, 1996, an exhausted and bitterly disappointed Richard Noble bowed to Mother Nature. Floods had turned Al Jafr Desert in Jordan into a lake.

After almost three weeks on the desert, Noble's creation, his massive Thrust SSC, had reached the speed of 331 miles an hour in a series of build-up runs.

Problems existed but they could have been solved. But man cannot beat the power of Mother Nature.

He made a brief statement:

"The Weather God is really mocking us today; outside we have blue skies and the beginnings of a hot day. Just five miles down the road the Jafr Desert is flooded. The course, which we had built so carefully, has been washed away and the local people know it will take at least three weeks to recreate the course. The decision to return home is clear cut. We can't last out here long enough to see the desert dry and the course re-established.

"It took us six hours to totally evacuate the site and when we left the water was two hundred meters away. I always believed that somehow the desert site was on higher ground, never vulnerable because the water would have to flow uphill to flood it. In fact, the next day the entire track system was lost."

So Richard Noble and his Thrust SSC team returned to England to regroup and prepare for a 1997 return to the Jordanian desert.

In a candid interview with the author, Noble tells what happened:

Question:

Tell me about the car. Is it as good as you had envisioned?

Noble:

I think it's going to be very good. It's very early to say yet. Basically, what happened is that we got out to Jordan and we got the car up to 330. It took two and a half weeks to get the track ready and the car ready. When we got out there we only got four runs before the desert flooded, so we had to go home, which is something we didn't expect at all.

Basically it's very good. It's very stable. It's very reliable. It looks to me as if it's going to be a real winner. We've got problems with the rear suspension where we were getting quite a bit of wheel shimmy. We're just coming to grips with that now. We'd eventually made the steering geometry changes. We weren't able to run the car with them before the rains came, which was a great shame."

Question:

Did you hit 330 with or without the afterburner?

Noble:

The burners. We did bring them in.

Question:

You did use the burners?

Noble:

Oh yes. We just established them and then we had to shut down.

Question:

Up to that point had the car been going straight as an arrow?

Noble:

Oh, yes, indeed. What was happening we were starting to get this wheel shimmy and that was destroying the stability. And, of course, we certainly couldn't go on like that. That's why Andy had to abort the run.

Question:

What kind of problem?

Noble:

It's a steering geometry problem. That's simply a matter of adjusting the toe-in and the caster.

Question:

Are we talking about minor or major?

Noble:

We're talking about minor, minor changes.

Question:

Had the weather cooperated, did you have the capability to make those changes?

Noble:

We made the first set of adjustments. It would have worked. We wouldn't know until we tried it.

Question:

How much warning did you get before the rains came?

Noble:

Very, very little, because what happened was it rained heavily the night before but it didn't rain on the desert. So we had to camp out on the desert. The people out on the desert said, 'It's fine... don't worry... it's gonna be all right'. By eight o'clock they suddenly saw the advancing water.

Question:

You basically had your own kind of Exodus?

Noble:

Yes. Absolutely. It took six hours to get off, but we got off. It was pretty tough actually because the last collection of people coming off the desert had to drive through nearly a quarter of a mile of water.

Question:

By how much did you beat the floods?

Noble:

It was about half an hour. What seems to happen is that the water floods over the hard surface. For a bit you can drive on that hard surface under the water, and then suddenly it all turns to porridge.

Question:

As for the basic design, is the car everything you thought it would be?

Noble:

It's pretty good. The car's kinda heavier than we thought. All the things we were worried about weren't problems. Like being able to select the two burners together – problems of actually hitching those two engines together and making sure that they accelerated together. The problems possibly of the rear fuselage being damaged by the acoustic noise from the afterburner. All that turned out not to be a problem.

Question:

Were the two engines in synch?

Noble:

Oh absolutely yes. They're very, very good.

Question:

If the engines aren't in synch is that a problem?

Noble:

That depends on the difference in thrust. Basically we've got a car with a big fin on it. It's a long, long way back from the center of gravity. That means it's got a big stabilizing moment.

In other words it tends to go naturally straight. If you've got slightly more power on one side than the other we've found that you can steer it out with the steering.

Question:

Was the rear steering any problem?

Noble:

It works very well except that we've got a shimmy problem. Once gotten through we'll be fine.

Question:

Is man going to solve the problem, or computer?

Noble:

We hoped that man would solve the problem because then we could run on the desert and prove it. Only it rained and we didn't get the chance to run on the desert. We're going to have to play around with the computers over here.

Question:

You had planned to go back to Black Rock Desert. Why Al Jafr?

Noble:

The fundamental thing was really this. We knew that the end of the Black Rock season was really coming up fast. It was taking us a long time to complete our car. We had hoped to go to Jafr in July, but the reality was that even at the end of October we still hadn't finished the car.

It's a very big car and it absorbs an enormous amount of man hours really. We didn't have a choice. The Black Rock situation was that the time was getting shorter and shorter before Black Rock flooded.

Question:

If the car had been completed in June or July would you have gone to Black Rock?

Noble:

We would have still gone to Jafr first and then probably gone to Black Rock if we could finance it.

Question:

Are the surfaces similar? Dissimilar?

Noble:

There are two factors. One is that the Jafr surface is much harder than the Black Rock surface. Certainly when we arrived it was much much harder. From time to time there were little bouts of rain and that softened it up a bit. But certainly it started out much harder than the Black Rock Desert. That means that the rolling resistance was considerably reduced, which made it a faster track.

The other thing was that it was reasonably easy to pick up the stones that were imbedded under the Black Rock surface. It was reasonably easy to pick up the stones. But at Jafr it was an enormous job. You've got to go along on your hands and knees with a screwdriver to get the stones out.

Question:

What is Jafr composed of?

Noble:

It's an alkali playa which has been washed off the nearby mountain. Washed over millions of years on to the desert. Sort of a sump where it cooks and bakes and it ends up like cement.

Question:

How did you hear of Al Jafr?

Noble:

Well, in 1948 an Englishman named Ken Warman was part of a survey party. He was driving a water truck and one day he happened to cross it. He saw one of our television programs. We were looking for alternative desert sites and he phoned in. Thank God he did. We wouldn't have found it otherwise.

Question:

Did you do the advance work?

Noble:

We did all the advance work. I went out there twice before we actually ran. My younger brother, Andrew, went out and did most of the advance work. He was out there for about two months. We had a lot of help from the Royal Jordanian Air Force.

Question:

It was seventeen speed lanes?

Noble:

That's right. We ended up with seventeen lanes, each 10.2 miles long.

Question:

Would the 10.2 miles have given you the distance that you needed?

Noble:

Certainly we think to have gotten up to about 650 or so. The problem was it was absolute distance. In other words there was no extra run-off distance at all.

Question:

Where would you have gone through the measured mile?

Noble:

We had to put the measured mile in the middle, as you know.

Question:

How much longer track would you require to go 850?

Noble:

The problem really is this. It's knowing how quickly you can stop the car. With our car we have a very low drag and quite a heavy car, so it becomes quite a problem to stop it.

What we've discovered now is that we can use our carbon fiber brakes at a much much higher speed than we thought we could. It well will be possible now. As soon as we get the car back we'll make a few modifications. It may well be possible now to start applying our wheel brakes at 300 miles an hour plus, which we hadn't banked on.

Question:

How quickly can your car go from 0 to 600?

Noble:

Well, at the moment we don't know until we've done it. We've got speculative numbers but I'd rather talk about real numbers.

Question:

Despite the end result, are you encouraged by 1996?

Noble:

Yes, I mean as far as we've gone, and we've only gone up to 330 miles an hour, which isn't very fast. The car is stable, it works well and it's reliable.

Question:

It's not exactly bragging rights at the moment?

Noble:

No, no, no. I think what we're going to have to do is do 700 and have an easy ride.

Question:

Do you plan to go back to Jordan?

Noble:

Yes. We've got to get on and finish this off. I don't know how soon we can get back to Jordan but we'll have to wait, I suppose, until the desert dries, and let's hope they'll have us back again.

Question:

You're talking about some point in 1997?

Noble:

That's right. Yes.

Question:

Is finance any kind of problem?

Noble:

It's always a terrible problem. Every team has got that. Craig Breedlove's had terrible problems. We've had terrible problems. The Australians have got problems already and they're just going out to run this moment.

Question:

All things being equal, when is the earliest you could possibly return to Jordan?

Noble:

When the desert dries, that's the thing. Probably April/May I would think.

Rosco McGlashan planned to return to Lake Gairdner, a huge salt expanse near Adelaide, Australia, with the sound barrier in mind, not just the land speed record.

Aussie Invader 3 is lighter, sleeker, more powerful than its predecessor for its supersonic adventure.

"The speed of sound, some 1270 kilometers per hour [789 mph] is our new goal," said McGlashan. "That's where the worldwide attention is at so that's what we are now chasing. Along the way we will collect the world land speed record.

"We are the most experienced team in the world. Our technology is tried and true. We have a sea-level venue – important for the challenge of the speed of sound."

Since the incident of March 1995, when the Aussie Invader 2 hit a timing light while chasing the land speed record, the team has been busy redesigning and rebuilding the existing car.

The new vehicle features a shorter chassis, revised nose section profile and intake, an all-new engine lifted from a nuclear strike aircraft and 'tweaked' to produce 36,000 horsepower and broader suspension setting options.

The new sleeker and lighter fiberglass/Kevlar body features a rounded upper body profile. A new tail fin would be added once final vehicle weights and gravity centers had been established.

For the transonic runs, a sonic probe has been installed with a sonic 'splitter' panel available if it proves more effective in directing the sound waves around the car in a programmed path.

Self-activating canard wings were under construction to provide additional downforce if required.

"Lake Gairdner hasn't been very kind to us," pointed out McGlashan. "Weatherwise so far and the logistics of moving the whole team across 3000 kilometers [1865 miles] are huge and expensive... but at present it remains our only option.

"To have a chance of getting the right track and weather conditions for some truly sensational high-speed runs we need to be on the salt for months, so our biggest challenge is to find a sponsor for around $300,000 [in Australian funds] associated with that long-term stay. We believe the entire national media exposure we can provide is worth millions, so we are confident."

McGlashan tried for several years in his home-built jet car, reaching an official clocking of 505 miles an hour and a peak speed estimated at 600.

He is considered a serious threat to Richard Noble's long-standing land speed record of 633.4 mph, set back in 1983.

While the media attention focused on the highly publicized Craig Breedlove–Richard Noble jet duel, contenders took to the Bonneville Salt Flats in 1996 to better the long-standing wheel-driven speed record of 409 miles an hour.

Bonneville veteran, Al Teague, who shares a piece of history with the late Bobby Summers, could 'only' muster a 345 mph run during Speed Week. Another disappointing season.

Nolan White, still racing at the age of sixty-six, became only the third man in wheel-driven history to surpass 400 miles an hour, a few years ago. Since then, he's lost that 'magic touch'.

Two long-awaited debates took place. Ex-motorcycle speed king, Don Vesco tried out his turbine-powered streamliner. The Burkland family, with son, Tom, behind the wheel, finally tested the salt with his potential 425 mph machine.

While all failed, no doubt they'll be back in 1997. After all, records are made to be broken... no matter how long it takes.

And for seventy one year old Arthur Eugene Arfons 'tomorrow' may never come... but then again he's beaten the odds all of his life.

Chapter Two

Faster and Faster into the Unknown

Man's obsession with speed seems inborn.

It began almost one hundred years ago with the advent of the automobile, and shows no sign of becoming just a faded memory... not as long as man can dream.

Many fantasize but only a few *dare* to turn that fantasy into reality.

A handful of daredevils have pursued the world land speed record in an exciting, sometimes deadly sport, which began in 1898 on a road near Paris.

In recent years, attempts have been few and far between.

Only four men have attempted high-speed record assaults since the jet duel of the 1960s between Ohio hot rodder, Art Arfons, and his younger rival, Californian Craig Breedlove.

Breedlove finally slammed the door on 'The Great Shoot-out' in 1965, crashing the 600 mile an hour barrier with his two-way average of 600.601 in his massive, jet-powered Spirit of America – Sonic I.

Five years after Breedlove's record, another Californian, the late Gary Gabelich, raised the standard to 622.407 in the rocket-propelled Blue Flame.

It would be another thirteen years until Gabelich's record fell, as Richard Noble of Great Britain pushed his Thrust 2 to 633.4 mph. Jet power once again reigned supreme.

Between the time that Gabelich raced into immortality and Noble ended his nine year quest, only one man took dead aim on the land speed record. Californian rancher, Slick Gardner, failed.

And for almost a decade, Noble awaited the challenge. Only two men between 1983 and the spring of 1995 picked up that gauntlet.

Arfons dug deep into his own pockets to build Green Monster No. 27, a task he completed in 1989. At that point, the mini-machine, weighing less than 2000 pounds, was a two-wheeler.

He went airborne in '89, changed his Monster to a four-wheel in 1990, but failed again. The effort was more respectable in 1991, but he went home empty-handed.

In 1994 and then in early 1995, Australian Rosco McGlashan tested his jet at a salt lake near Adelaide, Australia. His best effort: 505 mph.

However, men who pursue the land speed record do not give up easily. They may be beaten by the weather, by an ill-handling machine, by lack of funding, but they somehow manage to keep that dream alive.

So, like the legendary character out of Washington Irving's fertile imagination, Rip Van Winkle woke up from his long sleep, wiped his eyes and shouted, 'Let's party'.

And what a party that could be – at least half a dozen heirs apparent to Richard Noble's throne, including King Richard. The year 1997 could be the stuff of which fairy tales are made.

And if The Great Expectations fail to materialize, it's a good bet, the speed epidemic would still run rampant – to the edge of, and into, the 21st century.

What makes the great land speed revival more than just good copy is the fact that all of these contenders have been built or are nearing completion. There are five jets and one rocket racer.

Three of these creations boast supersonic speed potential.

First, a brief rundown:

Art Arfons

Approaching his seventy-first birthday – February 1997 – and already the oldest man to try for the record, Arfons has been waiting since 1994 to return to Bonneville. He was washed out by heavy rains in 1994 and at the opening meet (July) of the 1996 speed season. Politics sidelined him in 1995. He has reworked his 'balky' Monster, and conducted successful test firings of the J–85 engine. As he puts it: "Bonneville's the only place where I can afford to run for $400." Speed potential: 650 mph.

Richard Noble

When Australia's Rosco McGlashan appeared on the salt near Adelaide in 1993 with his jet Aussie Invader 2, Noble wasn't too concerned, as the car had sub-sonic potential. However, when five-time speed king, Craig Breedlove of California started building his latest Spirit of America, this development took on a sense of urgency. Breedlove's car boasted faster-than-sound potential!

A full-time crew of sixteen worked feverishly to complete construction on Noble's twin-jet, the longest (57 feet), heaviest (14,000 pounds) and most powerful (100,000 horsepower) in land speed history. This time, Noble would leave the driving to British fighter pilot, Andy Green. Target date at Black Rock Desert in Nevada was set for Fall of '96. Noble drove his jet-powered Thrust 2 to the record of 633.4 mph in 1983 at Black Rock. Speed potential: 850 mph.

Craig Breedlove

For more than twenty years, Breedlove, who celebrated his sixtieth birthday in March 1997, had tried to return to the land speed game. First in a rocket racer, and now in his forty-seven foot long, four ton Spirit of America – Sonic Arrow. The first man to average 400, 500 and 600 miles an hour, Breedlove also has his sights on the sound barrier in this five-wheeler. Spirit of America, his first record-setter, was a three-wheeler. Sonic I, the first car to hit 600, was a conventional four-wheeler.

Rosco McGlashan

In 1977, a little-known Aussie builder/driver, Ken Warby, gunned his home-made jet boat to a new world water speed record of 288 mph. A year later Warby went an incredible 317. His long-time friend, Rosco McGlashan – in his late forties – has tried since 1993 to break Noble's record in Aussie Invader 2, a jet that strongly resembles Arfons' Green Monster. Rosco hit 502 in 1994, and failed again in 1995. But now he hopes to be back in the chase with Aussie Invader 3. Speed potential: 650–700 mph.

Waldo Stakes

Stakes, a Californian in his late thirties, is an accomplished sculptor, specializing in metal. His entry into the land speed chase is perhaps the most intriguing. It is a mini (less than 1000 pounds) rocket sled, powered by an X–1 engine. While the machine could run on land, Stakes hopes to unleash his Sonic Wind on a frozen lake. The 'pocket rocket' is finished. He has hired a marketing specialist to find major financial backing. Speed potential: 900 mph.

Gary Swenson

Veteran jet-powered funny car driver, Rick Kikes of Oregon, has built a jet-powered LSR contender, American Eagle. The thirty-nine foot long car, which will be converted from a three to a four-wheeler, is powered by a J–79 engine, the same kind that Arfons used in his record-setting jet. Kikes has already done eighth-mile tests of 210 on the drag strip. But for the record attempt he has turned the driving duties over to his partner, Gary Swenson, another jet funny car driver. Swenson, in his late thirties, is from Washington. Speed potential: 680 mph.

These are the six known entities.

The most secretive project involves McLaren Racing of England, better known for Formula One than land speed racing.

The publicity mill worked overtime in 1993, as Ron Dennis of McLaren announced his company's plans to build an 850 mile an hour jet car. Mock-up of Maverick was unveiled.

The car would be powered by a British-made Rolls Royce Turbo Union engine found in a Tornado F–3 fighter plane. That engine would generate 38,000 horsepower.

Maverick would weigh some three tons, have four metal wheels and go from 0 to 850 mph in an estimated forty seconds, based on thirteen miles of track.

But just as quickly as the publicity faucet was turned on full blast, it was turned off. All that persists are rumors.

Chapter Three

'Gentlemen and Lyn, Start Your Engines'

When handsome Californian Craig Breedlove, then only twenty-six, rode a fiery chariot across the Bonneville Salt Flats more than four decades ago, 'THE GAME' changed forever.

Thrust-powered, meaning jet or rocket engine, created an entirely different beast, and captured the public's imagination.

400... 500... 600... to the present 633.4 miles per hour.

Big Numbers Equal Big Headlines.

Now that same young man who started it all back in 1963, and others like him, look far beyond to the sound barrier, and once again the general public is mesmerized.

750... 800... 850... 900.

Indeed, traveling through the measured mile in four seconds or less, titillates the imagination. It's simply mind-boggling.

Now who could get excited about a land speed vehicle traveling at say 425, 450 miles an hour? That's hardly worth a mention on TV, a few lines of copy in the daily newspaper.

Yet that 425 or 450 mile an hour ride in a car instead of a missile is easier said than done. MUCH EASIER!

Consider this. In 1947, England's John Cobb drove his pre-WWII Railton Special to a new two-way land speed record of 394 mph. It was pure car, power transmitted directly through the wheels.

It would be sixteen years later before Breedlove, driving his three-wheel Spirit of America, would exceed that average. And it was done with jet power. 407.45 miles an hour.

A year later, halfway around the world in Australia, England's Donald Campbell had to be content with a new wheel-driven mark of 403 mph. He wanted Breedlove's record, but came up short. Even though his Bluebird, was turbine-powered, the power was transmitted through the wheels. Campbell was a purist, even in the age of jet propulsion.

In 1965, a well-known California builder/driver named Bobby Summers gave the United States its first wheel-driven record since the late 1920s, by pushing his pencil-thin Goldenrod, to a two-way average of 409.277 mph. The car was powered by four normally aspirated Chrysler engines.

Al Teague and his Spirit of '76 (that's the year it was built) came along more than two decades later and went a tick faster at 409.986.

Many would say Summers still holds the wheel-driven standard because Teague didn't exceed Summers' effort by the prescribed one percent. That means Teague, or any other contender, would have to average 413 plus.

This is where it becomes a little sticky, technically speaking.

When all the Ts are crossed and the Is dotted, these cars compete in two different classes. Teague's single-engine machine uses a combination of fuels, including nitro. Thus, it is in the 'Blown' category.

Thus, Summers, who died of a heart attack in 1992, and Al Teague, his long-time friend, can both lay claim to the world's fastest wheel-driven vehicles.

What began as a ripple, meaning just a smattering of wheel-driven activity, has become a virtual tidal wave with legitimate challengers determined to carve out a new page in land speed history.

And even more on the way, drivers who are moving up to the 400 mile an hour class.

The field stretches from Florida to California – even a huge kangaroo hop to Australia.

The cast of characters:

Al Teague; his long-time rival, Nolan White; ex-motorcycle speed king, Don Vesco; Chet Herbert and his bright red four-engine monster; Tom Burkland and his two-engine streamliner; veteran Indianapolis 500 driver, Lyn St. James, in a 'ground-effects' creation; Australian Glen Davis, who is the mystery man in this equation.

* Teague, idle since 1992, competed in Australia and Utah during the 1995 speed season. Despite failure to go faster than his '91 record, this long-time land speed competitor is confident his time will finally come. It did not come in '96. He hit 300-plus, but blew two engines.

* White, from San Diego, California, is the 'old man' of the group. His sixty-sixth birthday was in January '97. White was the first since the late Bobby Summers to exceed 400 miles an hour. He did that in 1992 in a then twelve year old car (401.9). Since then, he's been 'in a rut'.

* Vesco, unlike Teague and White, did not compete in 1995. With turbine power in 1996, Vesco finally had enough horses. While he failed, this legend will be back.

* Long-time Bonneville fixture, Chet Herbert, debuted his massive machine in October 1990 at the World Finals. Theoretically, this is a 500 mile an hour car. But up until now, it hasn't performed up to that potential.

* Tom Burkland, with his No. 411 machine, is considered a genuine threat. He almost made it to Bonneville in '95. Although unsuccessful in 1996, the car shows great promise.

* Lyn St. James may be a 'rookie' when it comes to land speed racing, but she's no stranger to the high-speed scene. She's a highly regarded sports car/Indy 500 driver with more than thirty speed records to her credit. The second woman to qualify for the Indy 500 (Janet Guthrie did it in the late 70s), will be featured in a *National Geographic* special when this adventure is finally over.

* Rumors from Australia say Glen Davis has completed construction of his forty-one foot long missile, to be powered by a pair of twelve-cylinder engines, utilizing two four-speed automatic transmissions. He plans to run the car at Lake Gairdner, near Adelaide.

The wheel-driven record has been held by Americans for more than thirty years. The Americans owned the America's Cup Challenge for 132 years before an Australian team finally ended that supremacy on water. Who's to say Glen Davis won't do the same on land?

Al Teague (Brea, California)

Back in March of 1995, Al Teague made a bold decision to travel to Australia for a crack at the wheel-driven record. The lure of unlimited salt, far more than was available at Bonneville, was the major selling point.

He knew his ancient machine had the 'firepower', so he took the gamble. Unfortunately, it didn't pay off and cost him thousands of dollars in the process.

"Better salt conditions was the reason to go down there," says Teague. "They have miles and miles of salt. It's Lake Gairdner, near Adelaide. That's where Rosco [Australian Rosco McGlashan] has run his jet the past few years.

"A guy by the name of Dick Williams put the package together. A total of five American cars made the long trip. We had to pay our own way, and we did it.

"They put the cars in two forty foot long containers, plus all of our equipment, and flew it there before we went. It cost roughly $20,000. That included me, my car, two crew members. If you took more than two, it was about $2000 per crew member.

"About $7000 actually came out of my pocket. I got help. Two guys helped me finance the other $13,000. I guess you'd call it a calculated risk, but I thought it was worth it. Would I do it again? You bet.

"Instead of going to Bonneville and only having four or five miles to run on in each direction, we could have had an unlimited amount. If old man weather had cooperated with us, we could have easily had seven miles approach into the timed mile.

"But just my dumb luck, the weather conditions were bad... really bad. Every day we had a crosswind of at least twenty miles an hour. I'd get up to about 300 and it would blow the car off the course.

"You had to back off the throttle to get the car back on the course. Then make another run, get blown off course again. That continued all week.

"As it turned out, I ran only four miles into the timed mile. Parts of the course were dry, other parts were wet. They didn't drag it very well. If conditions had been good, I think I would have run to the car's potential.

"I was in third gear on my 360 mile an hour run, but I was off and on the throttle. In other words, I'd floor it, it would get off course and I'd get out of it.

"Tires have been a major problem for quite a while, not just with me but with a lot of other people. I ran the new Mickey Thompsons down there. They're made by M&H for Mickey Thompson. I ran the thirty inches and they seemed to hold up pretty well."

Teague was pleased with his car's performance, considering the conditions.

"The first two miles were good, and then it got soft. The car seemed to accelerate very well and I was really happy about that. I used one set of new tires down there, and they're in good shape. I've got one other set."

Al Teague returned to Bonneville in August 1995 for Speed Week, knowing track conditions were far from ideal – not just the shortness of the course, but the condition of the salt.

He made only two runs, hit 365 mph, then packed it up. He had accomplished what he had set out to accomplish.

"I really didn't plan to be any faster," he points out. "There was only one and a half miles to stop the car and really no chance for a return run.

"I entered the mile at 340 and left at 380. Considering the condition of the salt, the short track, I was very satisfied. The salt was loose all the way, but the car handled well.

"One of the reasons I wanted to run was to see how the Mickey Thompson tires would perform at Bonneville. They did as good as I could have hoped. I'd say I have about two more runs left in this set of tires.

"Reflecting a little, I'd call 1995 a good year for Al Teague. People kinda forget, but I haven't run since 1992, when I turned in a 417 during Speed Week. It was nice to get back in the groove."

When Teague ran in Australia, he installed a 540 cubic inch engine in his ancient streamliner. At Bonneville, five months later, he switched to a smaller 493, the same engine he used to set his record 409.986 in 1991.

When he returns to Utah in 1997, he's even considering using an even smaller 488 cubic inch power plant.

Why?

"It's a smaller-stroke engine," he says, "meaning you don't spin the tires as much and there's not as much torque. It's something I'm thinking about."

Al Teague planned to keep busy during the winter, hoping that 1997 will finally be the year he cuts loose from the shadow of the late Bobby Summers.

"I'll take the car completely apart, even re-paint it."

Teague is forever having to explain the fact that he is holder of the world's wheel-driven record, even though it would appear to the layman that he is not.

In 1965, Summers drove his Goldenrod, powered by four normally aspirated engines, to a record of 409.277 mph. Teague came along more than two decades later and went a tick faster.

On the surface, the rules say that while Al Teague exceeded Summers' speed, he did not break the record by the required one percent. That would have meant a two-way average of 413 miles an hour.

But technically, the machines were in two different wheel-driven classes. Teague's Spirit of '76 is powered by one engine burning a combination of fuels, including nitro. It is considered 'Blown'.

Thus, he and Summers are record-holders.

But until the day he can finally distance himself from his late friend, Al Teague will have to carry 'that monkey on his back'.

Building and driving the world's fastest wheel-driven, single-engine machine isn't good enough.

Nolan White (San Diego, California)

Nolan White, 'that grand old man' of wheel-driven land speed racing, was looking forward to a memorable last race of the 1995 speed season, the World Finals.

A participant at every meet at Bonneville, White figured the string of bad luck that has followed him since his 401.9 sortie in 1991 would finally come to an end.

Man, was he wrong!

A total of sixty competitors were needed to meet expenses for the last scheduled meet of the season. However, only thirty signed up and the meet was canceled.

That could have ended his season right then and there. However, when the SCTA (Southern California Timing Association) relinquished rights to the three day event, White turned to an old friend, Jack Dolan of San Diego, for help.

Dolan is head of LSA (Land Speed Authority), a group of speed enthusiasts formed during the past few years. He's the man who can get the proper paperwork needed to hold a last minute meet. He's also the man who can gain FIA approval should any car break an international record.

"All of the racers that had signed up for the SCTA meet, including me," says Nolan White, "were given a phone call telling us about the cancellation. I called Jack, and in a matter of two days, he had all the necessary documents.

"When I arrived at Bonneville, at the twelve mile international track that we had scrapped during a previous visit, the place was a mess. I believe a car company had filmed a commercial a week before our meet.

"Only thing is, they totally destroyed the middle of our course with the debris they left behind. Things like nails, wood. We had to call in tractors to dig up all the garbage. I'd say it took about twenty semi-truckloads to clean it up.

"I arrived on Thursday, and there went that day. It was completely wasted. We had to create a brand new twelve mile long course, and it wasn't until Saturday that anyone was ready to run. We had two days left.

"Because it was such a last minute deal, we never had much time to let everyone know about the new meet. I'd say twelve or thirteen showed up, but it was enough people to split the expenses and get on with it.

"We had to call out a surveyor from Salt Lake City to check out the course, and it turned out to be adequate. Don't forget Bonneville hasn't been in good racing shape for the past four or so years, so what we had wasn't any worse than what we had been running on.

"We had a full course. One end was a little dry and the other end a bit damp, but at least it was raceable. That big old red Herbert wheel-driven machine went 337 or 338. The Vesco/Nish entry set one FIA record of 320 with an unblown, small block Chevy.

"All of the guys that ran have told me they'd do it again, so it was a good meet in that respect. A couple of guys crashed, but nothing serious."

In two previous 1995 meets, Nolan White had clocked a top speed of 340 miles an hour. The car was fine-tuned for October, or so he thought.

"In all the years I've been running at Bonneville, I've never had a clutch fail.

"Never had a problem with my old equipment, but this time I decided to install a brand new clutch disc, and wouldn't you know, it failed in low speed during my first and only run. By then it was late Saturday afternoon, and it wasn't worth the bother, so I just packed it up.

"Sure it was a disappointment. I was hoping to give myself a real special [sixty-fifth] birthday present in January [1996]. I've learned that you take what life gives you. I can't complain. I'm still kicking, breathing, having fun, so everything's fine.

"The big plus out of the whole thing is that I don't have to depend on these other organizations anymore [Southern Californian Timing Association, Utah Salt Flats Racing Association] to have a meet. I know the guy to call [Jack Dolan]. He's the contact you need for any high-speed racing."

The year 1996 was a total bust. Nolan White hopes that all the pieces finally fit into place in 1997.

"I'll keep on doing it till I get it right."

Don Vesco (Murietta, California)

Call former motorcycle speed king Don Vesco the eternal optimist. Ever since he entered the wheel-driven automobile record quest in the early 1980s, he's been thwarted, by a combination of bad luck and lack of horsepower.

Now he's convinced he has finally found the magic formula for success. And this time around, he could be right.

The reason for his optimism, almost giddiness, is a 4000 horsepower gas turbine engine. This engine is usually used in a Lycoming helicopter. It is model T55–L–11ASA.

The single engine replaces a pair of four-cylinder Offys that Vesco has utilized during the past few years, but without success.

"The engine will cost me $30,000," says Vesco, a man in his late fifties, "but it will be worth it."

He is purchasing the engine from Tim Arfons, son of three-time land speed king, Art Arfons.

"I'm working on deals to sell several engines, and I'll do it," adds Vesco. "Tim sent me the dummy [or spare] engine a while ago, and it fits perfectly in the car. Now it's just a matter of coming up with the rest of the money."

Don Vesco had hoped to close the deal, and be ready to run his thirty one foot long streamliner during the 1995 speed season, but it wasn't to be.

"Sure it was tough watching Al [Teague] and Nolan [White] run, knowing they are the guys to beat, but they were literally spinning their wheels because of the lack of length and the poor salt conditions.

"And even if they, or anyone else, has broken the record, I'm more than confident I have enough horses in this turbine engine to do my thing."

"There's so much more technology available nowadays and more engines available. We're seeing middle-aged guys in their mid forties and up, who have good paying jobs, appearing on the scene with smaller class streamliners, hitting 300 miles an hour, and trying to step up in class. These guys will be our future competition, and I think that's great for the sport.

"Everything is more sophisticated today, and also more expensive. There's all this electrical stuff. You can't use an old Model A gearbox anymore.

"All of this money is coming out of my pocket, but I'm not complaining. To make a serious record attempt, I'll need seven miles – three miles into the measured mile, one through the mile and three to shut down.

"The car weighs less than 3000 pounds. I'll have to add some weight because there's not enough downforce."

Vesco returned to Utah with the turbine engine, but mechanical problems stymied his effort in '96.

But 1997 is a new year, maybe this time will be different? Maybe this time all the pieces will fit neatly into place.

Chet Herbert (Orange County, California)

It almost seems that Chet Herbert has been around forever.

Back in the 1950s, before he turned his attention to drag racing with partner Roy Steen, his cars which bore the name Beast were legendary.

Herbert runs his successful camshaft and hot rod accessories business in California while his sons, Josh and Clayton, run their machine shop at Idaho Falls, Idaho.

Herbert started campaigning at Bonneville in the 1950s. In 1954, his car broke the ten mile record.

"We had a fifteen mile course that year," Herbert fondly recalls. "Now, it's a drag race."

Four decades later, Herbert felt the itch to return to Bonneville and have a shot at the wheel-driven record. Construction of his four-engine 'beast' began in 1989. A year later, it was ready, with legendary Bonneville driver Don Vesco in the cockpit.

Herbert's bright-red creation, powered by four in-line mounted Chevy 8s, has grown in size over the years. It began 32 feet long, 48 inches wide, 28 inches high, with a wheelbase of 207 inches and a total weight of 8450 pounds.

It is now 36 feet long, 30 inches wide, 30 inches high with a 340 inch wheelbase, with a total weight of 9000 pounds.

The fuel-injected engines generate some 4000 horsepower and burn 25 percent nitro.

Initially, two three-speed transmissions were used, in conjunction with a third transmission used to minimize wheelspin and tie all four engines together so they could run at the same speed. Subsequently, the transmissions were modified to seven speeds. After their initial runs, the seven speeds were reduced to five.

Vesco drove the car when it had aluminum wheels and no suspension. The car vibrated so much on the salt, the '90 debut was over quickly.

That year, Herbert also tried some old Mickey Thompson tires, but they chunked rubber at speed. Transmission troubles also plagued the car that first year.

In 1991, Dan Soran replaced Vesco as driver. Roy Steen designed a suspension system and the car was fitted with seven-speed transmission. But by the time the car had been modified, the speed season was over.

In 1992, Nolan White and then Al Teague became the first drivers in more than twenty years to exceed 400 mph in a wheel-driven machine. Despite problems that year, Chet Herbert began to see a glimmer of hope for his car.

Young Clayton Steen, all of twenty-one years of age, averaged 364 miles an hour through the measured mile.

"We didn't get a return", says Herbert, "because we were still trying to get the bugs out."

In 1993, he made only one good run, due to poor weather. Weather and track conditions didn't improve much in 1994. Steen made only two runs. One was the stuff of which dreams are made.

"Clayton hit over 400 – 437 – in two and a half miles according to the tach," points out Herbert, "but we had to shut off before the lights. We had a bearing problem in the engines."

Another plus was the performance of the new Mickey Thompson, made by M&H.

Chet Herbert anticipated a productive 1995 season. It didn't happen. The car failed to reach 300 miles an hour.

It didn't happen in 1996. Despite the long journey, he still believes this car has 500 miles an hour speed potential.

Tom Burkland (Great Falls, Montana)

Talk about a bummer!

The night before the Burkland family was set to make the long trip to Bonneville in quest of the wheel-driven land speed record, (father) Gene and (son) Tom fired up the 400 mile an hour streamliner in the family backyard.

"We'd fired it up several times over the weekend, and everything went perfect," recalls Gene Burkland. "It was late at night when it happened.

"Tom said it sounded like a snap or a pop and it felt like something had hit his leg."

That something was a broken transmission shaft.

"We didn't know what it was until we tore it apart. The shaft, which is about fifteen or sixteen inches long, is made of 86-30 steel, but it was brittle like pieces of glass.

"As to why it broke, we're having tests done to determine the cause. The company that made it will build two new shafts to our specifications. We should be fine."

Gene Burkland doesn't want to think what could have happened if the problem didn't surface until his son was making a 250–300 mile an hour run during the September 1995 World of Speed meet.

"Sure, we were all disappointed," he says, "but thankful it happened in the back yard, and not on the salt."

The Burkland machine has consumed the last ten years of this Montana family's life.

"Gee," says Gene, "I don't even want to think how much money has come out of our pocket.

"We spent eighteen months on the major construction. Tom took that much time away from his job. Conservatively, let's say Tom and I worked ten hours a day, and that means seven days a week. But a lot of days, we worked sixteen hours on the car. That's not counting all the time Betty [Gene's wife] helped out."

Even if the car had been ready for the final '95 meet (World Finals), scheduled in mid-October, Gene Burkland said the record attempt will have to wait until 1996.

"We'll have the time to make sure everything is right. Heck, we actually waited three years for tires that will hold up at high speed."

Originally, the Burklands used tires from an F-16 fighter plane, as no major tire manufacturer had expressed an interest in supplying 400 mile an hour tires to just a handful of customers.

They found the tires at salvage yards across the country. But after a couple of tires exploded during testing on the Burklands' own home-made machine, they sought an alternative.

They are now using Mickey Thompson Performance Tire Company tires.

"They're twenty-four and a half inches by seven inches wide with a sixteen inch rim," says Tom Burkland.

"We've worked with the Thompson company almost three years on these high-speed tires. We've run them 8500-8700 rpm, up to 720 miles an hour, calculated at 502, 503 miles an hour for safety.

"We talked to almost every major tire company before we got lucky. That means Michelin, Goodyear, B.F. Goodrich, Firestone/Bridgestone, even some foreign ones, but none of them were interested. The only company we didn't talk to was Hoosier."

Under ideal circumstances, if there is such a thing, Gene Burkland envisions a 450 mile an hour speed potential.

"We're not looking to break the record [409] by the required one percent.

Tom is looking for a lot more than 413, but he certainly won't try 500 miles an hour first time out. Ideally, we need 10-11 miles of salt to do the total job. We'll peak in fourth gear, before the fifth mile.

I'm not trying to sound cocky, but if all goes well, we can hit 450 with relative ease."

The streamliner is 24 feet long, 41 inches high. Wheel base: 192 inches. Weight (without fuel): 4200 pounds. Weight (with alcohol): 5200.

"We plan to run strictly on alcohol," points out Gene Burkland, "but we could also run 20–30 percent nitro if we felt like it."

Unlike most high-speed cars, Burkland's car has no vertical tail fin.

"Tom figures a tail fin makes up for miscalculations in the car, and he feels we don't need that fin."

The car is powered by a pair of 444 cubic inch Donovan (aluminum Chrysler) engines, putting about 1800 horses each.

The Burklands hand-formed the body from steel, stainless steel and aluminum. The nose cone is a highly altered spun aluminum water tank and the fuel tank's stainless steel, formed to the shape of the car.

All the power is directed through two five-speed transmissions and two specially built 1-to-1 ratio gearboxes to all four wheels. The transmissions are air-shifted by an electronic switching system.

The car uses aircraft-type disc brakes, as well as two high-speed parachutes and one low-speed chute to slow down and stop.

Gene Burkland, a member of the Bonneville 200 Mile An Hour Club, was born in 1935. He was 'hooked' on cars as a youngster. He took a high school graduation trip to Bonneville in 1954 and returned three years later when his youngster brother graduated.

He first became involved in drag racing, driving a hemi-powered Ford Street Roadster and a slingshot dragster. In 1969, he took his wife and his young sons, aged five and nine, back to Bonneville and the 'flame was rekindled'.

Two years later, the Burklands had built their first land speed car, a 1953 Studebaker powered by a 370-Chrysler hemi. He went 186 mph that year, and upped the speed to 213 the following season.

In 1973 and 1976, he went an even faster 246.

The summer of 1975 was spent cleaning up their home after a disastrous flood. Three years later, Gene Burkland went 255.863. That car has been on display at the Donneville Speedway Museum in Wendover since 1980.

Does he secretly yearn for the chance to drive this potential record-setter?

"No, when I got my 255 in that old Studebaker, I called it quits. I'm not interested in driving. What I'd like to do is build a coupe so that Betty can make the club."

Betty Burkland, born in 1940, also had an early fascination with cars. She married Gene Burkland in 1959. Their son Tom was born a year later. She has always been involved with building and campaigning the family's race cars.

She drove their 1975 Datsun B210 competition coupe from 1983 to 1989 in an unsuccessful attempt to gain membership into the Bonneville 200 mph Club. Her fastest run was 247 in 1989.

Betty came close in 1986 driving the four-cylinder machine in D/CC class, coming within 1.5 miles of an hour of a class record. The Datsun was sold to Dan Webster of Carson City, Nevada, in November 1989 to finance construction of their streamliner.

Tom Burkland began his racing career in Soap Box Derby competition. While he won trophies for 'Best Paint', 'Best Upholstery', 'Best Brake System' for his Pinewood Derby car, he didn't win a race.

Burkland graduated from the University of Montana in 1982 with a BA in Mechanical Engineering. Since then, he has been working for the U.S. Government as an aeronautical/aerospace engineer on their F–16 maintenance and modification program. He now works at Hill Air Force Base in Salt Lake City.

Through the years father and son designed and built several dragster chassis, a pulling truck chassis, several street rod chassis and reworked a Jocko Johnson streamliner chassis, all in their Great Falls shop. Gene Burkland had been a welder for the Montana Air National Guard for more than thirty years, retiring in 1985 to open a welding shop at his home.

Tom Burkland's goal in 1980 was 300 miles an hour. It would be a competition coupe based on a Plymouth Arrow-shaped car. He found a Datsun B210 in a junkyard for forty dollars that looked like it would work and began building the car.

The car has a full belly pan incorporating 'ground effects' to keep it stable at speeds of 200 mph. It's design exerts 3000 pounds of downforce at speed. Tom drove the car in 1981 with a 372 cubic inch, four-cylinder Chrysler hemi and a front-mounted blower.

Rain washed out Bonneville activity in 1982 and 1983. In '84 he returned with a bigger Chrysler engine using alcohol. A year later, he was clocked 294.869, 294.368, beating the AA/Competition Coupe record by almost thirty miles an hour.

He was clocked through the quarter-mile timers at the end of his return record run at 300 miles an hour!

In 1986, Tom Burkland designed a small streamliner for Nick Mays, a Montana friend who wanted to run Rotax snowmobile engines. The car was aimed at 225 mph.

Nick set his record, with one 440 Rotax engine, at 179 plus in 1987. Three years later, Mays set the J/GS record – with two 340 Rotax power plants – at 210 and gained membership in the Bonneville 200 mph Club.

Plans to shoot for the wheel-driven record began in 1985. In May 1986, they purchased two 440 Donovan (aluminum Chrysler) engines, mounted nose to nose. The engines would run on alcohol.

Tom Burkland worked out the final design in 1987, but it wasn't until January 1990 that they actually began construction of the chassis. During that time, they test-ran one of the engines in their Datsun to work out some of the bugs.

Lyn St. James (Ormond Beach, Florida)

Lyn St. James isn't interested in playing 'with the girls'.

For all of her motorsports racing life, she's competed against the guys and done darn well. A veteran of the sports car scenes, St. James became the second woman in Indianapolis 500 history to qualify for the world's most prestigious race.

She finished eleventh in 1992 and was named race Rookie of the Year... at the age of 45!

In qualifying for her fourth 500 in 1995, she also set a women's closed course speed record of 225.346 miles an hour during official qualifications. During her long career, Lyn has set thirty-one national and international women's speed records.

Now she's taking dead aim on the land speed record for wheel-driven cars.

And even that has a definite 'Indy Connection'.

Back in 1977, Bob Riley designed the race car that A.J. Foyt drove to an unprecedented fourth Indy 500 victory. Now, more than two decades later, they have built a thirty-two foot long streamliner, boasting a 450 mile an hour potential for Lyn St. James.

Scott estimates the car will cost $500,000 by the time St. James is ready for testing.

"This is a new experience for us. Really. It is quite exciting. In the past, the land speed cars have been home-built."

The idea of a wheel-driven record car is the brainchild of Roger Lessman, a veteran Bonneville Salt Flats competitor. Back in 1989, Lessman set a record in the E/FS class at 292.19 mph in his own ground-effects machine.

St. James was first approached about being the project driver by Lessman in 1992. He was seeking a firm to build the car and St. James, who had known Riley for quite some time, suggested the firm.

Since that meeting, Roger Lessman and Lyn St. James have married.

Design and engineering began on the machine in September 1992. It is powered by a single engine, large-block Ford 572 cubic inch engine. Fuel choice is natural gas.

The weight of this machine, including driver, is 3000 pounds.

National Geographic is heavily involved in this project. A *National Geographic* explorer team will chart her unprecedented attempt at the wheel-driven record.

The crew will deploy as many as fifteen cameras, including cameras mounted on the car and inside the cockpit. The production will also employ aerial shots, super-long lenses and slow-motion photographs. The segment, to be aired on television, will also feature a time-lapse sequence showing construction of the car.

This marks the second time a car propelled by natural gas will seek a land speed record. In 1970, the late Gary Gabelich set the ultimate thrust record (622.407) in his rocket-powered Blue Flame, which used a mixture of Liquified Natural Gas (LNG) and hydrogen peroxide.

Lyn St. James's professional racing career began in 1979, in the Kelly American Challenge Series. In 1984, she was named Autoweek IMSA Camel GT Rookie of the Year.

A year later, she became the first woman to win a professional road race. In addition to the Indianapolis 500, she's also competed in the 12 Hours of Sebring, and the 24 Hours of Le Mans.

Lyn grew up in Willoughby, Ohio, and earned a piano-teaching certificate in St. Louis. She started racing in the Pinto her ex-husband gave her.

Her racing career progressed, her marriage was a casualty.

"Racing takes a lot out of you. It takes an intense personality, then you operate at a high level of intensity. I think [race couple] relationships require spouses who can provide that balance."

In her third Indy 500 appearance (1994), St. James qualified at 224.154 mph for a spot on the outside of Row 2, ahead of such 'hot-shot' drivers as England's Nigel Mansell, former 500 winners, Are Lynendyk and Mario Andretti and ex-national champion, Bobby Rahal.

Lyn St. James knows she's a role model for women, but that's not her sole purpose in competing.

"I hope it continues to strengthen the importance women's sports have in society.

"The fact is, I don't compete against just women. But that isn't the issue. The issue is to be a player, and not just a spectator."

She is indeed a player.

Glen Davis (Melbourne, Australia)

In 1994, five-time speed king, Craig Breedlove, journeyed to Australia's Lake Gairdner, a natural salt bed near Adelaide, to inspect the site for possible high-speed activity.

While in Australia, he met Glen Davis, went to Davis' shop and even sat in the cockpit of this wheel-driven record contender.

"I'd say Glen is thirty to thirty-five years old. He has some engineering and design background which is evident from seeing his car. When I was there a year and a half ago, the car was pretty much done.

"It has a lot of aspects that are very well done. He has a lot of potential.

"The transmission system is excellent. It was built by Allison. It's an all-automatic transmission and they're all set up by computer to shift together.

"The gearboxes are quite unique. He's got large, powerful transmission boxes that go to these Allison transmissions. I think basically they're big automatic truck transmissions, but they're electronically synchronized.

"The car has a steel monocoque frame which is kinda nice. It also seems to have a good suspension system in it. These are definite plus factors. Also, the lake bed down there will provide excellent traction for a wheel-driven car. The salt is extremely hard, and grips like mad. It's really, really tremendous.

"Horsepower should be no problem. He's using two Rolls Royce Meteor engines [twin supercharged V-12 power plants used in tanks]. He's built custom injectors and things like that for the engine.

"No one knows at this time, not even Glen, how much developmental problems he might have in getting all the fuel injectors to work. Assuming he can solve all his problems, he's a definite threat.

"The thing I found most concerning, and I told Glen so, was the extreme forward driving position in a wheel-driven car. A jet car is not gonna fishtail around on you, assuming you can build adequate stability in it.

"But with a wheel-driven car you tend to have a lot of wheelspin. If the car skates much around on him, he could get in trouble very quickly with the forward seating position.

"Why? Because you're not gonna know where the tail is basically. It can get quite a way out before you know it. Most of my jet cars have had a very forward seating position, but personally, when it comes to wheel-driven machines, I'd definitely have a strong disposition to sit in the back."

The methanol-powered supercharged V-12s each drive a set of wheels. Small tail fins flank the chisel-point tail. The body is a Kevlar/carbon fiber sandwich with balsa cores.

Each twenty-seven liter engine produces 2500 horsepower at 2800 rpm. Davis feels his Challenge boasts 500 mile an hour speed potential.

Chapter Four

Death... a Constant Companion

It's really confusing. I don't understand none of it.
I've had so many bad accidents, like the Baloney Slicer
should have got me in Carolina, or my crazy fifty mile an
hour crash in Pennsylvania, or certainly my 610 mile an
hour ride at Bonneville. But I'm still here. Others
haven't been as lucky.

Art Arfons

Art Arfons has defied death for five decades. The feeling is always the same.

"When I leave home, I wonder whether I'll be driving back. It's always on my mind... when the hell do they send the body back?

"I've never been afraid to get in a race car. I was a hell of a lot more reckless driving a dragster than I ever was setting three land speed records.

"I'd get consumed with horsepower and I could drive it into a brick wall if I had to go faster. I'd run where I bet my life on a chute at tracks that if the chute failed I'd be gone."

Whenever Arfons competed against arch-rival Don Garlits, "I admit I tried a little harder to beat that guy. Not very smart, but then again..."

At stake was $500 winner-take-all in Chester, South Carolina.

"I was driving Baloney Slicer then," Arfons vividly recalls. "Garlits went 157 and I went 155 or 156. Every time we'd get in the clocks, the front end would come up and sorta drift around.

"I thought to myself, 'Boy, if I just don't back out of it, I can get him'. So it come up and I stayed in it this time. The car went up 20, 30 feet, did 14 end-to-ends. Just completely destroyed it.

"There was no cockpit at all. It completely came apart. The engine was laying by itself. The Baloney Slicer ran like a bear. It just wasn't built heavy enough, but it was a good car."

The accident resulted in all of the tendons torn in Arfons' left hand.

"I still can't straighten out that finger."

For the records, Arfons beat Garlits on that final run and collected the $500 prize.

Was it worth it?

"Hell, no. That accident happened in the Fall, they operated on it and in the spring I had to put my hand in a cast so I could pull the brake lever on Number 11. I drove with a cast the first four, five weeks."

Now about that 50 mile an hour episode in Lancaster, Pennsylvania.

"I had a bubble shield on and they had lights right down on it, making it very hard to see. I left the line on my second pass. I got in it so hard. They had people sitting on the ground on both sides. It was packed.

"I got blinded and couldn't see how close I was to the people and I cut it back the other way. I wasn't going more than fifty miles an hour. Well, it rolled a couple of times and stopped upside down right on the track. It was an airport track.

"Gasoline was running out. Oil was running out. They [track crew] came out real quick and were gonna drag it off the runway. Ed [Snyder] reached in and pulled me out. He dropped me on my head and I was really hurting. I busted both ribs. I was really in a lot of pain that night.

"So, speed doesn't always kill," says Arfons, tongue-in-cheek. "It was pretty violent because it was a heavy car and it crashed down on top. I still got the engine."

Arfons is the only man in history to survive a 600 mile an hour crash on land, and he attributes credit for his survival in large part to the Bonneville Salt Flats.

"The salt is why. You can't dig in and get hurt like you could on dirt or water or something that you can't slide. With the salt you can slide for a mile and not make a sudden stop."

The late Doctor Nathan Ostich, first man to drive a jet car in land speed racing, was most fearful of fire. What about Art Arfons?

"My biggest concern, not fear, was a blowout. Tires became my biggest worry ever since I blew the first one. You'd sorta tighten up, wonder if you're gonna lose it when you really got moving.

"It's a funny thing, I never thought about a fire. The fuel tank was right at my back. I was practically sitting on it. Sure, something could have broken, triggering a fire. And I never carried an on-board fire extinguisher."

During Arfons' 610 mile an hour wild ride, caused by a frozen ball-bearing, the car flipped at least twice. Most of the damage was to the front and right side of the Green Monster. Arfons rode from the left cockpit.

"If it would have rolled one more time, the roll cage, everything would have collapsed in on me. If I was sitting up front, there would have been no chance.

"If I were driving from the right side like Richard Noble, I would have been flattened. I guess that means I was in the right place at the right time."

Arfons also gives part of the credit for his miraculous survival to his lucky black jacket.

"I took it out of my closet just the other day," he says, "tried it on and it still fits good. It's in pretty good shape after all these years. A lot better shape than me."

Art Arfons was wearing his very worn, black leather jacket that scary November day at Bonneville. In fact, he'd worn that same jacket for years.

Before returning for Bonneville in 1966, Arfons used a foot-pedal operated sewing machine to repair the jacket. And he says he's not really superstitious!

"I started wearing that jacket when I was running Cyclops, my jet dragster.

"I guess you just get used to wearing it. It becomes a part of your racing uniform. It becomes part of the man."

Following Arfons' 610 mph crash, he was flown to a Salt Lake City hospital. One of his few visitors was Jim Cook, Firestone's motorsports PR man. Cook had witnessed the horrible crash.

They talk about the crash, the car. Cook touches one of Arfons' forearms.

"Leather jacket saved me, you see? Not a scratch on my arms or body, right?"

Cook answers, "Right," blinking his eyes.

Only a few hours earlier, Cook had thought that Art Arfons was dead.

Unlike Craig Breedlove, his chief rival, Arfons didn't believe in slowly increasing his speed by increments. He always viewed land speed racing as Russian Roulette and as comfortable as he became in his Monster, he knew "the more times you pull the trigger, the greater your chances of blowing off your head.

"I was concerned and I had a lot going through my mind but saying I was shaking and afraid, I never was. If I was afraid, I wouldn't want to do it.

"I really don't understand Breedlove. I was there once and watched him make a run. They prepared the car and it sat on the track. They said the track was clear. He got in, closed the canopy and sat there for something like ten minutes.

"I thought something was wrong. He was psyching himself up or something. All of a sudden he waved he was ready, they wound up the engine and off he went."

Arfons, admits, however, that he was more than anxious the night before a land speed attempt.

"Before I did one record I hid in the laundry. I went to the Laundromat, did my laundry and tried to get tired. I didn't sleep real good."

Arfons was never concerned that the Green Monster would become airborne, unlike Breedlove's Spirit of America – Sonic I, which did a front wheelie at about 600 miles an hour.

"I knew my car was gonna stay on the ground. The wing was gonna keep it down so that really wasn't a problem worrying about it flying."

He considers crashes "just part of the game. I don't care what kind of racing you do, somewhere, sometime, you're gonna crack it up. You're gonna get hurt. Or maybe you're gonna get killed."

But the deaths of others still torment him today, more than twenty years after young Garth Hardacre was fatally injured at a drag strip in Pennsylvania, a reporter and two youngsters were killed at a Dallas, Texas track.

"If there's two things I could change in my life," says Arfons, "it would be those accidents."

Hardacre started out as an opponent, and he quickly became a friend.

"I used to run against him. He ran for a group called the Blue Devils at Massillon. They'd bring their little dragster up to run at the airport with us.

"He was competition and he started hanging around my shop. He started working for me part-time. Then he wanted to drive, so I put him in The Dud to start with."

Arfons was driving full-time on the drag circuit. In addition, Hardacre and 'Fast Eddie', "a roundie-round driver from Canton, also drove for me. He drove Super Cyclops, so we had three cars for about a year.

"After a while," recalls Arfons, "Garth wanted to drive a funny car, so we built a jet-powered Corvette. He helped build it. He was really a good guy, a good driver, real quiet and dependable."

Arfons will always remember that Sunday night phone call.

"Bud [crew member Bud Groff] was with him. I was home that Sunday night. I had run that weekend. Bud called and said, 'There's been an accident', but he wouldn't tell me Garth was dead. He just said, 'It looked bad, they took him to the hospital'.

"I kept calling and calling the hospital, and finally they said he was dead."

His voice still cracks as he talks about the incident, more than twenty years after it happened.

What caused the accident?

"Garth was hitting about 200 when it happened. Just outside the clocks there was a bad dip at that track and he came into the dip. When he came down, he was a little crooked.

"The Corvette was sorta short wheel-based and unforgiving. If you got crossed up, it was gonna go. Garth went through the fence and was killed instantly. The dip had been there for a couple of years. They filled it up later."

By 1971, Arfons was nearing the end of his drag racing career, even before his haunting accident at Dallas.

"When your reaction time starts to slow down in a sport where there's little or no margin for error, you can see the handwriting on the wall."

But Arfons wanted to go out as the first drag racer to reach 300 miles an hour in the quarter mile. He had hit 294 and there was still more horsepower to be squeezed out of his jet engine.

It was a twin-cockpit car, similar in design to his record-setting Green Monster. He drove from the left cockpit. The right cockpit was usually empty.

"I was running for IHRA [International Hot Rod Association] that year and as a pre-race promotion gimmick, we'd put a TV personality guy in the right cockpit prior to the meet and he'd do a story on what it was like to go 270, 280. I never thought anything bad could happen."

Art Arfons was so wrong!

An accident, with Arfons at the controls, would result in the deaths of three people and a $1 million lawsuit against Arfons.

Thomas Eugene Alfred, a thirty-one year old newsman from WFFA-TV in Dallas, who broadcast under the name 'Gene Thomas', was guest 'co-pilot' as Arfons prepared for his routine run at Dallas International Motor Speedway. He was one of the stellar attractions at the Texas open drag racing championship, three days of speed and thrills.

Arfons left the starting line about 2:45 that ill-fated Sunday afternoon.

"I'd just gone through the clocks and everything was fine. I was hitting 289 when a tire blew. I went through the clocks before it crashed. I was running about ten feet from the guard rail and went into the rail. There were eight-by-eight posts there and I took out 200 feet of 'em.

"Actually, we hit on my side of the car. We hit on the left side and if anyone should have been killed, it should have been me. After the car went through the posts, it rolled over and went on its top until it landed in a ditch. Then it burned. I managed to crawl out of the wreckage.

"The crash knocked my shoes right off. I injured my foot, my ankle and my shoulder. At that time all I knew was that they had taken my passenger to the hospital. They told me to go home. They got me a ticket and when the flight stopped in Chicago, I called. They told me the man had died.

"I said I'd come back and they said, 'No, you'd better go on home'. I also found out that two boys were also killed in the accident.

The boys had run over to see the car come through and they were standing right in the clocks against the guard rail. I never knew they were there."

The young men were identified as Robert John Kelseyp, (twenty), of Tyler, Texas and Sean Panse, (seventeen), of Dallas. Both were members of the IHRA staff.

Bill Dale, an IHRA spokesman, said Arfons was "almost through the quarter mile and was slowing down" when the car started smoking and suddenly veered into the railing.

"It looked as though, when he pulled the chutes, the left rear tire blew," said Dale. "It looked like it all happened at the same time."

Although there were several thousand spectators at the track at the time of the accident, only Kelsey and Panse were in the area when Super Cyclops went out of control.

They apparently died instantly as the car hurtled over them and plunged to the swampy area in the back of the finish line.

"There was a fire, but no explosion," said Dale.

The jet car ran on kerosene and carried only enough fuel for one run.

Thomas apparently was killed when the jet overturned after going through the rail, although no witnesses saw Super Cyclops overturn due to clouds of smoke coming from the dragster.

It was theorized that the blowout triggered the tragedy. The demolished car was shipped back to Arfons' garage in Akron, Ohio for examination. The left rear tire in question was returned to Goodyear for analysis.

A few days later, IHRA president Larry Carrier told a hostile group of Dallas newsmen that preliminary investigations had revealed that 'bead' on the left rear tire had caused the vehicle to veer out of control.

Super Cyclops, he continued, was forced from the right lane to the left lane of the strip. At 844 feet past the finish line, the jet car struck the thirty-two inch high guard rail on the left side.

Super Cyclops then catapulted up on to the railing, tore out 157 feet of it, then bounced on to a parallel return road where the two young men were struck and killed.

Super Cyclops continued bouncing, skidding and rolling sideways for 948 feet. It left the track near the escape road at the end, traveled

210 feet along the gravel shoulder and flipped over, finally coming to rest upside-down near a small water-filled slough.

"It was really scary looking at all those documents, 'State of Texas vs. Art Arfons' when we went to court in downtown Akron. All the lawyers showed up. It all boiled down to one thing. Goodyear never tested those tires.

"They told me they had run 'em up on their machine, tested 'em to 350. But they never ran a test. So, Goodyear paid the million. Until then, I had run only for Firestone, but Firestone was getting out of the deal.

"They [Firestone] were just giving me tires. I wasn't working for them anymore. Along came Goodyear offering me all kinds of bullshit. It was gonna be a good deal for me.

"Goodyear wanted new tires on the first car to go 300 in the quarter, so they made me a hell of an offer. They said they'd give me the tires before I'd run in Texas. They sent my tires down to Garlits [Don] and we picked 'em up over there, put 'em on and ran in Dallas."

It was Art Arfons' last drag race appearance.

For years Arfons had heard the claim that race drivers are all kamikaze pilots, operating with a death wish.

"It's aggravating. I hear it all the time. It's not right and we don't like it.

"If you're doing something enough times so that you get comfortable in it, it's really not that dangerous. I had a reputation of going out and hammering it at the Salt Flats. But I got so accustomed to the car. I knew no matter what kind of speed I hit, I could handle it."

Arfons, admittedly, enjoys the feeling of power.

"Them old Allison engines sure done something to me. They just sounded power. You could feel the piston engine vibrate the frames."

Later, he would set three land speed records, riding a 17,500 horsepower volcano that rumbled and spewed a long, fiery tail.

In all his years of drag racing, Arfons drove an open cockpit car. Not so with the record-setting Green Monster. It was a closed cockpit.

"I always had the feeling I was sitting in a coffin and they closed the lid on you. I was never in a closed cockpit in drag racing. I can remember my thoughts one time. I thought, 'Well, I'm over forty and I've lived long enough'. I thought if this is it, so be it."

A mental change took place when Arfons squeezed into the cockpit.

"Climbing into the car, they tell me, I'm white as a ghost. Then the motor winds up and it's a Jekyll and Hyde sort of thing. The whine becomes music and all I want to do is put my foot through the floorboard."

Back in 1979, Art Arfons knew something was terribly wrong. He was tractor pulling in Wisconsin and Michigan.

"I got handling weights on that trip. I'd handled a couple, damn near collapsed. I had to lay on the ground for about ten minutes. I'd handle a couple more and have to lay down.

"When I got home, I went to my doctor and had a cardiogram. I didn't know what the problem was. They had me go to the hospital after the EKG. I remember some gal telling me not to go anywhere without talking to my doctor.

"Before I got home she not only had called my house, but so did the doctor. They put me back in the hospital that day. My doctor said I'd better, or I won't last the weekend.

"I had triple bypass surgery. I had complete blockage in two arteries and one partial blockage in another. I wasn't scared. They told me the odds of surviving the operation were in my favor. And besides, I didn't really have a choice.

"The surgery took place at the end of the '79 season. I ran in January of 1980. They told me a bypass was good for about ten years, and I guess they're almost right. I've way exceeded that ten year limit.

"I've got two complete blocks right now. They said I've got hardening of the arteries. The only two that are operating are the ones they had patches on. He [my doctor] said it would be too risky to even try an operation.

"I feel okay, other than that I tire real easy. That's all. I've got nothing to bitch about."

Speed is his obsession!

"I think mountain climbing and land speed racing come under the category of sports. How many guys get killed in football each year? Why do they go out and run back and forth across the field to see who can get to the other end?

"Financially, I haven't gotten rich out of land speed racing. So why do I do it? I don't know how to explain it. It's really something I don't understand myself.

"It's obvious to anyone who knows anything about gambling that I'll never survive another 600 mile an hour crash. Everything is running on the ragged edge and it's just like you're balancing yourself. A couple of ounces can push you off."

Since 1960, three men have been killed in pursuit of the land speed record. Six others, including Arfons, have survived brushes with death.

On August 1, 1960, Athol Graham fired up his City of Salt Lake Special. Two miles into his run, the blood-red car went airborne and crashed. Graham, thirty-six, died two hours later at a Salt Lake City hospital.

On September 10, 1962, Glenn Leasher had already made one run in Romeo Palimedes' jet-thrust Infinity. On his second attempt, Leasher reached a speed of 250 when the car appeared to blow up. The jet crashed, killing Leasher.

For years afterwards, Leasher's mangled machine was left on the Flats. A deadly reminder of what could happen.

"I really wasn't aware of the car," says Arfons, "because they put it up against a fence. Then some movie company wanted me to pose by it. It was just sun-up and I was going out to make a first run. I asked if we could do it at night, afterwards, but they didn't want it that way. Since Firestone was paying for the movie, I did it against my own wishes.

"I'm walking and looking at the wreck. They're playing music. It was a weird feeling. I knew Leasher."

The last fatality took place in December 1970 when Noel Black crashed during the Bonneville Nationals. He was in pursuit of Bobby Summers' 409 mph wheel-driven record.

Black and his car, Motion I, made their debut in 1969 and reached a promising speed of 335.820. The machine was almost thirty feet long and weighed nearly two tons.

The car, designed for 450 miles an hour, was powered by a pair of blown Chrysler engines, each producing more than 1000 horses. Black sat behind the rear engine. The second engine was in the nose.

Because of its odd appearance, Motion I was quickly dubbed 'Rhinosaurus'.

In September 1970, Black returned to Bonneville and increased his speed to 352. However, rain washed out all activity the next day. After a twenty-four hour delay, action resumed.

Three accidents took place within a three hour period. The worst injury was a broken arm. Noel Black was next. The major problem was taking place between Mile 4 and 5. It was slippery.

Black reached a speed of about 330 miles an hour when Motion I veered sideways, rolled and exploded. Black was thrown out of the car and died five hours later at a Salt Lake hospital.

Arfons, Breedlove, Donald Campbell, 'Doc' Nathan Ostich, Gary Gabelich and Slick Gardner were luckier than Black. They all flirted with death at the Bonneville Salt Flats, but lived to tell the tale.

Campbell, Ostich and Gabelich would all die. But only Ostich died of natural causes.

Campbell invaded Bonneville in 1960 with his $4 million jet-powered Bluebird. He sustained a broken eardrum, ruptured middle ear and skull fracture as the result of his spectacular 360 mph slide. He blamed 'oxygen poisoning' for the crash. Campbell breathed pure oxygen. Following that discovery, carbon dioxide was mixed with oxygen.

"As we discovered much later," said Campbell, "there are certain people – and I was one of them – who experienced a form of drunkenness if they inhale pure oxygen at sea level.

"I knew she was going out of control. Felt it. Actually felt the tail spinning, and I knew what would happen. I knew I'd crash, but none of it seemed to concern me. I just sat there in that split second thinking, 'Well, this is the end'. And not feeling the remotest interest."

Four years later, Campbell drove the same Bluebird to a wheel-driven record of 403.1 mph at Lake Eyre in Australia. In January 1967, he was killed in pursuit of another world water speed record. Campbell was forty-five.

Ostich, a Los Angeles doctor who ushered in the jet age to land speed racing (1960) with his Flying Caduceus, skidded out of control after hitting 331 in 1962. Fortunately, damage to both the car and driver was minimal.

In 1964, Breedlove survived his wild ride after setting a two-way unlimited record of 526. His three-wheeled Spirit of America splintered a row of telephone poles and finally rested nose first in a small pond. He swam to safety.

One year later Breedlove's second jet – Spirit of America – Sonic I – gave the handsome Californian another scare when it went airborne at 600. The front two wheels lifted off the salt.

Arfons, who battled Breedlove for two stormy years (1964–65), miraculously escaped death on November 17, 1966 when his 17,500 horsepower Green Monster crashed at an estimated 610 mph. No broken bones, just facial cuts, abrasions and bruises.

More than twenty years later, in July 1989, Arfons, aged sixty-four, went airborne at 350 in his two-wheeled, 1800 pound, jet-powered Monster, the smallest and lightest car in land speed history. Injuries to both man and machine were repairable. Both would try again.

On October 11, 1970 – 12 days before he set the unlimited thrust mark – Gabelich rode out a 550 mile an hour ride which ended thirteen miles from the starting point, some four miles past where he intended to bring Blue Flame to a halt.

"It was a weird feeling," he said. "I tripped the toggle on the chute, then waited for the impact when it opened. Nothing happened, so I tripped the emergency chute. When nothing happened the second time I knew I was going a long way.

"I just flipped on the intercom and told the crew to come and get me. Man, it was scary for a time. I tried to steer left towards the mountains, but the car kept skidding to the right. My main concern was that the right wheel would dig into the salt and cause the car to roll.

"Finally, I skidded to a stop and all of a sudden the weird thought that my chutes hadn't deployed struck me. It struck me very funny. The car was covered with salt when it stopped. You'd have thought we were sponsored by Morton's the way it looked."

In 1978, wealthy Californian rancher, Slick Gardner, bought Art Arfons' jet-powered Green Monster, and made trial runs at El Mirage in California before going to Utah's Bonneville Salt Flats. Gardner was hitting 552 mph when the car suddenly veered sharp left. It was his only land speed attempt, but it marked the first appearance of metal wheels on a land speed car.

All of these men knew the danger involved in the high speed game, yet they risked their lives in pursuit of the land speed record.

Why?

Campbell once said, "There is no escape from record breaking and I know perfectly well that no record can ever be final. Once you have had a taste of a record bid you can never get away from it. It will be a sorry day when we no longer do something for the hell of it."

Ego, Campbell thought, played a major factor in his pursuit of both the land and water speed records.

"You know why I do this? Conceit," he said. "No other reason when you boil it down. The conceit of believing that this is something I can do better than anyone else in the world.

"I suppose it's the same reason with most artists or politicians. Everyone likes to think that they're unique. This is my way of proving it."

Campbell admitted that he never met anyone who wasn't afraid of death, including himself.

"At the same time one must keep the thing in perspective. One must realize that this is a very natural fear that the good Lord has built into every living creature and that it is possible, as many people do, to grossly exaggerate it."

Breedlove, now sixty years old, still dreams of a sixth land speed record. He fully realizes the risk.

"If something goes wrong at 600, you've really got problems. And the faster we go, the greater the danger. Driving at 600 miles an hour is very demanding, both physically and psychologically. You've got 8000 pounds of car going faster than a 30–30 bullet, or a cruising jetliner.

"Once I close the canopy, it's all business. You've got a tiger by the tail and you'd better hang on. The pressure acceleration is about 2 Gs – not too severe. But it gets as high as ten Gs when the drag chute goes out. You just hang on there in your seat belt. It feels as though the car is tipped over on its nose and you're driving upside down."

Prestige and not the lure of gold is the motivating force, says Breedlove.

"Let's face it. When you sit down in the cockpit, all the money in the world isn't going to make you drive that car if you don't really want the record. Believe it or not, speed really scares the stuffing out of me. I certainly don't crave it."

Gabelich admitted there was no sane reason for driving 600 plus.

"Speed, the feeling of going fast, has been part of my life since I can remember. I guess it's doing something a lot of people can't do or refuse to do.

"I've always had the secret dream to hold the land speed record. There's no greater feeling than being a winner. Land on the moon and you're a hero for one day. Set the land speed record and you're a hero the rest of your life. Sure, I accept the danger involved. It's part of my profession."

Gabelich spoke almost flippantly about death.

"If I should die because of my racing, at least my parents and close friends will know I went out with a smile on my face.

"I think of myself as a lion tamer. With all that horsepower, you try to utilize as much of it as possible without getting hurt. There's a fine line between control of the car and complete disaster. That's what makes it a challenge."

Gabelich enjoyed the feeling of fear.

"Many drivers express fear in different ways. My moment of fear comes just before the run. But when I climb into the car it's exhilarating – the adrenaline starts pumping. You think clear, you're in a world of your own. It's just out of sight."

Gary Michael Gabelich, holder of the land speed record for thirteen years, was killed in a motorcycle-truck accident in California in January 1984. He was forty-three. He left a wife and infant son.

Speed has also brought visions of death.

Arfons had a dream that he would crash. It came true at 610 miles an hour.

Campbell twice saw 'the messenger of death'.

"When I took Bluebird out to Bonneville in 1960, I was convinced that I was going to kill myself. I had a presentiment of death when I was on vacation just before I started the trip. It's the one time in my life I've had it, and sure enough everything went wrong from then on."

Less than forty-eight hours before his death in 1967, Campbell drew the Ace and Queen of Spades during a card game. For the fantastically superstitious Englishman, it was clearly a forecast of death.

Campbell appeared crestfallen.

"Mary Queen of Scots turned up the same combination and knew she would be beheaded. I know that one of my family is going to get the chop. I pray to God it isn't me."

The new playing cards were green-backed, the color Campbell believed was unlucky for him. Later that night, he told a close friend, "Well, I reckon it should be over tomorrow – one way or the other."

The premonition came true as the jet-powered Bluebird soared off the surface of Lake Coniston in England at a speed exceeding 300 miles an hour. The man who had set seven water and one land speed record disappeared into the pages of history.

Breedlove also had an uneasy feeling the day before he wrecked his Spirit of America during the return run that cemented a 526 record in 1964.

"I had a feeling that I was going to get killed. I couldn't sleep the night before. I was nervous on my first run, but I really hit it on the return. I could have gone 600 instead of 539."

One year later, Breedlove survived his second scare as Spirit of America – Sonic I veered off course at 600 mph. The racer careened off the official timing areas off the track, across wet salts through an opening in a line of telephone poles and finally rolled to a stop in front of a salt water pond – nine miles from where he left the track.

England's Richard Noble, who wrestled the record away from America with his two-way average of 633.4 in 1983, was practical-minded enough to take care of business years before he took his hopes and dreams to Bonneville (1981) in what turned out to be a three year quest for glory.

"Once we had decided to have a go, I saw my solicitor, sorted out the will and the insurance and that was that.

"If it was going to end, it would all finish with a very loud bang. I considered that on Day 1... and then forgot about it. If I hadn't, the men in white coats would have been waiting for me."

Chapter Five

The Great Race

They tried like hell to get it done in 1995.

But they simply ran out of time, and the money didn't always flow their direction.

Two legends of land speed racing, determined to be the firstest with the mostest: five-time king of speed, Craig Breedlove, a 'relic' of the glorious sixties, and England's Richard Noble, the fastest man on wheels. Both determined to officially break the speed of sound, unlike the controversial Budweiser Rocket of the late 1970s. Both hell-bent to do their thing in 1996 at Black Rock Desert in Nevada.

Sixteen men working full-time on Noble's massive machine, Thrust SSC (Super Sonic Car). A genuine beast measuring 57 feet in length, weighing 14,000 pounds, and powered by a pair of British jet engines churning out 100,000 horsepower.

Across the Atlantic, at Rio Vista, California, five men in the final stages of turning Spirit of America – Sonic Arrow from a sketch on a piece of paper to a fire-breathing missile on wheels. Forty-eight thousand horsepower.

Both machines projected at 850 miles an hour speed potential!

When Noble ended his nine year quest for the record in 1983 with his successful 633.4 effort at Black Rock, he returned home a hero, a man anxiously awaiting a challenge to his hard-fought record.

There was Thrust SSC in the back of his mind all the time, but he logically concluded he could not obtain financial backing for this colossal project until a challenger had stepped forth and made him ex-king Richard.

Three-time speed king, Art Arfons, Breedlove's rival in 1964–65, unsuccessfully tried in 1989–90–91 in his mini-sized Green Monster. Noble was at the Bonneville Salt Flats in October 1990, rooting the then sixty-four year old Art Arfons on to greater glory.

Noble did not want a long reign if that meant no competition.

But the competition came, not only from the United States but from Australia as well.

Aussie Rosco McGlashan entered the land speed chase with his Aussie Invader 2, and clocked 500 miles an hour at a salt bed near Australia.

Breedlove, who celebrated his sixtieth birthday in March 1997, began construction of his 'dream machine' back in 1993.

The threat to his record was real, so Richard Noble, that charismatic promoter, no longer faced the indifference of potential backers. Wave the British flag. Sing 'God Save The Queen'.

THE GREAT RACE had begun.

But this time around, Noble would let an experienced jet jockey take his creation through the sound barrier... RAF fighter pilot Andy Green. Call it being practical, and besides, Noble's wife, Sally, has been against her husband driving this car.

Breedlove, the first to average 400, 500 and 600 miles an hour in his two previous jet cars, Spirit of America and Spirit of America – Sonic 1 also wants to become the first to average 700, then set his sights on the mysterious sound barrier.

Realistically, Breedlove said, "I think the most we could hope for would be to get to 700 in 1996. If we can successfully do that, it would be a major accomplishment.

"Then, the plan would be to pull back and equip the car with autopilot and begin unmanned testing in 1997. If unmanned testing is successful, then we would do manned supersonic runs for the record."

Whether it be to better Noble's existing record or take dead aim at the barrier, Breedlove plans to do it as he's always done it – through the measured mile. The time-tested way. Strictly by the rules.

Not the way the Budweiser Rocket did it back in 1979 with stuntman Stan Barrett in the cockpit. First claiming a record that does not exist and never has, a one-way land speed record of 638 mph set through a fifty-two foot long speed trap, then unofficially clocking 739 that December at Edwards Air Force Base.

It is a so-called record still shrouded in controversy that casts a shadow over Breedlove and Richard Noble.

"Why would I be going through this exercise of building a supersonic car if someone had already done it," Breedlove asks. "That's a lot of trouble to go through if it's already been done."

"It's unfortunate that so much public relations misinformation was generated intentionally by these people to try to substantiate this claim. It's unofficial. It's unsanctioned. It was done with uncalibrated measuring devices that malfunctioned during the run. So now, what's left? The actual clocking was 666."

(The Bud Rocket episode is examined in another chapter.)

By late summer of 1995, it became apparent to Craig Breedlove that he wouldn't run that year.

"It wasn't even a decision," he points out. "It just wasn't completed in time for October as we had hoped.

"We weren't able to get our financing together in time to accelerate the work schedule enough to get it done. You only have so much cash flow to pay so many people.

"That car had been completed for quite a while from the engineering and technical standpoint. Everything in the car is hand-made. It takes skilled labor, and that's very time consuming."

And surprisingly, finding skilled workers turned out to be a major problem.

"There's actually a shortage of top people internationally in motorsports and because of that it's supply and demand. So you've got a twofold problem. One is just finding guys and secondly if you find somebody, trying to afford to get 'em. It has had a tremendous upward pressure on wages. I mean, a good drag racing crew chief is now making $125,000 a year."

Breedlove wasn't complaining, just stating the situation.

"The biggest problem was getting people that know how to form and shape aluminum. We've actually had to go to England to look for that kind of help. I knew the project would be big, and it has been."

He had hoped to complete Spirit of America – Sonic Arrow by February 1996, and begin preliminary testing at Edwards Air Force Base in California by April.

However, it wasn't meant to be.

Testing wouldn't come until the Fall of 1996 at the Bonneville Salt Flats in Utah.

Breedlove has made some minor changes to the car, but nothing major.

"We've done minor things from the initial concept. We've increased the ground clearance some. We've extended the boundary layer fences a little bit forward from the initial layout on the air ducts.

But essentially, it's exactly as we had planned it. Certainly it's a very spectacular car to look at."

Breedlove decided on a J–79 jet engine, the same type that propelled Spirit of America – Sonic 1 to a new record of 600.601 mph in 1965. It is the same engine that carried Art Arfons to three records – 434, 536 and 576 – on the ground and propelled Darryl Greenamayer to a low altitude air speed record of 997 miles an hour.

"Greenamayer set his record fifty meters above the ground in an F–104," says Breedlove. "The car is lighter and smaller than the aircraft by a substantial amount. The car weighs half as much as an F–104.

"The F–104 is fifty-eight feet long, has a much larger frontal area than the car, probably almost double. It does not have any rolling drag. However, it weighs 18,000 pounds. You have to keep it off the ground somehow and you do that with lift. Lift equals drag.

"So you've got more air drag in a plane than you do the car. The car has some rolling drag, so an offhand, very conservative analogy is that the car will have less drag than the F–104, and the F–104 went 997 miles an hour with the same engine the car has.

"My analogy is that the car should be able to go supersonic. That's just a seat-of-the-pants analogy, but it works for me."

Admittedly, Craig Breedlove hasn't had much time to worry about what Richard Noble, or the others, plan to do in his Unlimited Thrust class, but he's made it his business to learn as much as he can about the British car.

"I really don't know what Richard's doing. He's had his share of problems to solve, meaning money. I've never run out of money. I mean I have what I have and I need more."

In 1993, Noble returned to Gurlock, Nevada, to celebrate the tenth anniversary of his land speed record. Craig Breedlove was at that party.

"Richard did tell me a couple of years ago that he was planning to build a twin-engined car. I speculated on how that car might be configured, but frankly I was a long way off from what he actually did.

"I have seen some photographs of Richard's frame in his shop in England, and I do know his car will have rear-wheel steering. It's a very difficult way to steer the car.

"My objection to doing that myself would be in order to get the front wheels to steer one or two degrees in either direction, you have to yaw the entire fuselage two degrees.

"The front wheels are fixed. You move the back end of the car the opposite way that you want to go. In the back of the car you have a very large stabilizer that you've put up there so that the car won't yaw. But how are you gonna steer it?

"Assuming you get this thing up to 600 miles an hour and you need to steer it two degrees to the left and you've got a great big vertical stabilizer tail sitting right on the tail, how in the hell are you gonna move it over to a two-degree angle of attack? What's gonna move it? Those wheels aren't gonna move it. They're just gonna turn and push.

"It's certainly an approach I wouldn't have taken, but hey, let's just wait and see. Richard could prove me wrong. We have a well-planned program which I'm gonna try to stick to as best as I can. It's an untried, untested machine and we're going into speed ranges that no one has ever gone into before."

Breedlove's red, white and blue jet car is forty-four feet long, almost eight and a half feet wide, and weighs 9000 pounds (wet).

It is a five-wheeler powered by a J-79 engine, developing 26,650 pounds of thrust – or 48,000 horsepower – with four-stage afterburner.

"Basically we're looking at an initial record of 650 miles an hour. At that point we'll go for an unmanned test program. I couldn't tell you I'm going to break the sound barrier. I can tell you I'd like to.

"I think we have adequate power to do it. I think the design will also make it possible. It's a totally new design. It's very unique, quite revolutionary.

"It's easy to say how fast you can go, but very hard to do. Richard's record is 633. I can tell you what the drag numbers on the car are. I could tell you what the thrust is.

"I could tell you what an estimate of the rolling drag will be. I can tell you given a five mile approach the car has a potential purely calculating only drag, only power, that you have such-and-such potential.

"It's easy to click off the numbers like 600... 700... 750... but it's something else to do it when it counts."

He does not minimize the potential danger involved with the sound barrier.

"Sonic I was not an exploration into transonic airflow for me," he says. "Basically I learned a lot... the hard way.

"The air was actually going supersonic between the two front wheels underneath the belly. That was causing the nose to lift up at 600 miles an hour.

"My peak during the run was actually 640. It came way off the ground, about twelve inches in the air. I barely got the thing back. I think the sound barrier is a developmental problem.

"They've run sleds supersonic. Fire a bullet. It goes supersonic. I think when you take a vehicle and run it on ground-effect in a supersonic condition it has to be dealt with.

"There's nothing known about it. You don't have any people that have gone before you and done the same thing. At one time they had never done it in an aircraft. It was an unknown thing, but once they learned about it they knew how to deal with it."

As with his previous two land speed record-setting cars, Breedlove sits in front of the engine.

"It's a place that has an aerodynamic advantage. I can't figure out any way to sit in the back and get the same streamlining."

He has two fully operative J-79s at his disposal.

"We have a ready-to-run back-up engine if that becomes necessary. We'll be running a standard four-stage burner equipped with a specially designed, fixed nozzle."

His plan was to build two nozzles, "one of which will be somewhat restricted in that it will take me up to military power, which is just before afterburner. Then I'll have an open nozzle which is just for afterburner.

"We'll do preliminary testing with a military-power nozzle on it, and once we've done our preliminary testing we'll make runs with full power. What's it like to run that fast? I think it's ecstasy mixed with stark terror."

Breedlove's method of operations means countless runs made at progressively faster increments until it's 'showtime'.

As he puts it, "I think it's a good idea to make lots of runs. I don't think it's a sound idea to drive over 600 miles an hour with a total of three minutes experience under your belt."

His first hurdle was purchasing the J-79s.

"I'd been looking for the engine for quite some time to do a land speed project. Obviously, you need a pretty good shop because it's just like building a prototype jet fighter plane.

"I needed a facility which I purchased in Rio Vista [California], an old car agency. It's about 6500 square feet."

Until the cost and supply of rocket fuel became prohibitive, Breedlove was seriously considering going that route. He had driven his English Leather rocket dragster to a peak speed of 377 miles an hour in the quarter. ET: 4.65 seconds.

"Actually the car handled pretty well. It was a good car for me because it got me used to some real high acceleration rates. It was an excellent phase to go through.

"The Gs went from about 4.5 to about 5.5, and back to 5 at the end. I'd gone as far as building a mock-up for a rocket car, but that never materialized for two reasons.

"For one thing, the people who had agreed to sponsor the land speed car breached the contract. They sorta just left us holding the bag. The unbelievable cost of fuel was another factor.

"From the time I began running my rocket dragster until the time I stopped in 1974, the cost went up something like thirteen times. It got to the point where a single run on Unsymmetrical Hydrazene and Nitrogen Tetroxide would run about $35,000.

"The fuels were developed for NASA and the Air Force. However, various government agencies categorized the stuff very stringently and it took away my ability to transport and store the fuel.

"As the restrictions became tighter and tighter it became virtually impossible. You had to have a federally approved fuel depot for rocket fuels in order to store it.

"Then we changed the engine design from Hydrazine to Hydrogen Peroxide. That was okay at first, but they quit manufacturing Peroxide in the higher concentration in the United States.

"The only Peroxide available was in Europe and it was something like 72 percent concentration. In order to make that into suitable rocket fuel you would have had to go through a reprocessing phase once you got there. It became unrealistic to think that way."

Thus, Craig Breedlove's battle plan shifted to the J-79. He actually ran a J-79 in his 600 mile an hour Spirit of America – Sonic I, but that came equipped with a three-stage, not a four-stage afterburner.

Once he was forced to scrap the rocket car concept, "I just came up with a whole new design."

Goodyear Tire & Rubber not only supplied the wheels and tires for his record-setting cars, but was a major sponsor as well. Goodyear, however, is no longer in the land speed business.

Richard Noble and Art Arfons both ran metal wheels, but Craig Breedlove doesn't like metal wheels. His tires are made of Kevlar, an exceptionally strong synthetic material.

Breedlove had stated before construction began that he was wealthy enough to fund the project himself... if need be. But that didn't turn out to be the case.

Such American giants as Shell Oil, Chevrolet, Alcoa Aluminum, and Autozone jumped on the 'Breedlove Bandwagon'.

So did television/motion picture star, Craig T Nelson, who has purchased the film rights to Breedlove's life story. Nelson will write the screenplay.

In all of Breedlove's successful record runs (1963–65), USAC (United States Auto Club) was the official timer. This time, however, IMSA (International Motor Sports Association) would sanction and certify his record attempt, as authorized by the FIA (Federation International du Sport Automobile).

FIA sanctions vehicles with at least four wheels. Breedlove's car is a five-wheeler.

IMSA is more familiar to sports car racing. Its five series produce nineteen driver and manufacturer championships, paying more than $7 million in prize money and bonus awards.

Breedlove test-fired his back-up J–79 engine in February 1996. The static test delighted the five-time speed king.

"We were curious to see how the engine responded in terms of smooth throttle operation, exhaust gas temperature and vibration. Every expectation was exceeded, and yet the engine was well within manufacturer's specifications."

The test cell gauges climbed to a sustained 22,650 pounds of thrust.

"I was blown away by the amount of power we were making," said crew member, Tim McKinney. "Engines I've worked on in the past never made that much power running on jet fuel, let alone unleaded gasoline."

Five months later (July 1996), 'Team Breedlove' set up test headquarters at Black Rock Desert in Nevada to test the jet car's brake system.

The test was done by attaching the hydraulically actuated mechanism to one of the team's pickup trucks.

With Breedlove at the control lever the big-friction 'ski' made flawless contact on the dry lake surface, bringing the truck to a firm stop in simulating sixty-to-zero mph deceleration of the Spirit of America land speed car.

"I call it my 'Fred Flintstone' brake and it works," said a beaming Breedlove after applying the braking system numerous times at various test speeds.

Black Rock Desert, the largest dry-rock bed in North America – 250 square miles – is alkaline dirt, sun-dried to a flat hardness after a winter of heavy rains that turn the desert basin into a lake every year.

During his nine year odyssey of trying to capture the land speed record, Richard Noble had his goal set on Thrust SSC, a car designed to go supersonic. Thrust 2 was strictly subsonic, a stepping stone. Says Noble:

"John [Thrust 2 designer, John Ackroyd] and I began plans, almost immediately after I'd set the record, for Thrust 3, but it never proceeded past a preliminary drawing and an Olympus engine which we were given. This engine produces 36,000 pounds of thrust and is used in the Concorde.

"But honestly speaking, not only were we totally exhausted by the Thrust 2 experience, but so were our sponsors. I think everybody just wanted to enjoy what had been achieved.

"At the time, I was running my own aircraft company. While we were interested in doing it, there simply wasn't the enthusiasm, on any of our parts, to take it any further."

Noble's interest in a supersonic car was rekindled when he and five-time speed king, Craig Breedlove, spent three days together at Bonneville, watching Art Arfons unsuccessfully run Green Monster 27.

That was in October 1990.

"Craig told me he had purchased two J–79s, so I knew I had to take him very, very seriously. He's held the land speed record five times and set his first record at 407, and his last at 600. All within a three year period.

"Craig was the first to average 400... then 500... then 600, so I knew he wanted to be the first to average 700, and then go through the sound barrier.

"As much as I've admired Art Arfons over the years, I knew his latest car would never be capable of exceeding the sound barrier. I was truly hoping he'd go 650 at Bonneville in 1990."

Noble also admires Australia's Rosco McGlashan, who has unsuccessfully campaigned his jet-powered Aussie Invader 2 for several years.

"That car was intended to break my record.

"But Rosco's had stability problems which he's never quite solved. I spoke to him the other night and he's already got the frame built for Aussie Invader 3. He'll just take the engine out of the old car, and put it into the new car.

"He simply reached the point where he realized No. 2 couldn't do the job. He's always said his target was 1100 kilometers, which I believe translates to about 700 miles an hour. I don't think his new car will have supersonic capabilities."

With his crash program, the earliest McGlashan could take the salt near Adelaide, Australia was sometime in 1996... possibly as early as November.

In 1993, McLaren, famed English high-speed car builder (sports cars, Formula One) made the announcement it would build an 850 mile an hour car. Now that's a definite threat to Noble, so he took the publicity campaign quite seriously.

"People started ringing me and saying, 'McLaren's running around, spending an awful lot of money on this project. What are you doing?' And, of course, we were doing nothing.

"The story was running around in '93 and '94. It died in 1995 when they said they put the project on hold," adds Noble. "But with the Breedlove and McLaren threats, the time had come to get back into the fray."

Some $8 million has been poured into the Thrust SSC project, because of the sales ability of Richard Noble, the charisma of this natural born entrepreneur.

"The name of the car states the goal. SSC simply means Super Sonic Car. I knew the project would be immense, so that hasn't at all surprised me. We were hoping against hope to build the whole car in a year. The fundamental problem was we just couldn't keep the cash coming in fast enough to do that.

"This project is twice as big as Thrust 2. The cash has to roll in at sixteen times of what it did with Thrust 2. We've never run out of money, but we came close last August [1995]. Now we're going strong and hope to complete the car in late February or early March at the very latest.

"When we started construction, there was very, very little money in the kitty," admits Noble. "We didn't dare tell anyone. You have to be a salesman in this game.

"You can't possibly spend the rest of your life saying, 'Hey, we had the best land speed record and we threw it all away'. You've gotta drop everything and you've gotta do it."

Reluctantly, Richard Noble realized it would take a special kind of man to drive his supersonic car.

"It was a terrible decision to make," he says, "but I had to admit that a jet-powered, supersonic car needs a jet fighter pilot in its driving seat.

"He must have a cool, clear, uncluttered mind to concentrate on driving to win. He'll be in it for little money but a lot of glory. The person who does it has got to want to be the fastest man in the world more than anything else."

A 'Help Wanted' SOS was literally flashed across the United Kingdom, and thirty prospective candidates heeded the call. Of those thirty, the list was painstakingly reduced to five final candidates. Andy Green, a then thirty-two year old Tornado fighter pilot, was selected to drive Thrust SSC.

One of the finalists, Steve Warren-Smith, piloted his Tornado GR-1 on a bombing mission over Iraq during the Gulf War.

"Richard Noble wrote to each of us independently, explaining his project and the risks involved. He ranked them somewhere between high and very high."

Subjected to a battery of psychological and physical tests, including one that seemed a bit unusual at first glance, driving a Golf rally car – 190 b.h.p. – over the slippery Chris Berbeck rally school course in the shortest time possible.

Richard Noble explained:

"From 0 to 350 miles per hour, Thrust SSC will be in a permanent slide, like driving on ice down a fifty foot wide strip, so good car control is essential. What's more, the driver will have just forty minutes driving experience of SSC before attempting the record. He'll have to be a quick learner."

Each driver had four warm-up laps before going for three timed laps. The three fastest drivers would then continue to the final selection process.

Dick Downes, a thirty-two year old RAF weapons instructor, was first up, and clocked a promising best lap of four minutes, thirty-two seconds.

Andy Green was on deck.

"Andy's just clocked 4.34." said a voice from the track.

Green's time proved to be the quickest.

Announcement of Green's selection took place in February 1995, before three hundred guests at Brooklands Museum, adjacent to the legendary race track.

Said Green:

"Ever since Richard announced he was not going to drive SSC, I have been totally focused on occupying that seat. Now it's happened and it's hard to take in.

"Some people might think that I have enough excitement in my life already, but I can't get enough of it. I'm really looking forward to jamming that throttle wide open and aiming for the desert horizon.

"I know it's not very fashionable to admit it, but to attempt the land speed record in a British car, with a British flag on the side and a British team supporting me would make me extremely proud."

Andy Green is obviously blessed with a sense of humor.

"I passed the tests in intelligence, personality, control and fatigue. Fortunately, they didn't test me for sanity."

Who is Andy Green?

He was born July 30, 1962 in Warwickshire. He graduated from Oxford in 1983, then joined the Royal Air Force as a pilot. His flying career began at Oxford where he represented the University Air Squadron in flying competitions.

He gained his pilot's wings flying jets while in college, winning the course prizes for best student in both ground school and flying phases.

After a three year tour of duty in Germany, he was transferred back to England and converted to the Tornado F-3, a 930 mile an hour aircraft, in 1992. He is currently doing his tour of duty at Leeming.

To Green, relaxation means bungee-jumping, skiing, running marathons and tobogganing. However, he admits the speed record, and the sound barrier, will be his greatest challenge.

"Piloting a jet is pretty exhilarating and testing," he says, "but it comes nowhere near driving this car. It will accelerate three or four times faster than my Tornado. Under my right foot I shall have more power than anyone ever before."

An estimated 100,000 horsepower, generated by a pair of British-made Rolls Royce Spey 205 gas turbines from a phantom jet. Only twelve were produced, at a cost of three million dollars apiece.

Under full power, Thrust SSC will go from 0 to 100 miles an hour in four seconds, 600 in sixteen seconds. Within thirty-one seconds, the car will be at maximum speed and will have covered five miles.

It's estimated that the longest (54 feet, 7 inches), heaviest (14,000 pounds) and most powerful machine in land speed history will require 10.5 miles to come to a complete halt. A supersonic run would last sixty-one seconds from start to finish.

Speed potential is 850 miles and hour. That's Mach 1.1!

The speed of sound at ground level at Black Rock, Noble's proposed racing site, is 747 miles an hour.

The car has four wheels, two at the front and two at the back, offset. Steering is to the back wheels, which is considered highly unorthodox. The car's rear-wheel steering was successfully tested on two miles of straight road at the Motor Industry Research Association near Nuneaton, Warwickshire, to ensure it will not spin into a frenzied, cartwheeling crash.

The two engines were 'test-fired' individually and together on a jig, to prove they can be computer 'married' to provide a balanced output of thrust.

Thrust SSC was constructed with tubular steel space frame and composite outer panels. Dunlop Tires developed the four off-solid aluminum wheels to give the right amount of traction.

To design the car, Richard Noble turned to aerodynamicist, Ron Ayers, then sixty-two, who was lured out of retirement for this challenge.

A former chief aerodynamicist in the British Aircraft Corporation's guided weapons division, Ayers worked on anti-aircraft missiles before reluctantly leaving in 1967 to run the family printing machinery business. He sold the business and retired in the late 1980s.

After his wife's death, Ayers became involved in Thrust through a series of coincidences. He learned that the Brooklands Museum in Surrey, next door to the former site of the Vickers aircraft company, had acquired the archives of the Vickers wind tunnel and he volunteered to sort them out.

He made the 'amazing' discovery that Vickers had done wind-tunnel testing on pre-war land speed cars.

"That explained to me the UK dominance in that era," he says.

While pursuing his research more than three years ago, Ayers visited Kenneth Norris, designer of the late Donald Campbell's 1960s Bluebird turbine-powered car.

Delayed by traffic, he arrived there at the same time as Richard Noble. Noble was aware of Craig Breedlove's project and wanted to put together his own team, but didn't know how to design a supersonic car.

Ron Ayers fitted the bill exactly.

Ayers is largely responsible for designing the Thrust SSC layout, with twin Rolls Royce Spey 205 gas turbines from a Phantom jet flanking the driver. Stability, meaning keeping the car on the ground, is the crucial problem.

"You get all the problems you get transonically on an aircraft, particularly magnified because of its proximity to the ground," Ayers points out.

"You can always get the speed you want with a big enough engine. Our approach has been to start with the shape that gives most stability, then work out how to make it go fast."

In a single-engine configuration, with the engine behind the driver, he points out, the front track has to be narrow so the wheels do not throw sand into the engine intakes and the weight distribution is biased towards the back of the car.

But by using two engines, the center of gravity can be placed well forward between more widely spaced front wheels, recessed into the engine housings.

This makes the fin tail more effective, he notes, and should give good stability. He concedes, however, that the challengers, particularly Breedlove, should make a single-engine design work.

This $8 million project has blended industry, academia and racing expertise for one single purpose: to break the sound barrier.

For instance, a team from Leeds University developed the rear-wheel steering system. Two other universities and Cray Computers helped Ron Ayers in the car's design.

Dunlop developed the four metal wheels for Thrust SSC.

G-Force Engineering Ltd. of Fontwell, Sussex, is responsible for chassis construction, running gear installation, etc. etc. etc.

All told, more than eighty British companies are sponsors. Talk about national pride!

Jeff Luff, a model-maker in his late fifties, built the life-size model of this beast. Why a model almost fifty-five feet in length?

As he puts it:

"This is so important to us. This life-size model gave us a feel for the car. We could have done it on a computer, but we wouldn't have gotten the full impact.

"When you see the model you realize how brave the pilot has got to be, sitting between those two massive engines."

Built out of aluminum sheet wrapped around a steel frame, the model was made on a shoestring budget by special effects wizards and Ryan Hodges.

Jeff, who has worked on all the Superman movies, said, "This looks like the real McCoy."

He painted the model black, just like "the American Blackbird fighter plane."

A much smaller version of the car and the model was built to test Thrust's supersonic capabilities. The scale model tested on Pendine Sands in South Wales and burst through the projected Mach 1.1 sound barrier, reaching 66 miles an hour in 0.1 seconds, 130 mph in 0.2 seconds, 800 mph in 0.8 seconds and a terminal speed of 812 miles per hour.

The test rig, which was built to research underbody aerodynamics to ensure that the vehicle did not become airborne, costs almost three million dollars. But Richard Noble believes it was money well spent, and is confident that 850 can be achieved.

"If we succeed," he says, "it will be the biggest leap in the land speed record in ninety-six years. And that record has to be captured by Britain."

Noble calls his car "the most beautiful thing I've ever seen. We showed the car, minus the bodywork, at a recent London car show, and we moved about 250,000 to 300,000 people through the stand. The reaction was simply overwhelming. People are fascinated by the project, absolutely."

He gives full credit where credit is due.

"This car is the product of two very brilliant people, Glynne Bowsher and Ron Ayers. Glynne designed the wheels and brakes on Thrust 2. Glynne produced the definite plans for the tubular steel central chassis for the car's fuselage. He's an advanced engineer.

"Ron Ayers is the most wonderful character. He's basically a very talented, disciplined engineer. He's incredibly hard-working. He's really a pleasure to work with because he actually pulled the solution out of the hat.

"He started off by saying our chances of producing a safe, supersonic design are ten percent. He said he'd do the best he could, and by golly he came up with the right solution. When he did all the rocket testing and all the aerodynamics and we compared the results of the two tests, we found accuracy within three percent. And when we ended up with a safe design, he said, 'That's it, we've got a once in a lifetime chance'."

Comparing both Noble jets is like comparing apples to oranges. He explains:

"What happened when we built Thrust 2 was that we ended up with a car that was extremely stable. We had all sorts of problems at Bonneville with the metal wheels. You've got a very solid wheel with no give in it at all. And when you've got that and a hard surface, such as Bonneville, I was sliding all over the place.

"With some minor adjustments to the car, and the softer surface at Black Rock, it was almost like driving a taxi. I mean we're just going out and blasting across the desert at 620 and thinking nothing of it. I made eleven runs of six hundred miles or more an hour.

"Once you get the stability, you can use all the power that you've got, and believe me, there wasn't an ounce of power that we didn't squeeze out of that engine.

"On the other hand, if you haven't got the stability, you can't use the car to its full potential. It's gonna crash, or fly, or something. What we learned from Thrust 2 we tried to transfer to the new car.

"One of the key things we had in Thrust 2 was the position of the engine. We got sixty percent or so of the weight on the front suspension. That gave us good stability and pitch.

"What we wanted to do was try to repeat that with SSC, but we simply couldn't find any way of doing it, simply because you've got a very, very thin fuselage with the supersonic design and the engine had to go to the back.

"Because the driver can't sit behind the engine, we suddenly realized the solution was to use two engines. If you use two engines, then, of course, you get the engine well forward and you can get back to your position of having at least fifty percent of the weight on the front wheel.

"This also gave us many other benefits, one of which was that the car had now become quite wide, so therefore you had good stability and roll. And, even better, we could put a long, thin fuselage between the two engines and stick the rear wheels and the fin as far back as we could.

"That gave us tremendously good stability in yaw, directional stability, which we simply couldn't do with a conventional car because the actual length of the wheel base was being controlled by the length of the engine.

"We got away from that. We no longer had the wheel base controlled by the engine. Then the best thing of all was that the cockpit could be positioned near the center of gravity. By positioning the cockpit there you give the driver an enormous advantage.

"You can feel the car. It's like being a pilot, you can feel the whole thing. If, on the other hand, you're sitting up front or in the back of the car, it's not so easy. So, the whole thing started to come together."

However, by taking that design route, Richard Noble admits a major problem had to be solved.

"There wasn't enough room to get the steering mechanism in the car because you've got the intake duct and you've got the bodywork very close to the side of the engine."

Noble and his design team realized the logical solution was rear-wheel steering, which had never been attempted in a land speed car. He went to the experts at Leeds University for help.

"The idea of rear-wheel steer was really Glynne Bowsher's. But how do you determine that it will work? We took an old mini-saloon car, locked up the front wheels, built a sub-frame on the back. We had a rear-wheel steer car.

"After we got the steering right, it was extremely good. I could drive it quite handily at ninety miles an hour. After driving the car, I felt really good about the concept. It was quite clear this was a winner."

Does Richard Noble sometimes dream that he's in the cockpit, pushing Thrust SSC to supersonic speed?

"I'd be lying to say the thought doesn't occur to me."

Then he adds, "But it's only a fleeting thought."

Despite the enormous amount of money poured into this massive project, no one directly involved will become rich. They all know that.

"I didn't become wealthy after setting the record in 1983," says Noble, "and I won't become rich after we accomplish our goal.

"Fulfilling the dream is reward enough. And think of the experience. What a hell of an experience!"

Noble fell behind schedule because of modifications to the engine starting system.

Static firing tests were to be followed by 200 mile an hour runs at a British Air Force facility. Those tests were scheduled for August 1996.

Once completed, the high-speed runs would take off at Jafr Desert in Jordan. After that: Nevada's Black Rock Desert.

By early August, sixteen lanes had been carved out at Jafr, with more than ten miles of running room. All that was needed to complete the picture was Thrust SSC.

There are only a few places in the world suitable for high-speed racing activity. The glistening sand of Ormond Beach in Florida was the centerpiece in the roaring twenties. That gave way to Bonneville in the mid-thirties, and then to Black Rock Desert in Nevada in the 1980s.

Noble drove Thrust 2 to the current record of 633.4 mph at the desert course. Breedlove also planned his '96 assault at Black Rock.

The desert is very flat because each spring a lake forms from melting snow. In August, it dries to leave a flat surface. Conditions are suitable for about six weeks, but the unpredictable weather can reduce that 'window of opportunity' to just a few days.

Noble didn't set out to blaze a new trail. It just happened that way.

In 1981, Noble and his team arrived at the Bonneville Salt Flats with his jet-powered Thrust 2, in search of the land speed record.

He had traveled the same customary trail that others before him had taken, starting with the late Sir Malcolm Campbell in 1935, to travel faster than man had ever traveled before.

Campbell became the first to shatter the 300 mile an hour barrier at Bonneville, and since then every record, save one, had been set on the Utah Salt Flats between 1935 and 1970.

In 1960, Donald Campbell, son of the legendary Sir Malcolm, crashed at Bonneville at 360 miles an hour. Convinced the Utah track didn't afford him enough running room for his Bluebird, Campbell tried his luck at Lake Eyre in Australia.

He was flooded out in 1963, and barely beat the torrential rains the following year. While he bravely pushed his wheel-driven machine to 403 mph in 1964, it was four miles an hour slower than the 407 that Californian Craig Breedlove had traveled at Bonneville in 1963. Instead of the overall speed record which he really wanted, Campbell had to be satisfied with the wheel-driven mark.

When Bonneville became too rough for Noble's car, which utilized metal wheels, he sought better conditions elsewhere. That elsewhere was to Nevada, to Black Rock Desert.

After two frustrating and futile years at Bonneville, Noble carved his name into the record books with a two-way average of 633.4 mph.

The fate of Bonneville is uncertain. For years the racing conditions have deteriorated. The 'patient' is in critical condition. Only time will tell when Operation Save The Salt will return Bonneville to its former glory.

"The difference between Bonneville and Black Rock is like night and day," says Steve Garcia, an engineer from Camarillo, California. A long-time student of land speed racing, Garcia gets his speed kicks by preparing and maintaining "the world's fastest Volkswagen" at Utah speedway. This VW has hit 199 plus!

"Bonneville is a salt bed, while Black Rock is adobe, or clay, with a very fine surface dust, almost like talcum powder. Because of Bonneville's poor conditions for thrust vehicles, Black Rock is probably the best site for this kind of activity in the United States.

"Lake Gainard, a natural salt bed near Adelaide, Australia, would be ideal if we were talking strictly about a stable surface and enough length, but it's just too remote for any kind of a long stay. You just can't take your supersonic car off the trailer, fire it up, make two timed runs, set a new record and then go home.

"That's what Art Arfons, love him, used to do at Bonneville back in his glory days in the mid-sixties against Craig. But Craig's car and Richard's twin-jet are unknown entities. You have to have a well-planned strategy, and that means getting very familiar with the machine.

"Craig has always made a series of runs, increasing his speed by increments, until he's ready to go for broke. Theoretically, his car will accelerate faster than a top fuel dragster, from 0 to 350 miles an hour in four seconds. But as the speed increases, so does the drag. It could take twenty seconds to go to 500. I think you get the picture.

"Obviously the plusses that Black Rock offers are the length, the stable surface. But Black Rock's clay does have a negative side to it. If the aerodynamics aren't set up right, the car tends to plow. There's higher ground drag.

"Another thing, Black Rock is incredibly dirty, very similar to El Mirage in California, and I won't take my car to El Mirage for that reason. It takes weeks to get all that dust out of the car. It gets into everything.

"But the biggest problem could be the kind of winter we have and how the lake dries out. All of that water from the Sierra Nevada funnels out there. As I recall, Noble had a problem on his last run. The first half mile was kinda muddy."

Both Noble's Thrust SSC and Breedlove's Spirit of America – Sonic Arrow utilize metal wheels. Breedlove's concept, however, is different, according to Garcia.

"Craig has five solid aluminum wheels, but it has a Kevlar hoop to keep the wheel from fracturing. The top of the wheel is going twice the speed of sound, and without that Kevlar hoop that thing would fly apart."

Garcia believes a wheel-driven car using rubber tires would have more of a traction problem than these two massive jets with metal wheels.

"There's no adhesion problems," he says, "because these are thrust vehicles. And besides, after 350 miles an hour, the cars are basically not on the ground anyway."

Now for a little history about Black Rock Desert.

Sixty thousand years ago, Black Rock Desert (located in northern Nevada) was at the bottom of the ancient Lake Lahontan. As the climate changed, the lake started drying out. During periods when the climate stabilized, beach terraces were formed. They are still visible along the adjacent hills and mountains.

The desert is composed of the playa (the flat-floored bottom of an undrained desert basin that becomes, at times, a shallow lake), split into two arms by the Black Rock Range.

The playa is an extensive, flat and featureless plain, composed of silt. This differs from the salt playa at Bonneville. The Black Rock silt is as much as 10,000 feet deep in some areas.

Man probably first entered this area about 10,000 years ago. Legendary soldier/explorer, John Fremont, and his party passed through in 1843–1844. In 1846, Jesse and Lindsay Applegate established a new route to Oregon, using part of Fremont's route.

The Rock Range, after which the region is named, is a large, dark, volcanic outcrop and was a major guidepost for the early emigrants.

It's been estimated that half of the California gold seekers in 1849 used this route. Because of the remoteness and isolation of the area, much of the trail scenery remains as it was more than one hundred years ago.

In the 1940s and 1950s, the desert was used as a bombing range. Unexploded shells and live ammo are occasionally found. The military still uses part of the desert for low-altitude training runs.

Today, the principle use of the desert is recreational, especially by rock hounds, land sailors and history buffs. Wildlife enthusiasts head into adjoining mountains to look for deer, antelope and wild horses.

Spirit of America – Sonic Arrow

DESIGN CRITERIA

640 mph two-way average to return the Unlimited World Land Speed Record for Automobiles to America
Design envelope capability – ultimately exceeding 800 mph

DIMENSIONS

Width Overall: 8'6" (102 inches)
Length Overall: 47'1" (565 inches)
Height: 5'9" (69 inches) at tail fins
Weight: 8000 pounds (wet)
Wheelbase: 27'6" (330 inches)
Rear Track: 7'10" (94 inches)

ENGINE

Modified J–79 GE–8D–11 B–17
Fuel Capacity: 85.0 gallons unleaded gasoline
(Note: Gasoline utilized to show 'auto' inter-relation)
Water Capacity: 42.5 gallons
Thrust: 24,000 lb. (48,000 h.p.) afterburner
Oil Capacity: 2.5 gallons

CONSTRUCTION

Steel tubing-billet bulkheads/stressed aluminum skin
Composite-formed nose capsule and driver compartment
Composite air ducts and rear wheel fairings
Tires: bi-filament wound graphite-Kevlar
Wheels: aluminum billet hub, spun disk alloy heat treated
Fasteners: Titanium and other special alloys
Bearings: tapered rollers and other specific applications
Suspension/Front: coil over hydraulic shocks
Suspension/Rear: variable deflection beam
Steering: worm and sector
Parachutes: ring-slot Kevlar, mortar deployed
Brakes: hydraulic friction track
Telemetry Systems: control, transfer, multiple data acquisition

Thrust SSC

DIMENSIONS

Length: 54 ft (16.46 meters)
Width: 12 ft (3.65 meters)
Weight: 7 tons (7.11 tons)

ENGINE

Two Rolls Royce Spey 202s (development tests)
Two Rolls Royce Spey 205s (record attempts)
Output: 100,000 HP (75 Mw)
      = 141 Formula One cars
      = 1000 Ford Escorts

ACCELERATION/SPEED

0 to 600 mph (0 to 965 km/h) 16 seconds
In excess of 850 mph (1370 km/h)

CONSTRUCTION

Welded space frame chassis made from 2" x 2" (50 mm x 50 mm) T45 tubular steel supplied by Accles and Pollack, part of the TI Group
Body panels made from a combination of aluminum, carbon-fiber and titanium
Transmission: None
Wheels: Four solid forged aluminum, rear pair arranged in staggered formation
Steering: Worm drive acting on the rear wheels
Brakes (Primary system): At Mach 1 – single 7 ft 6 in (2.28 meter)
                         Irvin parachute
                         At 400 mph – triple 7 ft 6 in (2.28 meter)
                         Irvin parachutes
        (Secondary system): Front – 1 pair of 17 in (432 mm) carbon
                         discs with 2 piston calipers acting on each
                         wheel
                         Rear – Single 17 in (432 mm) carbon disc
                         with 2 piston calipers acting on each wheel

The *Green Monster 27* under construction. Art Arfons tries out the cockpit.
Photograph by Harvey Shapiro.

The *Green Monster* – poised and ready. Bonneville Salt Flats, Utah 1990.
Photograph by Harvey Shapiro.

The *Green Monster* at speed. Bonneville Salt Flats, Utah 1990.
Photograph courtesy of Buck Lovell.

Art and his wife June Arfons attending his induction into the Motorsports
Hall of Fame.
Photograph courtesy of Art Arfons.

The chassis of Richard Noble's supersonic car under construction, showing the basic engine-pod outriggers.
Photograph courtesy of Robin Richardson.

Reigning land speed king, Richard Noble *(right)*, and author *(left)* at Bonneville Salt Flats, Utah 1990.
Photograph courtesy of Waldo Stakes.

Frontal view of the *Thrust SSC*. This British car is capable of reaching a top speed of 850mph. It is powered by two Rolls Royce engines.
Photograph courtesy of Richard Noble.

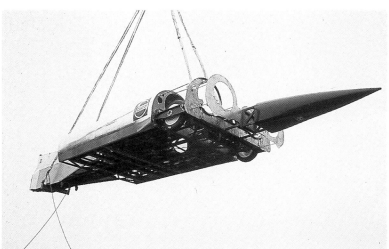

The *Thrust SSC* suspended in the air during shipment.
Photograph courtesy of Richard Noble.

Artist's rendition of Richard Noble's supersonic car the *Thrust SSC*.
Photograph courtesy of Richard Noble.

Static test – firing Craig Breedlove's *Spirit of America – Sonic Arrow*.
Photograph courtesy of Louise Noeth ©1996.

Scale model of the *Spirit of America – Sonic Arrow*.
Photograph courtesy of Craig Breedlove.

Craig Breedlove sits in the cockpit of the *Spirit of America – Sonic Arrow*.
Photograph courtesy of Louise Noeth ©1996.

Rosco McGlashan's *Aussie Invader 2*. Rosco, an Australian drag racer, built this jet car. It averaged 505mph in an unsuccessful record attempt.
Photograph courtesy of Rosco McGlashan.

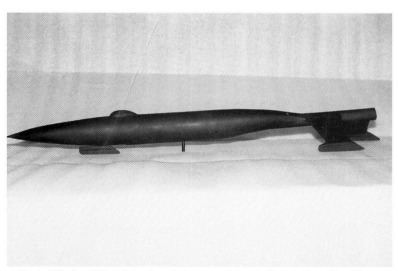

Sonic Wind, a 900mph rocket-sled powered by an X-1 engine. It will run on ice. *(Note the two runners.)*
Photograph courtesy of Waldo Stokes.

Rick Kikes of Oregon built this 680mph jet-powered car – the *American Eagle*. His partner, Gary Swenson, is set to drive the jet for the unlimited thrust record.
Photograph courtesy of Rick Kikes.

Al Teague's 'ancient' streamliner set a wheel-driven record of 409.986mph in 1991. He still wants to go faster. He built this car, the *Spirit of '76*, in 1976.
Photograph courtesy of Al Teague.

Chapter Six
Thunder 'Down Under'

(AUTHOR'S NOTE: In the long history of land speed racing, only one genuine Australian assault on the record had been attempted until Rosco McGlashan and his jet-thrust Aussie Invader 2 took his first crack in late 1993. He failed, but reached a speed of 475 mph. McGlashan would hit 502 in 1994, try but fail again in March 1995. However, he has vowed to try it again.

The only other entry dates back to 1931–1932 when Norman 'Whiz' Smith, an Australian endurance driver, was named to handle the Fred H. Stewart Enterprise, a twelve cylinder machine designed by Don Harkness and owned by wealthy businessman Fred Stewart, both from Sydney.

New Zealand's Ninety Mile Beach was selected as the race site. While the beach had seemingly endless length – some forty miles – the course was often soaked by heavy seas. There was also the problem of razor-sharp shells puncturing the rubber tires.

In 1932, Smith set a world record for ten miles, averaging 164.084 mph. But that wasn't the measured mile. The real goal: better Sir Malcolm Campbell's 244.897, set at Ormond Beach, Florida, earlier that year.

A year later, in 1932, Smith reached about 180 on a very soggy beach when a magneto shorted out and the run ended prematurely. That was the final attempt for Enterprise.)

Ken Warby knows what it is to be an underdog.

He wore that tag with honor in the late 1970s, becoming the first man to average more than 300 miles an hour on water. A builder/driver, Warby pushed his jet-powered boat, Spirit of Australia, to a record 317.6 mph in 1978. Only two men have tried to better his record, and both died in the attempt.

Although he also drove jet-powered funny cars and trucks on the drag strips both in his native Australia and the United States, he was never interested in the world land speed record.

Now, a fellow Aussie, named Rosco McGlashan, is amongst a handful of land speed contenders, and although he must be rated a long shot, Warby, an old friend, likes Rosco's chances.

McGlashan, a drag racer, completed building his jet car, Aussie Invader 2 in 1993. He reached 475 that year, improved to 502 in 1994. Again, there were poor track conditions at Lake Gainard, a vast salt expanse near Adelaide.

In March 1995, McGlashan returned to Lake Gainard, but failed once more in his attempt. A shortened course, due to heavy rain, created not only acceleration problems, but handling problems as well. He hit a marker on the course, damaging the Mirage engine.

However, Rosco McGlashan has vowed to return, and Ken Warby knows his friend is a man of his word.

"It's nice to come up with those fantasy figures," says Warby, who has retired from racing and now lives near Cincinnati, Ohio, "but saying and doing are two entirely different things.

"I always believe you go one little step at a time. You've got to go 640 before you can go 800 or 900. Breaking Noble's record will be hard enough, and I believe if anyone can do it, it's Rosco."

Warby isn't particularly impressed by all the hoopla surrounding the supersonic jet cars of Noble, an Englishman who went 633.4 in 1983, and five-time record-holder, Craig Breedlove of California.

Both were expected to be ready for the Fall 'shoot-out' at Black Rock Desert in Nevada in 1995. It never materialized.

"Quite frankly," snaps Warby, "it's all a whole lot of media bull. Let's see what happens when they get on the salt. Talk is cheap. Talk can also be expensive when you need money to put it out there.

"Admittedly, Rosco's limited by budget and by horsepower. It gets hard at times, and I should know. Rosco's got a whole bunch of volunteers. If you have enough belief in yourself, somehow you carry on.

"If anyone will do it, this boy will. He's all go. He's not afraid of the competition. In fact, Rosco's not afraid of anything or anyone. He's a wild man. He's into the martial arts.

"He's a bit on the small side – about five foot six – but he's crazy enough to take on Godzilla. That's how tough he is. He's confident he can break the land speed record.

"In 1994, Rosco averaged 502 on a short course. He was supposed to have twenty kilometers, but he wound up with a third of that because the course was soaked. But he peaked at 600 miles an hour. His problem was he didn't have enough land to keep it going. He'll go well over 600. He's not afraid of that speed.

"He's down a bit on horsepower, say, compared to the J–79, but with a full and dry course, he'll just start back further from the timing lights, another half-mile, or a mile.

"In March of 1995, he had all sorts of problems, hit a course marker and damaged his engine. He's got three engines altogether, so I'm sure he can come up with one healthy power plant.

"He's going back, make no mistake about that. This guy is dead serious. It'll be death before dishonor," Warby says chuckling. "HE WILL DO IT!"

Ken Warby has known Rosco McGlashan for fifteen years. One drag racer connected with another, so to speak.

"He used to have a V–8 powered motorcycle, a rocket-propelled go-kart, and many other toys.

"In fact, I sold Rosco his original jet dragster. I had two jet dragsters and two jet funny cars. I sold him a J–34-powered dragster built by Romeo Palimedes in 1982 when I moved out of Australia. I sold the other one to a guy in Texas.

"The J–34 is the same engine in my jet boat. Rosco used to hit around 260 in the quarter. He's come up the hard way, like a lot of us. Learn as you go.

"He's done it the same way I built my boat. He's literally built the whole thing himself. What he didn't build, he sorta sweet-talked people and conned, and did whatever had to be done.

"He did car burns all over the country [Australia] to raise money for his land speed effort with the dragster I sold him. Whatever brought in a buck to get the project going. He has a bunch of guys around him that helped do the fiberglass shell, all sorts of things.

"In January 1991 I stepped out of the jet truck and have never stepped back into a race car. But when I was racing in the United States, I always returned to tour Australia, and whenever I went back, I called up Rosco to drive one of my jet cars.

"We keep in touch. I call Rosco every now and then, or he sends me a picture or a bullshit letter just to let me know how he's doing.

"His car is capable, Rosco is capable. All he needs is a little luck."

(AUTHOR'S NOTE: Bob Jennings is a national award-winning motorsports writer for The Advertiser, *Adelaide, Australia's daily morning newspaper. But Jennings is much more than 'just' a reporter/writer. He is a seasoned driver. He began his amateur career in rallying, driving a variety of cars from Minis to Mazda rotaries, and more recently Toyotas. Now, he has turned his interest to circuit racing.*

"I run my own Australian Formula Two single-seater, and dabble in production car racing. I've also done two of the Targa, Tasmania, road races, one as a privateer entry with a Mitsubishi Lancer GSR, the other as a stand-in driver for the BMW team in a 325i Convertible."

In 1993, 1994, and March 1995, Bob Jennings covered Rosco McGlashan's land speed attempts at Lake Gairdner, a vast expanse near Adelaide.) In his own words:

Rosco McGlashan hasn't thought of much else other than breaking the world land speed record for the past decade, and he and his wife, Cheryl, and a dedicated group of followers in his home town of Perth share the vision.

McGlashan is short, nuggety and affable. He walks with a cocky swagger and talks with disarming frankness. In the searing heat of the Australian outback, his shorts and T-shirt reveal a set of comic-strip, simple tattoos, including a small circle on his ankle indicated with an arrow, and a notation, "oil here".

But speak to him and the subject never strays far from land speed record breaking and jet cars.

Like the bulk of the current generation of record breakers, his roots are in drag racing. Jet and rocket drag racing, including a rocket-powered go-kart which had Australian crowds blinking in disbelief.

He graduated to jet car racing and pursued the career in the U.S., but after a while found the experience in his beloved Aussie Invader increasingly frustrating.

"Every time we were getting up a bit of interesting speed at the end of a quarter while, we were shutting the thing down," McGlashan explains. "I just kept on thinking it would be kinda interesting to keep the thing going."

This was the birth of Aussie Invader 2, although the original Aussie Invader has been kept on as a meal ticket, doing the display circuit to raise funds for the LSR efforts.

The LSR effort really got underway when McGlashan picked up five Australian-made Mirage jet engines for the bargain basement price of $A5000 a piece at a Royal Australian Air Force auction in Sydney. He and his crew then designed their 4.5 ton car around the engine.

In between times and in the time-honored tradition of drag racers and record breakers, he hustled for sponsorship. He and Cheryl beat on plenty of doors, and have built a long-term relationship with Australian oil company, Ampol and the Perth Channel 7 television station which has dutifully recorded all three of his unsuccessful LSR attempts.

Each attempt has ended in disappointment, yet strengthened McGlashan's belief in his ability to top Richard Noble's record. And while there are more sophisticated cars being built with the same objective, McGlashan reckons that the simple, straightforward jet car – similar in appearance to Art Arfons' Green Monster – has the goods to run close to supersonic.

"We've run around 950 km/h according to our telemetry, and there's no sign of the acceleration curve tapering off, so we reckon we should be able to do 100 km/h more than that both ways over the mile," McGlashan says.

Each of his three attempts at the remote Lake Gairdner, in the low, rugged, ancient and arid Gawler Ranges of South Australia have been worthwhile in terms of experience gained, McGlashan explains. The more he has to do with the deceptive salt surface of the lake, the more unpredictable it becomes.

The fact is, no one has really studied the lake over a long period. The sheep station owners of Mount Ive, who hold the lease on the area, know it but don't study the surface the way a racer would.

Rain which sweeps in with sudden storms can give the lake the appearance of a conventional deep-water lake, but the depth is only a few inches. Only two or three days after a flooding such as this, and it can be driven on.

But it was a bit more than a rain squall which put an end to his first LSR bid in 1993. The lake was inundated, and the McGlashan crew was lucky to get its equipment out along the ten miles of muddy access road to the 'main' road which is simply graded dirt. Sixty miles to the east is the blacktop on which it takes around five hours to drive to the nearest city, Adelaide.

Although the lake surface dries out quickly, the surface can remain slushy for weeks, caking beneath the wheel arches of vehicles. Daily, the water table rises and falls beneath the crust.

During McGlashan's second attempt in 1994, the surface was at its best with a hard, dry crust in which his car's V-profile solid aluminum wheels left only the slightest indentation.

But there was an itinerant pond of shallow water at the lake's southern end which frustratingly kept wandering on to surveyed track, effectively reducing the length of the twenty kilometer track to a little under thirteen kilometers. This wasn't a huge problem on the northbound run (the furthest extremity of which ended in the thin and treacherous salt which covers the bulk of the lake surface) but it severely restricted the slow-down length.

This didn't phase McGlashan too much. Not much does. He staged back as far as he could, and let her go.

Popping the braking chutes early effectively gave them a one-run life, and a bit of a design problem meant they more often than not just blew themselves out.

Popping the chutes late meant hitting the water, which Rosco did on one occasion, sending up a massive sheet of spray which hid onlookers watching breathlessly. When the chase crews got to him, McGlashan was sitting on the bodywork, morosely eyeing the lake in which Aussie Invader was parked.

The journey through the water had peeled sheets from the sandwich-construction aluminum under-tray but amazingly had not entered the engine.

"Maybe we ought to claim the water speed record," said the laconic McGlashan, who then rushed to Adelaide to help fabricate replacement panels. He's very much a hands-on man.

The car was repaired, but the team ran out of time to wait for the water to go, and the fact they had also run out of braking chutes helped the decision along to once more pull out of the lake.

McGlashan left, bitterly disappointed, but such is the resilience of the self-taught engineer that he was back again in March 1995, with a fined-down team and even more determination.

The car had a higher stabilizer fin, which Rosco reckoned would give him better stability, and the braking chute system had been revised.

The salt surface wasn't good, and a couple of heavy showers of rain early in the month didn't help. The V-profile solid wheels cut deep grooves in the salt, and in reality one run on any one of the five tracks which had been surveyed and surface-prepared was enough to make it unusable.

McGlashan looked unusually thoughtful after his first exploratory runs. He explained the different track at the front of the car compared to the back meant that if the Aussie Invader veered away to one side, a rear wheel would drop into the track left by the front wheel and would 'tramline'.

It was almost impossible to shake the car straight again, although McGlashan didn't mind trying.

The snaking wheel tracks left in the salt were mute testimony to the 500 mph wrestling McGlashan was doing on the wheel. On one run he veered off-course and smacked into an orange plastic highway marker cone which was used to mark the edge of the track. Fortunately, McGlashan had shut down the engine, and the damage was superficial.

The intake vanes repaired and adjustments made to the 'petals' at the back of the engine. McGlashan made another exploratory run. Again, the car veered left, this time running way wide of the prepared surface and becoming bogged after breaking through the salt crust.

Back to the 'Bat Cave' – the Air Force temporary canvas hangar out on the lake, near the timing marks – for the car to be cleaned off and checked again.

Team Manager Peter Taylor was convinced the problem was with the salt surface and not the car. McGlashan looks serious as he explains calmly the frightening "left hook" the car has developed. But the speed is creeping up and with the weather looking good: McGlashan once more stages the car back for a fast run.

The weather's hot, hitting forty-five degrees centigrade in the middle of the day, and the fickle wind drops as the sun begins to set; enough for McGlashan to get serious.

Again the glorious sound of the engine firing, the distant speck of royal blue moving across the aching white salt. The impressive roar as the afterburner fires up and the Invader surges towards the timing marks.

Suddenly the noise stops; McGlashan has shut down as he enters the measured mile. But there has been a momentary puff of black smoke, and the mysteriously cryptic message crackling on the radio: "She's swallowed a light".

Once again the car had veered left, with McGlashan trying desperately to haul it back straight, but it had hit a foot-high metal pyramid containing a 9v battery and a little timing light at the extremity of the course.

The impact has been on the side of the jet intake at 850 km/h according to the telemetry, ripping away the thick fiberglass frontal bodywork, and the light stand's metal framework has gone down through the inside of the engine.

Amazingly, McGlashan has once more brought the car to a safe stop, but he knows that this is the end of the third attempt. His spare engines are bare; they need to be fitted up with pumps and ancillaries from the engine in the car. Then there has to be extensive bench testing.

McGlashan wipes tears from his eyes as his crew gives him three cheers when the car is pushed back to the Bat Cave. He is comforted by his wife, Cheryl, and the pair walk a little way distant on the salt as the sun goes down.

"I'm sorry fellas," says McGlashan.

"We'll be back," he promises the small huddle of press guys, shaking each by the hand.

He's uncharacteristically serious, lips set in a thin line, eyes narrowed. You can see the disappointment, but feel the determination.

Within weeks he's planned his next assault, later in '95, still convinced he's in a better position than the opposition to take the record.

"It doesn't matter if I only hold the record for a day. I'll be in the books, and I will have done it," he says. "The car can do it. I can do it. And we can do it at this place."

Looking into those eyes, you can only believe it.

Chapter Seven

Bonneville Salt Flats... Nature's Endangered Highway

I can remember when I was running at Bonneville in the mid-sixties and one of the Firestone engineers pokes an instrument into the salt to see how deep it would go before he hit mud. It was something like eighteen inches. When I ran in 1989–90–91, it was something like an inch to an inch and a quarter.

Unless something is done, and done now to save the salt, it won't last more than five years for the racers. It's a man-made problem. It's called greed. Big business is gonna destroy the Salt Flats because they want the money.

They're bleeding Bonneville dry, and it doesn't take a rocket scientist to figure out the consequences. I love this place. I'm comfortable running here.

Art Arfons

The patient is critical. Perhaps even terminal.

The major battle taking place in land speed racing is to 'Save The Salt'. That's the name of this movement, the battle cry.

And Rick Vesco, one of the driving forces behind 'Save The Salt' thinks the fight can be won.

"We should know in about three years," he says. "I'm cautiously optimistic."

For more than five decades the legendary Bonneville Salt Flats in Utah were synonymous with ultimate speed. From 1935 until 1983, all but one land speed record had been set on the Utah salt.

That exception took place in 1964 when the late Donald Campbell of England pushed his Bluebird to a wheel-driven record of 403.1 mph at Lake Eyre in Australia.

Richard Noble, another British driver, failed in 1981 and 1982 attempts at Bonneville. The metal wheels of his massive four ton jet, Thrust 2, couldn't hold a straight line.

So, in 1983, the determined Englishman moved his act to Black Rock Desert in Nevada, to a softer, more friendly racing surface, and became King Richard I. Average speed: 633.4. The land speed record was finally back in British hands.

Noble planned to return to Black Rock in late 1995 with his latest creation, a twin-jet with supersonic capability. Even five-time speed king, Craig Breedlove, who set all of his records in Utah, had forsaken his old stomping grounds for Black Rock in his heralded Fall 1995 record bid in Spirit of America – Sonic Arrow. Neither car, however, was ready.

Breedlove hadn't been to Bonneville in seventeen years when he returned in October 1990 to watch his old nemesis, Art Arfons, in Green Monster 27. He was stunned by the difference.

"Some of the course looked pretty decent," he said. "I'm shocked at the amount that diminished. This is not a new thing. I met with people from Stewart Udall's office [former U.S. senator from Utah] in the 1960s and there was really no interest in solving the problem.

"It's an obvious problem. They send eight rail cars a day, full of salt, down the railroad tracks, and over fifty years of mining, the salt's gone.

"It's a very sad thing for someone like me, or someone that's interested in this place, to see it happen, because it's a natural resource to the planet that probably took fifty million years to create from an inland sea, and we've practically seen it destroyed within our lifetime."

The statistics are startling, and in this case statistics don't lie!

An area once spanning 30,000 acres now covers about 19,000 acres. Land that once could be groomed into a race track fifteen miles long is less than ten miles in length.

The Bonneville Salt Flats are disappearing, and man has largely been responsible for the vanishing act.

According to 'Save The Salt', mining at Bonneville began back in 1900 with Montello Salt Company (potassium salt, 1900–1917) and continued with Sloway Process Company, 1941–1963, (potash and potassium), Kaiser Aluminum Company (1963–1988, potash and other chemicals) and Reilly Industrial (1988, potash and other chemicals).

A federal agency, The Bureau of Land Management (BLM), is the caretaker of this vast natural wonder. And for the longest time, BLM acknowledged there was a major problem, but shook its head as to what caused the problem.

What has seemed obvious to the racers utilizing the saline speedway was simply a mystery to the bureaucrats. And how do you solve a problem?

Conduct a long-range study. That's how.

In 1989, BLM reached the preliminary conclusion: "...the salt is disappearing," said Gregg B. Morgan, then stationed in Salt Lake City. "We're still losing at a rate of one percent a year. That's about 1.5 million tons of salt a year.

"The Salt Flats are fantastic. There's only a couple of other places like 'em, but they're so isolated. Access to them is so limited. It's almost impossible to reach except by plane.

"Nature does most of the work in preserving the salt. These are flood plains, so we're gonna be under water at least six months of the year. From the 1983 inundation of water we had here, about six inches of water, all summer long, rejuvenation of the salt came back.

"We've got about three inches of salt in thickness, the primary crust. We [BLM] just have to monitor the racing, filming activities. That's our primary responsibility. There are geologists in the district that have responsibility for the issues."

The three inches of primary crust that existed at Bonneville in the late 1980s, early 1990s, are only a memory less than a decade later, according to Vesco.

In early July 1995, Vesco and his tireless groups returned to Bonneville to access the situation following a harsh winter and a very wet spring.

"It looks pretty good. It was wet for a long time. There's about eight and a half miles of dry. We dragged it pretty darned hard. The drag and the big truck we used to drag with didn't even leave a mark on the salt. It's looking pretty promising at the moment.

"It was a cruise-in. We went out to survey our race track and test-drag it," he pointed out. "It was the first time we had a chance to see the Flats since last year.

"It was extra wet this past winter and extra cold this spring and summer so far. This is abnormal.

"The crust is about three-eighths of an inch, which is on top of what I call a vapor barrier of mud. It's real thin mud. Then it's hard underneath that, which is what we were running on in 1994. This is new, over the top of what we ran on.

"Our first meet of the season is scheduled for July 20. We have some one hundred entries. The real test will come in that meet, when all that power is applied.

"My feeling is that the guys will do well in the early meets of the season. The track will become real slippery later. Each year there are four events scheduled at Bonneville. Last year, we managed to run only two."

The forty-fifth annual Bonneville Nationals was the biggest casualty. It was canceled.

A terse note at the end of the Salt Flats access road read simply: "Speed Week Canceled Due to Salt." Almost all of the 400 competitors received notification in time. However, two didn't and showed up at Bonneville. One dejected racer had come from New Zealand.

The first meet of the '95 season, scheduled for July, was washed out.

A month later, 252 entries competed in Speed Week, with Al Teague capturing the top speed of 365 miles an hour. Teague made only two runs in his streamliner on the seven mile long course. Teague knew the conditions weren't suitable for a 400 plus run, so he called it quits.

"The track wasn't in good shape," says Rick Vesco. "We set up four lanes for the Long course [7 miles] and four lanes, also 40 feet wide, on the shorter course [four and a half miles]."

In August, some 130 ran during the World of Speed meet.

While the salt "hardened up a bit," as Vesco puts it, "the fastest trip was 'only' 359 mph.

From a personal standpoint, however, the '95 season has been a smashing success for Rick Vesco and the streamliner which Vesco's father built way back in 1957 and has been updated by his son.

Dave Spangler set a C gas record, reaching 302.6 miles an hour in the 371 cubic inch small-block Chevy-powered machine.

Then Terry Nish, driving the same Rick Vesco entry, set two records in the B gas category, 315 on gas, 330 with an added mixture of ten percent nitro.

"It was about an inch thick before we hit mud," says Vesco, "but a lot thinner on other parts of the course."

The final meet of the season, World Finals, was scheduled for October 13-14-15. If enough entries signed up, the meet was to take place on the longer International Course.

The season-ending meet was canceled.

On September 21, 1995, Save The Salt, Inc. issued the following press statement:

After thirty years the BLM has assumed the responsibility and has negotiated an agreement for the restoration of the world-famous Bonneville Salt Flats.

The Save The Salt board met today on the International Raceway of the Bonneville Salt Flats with the Bureau of land management to discuss the terms of the agreement for the Salt Lay Down Project.

BLM, along with the State of Utah, have signed the agreement and have forwarded it to Reilly Industries in Indianapolis, Indiana. We expect Reilly Industries to act on that agreement and sign it within the week.

The agreement calls for Reilly Industries to construct berms and ditches and to pump the waste salt from their abandoned evaporation ponds to the Bonneville Salt Flats which lie adjacent to their potash mining operation.

The project will be constructed over the next fourteen months and will be tested for the following four years. Waste salt will be pumped through the ditches to the Salt Flats with an expected gain of 0.44 inch annually.

To realize the magnitude of the salt loss from the Bonneville Salt Flats, it has been estimated that Reilly's evaporation ponds contain in excess of seventy-six million tons of salt.

Mining operations over the past thirty years have been identified as the major cause of over eighteen inches of salt loss from the historic raceway in several government studies.

Save The Salt, Inc. intends to monitor the project and have retained legal counsel to bring suit again Reilly Industries, BLM and the State of Utah if the project does not restore the Bonneville Salt Flats, which the BLM has designated as an 'Area of Critical Environmental Concern'.

The Utah Salt Racers Association sponsors the July (Land Speed Opener) and September events (World of Speed), while Southern California stages races in August (Speed Week) and October (World Finals).

"We call this present track 'The Alternate' area," points out Vesco. "It's not as long as the old course, but it seems to be better salt. The course where all the major records were set in years past is called 'The International Course' or 'The Long Course'.

"We're not in that area. We do cross it at one point. It's about at a twenty degree angle to the other course. We're just gonna move around and stay off the long course. We don't want to damage it.

"There's still miles around there that we can kinda move around and not do any permanent damage. If we see anything starting to happen due to our racing events, then we'll quit. We'll either move or get out of there completely.

"There are a couple of places you can go to get any mileage at all. It's not a great big oval. It's kind of an L-shaped thing because of all the trenches and dikes of the mining industry. So you're stuck with what you've got."

Vesco, and other concerned racers like him, started writing letters, not only to the BLM (part of the Interior Department), but to the State of Utah, as far back as 1961. In 1975, eight die-hards founded 'Save The Salt'. But while the group 'only' numbers in the hundreds, its influence carries the pack of a heavyweight champion.

"We've shown over the years that we just won't go away," brags Rick Vesco.

And finally, the message is being heard loud and clear.

"My Dad started racing at Bonneville in 1949. My brother [former motorcycle speed king, Don Vesco] and I followed the family tradition. The guys were complaining about the deteriorating salt in the 60s. In the 70s it became rather obvious that there was a problem.

"They've been doing studies for more than thirty years and nothing constructive came out of those studies. Trying to deal with Kaiser proved fruitless. They wouldn't even talk, but Reilly Industries is far more sensitive to pressure.

"In order to get any place nowadays, you've got to yell your guts out. We're not a passive group. We'll speak to anyone who will listen. Television, press conferences, letters, petitions, you name it.

"A few years ago I met initially with some of Reilly's people and they said, '...the reason we're talking is because you've been on TV and we don't like that kind of publicity. That isn't what our company's about'."

Vesco realizes it's now or never. Tomorrow will be too late.

"We're talking about huge overall losses over the years. We probably lost eighteen inches of thick salt. We're down to marginally nothing, comparatively speaking.

"In recent years, the salt has been very rough. It's been tearing up easily. In years past you would leave black rubber marks the whole way. Now, there's kinda dark haze to it.

"Instead of being hard, the salt granules look just like sand. It's the way the salt structures. It's what we're finding when we analyze the salt. The salt has a lot of magnesium chloride. We're looking at about eighty-nine to ninety-three percent pure sodium chloride. The good salt from the past is about ninety-eight percent pure sodium chloride without any magnesium in it. The magnesium is doing the harm.

"The magnesium affects the way the salt crystals grow. Instead of growing in a cross-mesh pattern, they grow linear, and when they grow linear, they fall apart. There's no strength to 'em.

"By all estimates, one to one and a half million tons of salt are mined each year. Reilly's main product is potash. Salt is really a waste product. But what they're also taking is brine water, and that's the key ingredient that replenishes the salt.

"While Reilly doesn't admit to any wrongdoings; Reilly has said on more than one occasion it just wants to be a good neighbor, that it didn't know when they took over the lease, that it wasn't aware of this issue, and now they want to do right by the racers.

"Reilly will continue its operation, but it will put back at least as much salt as it's now taking out. We probably won't see much change, if any, the first year. In two years we might see a little change. Three years after the project begins, we should know if the new salt is starting to bond right. I really think it's gonna work myself. I think it will work.

"But you can't initiate a project like this overnight. It will take about fourteen months to get all the equipment on line. In the meantime, we have to make out as best we can.

"Personally, I believe Reilly is right. When the lease was sold to Reilly, BLM never told Reilly exactly where they were and how they were getting into trouble with us [the racers]. Right now the BLM says it's worth saving; they don't have the money to do it and they acknowledge they were lax."

More than just the racers, BLM and Reilly are involved in this reclamation project.

Says Vesco:

"The intent is to improve the surface of the Salt Flats, and there's gonna be an overseer group, not just the racers. It'll be the racers, BLM, Reilly, the Utah Historical Society, the Technical Review Committee for the Bonneville Salt Flats, plus a group of engineers and geologists. Some of the colleges are also involved. People representing the state of Utah will also be involved.

"After thirty years of [the racers] yelling into the wind, others have heard the message, loud and clear." Then Rick Vesco adds, "Let's hope it's not too late."

Way back in 1936, a year after Sir Malcolm Campbell became the first man to exceed 300 miles an hour on land, the *Salt Lake Tribune* described Bonneville as "the fastest race course to be found in all the 197 million square miles that envelop the globe."

In 1983, Black Rock Desert in Nevada became the fastest race course on earth. Bonneville may never recapture past glories, but, hopefully, it will escape the obituary section.

From a historical standpoint, the Flats were named for Captain Benjamin L.E. Bonneville, a French-born officer in the U.S. Army who explored the Rocky Mountains region between 1833 and 1836. Whether or not he actually touched what is called the Bonneville Speedway isn't known.

Some historians credit a young scout by the name of Jedediah Smith and his party with being the first white people to touch their boots on the salt desert.

Smith established quarters on Bear River, and it was while returning there from a trip to California in 1827 that it is said he crossed the wasteland.

Later, in 1845, famed frontier scout 'Kit' Carson and three others, acting as a vanguard for colonel John Charles Fremont, explored western regions for the federal government. Some writers contend Carson was the first to actually cross the Speedway.

The following year, Lansford W. Hastings, a young frontiersman, mapped an eastward course which cut through the salt. The ill-fated Donner Party battled across the salt where the crust was thin.

They were forced to leave some of their belongings and their delay in crossing made them late in reaching the high sierras. Snow overtook them. Some froze to death; others died of hunger. Only forty-four of the original company of eighty-seven reached their destination alive.

It wasn't until 1896, the same year that Utah became a state, that the potential of the flats for racing was discovered. That's when W.D. Rishel accidentally came to Bonneville.

William Randolph Hearst, the publisher, had just opened a newspaper in New York City and thought it would be a great publicity stunt to send a message by bicycle. The message would be sent from Hearst's *San Francisco Examiner* to his *New York Journal*.

Rishel, then living in Cheyenne, Wyoming, received the assignment to blaze a bicycle trail from that town to Truckee, California.

Fighting thirst, sticky marshes and sweeping clouds of mosquitos, Rishel crossed the Flats in twenty-two hours. Four years later, he had the honor of driving the first car across the saline highway. The big Packard pushed its speedometer to fifty miles an hour!

In 1912, Rishel took A.L. Westgard, national Pathfinder for the National Trails Association, out to the beds. Westgard agreed the Flats were the "great speedway on earth". Though a well-known automobile figure, Westgard's statement drew no excitement.

Bonneville was forgotten until 1914 when a barnstorming fleet of nine racing machines were brought to Salt Lake City. Rishel and other local businessmen arranged for an exhibition race on the salt. One hundred and fifty-two tickets were sold for the event.

Teddy Tezliff, driving the famed Blitzen Benz which Barney Oldfield had previously piloted to numerous speed records, clocked a torrid 141.73. His mile run lasted 25-32/5 seconds.

Years later, Rishel vividly recalled the race.

"There was no electric timing device, so a good portion of the spectators brought stopwatches. A man with a flag was placed at each end of the measured mile, and we put the official timers in the middle so they could see both flags, which were waved as Blitzen Benz roared by.

"When the race was finished, the timers announced that the world record [25-3/5 seconds] had been bettered. Both the American Automobile Association and Automobile Club of America gave the record a chill shoulder."

Again, Bonneville faded into racing oblivion, until a young carpenter, named Ab Jenkins, from Salt Lake City came along. Jenkins first saw the salt in 1910 when he drove his motorcycle to a speed of 60 mph. He made a second visit on a motorcycle shortly before World War I.

"This time I drove a motorcycle with much more 'vinegar' in its system," he wrote years later. "I soon found myself bucking a strong wind, the first of which would not permit me to sit up in the saddle of the machine.

"So, I grabbed a firm grip on the two handles and spread my body straight out, as though driving a child's snow sled. I stiffened my legs and gave her the works... 50-60-70-80. That was traveling, and the ride gave my spinal cord more chills than any run I ever made on the Salt Flats."

It wasn't until 1925 that Jenkins brought worldwide attention to the speedway. His race against a train and subsequent twenty-four hour marathon against the clock would bring the likes of Cobb, Eyston and Campbell to Utah.

In 1925, the highway was completed. As an added attraction to the planned celebration, Rishel asked his old friend if he would race the special excursion train from Salt Lake City to Wendover, a distance of 125 miles.

Ab Jenkins said he would, provided there was $250 riding on the outcome. The money was quickly raised and the race was on.

Streaking across the Flats, Jenkins beat the train by five minutes. That run convinced him of the tremendous possibilities of the beds for racing.

Between 1926 and 1931 Ab Jenkins kept busy, not only setting cross-country marks, but American hill-climb records as well. During those years he never forgot his memorable race against a train.

In 1932, Jenkins returned to Utah for his first official races, peeled off the fenders of his Pierce-Arrow and the twenty-four hour marathon began.

Pierce-Arrow officials laughed before the race when Jenkins told them he was going to drive his Mormon Meteor 2400 miles in twenty-four hours. Instead, he clocked 2710 miles. However the '32 run never became official because it wasn't timed by the AAA.

In midsummer of 1933, he returned for the official twenty-four hour run. This time the achievement went into the record books – 3000 miles in 25 hours, 30 minutes and 36.62 seconds. The average speed: 117.77 mph.

Seven years later, Jenkins shattered all the world's circular track records from one mile to 3863.14 miles, the number he covered in twenty-four hours.

While his twelve cylinder, 750 horsepower Mormon Meteor III had a speed potential of 275 miles an hour, Jenkins never took a crack at the land speed record. He left that to a trio of daring Englishmen.

Born in 1883, Ab Jenkins died in 1956 at the age of seventy-three. His last assault upon his own records failed in 1951 because of car trouble. He was then sixty-eight years old.

Some of his numerous records included:

Year	Distance or Time	Miles Per Hour
1936	48 hours	148.63
1940	500 miles	177.229
1940	1000 miles	172.804
1950	200 miles	190.92
1950	24 hours	161.184
1950	1 hour	190.68
1951	100 miles	190.657

Sir Malcolm Campbell, who had reached 276 at Ormond Beach in Florida, was determined to shatter the '300 mph barrier'. In searching for a longer and smoother course, he arrived at the Flats in 1935.

On September 3, he recorded a new two-way record of 301.13. After the return run, Campbell called the Bonneville Salt Flats "the speed laboratory of the future".

Until 1949, the only forms of racing at Bonneville were Ab Jenkins' marathon runs, which began in the mid-twenties, and the land speed efforts of Sir Malcolm Campbell, Captain George Eyston and John Cobb, all Englishmen, starting with Campbell in 1935.

Dry lakes racing began at El Mirage (California) in the early 1930s, then moved east to the vast Bonneville Salt Flats when the Southern California Timing Association and Bonneville Nationals Inc. (BNI) staged the first organized time trials. It has become a tradition ever since – Speed Week.

Cancellation of the 1994 Nationals, by all estimates, cost the local economy $1 million.

From a geological standpoint, here's how it all began:

During the last stages of the ice age, some 70,000 to 100,000 years ago, when Utah's climate was damp and chilled and small glaciers flowed down the highest peaks, there was enough rain to form a huge lake.

Lake Bonneville, as large as Lake Michigan, covered Western Utah from Salt Lake city to Wendover. This lake was one hundred miles wide and nearly twice as long. The Great Salt Lake forms the edges of this vast lake.

To appreciate this lake fully, remember that both Wendover and Salt Lake City – 125 miles apart on opposite shores – rest upon their old bed. The water reached a depth of 1000 feet over both towns.

As the huge lake, without an outlet, continued to receive the water from the streams and huge quantities of water evaporated from its surface, the water turned brackish.

The lake dried up. More water evaporated than flowed in, and the water, still containing all the mineral salt, became more and more salty.

Today, the Great Salt Lake is twenty-five percent salt (table salt, Epsom salt, and other kinds), so salty it is almost greasy to the touch, and so dense, a human body will not sink in it.

Thus, the salt was formed by entirely natural processes over a long period of time. The Salt Flats and the entire Salt Desert near Wendover are solid crystalline salt left on the ground when the western part of the huge lake basin dried up.

Chapter Eight
Memories are Made of This

Art Arfons was nervous as he and a companion rode the elevator to the fourth floor of the fashionable apartment house in London, England.

As a youngster growing up in rural Ohio, Arfons idolized those dashing, daring British drivers who raced for the world land speed record on the glistening sands of Ormond Beach, Florida, during 'The Roaring Twenties', then moved their death-defying act to the hard-crusted salt of Bonneville, Utah in the 1930s.

Henry Segrave... Sir Malcolm Campbell... Captain John Eyston... John Cobb. Together, they combined for eighteen records between 1924 and 1947, including nine by Campbell.

Cobb, a wealthy London furrier, however, was Arfons' favorite. Cobb and his legendary Railton Special. Three records between 1938 and 1947.

In 1947, Cobb pushed his ancient machine to a new two-way record of 394.2 miles an hour, and in the process became the first to exceed 400 mph on land. Three years later he would die on water as his jet boat exploded in an attempt to set the record.

Now Arfons, this shy, soft-spoken hot rodder from Ohio, who would also 'write' his own chapter of racing history, was about to meet Vicky Cobb, widow of his boyhood hero.

"Richard set up the whole thing," says Arfons of his memorable spring 1995 meeting. Richard meaning England's Richard Noble, who raised the record to 633.4 in his jet-powered Thrust 2 at Black Rock Desert, Nevada (1983).

Richard Noble, that same entrepreneur who was feverishly trying to complete construction of his supersonic jet for a scheduled fall 1995 assault at Black Rock.

This time, Noble would leave the driving to British fighter pilot Andy Green.

"The meeting lasted about thirty minutes," Arfons fondly recalls. "She was a real classy lady. She looked like she was in her seventies. I think she and John Cobb were just married when he was killed.

"We sat in her living room and made small talk. I'm not too good at small talk. She seemed glad to see us and knew who I was. I kinda felt like a school kid. I was flattered.

"We talked mostly about Richard's project. It seems there's not a day goes by that there's not another story about Richard's car in the London papers.

"All of Europe, I believe, is very aware of what's happening in land speed racing. Certainly Mrs. Cobb is. The thing I most noticed was that there was no memorabilia in the apartment connected to her late husband. I wondered why, but I sure wasn't about to ask.

"Richard and I rode the elevator down. Mrs. Cobb took the stairs and darned if she almost didn't beat us. That lady's in a lot better shape than I am."

The London visit climaxed a two week trip for Arthur Eugene Arfons. A trip he didn't even plan.

Let him explain:

"For the past thirteen years, a promoter in Holland who stages a once-a-year track pull meet in his country has been trying to get me to come over and run my jet tractor. And every year I turn him down.

"It's really a world meet. There are seven countries involved, including the United States. When they said they wanted both tractors, meaning mine as well as Dusty's [Art's daughter is a well-known tractor puller in her own right], and would pay all expenses, how could I turn him down?"

So, Art Arfons, his wife, June, his daughter and son-in-law, Randy Sproggins, took the all-expense-paid trip.

"We sent the tractors two weeks before the meet, then flew from Akron-Canton Airport, to Detroit, then on to Rotterdam, Holland. All told, they had nineteen tractors. They had all the classes, including two-wheel drive, super stocks and a bunch of jets.

"They held two meets the same day, Saturday afternoon and then at night. Both were sell-outs. I'd say we drew about 5000 for each session. The meets were held indoors.

"Dusty and I made exhibition runs, and fortunately we both made full pulls right out the door. A full pull was about 260 feet. It would have been a little embarrassing if we had come up short.

"We spent ten days in Holland and had a great time. All the people were real nice. We got treated like royalty."

From Holland the party traveled to France, and then to England.

"We took the tunnel under the English Channel. It was a neat ride. The trip only took something like twenty-nine minutes."

Arfons was then escorted to the famed auto museum at Beaulieu, where he sat in the cockpit of two record-breaking British cars: Donald Campbell's Bluebird and Henry Segrave's Golden Arrow. It was the first car to exceed 200 miles an hour.

"Actually, they had four or five land speed cars there," recalls Arfons. "They even had a small model of my car. They had a tape running all the time, showing me and my Green Monster. I was shocked that they had me there."

Art Arfons and his family spent the night at the home where Richard Noble lives with his wife, Sally, and their two children. The next day, Noble drove Arfons to his racing facility.

This marked the second occasion since 1990 that these two land speed kings had spent time together. Noble, as well as Breedlove, spent three days at Bonneville in October 1990, as Arfons struggled with his mini-jet.

"Sally did the cooking. She's a real good cook. Richard was a perfect host, but he was real hyper. You could see his mind going a thousand miles an hour. He's really been hopping to get the car done on time. He's working his fanny off. He's got sixteen full-tine employees working on the car.

"I kinda feel sorry for him. He's gotta be on the run all the time just to keep this operation going. His shop is one hundred miles away from his home. It's a couple hours' drive and he doesn't get there too often.

"He's got some very good people working there. They're all experts with college degrees. When I spent the day with Richard, the chassis was done and they were starting to skin it.

"The engines were built somewhere else. They had one of the two jet engines when I was at the shop. Rolls Royce is furnishing the engines. They're a little bigger than my J-79 [which carried Art Arfons to records of 434, 536, 576 in 1964-65].

"The engines have about 25,000 pounds of thrust apiece. At altitude, it's a 2 to 1 ratio between horsepower and thrust. That means he's got 100,000 horses."

Arfons' J-79 had a four-stage afterburner, and he had to go through each stage to reach full power. On the other hand, Arfons believes Richard "...just goes into full power."

For one, Arfons isn't impressed with the big numbers, and that's the name of this speed game. Both Noble's twin-jet (57 feet long, 14,000 pounds) and five-time speed king, Craig Breedlove's newest creation, Spirit of America – Sonic Arrow, capture the public's imaginations on both sides of the Atlantic with their 850 mph potential.

Arfons simply didn't believe the impending jet duel at Black Rock between these supersonic jets would take place in 1995.

"I don't think either one of them will be ready. Ninety-six seems a lot more realistic."

(He was right.)

Art Arfons hasn't abandoned his dream of returning to Bonneville to push Green Monster No. 27 to his fourth land speed record.

He simply wants the title, Fastest Man On Wheels, if only for one day. Speed potential for this eight year old car is 'only' 650.

"Richard's car certainly has the horsepower, maybe too much power. They can do it if the car stays on the ground. They showed me the rocket test conducted with a model. They ran it up to 850 miles an hour. They had cameras that took 10,000 pictures per second. They could show the shock wave coming on the model.

"They figure it will go 850 in 21 seconds, and they'll need only two and a half miles to get up to that speed. To me, Richard's car is similar in design to a proposed car that Firestone drew up years ago.

"The driver will be sitting between two engines. They're using rear steering. What scares the hell out of me is the car's potential for flying. They're not gonna put the front down at all. I wish Andy Green [RAF fighter pilot/Thrust SSC driver] the best of luck. It scares me, really.

"I don't believe Richard wanted to drive it that bad. He enjoys putting together big packages. I think he enjoys doing that more than anything. I think the best he's got is a 50-50 chance.

"Richard, more than anyone, should realize how hard it was to get his land speed record. He ran for six years before he made it. He just ain't gonna go out there and run 850 right out of the hole. It just ain't gonna happen.

"I believe I can squeeze 650 out of my jet car. If someone goes 660, I'll forget about it. Maybe I'll just sell it to Slick," Arfons says, jokingly.

Back in the 1970s, and in need of cash, Art Arfons sold California rancher Slick Gardner his 700 mph Super Cyclops for some $125,000, a deal he has long regretted. Arfons maintains it was the best land speed car he had ever built, more aerodynamic and faster than his record-setting Green Monster.

After ill-fated attempts with Green Monster No. 27 in 1989–90–91, Arfons was ready to return to Bonneville for a three day meet in October 1994. However, the meet was canceled by rain, and that ended his record bid.

"I was sick when I got that call," he vividly recalls. "I wanted to go real bad. Bonneville is the only place I can run for $400."

He struck out in 1995 and in 1996.

But hope springs eternal. Maybe one glorious ride.

Chapter Nine
Alive to Tell the Story

Gee, I thought you had to be dead to be inducted into a hall of fame. Maybe they heard my old bones crackin' and figured they'd better do it now while I could still walk up the aisle. If they had waited until I was gone, it sure would have been easier on my nervous system. Dusty and I were at a tractor pull in Anaheim, California. Some guy I didn't know called and asked me over to his office for some pictures so they could get 'em in the program. I called home just to make sure it wasn't some kind of joke and spoke to June. She told me she was the one who told 'em how to reach me. He was with the Motorsports Hall of Fame.

Art Arfons

The legacy!

First to hit 150 miles an hour on the drag strip... developer of the braking parachute... holder of three land speed records in a jet car he built... only man to survive a 600 mile an hour crash on land... introduced jet-powered tractor to that sport... inducted into both the NHRA Hall of Fame and Motorsports Hall of Fame in the same year...

Arthur Eugene Arfons and his Green Monster, a matched set during the past five decades. You can't separate this very special man from his long line of brutish machines.

Just the kind of thrill-packed life that is the subject of a full-length documentary movie.

"But about the time you start getting impressed with yourself," says this living legend, "something comes along to put you in your place. And quick!

"Way back in the sixties, I was running at Kil-Kare Dragway near Dayton, Ohio, with my first jet, Cyclops. I don't think it was a full quarter. It had a very short shut-down area which had a sand trap.

"And if that didn't slow you down, you were in real trouble because there was a ravine after that. You really dropped into a hell of a hole.

"Well, the announcer really got me psyched up. The adrenaline was really pumpin'. He was screaming over the microphone, 'Arfons is really gonna nail it... he's gonna set a record'.

"I didn't want to disappoint the guy. I powered into the last light, locked up the wheels and put both chutes out. I almost made it through the sand trap to the ravine. Phew, it was close! I went 207 on that track. That was flyin'.

"They drove me back in front of the stands, and I was feelin' pretty good, waving to the crowd. A guy leaned over and yelled at me, 'You're not brave, you're stupid'. That really knocked the wind right out of my sails. I'll never forget that as long as I live."

Without a moment's hesitation, Arfons labels his land speed records as a career highlight.

"It's just as thrilling no matter how many times you do it. The last time was as good as the first time. It's never old hat."

Despite setting land speed records – 1964–65 – of 434, 536, and 576 in his jet-powered Green Monster, Arfons considers an old dragster as his best car.

"That was No. 11," he says. "It was the eleventh car I built. It was Allison-powered. It set top speed in a meet three years consecutive for NHRA [National Hot Rod Association].

"That's when they outlawed aircraft engines forever. It was such a good car they couldn't beat it, so they banned it."

Until a memorable showdown with Don Garlits in Florida, top speed for No. 11 had been 171 miles an hour.

"The Chamber of Commerce would bring in a new guy each week for Garlits to beat," Arfons fondly recalls. "I said to the guy, 'What makes you think he's gonna beat me? What will you give me if I beat him?'

"He said he'd give me a five year college scholarship but I said I couldn't use it. 'How about cash?' I kinda pressed the issue and finally he said they'd pay $500 if I could beat Garlits.

"That was enough incentive to haul all the way down to Florida. That was big money back in those days. We ran at an old airport, on a concrete runway.

"Concrete isn't slippery like asphalt. It was fantastic. It picked up one wheel right at the starting line. I went on three wheels all the way down, ran 191 and collected the $500."

A few years later, Arfons took his jet car to Europe.

"We ran in nine countries, including England, France, Austria, Sweden. It was part of a promotion for car shows which Jochen Rindt [the late Formula One driver] and his wife were putting on.

"We'd run at a local airport, and depending on the condition of the runway, make an easy pass or a hot pass. In England, the distance was probably some 300 feet more than the standard quarter mile.

"There was a photographer I'll always remember. He was the gutsiest, or the craziest guy I've ever met. Don't know which. I blasted down the runway and hit the chutes. I knew I had a good chute opening.

"I turned right to him and he never moved. I stopped about ten feet from the guy. Later, he showed me the shot. It was the best picture I've ever seen."

Arfons hit 325 mph on that run!

Another 'once in a lifetime' trip, however, failed to materialize. Therein lies another story.

"Back in the seventies it was one of those 'can't miss' sort of deals. I had my Green Monster, which I built after the record car was destroyed. This was a 700 mile an hour jet. Lighter, sleeker, better than the old Monster.

"Well, the Shah of Iran wanted a land speed record set on his soil... and he was willing to pay for it. He bought a C-5A, which is a mammoth transport plane, and they were gonna fly me, Mickey Thompson and Craig Breedlove over to Iran. Money was no object.

"Mickey had his wheel-driven car [Autolite Special]. I don't know what Craig would have driven. Anyway, Mickey said, 'Let me go over and see about this deal'. So he went. He gets one of the Shah's guys and he goes out and looks over their salt flats.

"He said, 'They've got the flats but that the country is so screwed up'. He wouldn't recommend that any of us take the deal. So, we didn't. Mickey said it was a shaky deal.

"He said, 'If we go over there and set a record that they'll never let us take our cars back home'. He was convinced they'd keep 'em. Within six months the Shah was thrown out, shot or whatever they did to him."

It was almost the stuff that dreams are made of.

There are times when Art Arfons reflects that he finds it hard to believe the path his storybook life has taken.

"I got into drag racing by accident and turned a hobby into a livelihood. How many guys spend most of their life in a job they hate and would quit in a second if only they could?

"The most I made in drag racing was $1000 a week, and I didn't run forty weeks in a year. I was satisfied. I bought and paid for a house. Money was never the main motivation.

"The most I ever made from setting a land speed record, and holding it for a year, was $75,000. I didn't have to sign a contract with Firestone. A handshake was enough.

"In fact, one year [1964], I actually set two records [434, 536 mph]. It was after setting the second record I went in to see Bill McCreary, who was top man in Firestone racing.

"He said to me, 'Now, did you understand we would pay you $75,000 for the year, or $75,000 for each record?' I said, 'No, it was just for a year'. I was honest and he didn't push it. That was more money than I had in my life. My God.

"I was never a big buck operation. But suppose I had the money, like Campbell. I'd have had more chrome and prettier cars, more money to spend on 'em. You couldn't get a better engine than the J-79. I guess if I had a million, my wife would have shopped more often."

Driven by a compulsion he doesn't understand, Arfons spent six years and $100,000 of his own money to build a pint-sized, jet-powered Green Monster in hopes of regaining the land speed record after twenty-four years.

He tried and failed in 1989, 1990 and 1991.

And even after celebrating his sixty-sixth birthday (February 1992), he couldn't shut the door on his land speed career. Maybe ninety-nine percent... but not all the way.

On one hand, he looks forward to the day when he can build an airplane and take his wife, June, on a cross-country adventure.

"No timetable, no nothing. Just spend more time with her.

"She complains that we've never had a real vacation, but I point out all the places we've been. She doesn't buy that bill of goods. She says, 'Yes, but we're always pulling that lousy trailer'."

But when Art Arfons walks into his office/workshop complex and looks at the twenty-two foot long jet car, he starts thinking about major changes to turn Dud II into a real 650 mile an hour Green Monster.

He dubbed his worst car, his most cantankerous car, Dud I. It was a jet dragster that underwent numerous major facelifts before it started earning its keep.

Arfons enjoyed playing the role of underdog, the guy with only three years of high school education, the guy with the junk cars. He thoroughly enjoyed going faster than Donald Campbell's four million dollar jet.

"I played it to the hilt. That was deliberate. My God, staying in Wendover wasn't good enough for Campbell. He'd have a helicopter fly him in from Salt Lake City [some 125 miles away]. Wendover was only eleven miles from Bonneville.

"He wouldn't stay there with us, and I resented his money a little bit. He was a nice enough guy to talk to though. They brought a whole room with spare this, spare that. I couldn't throw that much money away."

Since the early 1970s, Arfons made the transition from the drag strips to the indoor dirt arenas. He became a tractor pulling superstar. And, reluctantly, he's had to adjust to Father Time.

"I know I'm on the downside of my career. If I go another two to three years, I'll be lucky. My arthritis is gettin' worse. My hands and knees hurt. I've got a lot of damage to my legs, too.

"Before Dusty [Arfons' daughter] got into tractor pulling, I was on the road alone, driving all night. Putting in thousands of miles a year. I can't do that anymore.

"I drive seven or eight hours now and I'm really tired. I drive maybe until eleven o'clock and say, 'Dusty, I've had it'. We just pull in and sleep. It takes longer to get cross-country."

In 1991, at the age of sixty-five, Art Arfons received a double dose of immortality. First, he was inducted into the NHRA Hall of Fame in California. Three months later, he joined nine others named to the Motorsports Hall of Fame of America at ceremonies in Detroit, Michigan.

It was a virtual Who's Who of racing:

* Dean Chenoweth, unlimited hydroplane champ. Driver of Miss Budweiser.

* Dan Gurney, legendary Formula One, Indy 500 driver, car builder.

* Tony Hulman, the man who saved the Indianapolis Motor Speedway.

* Junior Johnson, NASCAR driver turned car owner.

* Joe Leonard, first a motorcycle star, then Indy car champ.

* Don Prudhomme, all-time drag racing star. Nicknamed 'The Snake'.

* Roscue Turner, legendary air racer of bygone years.

* Al Unser, Senior, four-time Indianapolis 500 winner.

Chenoweth, Hulman and Turner were honored posthumously.

Arfons called induction the highlight of his long career.

"The people I was inducted with," he says with astonishment, "well, they're up in the sky. I still can't believe it happened to me.

"Everyone got up and read their speech. I didn't. I should have. I spoke for a few minutes, whatever came to my mind. They had a projector on the wall and there was a little promo of what you did. A picture of my tractor running, a picture of my land speed car running.

"Each inductee had his own presenter. He was an announcer from tractor pulling. He's followed me since I ran my dragster at the Oklahoma State Fair in '57. He claimed I was his hero and he was thrilled to be there for my big moment. I still get a little choked up thinking about it."

For the record, Arthur Eugene Arfons did not wear a tuxedo on this most prestigious and formal affair. He wore a suit.

"I had a tuxedo once when Dusty was married. That won't happen again."

Arthur Eugene Arfons has touched the lives of many since he was first bitten by the racing bug way back in the early 1950s.

Some know him intimately. Others 'hero worship' from afar. But all cherish their memories of this remarkable man.

By Bob Russo

(Back in the 1950s, Bob Russo was probably the first full-time auto racing writer in the United States. He was also one of the driving forces in the creation of AARWBA [American Automobile Racing Writers and Broadcasters Association] and was that group's first president.
A long-time friend of the late speed king, Mickey Thompson, Russo not only runs his own public relations agency but is also involved with the Motorsports Hall of Fame of America at Novi, Michigan.)

I got involved when the Motorsports Hall of Fame elected and inducted Mickey. I had the honor of presenting the induction award to his son, Danny, and sister, Collene Campbell. I liked what I saw at that time, knew they needed help and offered my services (for free, of course).

To make a long story short, I gave them a bunch of ideas, which they adopted, and they made me Chairman of the Nominating Committee. I helped select that group of twenty-five persons and made sure we had a good cross-section and representation of *qualified* individuals with both a good general knowledge of motorsports and particular expertise in one or more of the categories.

I prepare the bios and ballot each year for the Nominating Committee, which, in turn, determines who will appear on the voting ballot for the Election Committee to consider.

Again, the Election Committee of about one hundred persons – journalists, former participants, recognized historians and other qualified persons – meet that criteria of being knowledgeable, like the members of the Nominating Committee.

In 1990, when I was updating bios, preparing the information, to send to the Nominating Committee for 1991 elections, I added an expanded bio on Art Arfons, using a lot of good stuff I got from my old friend, Deke Houlgate.

Anyway, the Nominating Committee must have been impressed because they nominated him, and the Election Committee elected him, and we inducted Art in June, along with such other greats as Dan Gurney, Al Unser, Tony Hulman, Roscoe Turner, Don Prudhomme, Joe Leonard and Junior Johnson.

The annual voting is usually done in late December, with the results announced in early January. The inductions center around the Detroit Grand Prix Indy car event.

In January 1991, H of F Executive Director Ron Watson called me and said he needed a mugshot of Art Arfons and I told him to call Art at home, whereat Ron replied, "He's sitting in your parking lot right now!"

It was true. Art and his daughter, Dusty, and crew were at Anaheim Stadium a couple of days before a scheduled tractor pull.

So I went down to the parking lot, hunted them up and gave Art the glad news of his election. I think both he and his daughter were stunned by it all, or didn't know if I was pulling their legs. I'm sure they hadn't heard about the Motorsports Hall of Fame of America before. A few days later, of course, they got their official written notice with all the details.

I didn't see them again until the reception for the 1991 inductees at the Novi Hilton the night before the banquet. Art, God bless him, was very impressed.

It was so obvious that he was in awe of all this attention, plus other racing celebrities and families – Gurney was there, Joe Leonard, Wilbur Shaw's son, Billy, the widow of Roscoe Turner, etc. But I could also tell that he was inwardly proud that such an honor was happening to him.

His family, what great people, were equally humble and gracious. I spent lots of time talking to them, trying to make them feel more at ease.

At the banquet, it was the same. Very humble and gracious during the dinner. And when it was his turn to receive the Induction Award, I think Art won the hearts of everyone in the room by his sincerity and gracious acceptance. He got one of the biggest hands of the evening.

I think everyone that got to know him or even see and hear him for the first time realized what a truly great individual he is, and gained a new respect for his accomplishments – all of which came through his own self-education and love of machines.

I think he, in turn, regarded that evening as one of the highlights of his life, more so than the NHRA Hall of Fame (also in 1991) because this one placed him on a level with so many other motorsports greats from other eras and other phases of the sport. That means a lot to him and his family.

Art was elected, by the way, in the At Large Category which encompasses individuals who do not necessarily fit into other, more specific categories such as Open Wheel, Stock Car, Drag Racing, Sports Cars, Power Boats, Motorcycles, Air Racing and Historic. It included other LSR competitors like Campbell, Gabelich, etc. and is the category in which Mickey Thompson was elected in 1990.

By H.A. 'Humpy' Wheeler
(President/General Manager, Charlotte Motor Speedway)

(Wheeler was Director of Auto Racing Public Relations at Firestone Tire & Rubber Company, Akron, Ohio, when Art Arfons was on his record-setting rampage in 1964–1965.)

Art is unquestionably one of the most extraordinary human beings in the history of mankind. While lacking a high school degree, he probably knows as much about land-bound aerodynamics as anyone who ever lived. If he were in charge of the space program, we might be on Mars now.

His famous 'Duel In The Sun' with Craig Breedlove at Bonneville will be looked at by motorsports historians in the next century as perhaps the highest drama in auto racing in the twentieth century.

What makes him so interesting is not only his natural engineering brilliance but his tremendous integrity and courage. Any time a sane man crouches low to begin running the 'flying mile' for the world land speed record, he must fight, for a few moments, his own mortality, and that is what makes these men so rare, and Art is the rarest of the rare.

Buddy Baker once told me that as far as he was concerned "those are flying coffins on four wheels." That statement from a driver, who, in the last twenty-five years, has gained the reputation of being one of the greatest drivers to run the 200 mph NASCAR tracks – Daytona and Talladega.

I introduced Art to Mario Andretti at Indy in 1966. Mario later remarked to me that "those guys really have steel nerves." My first impression of Art when I met him was that he has instant charisma, probably like the kind that Daniel Boone and Davey Crockett had, rough-hewn but a man of action.

Art's lineage of Cherokee and Greek also contributes to his charisma. He looked like a man who feared nothing. His personality is warm and hospitable. After breaking the land speed record (1964), I took him on a nationwide tour. He handled the press extremely well.

In the mid sixties, athletes were beginning to wear Brooks Brothers suits, speak English like someone from Evansville, ride in limos and appear on television selling antiperspirant, hairspray and cough-lax.

He was a guy who was down-to-earth and totally humble about his death-defying exploits and his, 'Aw, shucks, it wasn't nothing', in a new age of high tech.

At one press conference in New York, the late Howard Cosell, after an interview with Arfons for ABC, told me Art was the most humble sports person he had ever met.

I still remember this incident like it were yesterday. We were in New York, walking down 50th Street near St. Patrick's Cathedral and a taxi cab had broken down. The driver was holding up traffic. Horns were blaring.

Art, in a brand new suit, went over and asked the driver what was wrong. The amazed cabbie said the motor wouldn't run. Art lifted up the hood, saw that the choke was sticking, fixed it and closed the hood. He had never seen anybody do anything like that in New York. He didn't know Art.

As I said, I'd never seen Art experience fear. He approached the land speed record like he fixed the cab. Just something to do. I'm not surprised that he tried for the record in 1989, when he was sixty-four, and tried again in 1990 and 1991. Arfons retire? Don't bet the farm on that.

As far as his crashes were concerned, the first was the worst I've ever seen in all my years in racing. I was driving the 'chase' car which was a Highway Patrol-issued Dodge or Plymouth with a 426 Hemi engine.

I took a *Sports Illustrated* photographer and a doctor along for the ride since we were the only vehicle allowed within 1000 feet of the actual course, or as we called it, 'the black line'. I taxied the car up to the Green Monster and Art and I had some sort of a weird signal that I would take off at full speed so that he could take off moments later and pass me as both vehicles approached the measured mile.

First, it is almost impossible to describe the sensation of a vehicle with 17,000 horsepower passing you at 500–600 miles an hour.

I can best describe it as a terrible noise, particularly if he hit the afterburner, fire belching out the rear of the jet and salt spray one hundred feet in the air.

It was like watching something out of the fires of hell as it stretched past. I used to think, surely a human being cannot be in that quail-green thing. On this particular day we were fighting a bit of a crosswind as I approached the entrance of the measured mile.

A peak at my speedometer showed 140 plus. I was on the left side of the Monster, about 500 feet from 'the black line'. As Art hit the mile, the afterburner and this Green Monster from the dark, surged even faster.

He was halfway through the mile when he hit the next stage of burner and at that point I started hearing sounds like an automatic elephant gun – crack, crack, crack. That's when I saw a huge, unnatural spray of salt.

The next thing I saw was a flash of green high up in the salt spray. I knew then that Art was airborne when the Green Monster hit the salt. All I could see were clouds of salt darkened by sounds of metal as the car went into a series of rolls.

I didn't panic because I had mentally gone through a crash like this many times and Art and I talked about it many times. He said if he were to crash, to look for a capsule of steel tubes which was the driver's compartment, made to break away from the engine. It looked like a high-speed aircraft had crashed. I thought no one could survive.

When I got to the crash site, I saw a mass of tubes and went straight for it. Art was in it. We jumped out with the doctor. Art was unconscious and his eyes were dilated. Surely, no one could survive. We kept a twin-engine medical transport aircraft during the runs since Salt Lake City was the closest hospital, over one hundred miles away.

We put Arfons on the plane and it took off. Even though his vital signs appeared fair, he was still unconscious. He woke up some twenty minutes into the flight. Incredible!

We checked him into the hospital where all sorts of tests were made. They probed everything in Art and found no more than a mild concussion and many bruises. He had not only survived the highest speed crash in the history of land speed racing, but left the hospital the next day no worse for wear.

How did he survive this incredible accident?

He built the car to survive. He is also an extremely tough human being. However, I think the most telling thing about the accident was that mentally when he was building the car he thought about what *could* happen. What could, did, and he saved himself simply by building a machine that could give and break apart in the most critical area, and that was the driver's compartment.

By Bob Motz

(He is one of drag racing's most exciting performers, driving a 7000 pound, jet-powered truck at speeds reaching 200 miles an hour. Before Motz decided to 'do his own thing', he drove jet dragsters for both Art and Walt Arfons.)

Seems like I've known Art forever. I actually started out working for Walt in the 1960s, helping with the JATO system on that rocket car. Then I drove one of his dragsters for a year, a Camaro with a J–34 engine.

I guess it was 1969 or '70 that I approached Art about maybe driving for him. Art and Walt had buildings just yards apart, but I really didn't know Art. You never went between buildings.

We talked and he gave me a ride in a jet car he called The Dud. It was a long, slim-nosed car with skinny tires. The driver sat in the middle, with the engine behind. Actually, it was a very good car. I drove it for three to four years and actually ended up buying the car from Art.

I'd run the quarter in around 6.50, probably hitting 250. I'd travel all across the country, working on, hauling and driving that car. It had a J–34 and a burner that Art made.

We ran against each other for four years at match races and I never could beat that s.o.b. I remember one time at Bristol. I was first off the line and figured I finally had it won, but I could hear those thundering hoof-beats. He just beat me. Close doesn't count, damn his hide. I'm only kidding.

Art just doesn't give you an inch. You have to earn that victory. That's what I call a competitor.

I've never really seen a change in him in all these years. Sure as heck doesn't hold any grudge. Two years in a row, I crashed his Super Cyclops. It was a mean machine which could have hit 300 real easy. It was powered with a J–52 with burner. I figure it unleashed 12,000 to 14,000 pounds of thrust.

The last crash was at Dragway 42 (in Ohio) and I still don't know what happened. I shut it off after only 500 feet and was still running like 272. I rolled four times and took out a guard rail. Art was there that time and he didn't want to come up to the car.

Hurt, no. Embarrassed, yes. He built a lot of safety into his car. Heck, he survived a 600 mile an hour crash at Bonneville. That's how strong his cars were built. When I was kicking around the idea of a jet-powered truck, Art's the one who helped me build it. We've always gotten along fine.

If I could afford to do it, I'd work for him for nothing, What he can do with nothing is amazing. He's never had the luxury of a big buck sponsorship whether it be land speed racing or tractor pulling. He's built more, done more with so little.

He knows how to make it work, that's why I'm really surprised he didn't set a land speed record with that little jet. Maybe that really shows he's human after all.

I'm about fifteen years younger than Art and I don't have the stamina I used to have. But Art keeps on ticking, appearing at all those tractor pulls, and yet he put all that time into building that little Monster. Maybe he has to push himself a little more, but he still gets the job done. One of a kind!

By Roger Gustin
(Drag Racing Legend, Jet-Powered Funny Car Driver)

(As a boy growing up on a small farm in rural Southern Ohio, Roger Gustin dreamed of becoming a race car driver: "...but I didn't tell anybody. I didn't want to get laughed at." He started drag racing in 1957, driving his '49 Chevy. He was just seventeen. By 1972, Gustin made the big jump to jet-powered funny cars. Now retired, he is a successful car owner.)

As a kid crazy about cars, who didn't hear about the Arfons Brothers and their famed Green Monsters? I don't know how many times I'd seen Art compete – it was a bunch. I'm just sorry I never had the privilege and honor of personally running against him.

But I did run against his cars that were driven by Teddy Austin and Bob Motz. And through the years, we've become friends. He'll always be a hero to me. Kids today – supposedly – are having a hell of a hard time finding heroes to look up to.

Look at Art. At a time in life when most men his age are retired, he's driving his jet-powered tractor on the circuit and hasn't given up his dream, his passion, for setting another land speed record.

Art never needed the drugs and the bullshit that went on in this country over these last years. The guy went out and did what he wanted to do for a living. He's enjoyed his life, so that makes him a rare human being. There's not a day that goes by that I'm not thankful for what I've been able to do, and I owe so much of it to the Arfons Brothers, Art and Walt.

I might not have been in racing the last twenty years if it weren't for these guys. I don't think I would have gone out, bought an old salvage jet engine and put it in a race car. But that's what they did. They were the pioneers. They blazed the trail for the rest of us.

When you look at the piston cars, as sophisticated as they are today, they're still using an engine that was built in the 1900s, this old piston-type engine. But look at the Arfons Boys. They took a jet engine that was designed for a fighter plane. Those are the guys that did it from scratch.

Basically, guys like myself came along a number of years later. I didn't know anything about a jet, so I bought a car from one of these guys. I bought a car from Walter. I had to learn the jets. These guys already proved the concept would work. They had proved it long before I ever came along.

They laid the groundwork for us. Just think about all they've accomplished. They were the first to use a parachute in a race car. They had more innovative ideas, and I'm sure neither one of them had a day of engineering school. They just did it the good old-fashioned, common-sense way.

I was driving a fuel funny car in '72. The first jet funny car I bought was built by Walt Arfons. It was a good car. I ended up having a horrible crash in that car in the spring of 1974. I flipped it seven times, down in North Carolina, and got busted up pretty bad. Broke a lot of bones.

Back in 1971, despite sponsorship, running a fuel funny car was becoming a losing proposition and it had me worried. The arithmetic was getting terrible.

When it got to the place where you go out and win $2000 and then spend $3000 getting your car ready to race again the next week, that's scary. You're not supporting yourself, really, let alone your wife and your family.

By then I'd been in the business a whole bunch of years, was good at what I was doing, but was starting to consider, at least in my mind, other ways to earn a living.

That was when Dave Corey, a friend of mine from Dayton, pointed me in the direction of jet funny cars. Before the end of the 1972 season, I was racing Dave out in Seattle and he crashed and lost his life.

I can remember seeing Art at Great Lakes Dragway in Union Grove, Wisconsin. I think it may have been Labor Day weekend in 1972. By then, as I recall, Art had basically quit drag racing. Teddy Austin was driving his dragster, but he had that awesome Bonneville car and was going to make a pass during the big jet show.

That, I believe, is the car he later sold to Slick Gardner. It was powered by a J–79 and I'll bet it could have gone 650 or so at Bonneville had Art ever had the chance to run it for the record.

I was up in the tower when Art was moving up to the starting line. Don't ask me how I saw it, but I saw the flap fall open for the main parachute while he's moving up to the line. I just happen to catch it in all that smoke and thunder back there.

I go flyin' down the steps and run out on the track, right in front of Art's car. Officials are screaming at me, because they don't know why this crazy man is out there on the track, waving his hands.

They sure as heck don't know what's wrong. I'm frantically giving Art the signal to shut it off. I knew the main chute would come up the minute he started his run. He never hesitated and shut it off. When he opened the canopy and took off his helmet I told him what the problem was.

He smiled, then thanked me very much because more than likely he would have crashed had he made the run. As big and heavy as that car was, he never could have stopped without the main chute and that would have been burned off by the afterburner blast.

Through the years, I've kept in touch with Art. A few years ago, I was just passing through and decided to stop off in Akron, just for a quick hello. But that quick hello lasted for most of the afternoon.

Art has always been good to me, nice to me. Anytime that I've ever needed advice, I knew I could just call him up and Art would give me straight, honest answers. He's a no-foolishness type of guy. I wish I had the time to just go up to his shop and hang out for a while. He's a pure racer, a smart man, someone to look up to.

I know what another land speed record means to him, because if I could do it, I can't think of anything else I'd rather accomplish than taking a car to Bonneville and going for the record myself.

I wanted to do that years ago, honest, and secretly I still do today. But I've got to be realistic. With my hectic schedule I just can't devote the time necessary for such a project.

Even today, I don't know how Art can still keep perkin' on eight cylinders, how he could haul his tractor across the country, come home for a quick pit stop just to work on the land speed car, then hit the road again. I'm some fifteen years younger than him and I know I couldn't keep up with that grind.

I was very close to Craig (Walt's son, Art's nephew). In fact, Craig drove one of my funny cars every weekend the year he was killed going for that damned world water speed record.

Craig was killed in July 1989 and a few days later I flew to Florida for the memorial service. Art was there and we spent a lot of time talking. He was leaving the next week to go to Bonneville with his jet car, which was then a two-wheeler.

Art was badly shaken by Craig's accident. We all were. It took a real pro to put his grief aside and go out and tend to business. I worried myself sick when Art crashed until I heard he was okay.

Personally, I'd like to see him retire, but having been in the business for more than thirty years, I can understand what's driving him. Each time I got into my jet car, it's like I was a kid with a new toy. I just couldn't wait to get it on.

If Art said, 'Roger, would you like to drive the car?' I'd jump at the chance, the chance to do whatever it takes to get that land speed record. I can tell you this, if I ever built a car, it would look a whole like his Green Monster.

Somehow, I don't quite picture guys like Art Arfons retiring, at least not when it's still unfinished business. As long as he's healthy and still has the desire to get back that record, he could be doing it when he's eighty. And God bless him, I hope he does it.

What's been the secret of Art's long success? He's had a good mind for what he's wanted to do, what he wanted to build. He had the old-fashioned dedication to go make things happen. Just honesty and hard work. That's been the key to his success.

He's one of a kind. He's a dinosaur, a relic from another time. A hero in the true sense of the word.

By Thomas Palm

(This young man from Minnesota dreams of driving his jet-powered car 450 miles an hour to a new wheel-driven land speed record. The dream began when he was twenty-one, and a decade later he hasn't given up that quest. Back in 1981 and 1983, he spent parts of his summer working as a volunteer member of Richard Noble's crew. "Even though I was only twenty-one at the time," he still recalls, "Noble never talked down to me. He gave me encouragement to go for my own dreams.")

I first met Art Arfons in 1984 when I was coming back from a vacation in Florida with my family. They dropped me off in Dayton and I took a bus to Akron.

I had talked to Art briefly over the phone, and to his son, Tim, quite a bit before that to get information about GE T–58 turbine engines for use in my land speed car.

The morning I arrived, Art was gone but was going to return that afternoon. I met Tim and showed him some of my drawings and a small model I had brought along of my car. He showed me where the T–58 engines he was working on were and showed me around the place. Wow! I had never seen so much stuff relating to jet engines and cars, and after the mini-tour I got down to business, taking about thirty pictures of T–58 engines, engine parts and some of the jets and turbine tractors that were in the one shop.

About the time I finished getting some measurements from one of the engines, Art came in. I said 'Hi', and introduced myself. He said he remembered talking to me on the phone and asked me about my project.

I took out the model of the car and we sat down, analyzing it. He seemed to like the shape and look of it and made some good suggestions and changes I could make to improve the design.

He then took me on a tour of his offices, showing me all kinds of pictures of his previous Green Monster cars, including the wheel-driven car he raced at the Flats in the early sixties. Then he showed me some stuff in one of the shops that looked like long drop-tanks from jet aircraft.

He said he was planning to build one last Green Monster record-breaker with the engine he had suspended above the floor. He also told me jokingly not to tell his wife since he would catch hell if she found out he was building another LSR car.

It was getting close to dinner time so he invited me to go out and eat with him, his wife and daughter. That was fun. I couldn't really believe I was eating with Art and his family, and talking, not about racing, but day-to-day stuff.

After dinner we returned to the shop. Since Art had some other things going on, Tim drove me to the bus depot.

We met again in 1988 when we showed up with our full-scale mock-up on our twenty-four foot trailer at his shop. Myself and team member, Tim Kasper, were on our way back from a car show in Toledo and decided to make a detour to Akron and see what was happening.

Art was impressed to see the mock-up and made some good observations and suggested some changes to the car that later would be incorporated into the present design.

We then went inside the main shop to see his latest creation. It was really impressive to see how the car had progressed in four years.

We stayed about three hours, talked a little about his custom aluminum wheels and the design of the intakes, which would later be one of the big problems with the finished car.

I saw him and the car at Bonneville in 1991 but didn't get a chance to talk to him since it was the day we were leaving and he had a mob of people around him, including reporters and camera crews.

I would love to meet him again and maybe be involved with a future LSR project, maybe with Art and I doing the design work, Art building the car and me doing the driving. Who knows?

By Donald Davidson
(Historian, United States Auto Club)

(Once upon a time, as the story goes, a young man from England who lived and breathed auto racing came to the United States in 1964 to attend his first race, the Indianapolis 500. He stayed for the entire month of May, then returned home.
A year later, he returned to Indianapolis, but without a job, contacted USAC [the official sanctioning body for all of Art Arfons' land speed attempts between 1960–1966] about a possible position and the rest is history. He became historian at the 'ripe old' age of twenty-two and has lived his fantasy ever since.)

In anticipation of raised eyebrows over the fact that Donald Davidson is being included in this personal tributes section, let me be the first to admit that I've never met Art Arfons. I've never seen him compete and I've never even seen him in person.

The best I can claim is that I've had two or three telephone conversations with him, those being when he called the USAC office, for information and I happened to be given the call. But I can say I did know who he was several years before his Land Speed Record days at the Bonneville Salt Flats.

It came about late in the summer of 1958 when, as an English schoolboy with a passion for American motorsports, I discovered to my delight that a local magazine shop was carrying an American publication called Speed Age.

Each month there was a drag racing column – 'Dragging It Out' by Robert Lee Behme – and that's where I first learned about people like Calvin Rice and the Chrisman Brothers and Don Garlits (who was then 'Swamp Rat' rather than 'Big Daddy') and Art Arfons and his Green Monster.

Although the British were always captivated by the Land Speed Record, Arfons' breaking it in 1964 only merited a couple of lines in a newspaper paragraph. Craig Breedlove fared a little better, but not much.

It was England's Donald Campbell who was continuing to get all the publicity, and I think it is safe to say that for several years in the late 1950s and early 60s, his name was a household word over there.

In fact, I'd go so far as to say he was as well-known as any of the leading half a dozen personalities in English sports, period.

This was of particular amusement to my friends because my middle name happened to be Campbell. I was often asked if my parents had named me for him. They had not, of course.

Once I moved to the United States and was employed at USAC on a full-time basis, it was obvious on this side of the Atlantic that Breedlove was far better known than Arfons.

Craig was sort of like the figment of a PR man's imagination. He was the good-looking, all-American boy with the sharp uniform and the Stars and Stripes who always seemed to have a film crew and television crews in tow.

It was almost as if he were really an actor playing the role. Even his *name* sounded made up. That's not fair, of course, because he was a very dedicated racer, but that's the way I think he came across.

On top of that, he was taking the scientific approach, surrounding himself with engineers and experts in telemetry and so forth. Arfons, on the other hand – and I say this with admiration – came over as the mysterious, silent gunfighter who did the job with little fanfare and sheer brute power.

Breedlove would make explanatory runs and build to speed in gradual increments. Arfons would seemingly show up, unload and then run 400 or 500 on his first pass! Breedlove would try an aerodynamic refinement. Arfons would simply crank in more power.

Together I think they authored one of the great motorsports battles of all time, backed by Firestone (Arfons) and Goodyear (Breedlove), each camp trying to outdo the other.

For heaven's sake, the Land Speed Record has only been broken once in the last twenty-one years and yet there was a time back in October 1964 when it was broken four times in two weeks, plus a fifth time before the month was over!

Then there was the classic one-upmanship struggle in 1965 when they'd pack up and leave Bonneville and then sneak back after the other was gone.

It was getting later and later in the year. The ideal salt conditions were supposed to fade on into October so that late in the month was really pushing it. But they kept up their cat-and-mouse game far into November!

I'll never forget the day Joe Petrali called from Bonneville with the really stunning news. It was lunchtime on an unseasonably warm and sunny mid-November day when the phone rang. I was the only person in the office.

"Hey, Donald," he began very excitedly, "is Henry there?" (Former National Champion Henry Banks was USAC's Director of Competition at the time.)

"No, Joe," I replied. "Everybody is at lunch."

"Listen," he gushed, "Breedlove just did 600!"

Wow. I got shivers just thinking about it. It just happened out there and I was one of the first people in the world to know about it!

As far as the see-saw battle between Breedlove and Arfons was concerned, that was about it. Art remounted further challenges but he never got the record back.

I've always treasured the behind-the-scenes stuff and insight into the private moments. There is a passage in the excellent book Bill Neely did with Craig Breedlove that really stayed with me.

There is this wonderful word picture of Breedlove finishing an early supper in anticipation of an early bedtime, contemplating a very early start the following morning, but being not quite ready to turn in.

He decides instead to go for a stroll... alone. The light is fading and the wind has picked up as he walks for several blocks, back and forth around tiny, deserted Wendover, Utah.

He is jamming his hands down in his jacket pockets, trying to relax himself and get his thoughts in order when he turns a corner and bumps into who has to be the only other person out on foot.

Of all people, it is Art Arfons, doing exactly the same thing as himself!

I've carried that picture in my mind for years. It will often come to me when I'm out walking myself or perhaps driving on some trip. What a great little vignette. What a neat, intimate slice of life. But, horror of horrors, supposing it weren't really *true*?

Well, a couple of years ago, during one of the occasions on which Art called USAC for information, I asked him if he recalled such an incident.

Happily, he chuckled and confirmed that it was exactly as Breedlove had said.

By Don Vesco

(One of the legends of racing at the Bonneville Salt Flats, Vesco has been competing there since the early 1950s, on two-wheeled bikes, four-wheeled motorcycle-powered streamliners and 400 mile an hour, wheel-driven creations. In 1978, he averaged 318 mph in his streamliner, powered by four Kawasaki motorcycle engines. It was a world record.)

I guess I first heard of Art around 1954. He was driving his Green Monster No. 11 on the drag strips with that big Allison aircraft engine. I thought, 'Wow'. I've always wanted an Allison. I was road racing, then drag racing.

I remember seeing that Allison-powered land speed car at Bonneville in 1960. It was kinda odd-looking, but it definitely had 400-plus potential. As I recall, he had transmission problems and 'only' reached the low 300s.

I really didn't have any contact with him until 1988 or 1989 when he called me. I was doing my thing all those years, and he was doing his. But when you're in the speed business you're keenly aware of what everyone else is doing and plans to do, whether it be lakesters, streamliners, jets or rocket cars.

Was I surprised to hear from Art? You betcha. He told me about the bike he was building. I gave him a little bit of advice, but Art doesn't always heed it. I told him he was sitting in the wrong place.

You don't sit in front of the front wheel. You can't feel the bike, what it's doing. There were a few other things I thought he was doing wrong, only because I've thought about those same things during the years... and they didn't work.

I honestly thought the bike was doomed to failure. With some modifications I think it can beat Richard Noble's land speed record, and I'd love to be the one to make those modifications and drive that Green Monster.

I was at Bonneville in 1989 when he tested the two-wheeler. That bike had no stability the first two runs. No balance. Art and I talked. He listened. We put plates on the bottom of the two skids so it would sit level, not lean left or right.

Before, the skids were off the ground and the bike would flop from side to side. The bike looked good and steady during the third attempt, but that's not in his vocabulary. Once he got it going, he hit the burner and went airborne at over 300. Again, he was lucky.

The man must be like a cat. He has nine lives. Two days after he survived that 610 mile an hour crash in November 1966, I was at Bell Helmet and they had Art's helmet. They were studying it. It was delaminated, meaning some layers of fiberglass had been separated, either when his head hit the ground or from salt spray. Like I said, he was born lucky.

I'd say the odds of succeeding in this business seem like twenty to one against you and Art's sure beaten those odds over the years. The thing I probably most admire about him is his persistence, his desire. He keeps pressing, pursuing it to the end. He's always given it all he has. He might go on forever. He has my respect.

By Mike Galloway

(In July 1991, Art Arfons was inducted into the Motorsports Hall of Fame at Novi, Michigan. Here is the complete text given by Mike Galloway, who presented Arfons as an inductee.)

This is probably the most exciting night of my life because very seldom does a fan get to talk about his hero, and that's just what I'm getting to do tonight. Talk about my hero.

I first met Art Arfons in 1958. I was a child. Well, okay, I was a young kid. Well, maybe I wasn't that young. But I was standing behind the fence watching him work on one of his Green Monsters. He took the time to... he came over and shook my hand. And he became my hero. I followed him through his land speed record attempts as he went to Utah, and he built the car that fit inside the bus, that had the 1937 Dodge front axle. It wasn't because that was the best axle, because that was the axle he had at the time.

And I watched him as he built the car that when the parachutes came out they sucked behind the car. So he cut off shotguns and put them in there and fired the shotguns that blew the parachutes, but stopped the car.

He did it three times, he set the open-wheel land speed record that still stands. The car is on display out at Novi. Then he built a car to go to the salt and race on its own. He set the record at 434 and it didn't last very long.

He had to turn around a couple of weeks later and go back to Utah. It's not going across the street because the man's from Akron, Ohio, but when he went back the next time he pushed the record to 576 and that stood for a while. It stood until he went back two years later in 1966 and crashed the car at about 600 miles per hour.

I just followed him through books and magazines and news reports up to this time, but in the early 70s I met Mr. Arfons and shook his hand and became a personal friend in tractor pulling. At that time he was the most feared name in tractor pulling with a single-turbine engine. He was awesome.

Today, he is just as awesome as he was then. Almost weekly this man pulls into an arena and runs his tractor with the very best. And every time he goes he has the capabilities, and many times he does win.

And if you read your program tonight, it said that he went to the Salt Flats last year and didn't break the record and retired. This is a lie. Because in August of this year he will go back.

Why not? He's just a youngster. On Friday of this week he and his lovely wife, June, will have been married forty-four years. They have three lovely children, Ron and Tim and Dusty, and they're all here tonight. Ladies and gentlemen would you please put your hands together for my hero, Mr. Art Arfons.

By Art Arfons

(This is Art Arfons' acceptance speech.)

Thank you, Mike. He didn't leave nothing for me to tell you. My whole family is here. I've got two grandsons, too, and the Arfons clan has arrived. Dusty and I drove the bus. We still have a bus.

We drove to Anaheim in January and we took our two tractors out to run Anaheim and San Diego. While we were out there, Russo come down, Bob Russo from the office, and said I had been inducted into the Hall of Fame.

And I really was in awe. I didn't know what this was all about, and when I seen the roster, men like Glen Curtis and Roscoe Turner and some of the great people that I've read about, I thought they'd made a mistake. Uh-oh, I'm really in the wrong league here.

The last car I built, I built as a motorcycle. I laid down in front of the front wheel, and I can't feel it as a bike, so I couldn't stay upright.

I made it into a car now and I've got, uh, it's a three-wheel... it's a four-wheel car but it's in a three-wheel configuration. That's what I'm going to try and run again this year.

Special thanks to my wife. She puts up with this and she has for forty-four years. I'm very much appreciative for being chosen for this. I, I didn't prepare a speech 'cause I don't speak very well. Thank you, everybody. I appreciate it."

Chapter Ten

No City Slicker, Not This Boy

When Pearl Harbor struck [December 7, 1941], I was almost sixteen. I wanted to join the navy. When I turned seventeen, I thought I was gonna miss the war. I quit school and enlisted. It was a hassle, but Dad signed the papers. It seemed like something exciting to do. I didn't see any sense in wasting my time. But no seventeen year old kid is thinking about the realities of war. There sure as hell ain't nothing glamorous about it. You're scared all the time.

Art Arfons

Art Arfons was a child of 'The Great Depression', growing up in rural, northeast Ohio.

"We were definitely poor, but so was everybody else. I was telling June (my wife) just the other day we had an outside toilet, an outside water pump.

"Things were tough. Dad would walk from the Firestone plant to save a nickel on bus fare. We never had the extra nickel. My mom used to give me a dime to get a big box of Post Toasties and she said I could have three cents for candy. I'd get the whole bag of candy."

Arthur Eugene Arfons was born on February 3, 1926, the son of Tom and Bessie Arfons. He was the youngest of four children. Brothers Walt and Dale were born to Bessie from a previous marriage. Lou was the only girl in the family.

Walt was ten years older than Art, Dale eight and Lou eighteen months.

"Dad was born in Greece," says Art Arfons. "My mom was one-half Cherokee. Dad came to this country when he was fourteen.

He couldn't speak a word of English. He joined the army when he was fifteen and was a cook in World War I.

"Dad was quiet and it took a lot to get him mad, but once he was mad, look out. He ran his own feed mill. Everybody had their own chickens, their own pigs. They tried to raise their own meat. That's why the mill was so successful. He also sold fertilizer.

"He was a pretty good size, about my size [5'10"]. I guess I resemble my dad. So does Lou. Mom was more outgoing. She handled the money for the mill and she made the financial decisions."

Art and his sister were close through their childhood and they still remain just as close.

"It was always a close family," she says.

"My given first name is Gresola, Lou was my father's mother's name. When I went to school everybody made so much fun of it. I decided when I went from the eighth grade to the ninth grade to change my name, so I started writing Lou, and it stuck.

"Our daddy died shortly after his fifty-second birthday in 1950 and I still feel cheated. Mom died in 1984 at the age of eighty-four. She really ruled the roost. I can still hear Dad saying if anyone of us had done something that we should have been punished for, 'Beginning tomorrow if you do that you're gonna get a licking'. But, of course, tomorrow never came."

There weren't too many children Art's age as a youngster. He recalls, "Ed [his best friend, Ed Snyder] lived next door. The Becker Boys were about the only other boys our age. They lived about a mile away. Kids nowadays grow up as kids. I think we had to grow up a lot quicker, take on more responsibilities, because of the tough times.

"I came home right after school and my job was to sweep the mill. We had the cider press running in the fall and it was my job to wash the press. I'd come home about 3:30 in the afternoon and work until nine or ten at night."

Admittedly, Art Arfons wasn't an honor student.

"I really didn't care for it, only certain subjects such as arithmetic. Somehow, that stuff came easy to me. Don't ask me why."

Despite the fame, the status of a living legend, Art Arfons hasn't changed over the years.

"I remember right after he set his first land speed record," says his sister, "I was at their home. Arthur was popping corn for the kids one night. He put the popper down and burnt a hole on the new carpeting.

"He picked it up, looked at it and said, 'You know, I thought when I broke the record I'd feel different. I'm still me. I don't feel any different.' He's absolutely the same all these years. He's just a wonderful person.

"In his own way," says Lou Wolf, "Arthur was very studious. I can remember lots of times he'd jump in his car, or ride his motorcycle, depending on what vehicle he had at school, ride home from school to get a book, return to class to prove a point to his teacher. He just had to show that he knew what he was talking about."

Despite their closeness, his sister doesn't ever recall "Arthur telling me what he wanted to be when he grew up, but I knew it would be something different.

"Arthur was always very special. I mean he always knew things. He was never at a loss for anything he wanted to do. He just started and he would do it, like taking care of the diesel engines at the mill, like building all those race cars.

"All the boys worked at the mill. I worked at the mill, in the office. I didn't like it. I wanted to work with the boys, but Daddy wouldn't let me.

"I can remember we had a water wheel and we would run out of water. Arthur talked Daddy into getting some diesel engines when he was fourteen years old. Arthur put in all of those engines and got the machinery working. Later, we turned to electricity. Arthur worked at the mill until he went into the navy."

Funny guy, this Art Arfons. "It really wasn't work to me. It's not work if you love what you're doing. I don't remember my brothers helping at night. I think they were running around. It was a lot of belts and stuff. You had to be slicin' belts and doing a lot of that kind of work.

"When we had a dry season, we didn't have enough water to run the mill. So we'd use car engines. I worked with my dad. We took a Buick engine and made it into a stationary power plant. It required constant work. I'd help him tear it down at night, put pieces in it and keep it running.

"Even today, I'm down in the shop and June thinks I'm working. I've got a day off and I go down and just piddle. Like trying to figure out a problem with Tim's [Art's youngest son] jet jumper. I just enjoy doing this kind of stuff."

Arfons passed his driver's test when he was fourteen. His father needed that kind of skill.

"Dad needed me to go to Massillon twice a week and get feed. He had an old four-door car and [I had to] haul about 1200 pounds of feed. We had a truck later, so I drove the truck and got the feed. I went to Alliance and Marietta, Ohio.

"Before Dad got married, he had a Pierce-Arrow. But growing up, we were lucky to have a car that ran. We had a Diana. It's a real old car. We had one radio in the house. We had a coal stove in the living room and one in the middle of the house. Dale and I shared a bedroom. Lou had a bedroom. It was just a divided room upstairs in an old farmhouse."

At Springfield High School, Arfons signed up for a special night class in welding and mechanics.

In 1943, at the end of his junior year of high school, Art Arfons joined the U.S. Navy and was assigned to diesel mechanics school. He was assigned to "attack landing craft" in the Pacific.

"I was a mechanic and I operated the door. I dropped the door and let the troops out, then wound it back up. I also kept the diesels running. The landing craft could hold fifty troops.

"We also had a gunner's mate on the landing craft which was equipped with a pair of fifty caliber machine guns. You lowered and raised the huge steel door with a big double crank. He got on one end and I got on the other. We had armor plate around and if you could stay down you were pretty safe.

"But it was a slow, tedious process. From the enemy's point of view, it was a real shooting gallery. Head pops up and bang. Easy pickin'. So I decided to do something about it."

That something was lowering and raising the door mechanically.

"I kept a starter motor and put a cable in it. I'd lay down, just touch a button and the old door would just fly open. It went down quick and came up quick. It was neat."

Arfons was involved in two massive invasions, including the bloody battle of Okinawa.

"You go up on shore and drop the ramp. The troops run off. The day before the landing at Okinawa, the navy had shelled the enemy with the big ships. When we landed, we didn't see the enemy on the beach. They were all back, maybe half a mile. But the enemy planes were strafing and bombing.

"We were all scared to death. But we did what we had to do. I can remember one incident like it was yesterday. There was one ensign who freaked out.

"You had to climb down this net to get into the landing craft. When it was the morning to go, the ensign said he wouldn't go. He was crying. The captain came down with a .45 and tried to force the guy to climb the net. But he still wouldn't. I never seen that man again. They put him in his quarters. I don't know what happened to him. He was an officer and he broke down. He couldn't make it."

Art Arfons was discharged from the navy after a three year hitch. He was a second class petty officer.

"I've always loved planes, and really wanted to be a pilot. I wanted to enlist in the navy, and learn to fly, but they said I was too damned old. I was twenty-seven. They were still flying Corsairs and Mustangs then."

After service, he returned to Akron, back to Arfons Mill, as if he hadn't been away at all.

Before he went off to war, Arfons dated a young woman named June La Fontaine.

"I met her at a roller skating rink. I could skate a little bit. June was the prettiest girl I'd ever seen and I liked her instantly.

"I went with a friend of mine that night. My plan was to leave the rink, sit in the car and wait for her to come out. She came out and was running after a car going down the street, hollering like she's trying to get another guy.

"She came over and talked to me. I asked her if we could take her home. We took her home. I had a date with June the next night."

Shortly after that, Arfons joined the navy. He wrote to June, "but she never did answer." Once back in Ohio, Art and June resumed dating. They were married a year later.

That 1947 marriage would produce two sons – Ron and Tim – and one daughter – Dusty Allison.

"Dad and I worked at the mill, along with two or three other workers. When I first came back from the navy I was making thirty-five dollars a week. It was a tough, dusty business.

"There were two other mills within a two mile radius, all looking for the same business. A good profit was ten dollars a ton. It was a tough way to make a living."

By 1952, Art Arfons had a wife and an infant son. He was earning fifty dollars a week.

"I guess I was never money motivated. It was a living. When you've been brought up in the Depression, you watch your money kinda careful. I was satisfied."

Chapter Eleven

Just a Sunday Afternoon Drive

Drag racing is a major sport. It draws huge crowds, big purses. If you want to be competitive in the fastest division, meaning Top Fuel, it's gotta cost a fortune just to run. Unless you're a real rich guy who can support your own habit, you need major sponsorship.

If you have that kind of money, you go buy the best of everything. Everybody's got the same power. Not like in the days when I first started. Everything was different then. You didn't see two cars alike, and a guy like me could race on a shoestring. I'm glad I was in it at a time when you could bolt an engine to a frame and go racing.

Art Arfons

The handwriting had been clearly written on the wall.

Back in 1990, Gary Ormsby smoked a 296.05 mph run at Topeka, Kansas. Insurance companies pressured NHRA (National Hot Rod Association) to slow down the Top Fuelers.

NHRA, however, obviously felt the slingshots were safe and the speed continued to inch closer to the magic 300 mph barrier.

In March 1992, at the Gator Nationals, veteran funny car driver turned Top Fuel chauffeur, Kenny Bernstein, stormed into drag racing history. Peak speed: 301.70.

And to prove it simply wasn't a mirage, Bernstein clocked off a 300 burst at the Summer Nationals. Bernstein has since hit 318 in the quarter mile! Can 320 be far away?

Unless a speed restriction is put on drag racing's most exotic machines, the cars of the future will keep soaring. Such is the nature of man.

Drag racing legend Don 'Big Daddy' Garlits wouldn't have it any other way.

"Advances will be smaller, but I see no limit. The engine and clutch management systems are so much better than they've ever been and that's made a big difference."

Garlits, forced to retire because of an eye problem, turned in a top career speed of 287.81. He won a record-setting thirty-five NHRA meets.

He, too, has seen the sport grow from its grassroots beginning, "and it boggles my mind. I think this is as big as it can get, and the sport keeps on getting bigger.

"Back in the days when it didn't cost much to compete, winning $500 or $1000 was a big deal. Now, it costs $1 million a year to be competitive in Top Fuel."

The NHRA attracts almost two million fans nationally on its coast-to-coast tour. That's an average attendance of about 90,000 per event. The sport draws big at-home TV audiences.

The American phenomena is that drag racing had its roots in dry lake racing. In California, naturally!

Muroc Dry Lake. El Mirage. Run what ya bring!

"The early guys who drove there," recalls Wally Parks, the founding father of NHRA, "drove all night, then they took off the fenders, took off the headlights, took off the windshields and then went racing.

"It was a mixed bag of machines. There was no attempt to classify cars except for the speed performance. For instance, if you went 86 miles an hour, you were in the 80–90 class."

There were no medals, no prizes, just the satisfaction and thrill of hitting top speed.

It was quite a collection of hardware. Model A Ford roadsters, Ford flathead V–8s, Chryslers, including couples, streamliners and various hybrids. They raced across the dry mud flats through 1948. That's when Stu Hilborn's semi-streamliner hit 150 miles an hour.

One of those driving a lake machine was a young man named Wally Parks. Remember that name.

Ak Miller borrowed his brother's 128 Chevy roadster and hit top speed of 92 mph at Muroc in 1934.

"It extended for miles and miles. No leather helmets, no roll bars, no nothing. What a thrill."

Southern California was flooded with car clubs. In 1937, the Southern California Timing Association (SCTA) was formed to supervise the so-called 'hot rod' activity at Muroc. Meets were held four times a year.

"It was a very primitive operation," recalls Parks, "but one that had a magic to it."

Many of these lake racers would take their talent and cars to the drag strips, competing under the NHRA banner with Parks as founder and first president. Miller was named vice president.

NHRA started in 1951.

For years illegal drag racing took place in California.

"It was after-dark street racing," says Miller. "Some 300–500 cars would drag it out. It was an eerie sound, with all those cars lining both sides of the road. Top speed was 90–100."

The first legal drag race took place at Goleta, California in 1948. It was staged by the Santa Barbara Acceleration Association. In November 1949, SCTA staged its event at the Santa Ana Navy Blimp Base. Earl Evans, driving a wing tank lakester, hit top speed of 121 miles an hour.

A week later, C.J. Hart leased Orange County Fairgrounds. It became the first commercial strip.

"It costs ninety cents to run," says Parks, "and ninety cents to get in. It was kind of a mad house. They'd run it fifty weeks a year, but it was a way to get boys and girls off the streets.

"Our plan was to unite the car clubs and provide various forms of activities. We hoped for a national run-off. We put on a major race schedule at the Los Angeles County Fairgrounds and held our first West Coast championships. Admission was fifty cents. We had 200 people in the grandstands."

By the end of World War II, a lot of young men came home. They loved cars. The time was ripe for a magazine called *Hot Rod* (1949), then for a drag racing organization.

By 1955, more than 300 entries poured into Great Neck, Kansas, to compete in the NHRA Nationals. It had become a true national event. An Ohio hot rodder named Art Arfons was all the rage with his sixteen-cylinder Allison aircraft engine. Another racing legend, Mickey Thompson, drove a streamliner.

But let's backtrack to 1952.

Art Arfons and his older brother, Walt, were working the family feedmill. Both were licensed pilots and had purchased five planes, which they took turns flying.

It was a Sunday afternoon and Art was heading for Akron City Airport.

"It was a trainer, an old army airplane," recalls Art. "We bought it in pieces and put it together behind a friend's house. If Walt wasn't flying it, I'd take it around the field a couple of times.

"June was with me that Sunday. We were heading towards the airport, but the highway was closed where we go into the airport. You could hear the noise, so we went down to see what was going on.

"We saw a crowd of people and a drag race was going on. I wasn't aware of drag racing until that day. It was fascinating, the smoking tires, the screaming engines. A lot of horsepower running wide open.

"When I got back home I told Walter about it. He hadn't heard about drag racing, but he was excited. I looked around the mill and found engines that we used for power.

"There was a six-cylinder Oldsmobile engine laying there. There was also a nose wheel off one of our planes. I welded a frame, stuck this nose wheel in front of the engine. I got a Packard rear-end and bolted it to the back of the engine. It was just a three-wheel thing. We put it together in a week."

They topped it all with some green tractor paint. It was the only paint the Arfons Brothers had available at the time.

"The next week I took it over to the drag race."

In its maiden run, the three-wheeler shut down halfway through the run. On its second try, Art Arfons hit 85, but the winner's speed was 105. Thus, his first day as a drag racer had ended in failure.

During its first appearance, the car drew laughs from the crowd. "It's a green monster," someone yelled.

"That's a mighty fine description," agreed the track announcer. "Okay, folks, here it comes – the Green Monster."

"This thing would scream out of the hole. I could beat anybody at the start, but it got to about 80 miles an hour and started crackin', poppin' and backfiring through the carburetor. I had devised a two-position speed shift. I could shift faster than anyone with an automatic.

"But I didn't know anything about gear ratios. A guy told me I didn't have the right gear ratio. I had a big type of rear-end and was geared way down, like five-to-one. The little engine just couldn't handle it."

Arfons' debut came during the last race of the '52 season, but it was enough to whet his appetite.

By 1953, Art and Walt Arfons were consumed by drag racing. By the middle of the season, Green Monster No. 2 was hitting peak speeds of more than 100 miles an hour!

"Number 2 had two forward rear-ends facing each other. It was a six-wheel car. The Allison sit down and I had a chain drive down to the two pinions."

It was built from parts from airplanes, army tanks and automobiles. The twenty foot long beast was powered by the 2000 horsepower Allison V-12 engine from a P-51 fighter plane.

The power was transmitted through a hydraulically operated clutch taken from a thirty ton tank, and a chain drive to two rear axles mounting four drive wheels. The Arfons brothers used the unusual tandem-wheel drive for better traction.

They estimated top speed of the car at 270 miles an hour. Acceleration was estimated at 0 to 140 in about eight seconds.

The front was painted to resemble the feared Flying Tigers emblem. The legendary Tigers flew P-40s against the Japanese prior to America's formal entrance in World War II.

"My mother painted the mouth of that car," says Art Arfons. "That was her idea. In fact, she always wanted to drive one of 'em. She was really enthused about racing. She jumped up and down. She liked it."

The Arfons brothers didn't stray too far from the airport strip.

"We never had a trailer. We just took it out and drove it from Pickle Road to the track. The cops never bothered us. I don't know why. We drove in, pulled up to the line and made a pass.

"One time I went back to get my timing slip and a guy says, 'I want to see you guys in the tower'. So Walt and I climbed to the tower. The guy there told us the clocks malfunctioned, so he couldn't record a time.

"I pulled around, made another pass and went 132. It was just ten miles an hour off the world record. I had 616 car tires. One of them was really safe at 50 miles an hour and here I was running at 132."

At the first World Series of Drag Racing at Lawrenceville, Illinois, Art Arfons showed it wasn't a fluke as he took top speed honors with a run of 132.35 mph.

"We ran at a military air base," he recalls. "There were cars from all over the country. There must have been twenty cars, all types, including dragsters. It was the first time we'd seen how some of these real cars were built.

"I was running gas, but we could run for top speed in the meet. That's what paid the most money. I was using an Allison. I had real good luck with airplane engines. All these other guys had car engines that were hopped up.

"They even had flathead V–8s. They had overhead valves and great big engines. A lot of 'em had hemispherical pistons. At the time I was making fifty dollars a week, was building a house and raising a family. I didn't have any money, so I had to go with this junk."

But Art Arfons was going faster!

"In the early days of drag racing," says Arfons, "NHRA would go around the country conducting what they called a Safety Safari. They called me and said, 'We'll time Arfons'. At the time someone on the West Coast went 144. When they were timing me, I went 145.16 in No. 2. That was a world record. *Hot Rod* magazine even publicized it."

In 1956, he made drag racing history in Green Monster No. 6.

"It was a big heavy tank. It was powered by an Allison, had six wheels, duals in the back and front-wheel drive. We had truck tires on it."

Hot Rod was looking for the first driver to his 150. The prize: a jacket.

"I've got the No. 1 jacket for the 150 Mile An Hour Club. A funny thing, two of us did it on the same day.

"I went 150 at Kansas city and some other guy went 152 on the West Coast. By the time the year ended, I think there were four of us in the club."

Art Arfons still has that cherished memento.

There was never anything 'conventional' about those dragsters. No, siree.

Take Green Monster No. 9 for instance. It was powered by two helicopter engines, developing some 800 horsepower. The engines were mounted over the rear axle, the crankshafts joined by two pinions and a ring gear. Fluid clutches were inboard of the wheels. It was a three-wheeler.

By the late 1950s, the Arfons brothers had gone their separate ways. Years later, Art and Walt Arfons would become speed rivals, each seeking the world land speed record.

Art Arfons is about six years older than Don Garlits. He started his illustrious drag racing career before 'Big Daddy'.

"I was racing as a kid in 1950, never leaving the state of Florida," recalls Garlits, the first driver to exceed 250 mph (1975) in a Top Fuel dragster. "I turned professional at the World Series of Drag Racing in 1957.

"Art had been racing before me. He was like a hero to me. I always looked up to him. The Allison was on gasoline, I drove fuel dragsters. We were in different classes, so we didn't run against each other side by side.

"But in those early days, more money was paid for top speed, and Art was very competitive with his Allison-powered cars. He was way ahead of his time. Back in the 1950s, his cars had a lot of aerodynamic characteristics with that little pointed nose.

"And those Allisons, I'll always remember those beasts. The motor was bigger than my whole race car. I learned a lot from him back then, mostly on suspension. Our engines were so different.

"I can remember at one meet I outran Cook and Bedwell. They were the world champs from California. I remember I was running a two-speed transmission and I was talking about going to high gears removing the two-speed.

"Art came over to me and said, 'Donald, don't ever take that two-speed transmission out of your car. All fuel dragsters will have them'. I didn't touch a thing because Art Arfons told me not to.

"He was a very personable guy, always helping others, a really nice guy. He used to smoke his tires so hard, they'd spin and get away. But then he began to get tires good enough to hold that power. He was getting ready to be really dangerous, top-speedwise.

"The NHRA was going to hold its big meet in Detroit in 1959, but they didn't want airplane engines coming into the motor city, so they outlawed the Allisons. They outlawed Arfons and his No. 11."

During those years, Art Arfons and Don Garlits would lock up for top speed honors.

"I can remember when we battled it out at Chester, South Carolina. Art had that Baloney Slicer. I was one of the first guys to get to him when that car came apart."

Arfons considers that his worst crash.

In 1991, Art Arfons was inducted in the International Drag Racing Hall of Fame at Ocala, Florida. The induction ceremonies took place at Don Garlits' Museum of Drag Racing.

"I hadn't seen Art for quite a while and the thing that really surprised me is that he hadn't changed one bit in all the years. He's still a little shy, not much of a talker.

"I got a kick out of his little statement which went something like, 'I'm so glad you people honored me when I was still alive and could enjoy it'. There's certainly none more deserving.

"Nothing that man has done surprises me, not even him going back to Bonneville after all these years and trying to get back his land speed record. He's just that kind of guy.

"I'd never been to Bonneville until 1988 when I went there to run a streamliner with a flathead Ford. I went over 200 in the F/X class. I can see Art's fascination with the Salt Flats.

"It's an awesome place. It was such a wonderful feeling, to go on and on. It's so quiet, so very different from drag racing. I'll definitely go back."

As for drag racing, he feels the sport has never been safer, despite the ever-increasing speed.

"In '85, '86 and '87, I had crashes, all over 250 miles an hour, and walked away. Let 'em run as fast as they can. That's what it's all about, isn't it?"

Art Arfons would certainly say 'Amen' to that!

Chapter Twelve
Man and His Incredible Machine

I read everything about John Cobb. When he and Eyston battled back and forth in 1939 I thought that was really something just for the man to climb down into a car wearing an old cloth helmet and goggles in a car that had no roll bar, no protection.

Art Arfons

What is land speed racing?

It is a test of man and machine. It is a projectile launched at speeds that only a split second electronic timer can record. It is a lonely ride that lasts an eternity.

Until 1910, only one run was required for the land speed record. Since then, however, a driver must make two runs in opposite directions within sixty minutes for the attempt to be considered official.

In addition to the time for the measured, or flying mile, the time for the kilometer is also recorded. The kilo is the final five-eighths of a mile. The times for both runs through the measured mile are calibrated, then translated into miles per hour to determine the average speed.

Man's quest for the land speed record usually takes place early in the morning, just after dawn, when the winds are calmest, the salt the driest, the air the coolest. Engines breathe better in cool temperature.

Although the track may be as long as twelve miles, only the speed through the flying mile – at the midway point – is timed. A black line, twelve inches wide and as many miles long, gives a driver a guideline. Just aim and blast-off!

In order to set a record, a driver must exceed the existing mark by one percent. Between land speed runs, a car is refueled, parachutes repacked and tires checked for wear. Or in this age of metal wheels, scraped of excess salt build-up.

Land speed attempts are permitted with wind gusts exceeding five miles an hour. Much too dangerous!

The sensation of speed means different things to different people. For instance:

* Sir Malcolm Campbell: "It was as if the world had been reduced to a small elliptical surface, which traveled along with me. At no time could I see more than a few hundred yards down the salt."

* John Cobb: "I had the odd sensation of driving up a steep hill."

* Art Arfons: "When you're only three-quarters of an inch off the ground, the sensation of speed is tremendous. The land markers go by awfully fast. It takes only two miles to accelerate to over 500, so the pull on my body [G forces] is tremendous."

How does a driver know he's approaching the measured mile?

Because of the speed involved, Arfons designed specially colored signs to indicate when he was entering and leaving the measured mile. In his case, the sign approaching the flying mile was painted black with a green cross. He knew he was leaving the mile by a huge sign painted with red and black checks.

The course is usually ten to twenty yards wide.

Once upon a time, a land speed machine was a car, power transmitted directly through the wheels, four wheels. But in the 1960s, all that changed with Craig Breedlove's three-wheeled, jet-powered Spirit of America.

But with the space-age creations, the Federation International de l'Automobile (FIA) and the FIM (international motorcycle sanctioning body) redefined the rules.

Four-wheel attempts would be controlled by the FIA, two or three-wheel assaults would be controlled by the FIM. In addition, two classes were created – wheel-driven and pure thrust.

Richard Noble of England set the unlimited thrust record of 633.4 in his jet-powered Thrust 2 back in 1983. Bobby Summers, a Californian, averaged 409 plus in his wheel-driven Goldenrod back in 1965. His record is in definite jeopardy.

Veteran California driver Al Teague, in his single-engine streamliner, averaged a shade better than Summers during his 1991 assault at Bonneville. While he did not exceed Summers' effort by one percent, he nevertheless set a record because the cars were in different classes... technically speaking.

Land speed racing was born in Europe, almost 100 years ago. The French Automobile Club was formed in 1895. Three years later, one of its founders, Count de Chasseloup-Laubat, carved his name into history with the first ever run for the record.

He drove his electric-powered car through the flying mile at an unheard of 39.24 miles an hour. His time: 57 seconds!

His claim to the land speed record, however, incensed Carmile Jenatzy, a red-bearded Belgian inventor, who knew his electric car was faster.

Jenatzy, who would later become a successful driver for the German Mercedes team, wheeled to a new record of 41.42, racing over the same straight stretch of road at Achères, outside of Paris. However, before the day was over, Chasseloup-Laubat came back with an even faster 43.69 before burning out his motor.

Jenatzy, his car's batteries exhausted, waited ten days before making a crack at regaining the world land speed record. He sped through the flying mile at 49.92 for the glory of Belgium.

A month later, however, the fearless Frenchman went 57.60 and Jenatzy realized that his car could never top that speed. So, he returned home and designed a new bullet-shaped automobile, the first streamliner in history, and called his creation 'Jamais Contente' – Never Satisfied.

On April Fool's Day of 1899, Jenatzy and his Never Satisfied blazed down the road at Achères at record speed. However, the French timers had failed to clock the run.

One month later, Jenatzy returned to Achères, lectured the timers and shattered two barriers: 65.79 for the mile and 105.38 for the flying kilo.

By 1902, the Americans entered the speed game on the glistening sands of Ormond Beach, in the northern section of Daytona Beach, Florida.

At that time, guests at the luxurious Hotel Ormond engaged in the earliest beach motor car tests. Ranson E. Olds, pioneer auto builder, and U.S. race champion Alexander Winton tied at 57 miles an hour in their wheel-to-wheel duel. The following year, Winton hit 68 for a world record.

This heralded the start of racing at the famed Florida strip. In the next thirty-two years, a total of fifteen land speed records were set on the sand. Other speed marks were established at such places at Lake St. Clair (Michigan), Nice (France), Brooklands (England) and Pendine (Wales).

In 1904, Henry Ford powered his hand-built, six cylinder Arrow across a frozen lake outside Detroit at a speed of 91.370. A month later, however, William K. Vanderbilt wheeled his German-built Mercedes to a faster clocking – 92.307 – at Ormond Beach.

Halfway around the world, in Nice, Louis Rigolly of France became the first to shatter the 100 mile an hour barrier with a 103.55 clocking.

That same year, in Florida, Arthur MacDonald and his six cylinder, 90 horsepower Napier churned down Ormond Beach at 104.65. On another run, he traveled five miles in three minutes and seventeen seconds.

In 1906, Fred Marriott gunned his Stanley Steamer Rocket to a blistering 127.66 at Ormond Beach, thus becoming the first man to drive an auto more than two miles a minute.

But later that year, Marriott wrecked his car and he was lucky to come out of it alive. Several of his ribs were broken, his face cut and one eye was hanging limply on his cheek. It marked the last time a steam-propelled car would contend for the land speed record.

When asked about the spectacular crash, he said: "I looked the beach over and found some depressions in the sand. This was not good, but I was determined to run anyway. So after taking a seven mile acceleration run, I hit the measured mile wide open.

"I ran through the first depressions without trouble, then suddenly I hit some that felt like running into a curbstone. The car went up like a kite and I sailed through the air one hundred feet. The car broke in half when it landed and I was in the front half with my head in the water."

From 1909 to 1920, the German-made Benz dominated the speed scene. The famed Barney Oldfield drove his Blitzen Benz to a two-way average of 131.72 at Ormond Beach in 1910.

Although another American driving champion, Tommy Milton, clocked a sizzling 156.03 in 1920, his record was not officially recognized. He made only one run in his Duesenberg, powered by side-by-side eight cylinder Duesenberg engines. Each engine drove one rear wheel through its own independent driveshaft.

Across the Atlantic, the British were readying for the challenge. The car was the famous 350 horsepower, single-seat Sunbeam, powered by a World War I aircraft engine.

The 350 HP Sunbeam first appeared at Brooklands in 1920. Two years later, K.L. Guinness reached 144 around the flying half mile at Brooklands.

On May 17, 1922, Guinness set a world land speed record of 133.75. It was the same car that Sir Malcolm Campbell would buy and use to set the first of his nine land speed marks. No one has come close to approaching that record (American Craig Breedlove set five records between 1963–65 in a jet car).

Campbell was born to set records. Even as a youngster, speed was his obsession.

"When I drove my first seven horsepower car, I craved for ten. I wanted to experience the sensation of traveling faster."

Born March 11, 1885 in Chislehurst, Kent, England, Campbell showed an early enthusiasm for speed. As early as 1905 he was winning medals in motorcycling events and in 1909 tried flying. Building his own airplanes he flew for a time, but successive crashes proved to be too much of a drain on his savings.

The year 1910 marked his first official automobile race at Brooklands, England's famous track, and the appearance of the name Bluebird for his cars. That year, Campbell took a Darracq car which had won the Vanderbilt Cup in America the year before, painted it blue and went to Brooklands to win the race.

Entering World War I soon after the declaration of hostilities, he became a dispatch rider, then was made a commissioned officer. Campbell transferred to the Royal Flying Corps and was discharged in 1919 with the rank of captain.

He immediately re-entered the racing game, taking part in many contests, and then, fired by the record speed of 142 miles an hour set in 1911 by 'Wild Burman' at Ormond Beach, he began to make the world record his own. The best European mark was then 109, made by Georges Boillot in 1914.

Campbell never talked of what speed he might make, but his wife admitted that 300 miles an hour was his goal. His first assault on the land speed record was made with a borrowed car in 1922 at

Saltburn-on-Sea, Yorkshire. He averaged 135, but the mark wasn't accepted.

Unfortunately, Campbell's speed had been timed with a hand-held watch instead of by the electrical timing device required by official rules.

At that time, K. Lee Guinness, also of England, held the official record at 133.75.

A year later, after having purchased Guinness' 350 horsepower Sunbeam, Campbell entered the international speed trials at Fanoe, Denmark. On June 24, 1923, he reached 137 mph but again failed to win recognition as the timing equipment did not meet international approval.

Twice in two years he had bettered the land speed record, but twice he was denied.

In 1924, he again returned to Fanoe. Storms had swept Denmark. The beach was in poor condition, littered with debris. He was nearing the start of the measured mile, hitting 150 miles an hour when Bluebird suddenly started sliding sideways. His tires flew off, one tire flying into the crowd and hitting a thirteen year old boy who died later at the hospital.

Campbell and his crew were initially arrested, but released when the investigation was concluded. The meet was canceled.

"It was fantastic to see those two bloody tires hurtling by me", said Campbell, "as I grappled to keep the bitch straight."

Undaunted, Campbell returned to Pendine in the fall of 1924. But not before 1914 Indianapolis 500 winner, Rene Thomas of France, clocked 143.26 at Arpajon in France for a new two-way record. Four days later, Ernest Eldridge upped the mark to 143.8. However, Thomas lodged a protest, claiming that Eldridge's car was not fitted with a reverse gear, as was required by international rules.

Within forty-eight hours, a reverse gear was fitted on the six cylinder Fiat. This time, Thomas could only watch as Eldridge clocked an even faster 145.897. This time there was no protest.

On September 25, 1924, Campbell finally beat the 'jinx', setting his first of nine land speed records with an average speed of 146.16. Ten months later, also at Pendine Sands, he became the first to shatter the 150 mile an hour barrier; his speed: 150.87.

THE RECORDS

September 25, 1924	Pendine Sands, Wales Speed: 146.16 mph
July 21, 1925	Pendine Sands, Wales Speed: 150.87 mph
February 4, 1927	Pendine Sands, Wales Speed: 174.88 mph
February 19, 1928	Daytona Beach, Florida Speed: 206.06 mph
February 5, 1931	Daytona Beach, Florida Speed: 246.09 mph
February 24, 1932	Daytona Beach, Florida Speed: 253.97 mph
February 22, 1933	Daytona Beach, Florida Speed: 272.46 mph
March 7, 1935	Daytona Beach, Florida Speed: 276.82 mph
September 3, 1935	Bonneville Salt Flats, Utah Speed: 301.13 mph

From 1924 through 1947, British drivers set twenty-three land speed records. Only once was that string broken, when Ray Keech of the United States averaged 207.55 in the massive Triplex on April 22, 1928. Keech, also an Indianapolis 500 winner, later lost his life during an auto race at Altoona, Pennsylvania.

The great battles pitted Englishman against Englishman. Campbell vs. Segrave. Cobb vs. Eyston. The speed would increase almost 250 miles an hour. What a shoot-out!

The famed Florida sand was the primary playground during the Roaring Twenties, the so-called Golden Age of Sports. As many as 50,000 people lined the beach to see these daring men in their muscle machines.

However, no driver captured the public's imagination more than boyish-looking Frank Lockhart, a young Californian, and his tiny streamliner.

He passed through like a meteor. Death came at the tender age of twenty-six. He was a small man, not weighing more than 135 pounds. But could he handle a racing machine.

He was born March 8, 1903 in Cleveland, Ohio. When his father died six years later, Lockhart's mother moved the family to California. By 1923, he launched his racing career in a Model T Ford, named the McDowell Special.

It wasn't long, however, before he started beating all-comers at the famed Ascot Park oval. By 1925, he joined the Automobile Association of America (AAA), a duly sanctioned racing body, and attracted the attention of Harry A. Miller who gave the youngster a 183 cubic inch Miller to campaign on the dirt tracks.

By the end of 1925, Lockhart was considered one of the top dirt track drivers in the country.

In May of 1926, Lockhart went to Indianapolis without a ride, hoping to sign as a relief driver in the Indianapolis 500. That would have been good enough for the twenty-three year old.

But, Fate had other ideas. He sparkled in borrowed cars, actually set an unofficial one-lap record in Bennett Hill's car and signed on as Hill's sub. That might have been it for Frank Lockhart.

However, another driver, Peter Kries, was hit by pneumonia. Lockhart quickly jumped into that car and on May 27, 1926, set an official one-lap record of 115.488. On the second qualifying lap, the right rear tire shredded and he was forced to abort that attempt.

Later in the day, Lockhart's car developed engine problems during his second try. On his third attempt, he coasted to a twenty-place start with his unimpressive 95.783.

Yet, he was in the Indianapolis 500 field. After lap No. 1, he moved all the way up to tenth position. After five laps, he was fourth, and by lap No. 10 had moved into third place. On the sixtieth lap, Dave Lewis, the pacesetter, pitted, and Lockhart assumed the lead. He would hold it for thirty-three laps, then take over the lead on lap

99 of a scheduled two hundred lap race. He was still leading the pack when rain halted the event after 400 miles. His winning speed: 95.904. It would be twenty-six more years until a driver younger than Frank Lockhart would take the checkered flag at the famed 'Brickyard' – twenty-one year old Troy Ruttman in 1952.

Lockhart was modest following the race.

"Perhaps I am the most surprised man of all those here because I won the race. I want to give plenty of credit to the Miller Special. It worked perfectly. I had to come into the pits but one time, and that was for oil, gas and water. It's a great car. What will I do with the money? I hardly know, for I haven't had time to think about that.

"All I have been thinking about was winning the race. I came here without a reputation and I had everything at stake. I am glad I won and thankful to those who helped me in every way they could."

A record crowd of 135,000 watched Miller's cars completely dominate the 500. Six of his creations finished in the Top Ten. Harry Hartz was second in a Miller Special, some thirty-three seconds off the pace.

With that same ninety-one cubic inch Miller, Lockhart went out to Muroc Dry Lake in California, located about sixty-five miles from Los Angeles, and on April 13, 1927, averaged a sizzling 164.285 mph in a two-way run through the one mile speed trap.

Going against the wind, he was clocked at 157.549, and with the wind at his back an amazing 171.021. Thoughts of a world land speed record entered his mind. On July 26, 1927, Lockhart told the world that he would begin building a land speed record car to break Sir Henry Segrave's mark of 203.790, set March 29 of that year at Ormond Beach.

Sir Malcolm Campbell had hoped to become the first to break the 200 mph barrier. However, his fellow countryman and fierce rival beat him to the punch in his Golden Arrow.

In 1926, England's Parry Thomas, driving Babs was the fastest on wheels with his record of 171.02. A year later, he would die during a land speed attempt.

He had made two fast runs and was back for the fatal run. Eyewitnesses said black smoke poured out of the car before the driving chain broke, was propelled into the cockpit and almost beheaded Thomas. A wheel came off, the car slid upside down and burst into flames. His chief mechanic suffered burns pulling Parry's lifeless body out of the cockpit.

The car, along with Thomas' coat and driving helmet were buried in the Pendine Sands. Some forty years later, the car was exhumed from its grave.

Segrave's record-setting machine was powered by two Matabele airplane engines, one fore and one aft. Campbell's Bluebird, under construction, would not be underpowered. It was a 940 HP Napier-Lion airplane engine, developed for British entries in the prestigious Schneider Trophy Air Race. In the air, the speed was 281.49.

By the 1928 speed season in Florida, Lockhart, Campbell and Keech were ready to challenge Segrave. Lockhart's Stutz Black Hawk was the most expensive car in land speed racing, a $100,000 'space age' creation weighing 3000 pounds. Its engines consisted of two Miller 91s mounted on a common crankcase. The horsepower rating was 385 at 7000 r.p.m. Total frontal area was only 10.26 square feet. The car had no radiator. Instead, it used seventy-five pounds of crushed ice as the coolant.

Keech's Triplex weighed 8000 pounds as did Segrave's machine. Campbell's Bluebird was a bit lighter at 5600 pounds. Total piston displacement: Lockhart (181 cubic inches), Segrave (2760), Keech (4950) and Campbell (1360).

When Keech's car first showed up, it was barred from competition as it lacked a reverse gear. And when the car did pass muster, a water connection busted, badly scalding Keech. He was taken to the hospital to heal.

Keech would return to combat and persevere, setting a record of 207 during a hairy ride in which his car flew fifty feet through the air.

In early February, Campbell's Bluebird hit a bump, leaped thirty feet in the air, landing hard on four wheels. The result: damaged springs, shocks and underside of car.

But on February 19, 1928, he set a land speed record of 206.956 with bursts of 199.667 and 214.797. The next day, Lockhart went 200.22 mph against the wind, but clutch trouble on the return run ruined his record bid.

Three days later, he tried again and the attempt almost proved fatal.

A mist made visibility difficult at best. Lockhart was reluctant, but the huge crowd on hand changed his mind. All appeared well as Lockhart passed the 200 mph mark. But suddenly, the car swerved sharply left, towards the crowd. Then the car moved to the right, toward the ocean. The Stutz Back Hawk hit a four foot wave and skipped over the water some forty feet, rolled over and finally came to rest upright some one hundred yards off shore.

The car was fully submerged. Lockhart was trapped and semi-conscious. Spectators tried to help, but the sea proved too strong, as heavy waves beat them back. Finally, a small mob surrounded the car and managed to push it to safety.

With the use of chisels, drills and blow torches, Lockhart was freed. At first it was thought he suffered a broken arm. He did not. Three tendons in his left wrist had been severed, but outside of some severe bruises and cuts, he was basically okay.

He was taken to the same hospital where Keech was recovering from his burns.

In the hospital he said, "I was feeling my way, wide open in the mist and started instinctively pulling the car higher on the beach, away from the ocean. When I struck soft sand, I knew I was too high and pulled her down again – but too quickly. The next thing I knew, I was in the water."

The accident did not check his determination. He wanted repairs on the car to begin as quickly as possible. The streamliner was taken back to Indianapolis for repairs, and when the speed trials were resumed in April 1928, Lockhart's tiny car was ready.

So was Ray Keech and his massive Triplex.

Keech averaged 202.702 on two runs while Lockhart made some easy shakedown attempts. On April 22, Keech gunned his Triplex, powered by three Liberty-type V-12 aircraft engines to a new land speed record.

On April 25, after taking three sorties of 147.23, 193.34 and 203.50, Lockhart was ready for a record attempt. His third run had been made into the wind, so he felt confident. Running with the wind should add some fifteen miles an hour to the overall speed, more than enough for the record.

He started his fourth run about eight o'clock in the morning, and when he was about 500 yards from the first official timing trap, the right rear tire blew. Lockhart was traveling at an estimated 225 mph.

The car went into a fifty-seven foot sideways slide, then took seven bounces ranging in length from 33 to 140 feet. On the last bounce, Lockhart was thrown from the car. He was found fifty-one feet from the wreckage, breathing heavily and bleeding profusely. His wife, Elia, was one of the first to reach him.

Lockhart was taken to Halifax Hospital where he was pronounced dead at 8:35 a.m. He was twenty-six years old.

Within another year, land speed racing would claim another fatality. Lee Bible, driving the same Triplex which Keech drove to the speed record, was killed at Daytona. The out-of-control car also killed a newsreel photographer.

While Segrave decided to return to Florida for the 1929 speed season, Campbell journeyed thousands of miles to Verneuk Pan in South Africa.

On March 11, 1929, Segrave gunned his Golden Arrow to a new record of 231.44 mph. Verneuk was some 2000 feet above sea level and that condition created carburetor problems for Campbell's Bluebird.

While the dried lake bed seemed the ideal place, the surface was less than ideal. The solution: to lay a mixture of mud on top of the shale; but the nearest water hole was five miles away.

Campbell, a seasoned pilot, crash-landed his plane during one of his flights from Verneuk to Cape Town, some 500 miles away. He suffered injuries to his nose and mouth. He would have to heal.

In the meantime, Segrave hit 231. Campbell's Bluebird had a speed potential of 230 mph. Close, but not good enough. So he salvaged the South African assault by setting a five mile record of 211 mph. He also bettered Segrave's five kilo record which had been set during his record run.

Segrave returned home amid triumph. He was knighted, then turned his attention to the world water speed record. Segrave built Miss England III, a massive boat powered by two Rolls Royce aircraft engines.

On Friday, June 13, he made his attempt on Lake Windermere. He made a total of three runs, his second a swift 98.76 mph. During the third attempt, Segrave's boat hit a submerged log, capsized and sank. He died shortly afterwards in a hospital. Of the two engineers also on board, one was killed. His final run: 119.8 mph.

All during his racing career, Segrave competed with a handicap. As a World War I pilot in the Royal Flying Corp, he was shot down in 1916. Silver plates were inserted in his left foot.

Campbell spent most of 1930 remodeling his Bluebird. The car was given a new body and new engine, a 14,500 horsepower Schneider racing type. He returned to Ormond Beach and on February 5, 1931, covered the flying mile at 246.153 mph.

England went wild. The returning hero was still on board ship when he was notified that knighthood had been granted him.

Sir Malcolm rest on his laurels? No way. Bluebird was altered again. It was given a new streamlining and an engine of the same type, but developing slightly more horsepower. He returned to Ormond Beach and on February 24, 1932, drove at 253.96.

Returning to England, Sir Malcolm once more rebuilt the car. When it was completed nine months later, Bluebird was longer, heavier and more powerful. A new streamlined body had been fitted, and under the hood was a twelve cylinder, 2500-HP engine.

With this machine he set his 1933 record of 272.463.

When the sands of Ormond Beach had outlived their usefulness, Campbell searched for a longer and harder surface. He found it at the Bonneville Salt Flats in Western Utah.

The date: September 3, 1935.

More than 1000 spectators were on hand as Sir Malcolm began his run down the thirteen mile long course. But just as the three ton beast streaked passed the last measured mile marker, the left front tire blew.

Exhaust fumes filled the cockpit. A film of oil spread over the windshield. Bluebird swerved, but Campbell calmly managed to twist the wheel and straighten out its course. He applied a heavy foot to the brakes to finally stop the car, leaped out of the cockpit with a fire extinguisher and put out the tire fire.

Speed for the first run: 304.111. Time through the flying mile: 11.63 seconds. But in order to set a record, he had to make a return run within a sixty minute time limit.

"Hurry, boys, hurry," Campbell told his mechanics. "We've got to make a quick change or the hour will be up."

Eight minutes remained on the clock when he climbed back into the cockpit.

At first, speed of his return run was announced at 295.566 for a two-way average of 299.875. Then, officials made a correction. The second burst was actually 298.013 for a two-way land speed record of 301.337 mph.

Sir Malcolm Campbell had shattered the 300 mph barrier.

Afterwards, T.E. Allan, secretary of the contest board of the American Automobile Association, issued the following statement:

> *The run northward over the measured mile was made in 11.83 seconds, or at a rate of 304.331 miles an hour. The trip southward was actually made in 12.08 seconds instead of the 12.18 seconds he was credited with.*
>
> *The method of computation of such records is to take the actual time that the car comes in contact with the timing wire at the beginning of the one mile stretch and the exact time it makes contact with the trap wire at the end of the mile. These times were 49 minutes 50.92 seconds and 50 minutes 03.00 seconds respectively.*
>
> *In subtracting these two readings the calculator made a difference of 12.18 seconds instead of the correct figure of 12.08. These records are all shown on the original timing machine tape, which goes to the International Sporting Commission at Paris for checking and ratification.*

Obviously, Campbell was elated with the news.

"The old car stood up beautifully. I couldn't have expected more. Now it's going home with me... we're both going to rest."

Then he added, "No. I have not set a record I cannot beat. I can build a car that will go much faster, and I shall probably do that. Nor have I set a record that another driver can't beat. No man could do that, for what I can do another man can do."

How fast can a man travel on land?

"Given the right surface, a long enough run, and a car designed for the work, a man may even reach 500 miles an hour. The limiting factor to ultimate speed will be the difficulty of finding a suitable course, not in the cars themselves or in the human element."

Sir Malcolm had achieved all that he had set out to do on land, so he turned his attention to the water and set four records between 1937 and 1939.

Bluebird is on display at Talladega, Alabama museum on the same ground where the 2.66 mile super speedway is located.

The car is thirty feet long. At the time, the V–12 engine was the most powerful ever installed in a car. The engine alone cost the British government more than $75,000. Specially built tires with a life of just seven minutes cost $1800 each.

Bluebird, which used three gallons of gas a minute, had three speeds and could run 175 miles an hour in low gear. It is only three feet high at the cockpit and the driver's seat is just eighteen inches off the ground. The highest part of the car is the top of the stabilizing tail fin, which is five feet high.

RECORDS ON WATER

September 1, 1937   Lake Maggiore, Italy
                            Speed: 128.30 mph

September 2, 1937   Lake Maggiore, Italy
                            Speed: 129.50 mph

September 4, 1938   Lake Hallwill, Switzerland
                            Speed: 130.94 mph

August 19, 1939   Lake Coniston, England
                            Speed: 141.74 mph

With the start of England's war against Germany, Campbell was back in the army in 1939. Six years later, Sir Malcolm was out and his thoughts turned to 200 miles an hour on water.

His Bluebird, built by Reid Railton in '39, was updated. The Air Ministry allowed Sir Malcolm to borrow a 4000 horsepower Goblin jet engine (1946). By 1947, reconstruction was complete and Campbell returned to Lake Coniston for a record assault.

However, his bid was short-lived. At 100 mph, the jet boat swerved off course. A year later, he returned to Coniston, but this time handling problems plagued him. Campbell was now sixty-two and in ill-health.

A year later, England's greatest speed king was dead.

While one gallant Englishman had faded from the land speed picture, two others picket up the gauntlet.

John Cobb and Captain George Eyston waged a fierce battle between 1938 and 1939.

Eyston began his speed pursuits in 1923 in European road races. Later, he set numerous distance records in his car, Speed of the Wind.

On November 19, 1937, the shy, retiring driver piloted his ten wheel, seven ton Thunderbolt to a new land speed record of 311.42.

Less than a year later – August 27, 1938 – Eyston upped his speed to 345.50. Thunderbolt, painted black to overcome a glaring sun, hit 347.49 on its outward trip and 343.41 on the return jaunt.

"Thunderbolt was by no means at full throttle," he said. "I had a very comfortable ride and not once did I feel there was any danger.

"I'm getting rather used to the sensation of high speed now. I seem to go through that measured mile like it was a mere 100 yards. Things fly at you tremendously fast. The sensation I used to have when I first went over 300 is wearing off. I don't feel as though the salt is curving down in front of the car and I'm going downhill. I just seem to be whistling through space. I really don't have much time to think about sensations."

He admitted he was hooked on speed.

"Record-breaking is a lure which is all its own. I cannot compute the enjoyment I have got out of my record-breaking quests.

"To have set a difficult goal and to have achieved it; to have overcome all difficulties which beset an attack on the 'best ever' – believe me, it is glorious.

"So far as speed is concerned, there is no mechanical limit. Engines can be built and I have no doubt that vehicles could be designed which would give us speed beyond the endurance of man's senses.

"Remember those nineteenth century medicos who theorized on the impossibility of breathing at sixty miles an hour. How can we know what our faculties will stand until we test them to the limit? And where is the limit?"

Eyston wasn't about to speculate.

"No, I think we shall do well to content ourselves with the present and the all-absorbing possibilities of the near future. To do more is to wander sightlessly in a world which is beyond our ken."

His prime concern was a chap named Cobb.

Two weeks after Eyston stretched the speed to 345.50, Cobb averaged 350.20 in his turtle-shaped Railton Special.

But no sooner had Cobb enjoyed the fruits of his victory than Eyston powered his mammoth twenty-four cylinder creation to a new mark of 357.50. The land speed record had been broken twice within twenty-four hours.

Eyston's seven ton car had been extensively remodeled for the record run, the big tail fin removed and the square nose given a tear-drop streamlining.

"She's got more speed left," he said. "But we're getting the speed so fast now that we're treading on very dangerous ground each time we try to jack it up a bit."

Eyston made the north run at 356.44 mph and returned at 358.57, requiring 10.04 seconds for the measured mile. It was estimated the car reached the velocity of 525 feet per second, comparable to the 700 feet per nuzzle velocity of an ordinary .45 caliber revolver bullet.

Cobb was sound asleep when Eyston started his dawn assault. When he heard what his rival had done, he said, "After due deliberation, we have decided to abandon further quests for the world land speed record so far as this visit is concerned."

He paid his compliments to the tall, tense, retired British Army officer and declared his Railton Special had been built with a 350 mile an hour potential, and had attained that goal.

Did that mean the end of Cobb?

By the 1939 season, Reid Railton had unveiled a new car, a 2600 horsepower, twin-engined Railton Special. Cobb's twenty-nine foot long, turtle-shaped machine featured a unique four-wheel drive in which the rear engine drove the front wheels and the front one the rear wheels. A 400 pound, removable aluminum-alloy shell completely streamlined the car.

Started by pushing, the three-speed, reverseless machine shifted into second at 140 mph and into high at 240. Weighing in at close to four tons, it required special transmission brakes, and wore out a full set of forty-four inch tires on every run.

Although eight feet wide in front, the Railton Special tapered to a beaver-tail rear-end. Lacking the conventional radiator in front, the Napier twelve cylinder engines were cooled by water and ice in a seventy-five gallon tank. Fuel capacity was eighteen gallons.

Wheel base was 13.5 feet. The car was only fifty-one inches high. Its front wheel track measured 5.5 feet, the rear 3.5 feet.

Cobb sat in an enclosed cockpit in the nose of the car, forward of the front axle. The power plants were behind him. He had four pedals for his feet, a throttle, brake pedal, locking pedal for free-wheeling and a foot-rest.

Brakes were on the propeller shafts instead of on the wheels and each brake was cooled by water discharged from the engine cooling systems. Clouds of steam shot out from the rear of the car when the brakes were applied.

Braking was the trickiest part. Cobb applied the brakes in short bursts after the car slowed down to 300 miles an hour. Each application caused such a violent deceleration that the driver was thrown forward in his cockpit.

Oddly enough, Cobb's car had an ordinary electric horn. He used it to signal the push truck that he was ready to start. The car had no starter and was pushed along the course in gear until the engines began to fire.

Railton built the car to exceed 400 miles an hour.

For one year, Captain George Eyston enjoyed the title 'Fastest Man On Wheels'. On August 23, 1939, John Cobb streaked across the Bonneville Salt Flats at a two-way average speed of 368.90 mph.

Cobb's track was twelve miles long.

Railton said: "He used 5.5 miles to accelerate, reaching 300 miles an hour within three miles of his start.

"After going through the measured mile, he used the last 5.5 miles to brake to a stop."

Railton and Cobb were satisfied... for the time being, that is.

Cobb would have to wait until after World War II to take a crack at the 400 mile an hour barrier.

During the war, he was in the Royal Air Force, serving as a ferry pilot in the British Air Transport Auxiliary. In 1947, at the age of forty-seven, he returned to Utah.

Except for minor changes, his Railton Special was essentially the same car that had smashed the world land speed record eight years before.

On September 16, Cobb started the two engines, working up 1,250 horsepower apiece. Slowly, the car gained momentum.

Cobb's first run through the measured mile was 385.645. It was fast, but not fast enough to suit him. Less than an hour later, John Cobb began his south-to-north return run. In the span of nine seconds he had blasted through the flying mile. Official speed: 403.135. His peak speed at one point was 415.

His two-way average was 394.196 for the mile and 393.836 the kilometer. It had taken him seven long weeks to break the record.

Asked how it felt to drive at 400 miles an hour, he replied laconically: "It feels bloody quick."

While he wanted to go faster, two factors prevented any further runs – condition of the car and the weather.

"Owing to the terrific punishment the car has taken for the many tests required preceding this run," he said, "it has been decided not to risk further serious damage which might possibly result from any attempts to establish records for five miles and ten miles."

Despite setting the record, he called it "the roughest ride I have yet had on the Salt Flats. It felt like I was riding inside an infuriated vibration machine."

Less than twenty-four hours later a heavy rainfall flooded the Flats at a depth of 2.6 inches.

Reid Railton, Cobb's long-time friend and creator of the British car, felt there was probably another sixty miles an hour left in his creation.

Cobb agreed. "I think the topmost speed for an automobile lies somewhere between 400 and 450 miles. Tires just won't stand up under the heat generated by friction in speed much above 400."

The Railton Special's (Dunlop) tire treads were almost paper-thin.

In 1949, Cobb said, "I don't think I'll be very active in high-speed work any more. The record? I've got it. I won't bother again unless someone else breaks it."

Like Henry Segrave and Sir Malcolm Campbell, Cobb then turned his energies to the world water speed record.

By 1952, America's Stan Sayre pushed his propeller-powered boat to a new speed mark of 178.427 mph at Seattle, Washington. Cobb knew he had the craft to easily eclipse that mark.

Cobb's thirty-one foot racer, Crusader, was jet-propelled, powered by a De Havilland Ghost turbo jet engine. It weighed three tons. He was shooting for the 200 mph barrier.

Instead, he was killed on September 29, 1952 on Loch Ness.

John Cobb was born December 2, 1899, and educated at Eton and Trinity. He was a businessman who amassed his wealth from his fur-broking interests.

He first appeared on the racing scene in 1925, at the wheel of a ten liter Fiat at Brooklands.

By 1935, he turned in the fastest ever lap at Brooklands, 143.444 mph, and the fastest speed (almost 152) ever recorded on that high-speed layout.

In July of 1935, another driver, Freddie Dixon, took Cobb's car, powered by a twenty-four liter, twelve cylinder Napier-Lion aircraft engine to the Bonneville Salt Flats for a shot at the twenty-four hour endurance record.

Dixon averaged 134.84 mph, without a hint of mechanical trouble.

By 1939, Cobb was at Bonneville with his land speed machine.

The rest is history.

Chapter Thirteen
No Holding Back the Flood

My first land speed attempt was in 1960 with Anteater. It was Allison-powered. There was about $10,000 in the car.

Then there was Donald Campbell's $4 million Bluebird, a truly beautiful car. Even by today's standards it was streamlined.

Campbell seemed like a real nice guy, but he really wasn't too familiar with the car. He had radio contact with his engineer, a guy named Peter Carr. One time when Campbell was going about seventy, he says, "Peter, there's a red light on in the center of the dash." And Peter said, "Donald, your parking brake is still on."

Art Arfons

John Cobb was dead. Long live the king!

And with his passing came the end of a romantic era in land speed racing. Just as the rear-engine racer would replace the upright roadster at Indianapolis, the shrieking power of the jet engine would usher in a new chapter in the high-speed game of Russian Roulette.

For more than a decade, Cobb's two-way average of 394 mph was the standard by which any land speed challenger was measured; this marvelous pre-World War II relic, this British-built Railton Special. The power of its two Napier engines transmitted directly through the wheels.

For the purist, it was a wheel-driven masterpiece.

But nothing lasts forever.

Progress rolls on relentlessly. It cannot be turned back.

Steam pushed aside electric. Piston replaced electric. And the speeds increased dramatically... 100... 200... 300... 400...

By the late 1950s, piston power was still a formidable force, but the handwriting was already on the wall. Jets were already performing on the nation's dragstrips.

While no British heir to Cobb's throne would step forward, more than a handful of willing and capable Americans would take up the quest.

Well-known hot rodder Mickey Thompson set an American flying mile record of 363.67 in his four-engine Challenger I in August 1959.

Four months later, little-known Athol Graham of Salt Lake City, a one-time Mormon missionary, drove his home-built City of Salt Lake to a top speed of 344.761. The $2500 racer was powered by an Allison aircraft engine.

He too was in the hunt as a new era would dawn on land speed racing. It was 1960. The jets are coming... the jets are coming!

The name of the late Dr. Nathan Ostich doesn't appear in any land speed record books. It's not because the Los Angeles baby doctor didn't try. For three years, he waged a game battle in the world's first jet-propelled land speed contender, Flying Caduceus.

Ostich caught the speed bug in 1949. No stranger to the Flats, he had raced there for ten years and traveled 189.98 in a modified sedan – "as fast as the car could go".

But his "Flying Caduceus" was no modified sedan. It was a twenty-eight foot long, needle-nosed car, powered by a GE turbo jet engine, the type used in B-36 bombers. Two years in the building, the jet boasted a 5000 horsepower punch. Wind tunnel tests at Cal Poly Tech showed the car had a speed potential of 500 miles an hour.

"Our goal is 500," Ostich said in early 1960. "We expect to begin testing within a couple of months."

Then he explained that his $100,000 creation differed from Thompson's Challenger I.

"We will be straight jet-propelled, eliminating the problem of a transmission which Mickey had. We also will have open wheels. The car looks like an airplane fuselage on wheels."

Ostich would be joined in the 1960 chase by England's Donald Campbell, Graham, Thompson, and drag racing star, Art Arfons.

On August 1, 1960, the thirty-six year old Graham was killed. He had dreamed from boyhood of becoming the first American to drive 400 miles an hour.

Graham was two-thirds of the way between the starting pit and the measured mile, traveling at an estimated 300, when his 4200 pound car skidded and flipped.

When it came to a halt upside down, the car's body was broken and the wheels bent. A tow truck lifted the battered, bright red racer on to its right side, and Graham was removed.

Graham, with a fractured skull, collapsed lung and other injuries, was flown to Salt Lake City, some 125 miles away. He died at the hospital. His twenty-nine year old wife, Zeldine, was at the finish line, waiting for him to complete the first run.

"The car started to disintegrate," she said, "then it turned over. I couldn't see anything for the dust."

A crosswind, with gusts up to twenty-five miles an hour, was buffeting the track during the attempt and was blamed as the major cause for the crash. Less than two months after the tragedy, Zeldine Graham said she would rebuild the car.

Ostich was next on the Flats. However, his 5000 horsepower jet was plagued by technical problems. Although the Californian doctor pushed the car to 300 mph, violent vibrations forced him to return home for repairs.

While the Flying Caduceus failed, the jet era had been officially launched.

Arfons made his first land speed appearance with his Allison-powered Anteater, but was knocked out with clutch failure. Top speed was a disappointing 260.

He prepared himself for Bonneville by running his car, minus body panel, at nearby Akron Airport, hitting speeds of 100 miles an hour, "...just to see if I could go and stop".

Back at Bonneville in 1960, Thompson had added a supercharger to each of his four Pontiac engines. In addition, he covered the front wheels to improve streamlining.

Everything had gone wrong for three weeks. Then, on September 9, 1960, Thompson gunned his Challenger I to a speed of 406.60, the fastest ever recorded through the measured mile. However, a broken transmission shaft aborted his return run, thus preventing him from a new two-way record.

Now it was up to Donald Campbell, son of the legendary Sir Malcolm, and his jet-powered Bluebird.

Like father, like son.

Campbell came to Bonneville with no high-speed racing experience on land. He was a record-holder on water. Call it on-the-job training.

Donald Campbell was only fifteen when his father shattered the 300 mile an hour barrier at Bonneville. The youngster was there. Moments after completion of the return run, he embraced his father. Tears were in Donald's eyes.

During World War II, he tried to join the RAF but was turned down because of boyhood rheumatic fever. So, he went about his life as an engineer.

But within two weeks of his father's death in 1969, Campbell told Leo Villa, who had served as Sir Malcolm's chief mechanic for more than forty years, that he intended "to start where the old Dad left off".

At that point, he had no racing experience whatsoever. But he would learn. He would set records. He would carry on the family honor.

His father's unsuccessful jet boat was taken out of mothballs. A proven piston engine replaced the jet power plant.

Three weeks later, he thought he had eclipsed his father's record of 141.74. However, there had been a mistake in the timing.

A year later, America's Stanley Sayre raised the water speed record to 160.32 mph.

In 1951, Campbell took Bluebird to Lake Coniston, reached the record speed of 170 when the jet boat spun into the air, hit water and began to sink. He had to be fished out of twenty-five feet of water.

The boat was gone. His finances were gone. Donald Campbell returned to engineering. Leo Villa went with him and remained by his side until Campbell's tragic death in 1967.

By 1955, Campbell was ready for the water wars with a brand new Bluebird, but by then, Sayre had pushed the record to 178.

On July 23, 1955, the intensely superstitious driver who believed his father's spirit was always with him, set his first of seven water speed records, averaging 202.32 mph on Lake Ullswater, England. He was the first to exceed 200 mph on water.

Less than four months later (November 16), he boosted his own record to 216.25 mph at Lake Mead in Nevada.

That would be followed by: 225.63 in 1956, 239.07 in 1957, 248.62 mph in 1958, 260.35 in 1959, and 276.33 in 1964.

He was convinced that on several occasions his father's intervention had saved him from disaster. The first time was Lake Coniston in 1957, just before he raised the water speed mark to 239.07.

A medium at a seance had warned him of unspecified danger. Campbell believed the message originated from his father and ordered a complete overhaul of Bluebird before he made his run.

The second occasion was also at Coniston, a year later, when the steering failed and he found himself heading for a pier at high speed.

"Suddenly," he said, "the throttle opened wide, the launch answered to the helm and we were clear of danger. Again, I knew someone had acted for me."

He also believed his father was with him during his heralded land speed debut at Bonneville.

The huge entourage brought 35,000 tons of equipment, transported 6000 miles from England. Support vehicles included refueling vehicles, specially equipped Land Rovers. The largest tires in land speed history, some fifty-two inches in diameter, were made especially for Bluebird. Almost one hundred such tires were stored in an old Air Force hanger in Wendover, some eleven miles away from Bonneville.

The 'assault force' included engineers, technicians, representatives of the eighty British companies which finally backed Campbell's $4 million project.

The massive car – 9600 pounds – was powered by a 4250 horsepower Proteus gas turbine engine. However, technically, Bluebird was considered a wheel-driven car because forty percent of the power was transmitted directly through the wheels.

Speed potential was 500 miles an hour, according to co-designer Lewis Norris.

"It's hard to see how any vehicle driven through the wheels can have a higher potential than this one. You can almost say this is the end of the road."

On September 5, 1960, Bluebird made easy preliminary runs in the 120–170 speed range. Four days later, Thompson hit 406.

By September 15, Bluebird was back on the salt after modifications and Campbell upped the speed to 250. The course was rough but the British car handled well.

The next day he was ready for an acceleration test. The car was refueled at 7:12 in the morning. It would be a 360 mile an hour crash.

Bryan Cooper, public relations officer for the project, described the run:

"Within 1.6 miles of the start, the telemetry dials at the north pit showed that Bluebird had incredibly accelerated to a speed of 365 miles per hour. At this point, the car began to slide towards the left of the track.

"The cause of this was a combination of factors – the effect of a gushing crosswind, the bad conditions of the salt on that part of the track, and higher torque values than were expected, making it more difficult to prevent the wheels slipping, a difference in adhesion between the left and right wheels gave a rotational effect to the car and caused it to spin to the left side of the course.

"At a point 1.9 miles from the start, the right-hand wheels went into rough salt beyond the course and the car crashed on its right side, almost at right angles to the course.

"With its length facing the wind like a huge airplane wing, Bluebird took off from the ground and twisted crazily into the air. The first vicious twisting motion caused Campbell to lose consciousness. He [Campbell] next remembers banging his head very hard and was then semi-conscious as the car rumbled to a halt and he was pulled out of the cockpit.

"After leaving the ground", he continued, "Bluebird hurtled through the air for about 200 yards – four tons of metal traveling at over 350 mph. It touched down again on its tail, then on to its right wheels five yards further on. Three more times the car bounced to the ground within a distance of seventy yards, then went into a 200 yard 'S' slide and came to rest facing the direction it had come.

"Strewn over a wide area were pieces of twisted metalwork and also two of the huge tires and wheels. Despite the tremendous impact when the car bounced, not one of the tires burst."

Campbell escaped the hairy ride with a hairline skull fracture. The car would be rebuilt.

Later, Campbell told a friend that his father's face appeared at the windshield during the crash and said, 'Don't worry, Donald. You'll be all right.'

What caused the crash?

One theory blamed the oxygen mixture that was being fed to Campbell, who wore a full mask. Pure oxygen has the effect of making one drunk.

Some friends believed his character changed after that. The possibility of another crash became an obsession with him. Others questioned his courage. They wondered whether he could ever push a car or a boat to the limit.

Despite his superstitions, Donald Campbell would show the doubters and the world his special brand of courage.

When the 1960 speed season ended, John Cobb's 394 record had successfully withstood the challenge.

Poor salt conditions in 1961 virtually eliminated all record attempts. However, Art Arfons managed to hit 313.78 in his piston-powered Anteater before a burned-out clutch knocked him out of contention.

It was the last time this wheel-driven contender would run at Bonneville.

More than thirty years after that inauspicious debut, Art Arfons is still convinced Anteater had the stuff to set a land speed record.

"The car has the potential of 450 miles an hour," he insists. "Years ago, I made a mistake and sold it to Bob Motz who used to drive for me. I offered him $7000, but he wouldn't sell.

"If I had the car today, there's several things I could do. The major problem was the clutch. It just wasn't strong enough. I'd beef it up. I had a two-speed transmission, but I never did get it into high.

"I could drop in a pair of turbine engines that would drive the wheels, or if I extended the body by about twelve inches, I could put in a twin-Allison.

"It was a good handling car. I sat way up front. It's scary. You can't see nothing except salt rushing at you. It really gives you the sensation of going fast.

"What's bad about sitting so far forward is that if something happens and the back end starts to drift out, you wouldn't know it until it's too late. You wouldn't have the feel."

It cost about $10,000 to build Anteater, which resembled John Cobb's Railton Special from the rear.

"The biggest expenditure was about $4000 for the body, and Firestone paid for that. I probably had $5000 in the rest of it."

Arfons' formula was simple. Surplus parts. Junk parts. Put together, and presto, a speed machine.

"When you grow up in a depression you watch how you spend your money. Most of the major components were army stuff I picked up.

"A friend of mine made the canopy out of an F–86 canopy. He cut out a section. The hubs were all Dodge power wagon hubs. I sorta used 'em on everything except my land speed car. I had Hallibrand wheels which weren't special. The tires [thirty-one inches in diameter] were specially made by Firestone."

Anteater used 100 octane gasoline as the fuel for its 1500 horsepower Allison aircraft engine.

"The Allison really came out of the P–38s, 39s and 40s [all World War II fighter planes]. You would buy 'em cheap for about $200 each. I've still got thirteen of 'em."

The Allison engine was five feet long, two feet wide and weighed 1260 pounds. One novel approach that Arfons took was running ice water through the cooling system, "just like Railton did with Cobb's car, so I wouldn't have to hang a radiator out in the air stream."

During the two year period that Arfons campaigned Anteater at Bonneville in search of the world land speed record, he took a little side trip to Daytona and the two and a half mile, high-banked race track.

"There was a standing offer, $10,000 to the first guy that goes 200 at Daytona. So I took it down there, 'cause there wasn't anything in the rules that said I couldn't run for the money.

"I put a tether chute on the top so when I got in the corner it would keep the car down. I went out and made an easy lap. Then, as I was coming down the back stretch I put it up to 190 and almost lost it.

"I went into the third groove and that corner didn't look good at all. I hit a patch and all of a sudden I'm within inches of the rail. That was all for me. I didn't want to do it.

"That's when one of those race drivers [Brian Naylor] got in it and he got his ass burnt. I told him if it gets to 200 degrees he'd have to pull in because the water line would blow.

"He made one good lap, but musta misread the needle, because on that second lap the water line blew and he was scalded."

Art Arfons' debut as an oval track driver ended quickly, but not uneventfully. That's just not this man's style.

Pre-race publicity heralded 1962 as a banner year, with no less than ten competitors, including seven jet cars. The cast included Thompson, Arfons, Ostich, Craig Breedlove, Glenn Leasher, Bob Knapp, Bill Fredrick, Ernie Immerso and Bob Funk.

In addition, the car that carried Athol Graham to his death in 1960 had been rebuilt and was reported ready to return to Bonneville. It was quite an array of hardware.

Breedlove, a twenty-four year old Californian, was building his three-wheeler, Spirit of America. Arfons had abandoned conventional power and was readying his jet-thrust Cyclops. Dr. Ostich was back with Flying Caduceus. Leasher was set to drive the jet-powered Infinity. Thompson couldn't wait with Challenger I.

In addition, Knapp was constructing a four ton monster, propelled by a pair of J–47 jet engines. Fredrick was also relying on jet power, but his entire machine was to weigh 2960 pounds, including fuel.

Immerso had a car driven by four Ford engines. It was a scaled-up version of his old twin-engine creation. Funk was also working on a four-engine contender.

But by countdown, five jets, plus Thompson's Challenger I, and Graham's City of Salt Lake were involved in the dangerous game.

By August 9, 1962, Flying Caduceus had progressively increased its speed from 296 to 324 miles an hour. Now, Ostich was ready to turn on full power.

Reaching a speed of 331 after about seven miles, the car suddenly went into a spectacular slide. The left front wheel snapped off.

Finally, the fifty-two year old driver deployed his safety chute and the 6500 pound car came to a halt. Ostich said he sensed trouble when the racer began veering to the right as he passed the three mile marker on the twelve mile long straightway.

"I had trouble pulling it back on course," he said, "and then started shutting off power. It still wouldn't come back so I popped the chute.

"I felt the car spinning and I thought I was going into a roll. I did everything automatically – the things I had learned in numerous practice runs. I didn't know I lost the wheel until I felt the car go down."

Ostich had only one thought during the slide.

"I didn't want to burn. That was the one thing on my mind and I remember grabbing for the extinguisher overhead."

Although he wasn't injured and the car sustained minor damage, Ostich and his crew returned to California to modify the jet. He was through for 1962.

"At high speed", he explained, "it is impossible to control the car with wheels. At speeds between 319 and 324, it handled perfectly. But if you get the least little bit out of line, say only two degrees, there's 19,000 pounds of pressure pushing on one side. There's just no way to hold it. At high speed the only thing you can do is control it with a rudder."

Why the crash?

The left front wheel spindle had broken off, causing the wheel to come loose. As a result, the excessive transfer to the left-front of the car when it began slipping sideways caused the break. It marked Ostich's thirteenth run on the Flats.

Next it was Arfons and his 8000 horsepower Cyclops.

By 1962, Arfons was campaigning his one-eyed monster on the drag race circuit, hitting the 260 mile an hour range in a run that lasted less than six seconds.

"I knew I was going to go fast, and if I had five more gallons of fuel, I'm sure I would have gone 400," says Arfons.

Fuel tank capacity was twenty gallons. That's fine for a drag strip, but not when your car is perched two miles away from the measured mile.

"I was running there during a meet. It's get in line, wait, then make your run. You had to start two miles out. One mile closer..."

Arfons, nevertheless, averaged 330.013 for the mile. It still may be the fastest anyone has ever gone in an open cockpit car.

"It was really a bitch, but I couldn't put a canopy on it. If I'd have closed it in, I'd have taken air away from the engine. I was sitting right down in the engine.

"A friend of mine, Charlie Nesbitt, taped my glasses to my helmet 'cause it [the wind] was tearing my glasses off every time. If my head got turned, I couldn't straighten it. Some fun."

The jet was unique in that it was the first time in land speed racing that a wing was utilized. It was situated right behind the cockpit.

"The car wasn't streamlined and I was afraid that the ground effect air would pick it up and make it light where it wouldn't steer. So I put a wing to hold it down. It was geared into the suspension, just like my record-setting Green Monster. It was a huge wing on Cyclops, but it did the job."

Arfons dubbed the jet Cyclops after he started drag racing.

"I ran at a lot of strips where the lights were really bad in the shut-down area, so I put this landing light in the nose. I had it rigged to the same switch as the burner. When I lit the burner, the headlight would come on."

Cyclops was Arfons' first jet car. It was propelled by a J–47 engine. Later, he would install a more powerful J–79.

"With the 47, I'd run it at one hundred per cent. When I put in the 79, I didn't. I ran that car for four years and never had a problem. No scares. It was dependable. I ran it until I hired a driver and he ran it into a telephone pole and lost the engine. That's when I put in the 79."

In those early days, there were few jet dragsters on the circuit.

"I'd make mostly exhibition runs, but there were those dumb times when I'd run against the hottest local guy.

"We'd put the hotshot halfway down the track and the flagman would go down there. I'd be at the starting line and when the flagman waved the flag, we'd race.

"Life was good back in those days. I was in demand and raced as often as I wanted to, and I was running just about every weekend. I'd take some time off during the winter. I was making what seemed like a ton of money back in the sixties."

Even with limited fuel capacity, Cyclops was still a formidable land speed threat. His peak speed through the flying mile was 366, big numbers for those times.

"I was tickled pink with the car's performance. It only made me all the more anxious to want to go even faster."

Otto Anzjon, a nineteen year old mechanic from Salt Lake City, had rebuilt Athol Graham's City of Salt Lake.

According to Zeldine Graham, "...the idea of rebuilding the car was all Otto's. I would never have asked him to race, but he has expressed a strong desire to fulfill Athol's lifetime dream."

But what she did not reveal at that time was that young Anzjon was suffering from leukemia, that the death of Athol Graham had left him depressed, that his health was failing.

"I guess I should be scared but I'm not," said the teenager. "My parents say it's okay and I'm most eager to drive the car."

Anzjon successfully passed the 250 mile an hour hurdle when the car suffered a blowout. The only damage was to the skin, which was ripped by the pressure of the blowout.

In the winter of 1962, Otto Anzjon died.

Breedlove, a veteran at El Mirage Dry Lake but a newcomer to Bonneville, drove a three-wheeler, which looked like an exotic plane without wings. Plagued by steering troubles, he reached only 300.

Now the spotlight was on Glenn Leasher and Infinity.

The twenty-six year old drag racer and part-owner of Infinity was two-tenths of a mile through the measured mile when his jet car exploded at speeds exceeding 300 miles an hour.

Observers said he entered the mile with afterburner on, but shut it off after passing the marker. Whether or not he sensed trouble and was cutting the engine could not be determined. He was killed instantly as Infinity was turned into a mass of twisted metal. The date: September 10, 1962.

Two land speed fatalities in three years. Who would be Unlucky Number 3? After all, tragedies come in threes.

"Everything appeared to be working all right when he suddenly disappeared in smoke and flame," said USAC's David Petrali, who was manning the telephone nearest the crash site. "Then the car started tumbling."

Leasher, who had been driving dragsters and jalopies since he was fifteen, was attempting something revolutionary in land speed racing.

He revved up the engine while keeping the wheels locked with the brakes and gave himself about a half-mile running room before entering the measured mile. While this practice was common in drag racing, it was new on the Flats.

In August 1962, twenty-three year old Chuck Hatcher of North Hollywood, California, had recorded a 300 clocking on a test run.

Bill Fredrick, the twenty-one year old builder/owner from Woodland Hills, California, felt confident his Valkyrie I would crack the existing land speed record.

"She drove straight as an arrow and I know she'll go faster," he said.

However, as a result of Leasher's death, Fredrick found himself without insurance.

"The accident soured them [insurance companies] on another try now with a jet. Jet cars are a new thing and they aren't used to them yet. We'll just have to wait for next year."

Despite his optimism and the speed potential of his car, Bill Fredrick did not return to Bonneville in 1963. As a matter of fact, he never did challenge the world land speed record with jet propulsion.

But that's another story!

A determined fifty-five year old doctor, a humiliated twenty-six year old drag racer, a forty-six year old veteran, the widow of a land speed aspirant. They all came to Bonneville in 1963.

Dr. Nathan Ostich was once again at the Flats with his Flying Caduceus. Breedlove and his Spirit of America, a wingless F-104 Starfire, were a big flop in 1962. Now he was back with this modified monster.

Walt Arfons, the Ohio grandfather who built the first jet dragster in 1959, was making his first Utah appearance.

Zeldine Graham had rebuilt her late husband's piston-powered car. Driver Harry Muhlbach would try to fulfill Graham's dream of a land speed record.

Before a heart problem ended his driving career Walt Arfons had hoped to sit in the cockpit of his jet-thrust Wingfoot Express. But that was not to be, so thirty year old Tom Green of Wheaton, Illinois, was given the chance of a lifetime.

However, the 8000 horsepower jet was knocked out of contention after only four runs when salt was sucked into the engine.

Next it was Breedlove's turn. He was hoping for better things, and not a repeat of 1962 when his mechanics couldn't even get the jet engine started.

Steering problems had developed in the car's radical guidance system, which used wheel brakes and a canard fin with all three wheels fixed.

Newsmen gave up after the three-wheeler failed time after time to even make it through the timing clocks. One run was a 240 success. The rest of the time Breedlove veered from the course at speeds up to 300 miles an hour, by his own estimate.

Breedlove and his Spirit of America became the butt of countless jokes about 'Speedlove's Folly', 'Shell's White Elephant' and 'Goodyear's Goat'.

It was widely reported that Ostich, who lost a wheel off his four-wheeled jet at more than 300 mph, walked around his disabled vehicle and said, "Tell Craig that three wheels aren't enough."

In reflecting on 1962, Breedlove admitted, "I was extremely disappointed." But this was another year, and a new Spirit.

The front wheel was made steerable through two degrees in each direction; a six foot high vertical tail fin was added to increase stability and move the center of pressure to the rear; the industrial-type disc brakes were rigged to work from a single brake pedal; the throttle linkage was arranged for either hand or foot operation, where formerly it was operated only by hand.

Late in July of 1963, Spirit and her crew were back at Bonneville. Numerous test runs and minor adjustments were made. On July 31, Breedlove drove the thirty-five foot long jet to a speed of 276 and reported no problems. In all, he made twenty-two practice runs before he was ready to shoot for a record that had stood for sixteen years.

On August 4, 1963, Breedlove unofficially hit 365.93 and set five records in the newly created USAC (United States Auto Club) jet class. His marks were 335.6 in the kilometer, 356.4 in the mile, 330.52 for five kilometers, 313.1 for five miles and 287.36 for ten kilometers.

He was confident of faster things to come.

"We have a steerable nose wheel now and it has been great in practice runs. The six foot high tail fin has been a big help in guiding the Spirit."

It was August 5, 1963. At 3:30 a.m. the crew made the eleven mile drive from Wendover to the Salt Flats to make last minute preparations. About two hours later, Breedlove arrived. He was in high spirits.

"I had a sip of water for breakfast and I feel fine."

He joked with his crew by putting on an old GI helmet shortly before he stepped into the cockpit at 6:30. He turned to a crowd of photographers and newsmen.

"I don't know why everyone is out here. We're just continuing our normal speed build-up."

But everyone there, including USAC and FIM (Federation Internationale Motocycliste, since his three-wheeler was technically classed as a bike) officials knew otherwise. They knew this would be a run for the record.

In a raspy voice, USAC official L.T. Torros announced: "Zero [wind] at the south and she's all clear."

Slowly, Spirit of America began to move. Then it gathered momentum and in a matter of seconds was out of sight.

"The measured mile was eleven miles long, but the first two miles were too rough to use. I was starting at the two mile mark, and even so, the salt was bumpy enough to bounce the Spirit several times while accelerating toward the other part of the track ahead of me.

"Salt began whirling around the cockpit, whipped up and powdered by the front wheels. In spite of the cotton I had pushed into my ears inside the crash helmet I could hear the scream of the jet's compressor and some of its exhaust roar.

"The hard tires crunching on the salt, even the rattle and the bang of components inside the car were audible. And the ride, like all the others, was rough as well as noisy."

Breedlove's first run, using ninety percent power, lasted 9.267 seconds through the measured mile. The speed: 388.47.

"I started the [first] run several feet to the right of the center stripe and the wind soon drifted me across the line. I stayed there. The car was still accelerating when I went through the light beam that marked the end of the measured mile and the kilometer. But by now, only four miles of salt were left and it was time to start shutting down.

"I took my foot off, coasted until I was approaching the ten kilo marker and then pushed the steering wheel knob that flames out the engine and jettisons the drag-chute door.

"When the door popped open it deployed an eight foot chute that served as a high-speed brake. The chute whipped around quite a bit and swerved the car from side to side, but I wasn't nervous.

"When the speed got down under 150, I began using the foot brakes and rolled to a stop alongside the vehicles at the far end of the course."

For the all-important return run, Breedlove increased the power setting to ninety-five percent.

"By now the wind was freshening. Gusts were spilling out of a canyon west of the Salt Flats and creating crosswinds of seven and eight miles an hour on the course.

"I waited in the cockpit for a while, then the reports showed that the wind had dropped to five miles an hour (the legal limit). It was time to go.

"I started the run well over to the right of the center line and it's a good thing I did. By the time I entered the measured mile the wind had drifted the car forty feet to the left, close to the markers and the rough salt outside the smoothed course. I corrected slowly and kept my foot on the floor, still accelerating.

"The Spirit was traveling about 440 miles an hour at the end of the measured mile and I was taking my foot off the throttle when the car began a slight weaving motion."

He knew what the trouble was at once – the chute door had popped open again and released the chute. Breedlove felt sure of a new record for the mile, but thought he might miss new records for other distances. The chute was dragging the speed down rapidly.

There was a long wait at the south end after Spirit came to a stop. Joe Petrali, the man in charge, and his USAC timing crew were inspecting the tape, averaging the time and translating it into speed.

The word came to Breedlove the same time Petrali was making an announcement to the press at the timing stand: "Gentlemen. We have a new land speed record!"

Craig Breedlove had blasted through the measured mile in 8.404 seconds, or 428.37 mph. His two-way average: 407.45.

The young, handsome Californian was jubilant as he emerged from the cockpit. "It feels great," he told the two hundred spectators. "I had a lot of throttle left and the car came through in fine shape. I'm certain I can go much faster."

While Breedlove wanted to stick around to increase his speed record, Shell Oil, his chief sponsors, decided to leave well enough alone.

Technically speaking, the late John Cobb still held the wheel-driven record of 394. But to the world, Craig Breedlove was the fastest on wheels.

Dr. Ostich tried to quiet the critics: "The main thing is you have to just get up there and drive."

Even a disappointed Donald Campbell, who had traveled to Lake Eyre in Australia for a land speed assault, praised Breedlove's performance. He called it a "jolly good effort".

Breedlove's car had three wheels instead of the conventional four. In addition, Spirit of America was propelled by pure thrust, rather than by a piston engine that transmitted its power directly through the wheels.

"I don't think this is really important," added Campbell. "Technically, yes. But in the eyes of the world, no. If we were to succeed in beating Cobb's record with Bluebird and fail to break Breedlove's as well, then in my mind, we have failed."

Campbell was back home in England when Breedlove went 407.

Three months earlier, Campbell had taken his big gamble and failed. He had laid much of the blame for his 1960 crash on the length of the Bonneville course – eleven miles – because the placement of the measured mile at midpoint left little room for braking.

He wanted a longer speedway and narrowed the choice to three sites – Lake Eyre, a dried-up salt lake in Australia, a site in the Caucasus Mountains and a site in the Trucial of Oman in the Persian Gulf area.

Campbell ruled out the Trucial of Oman site because it could not be reached by road or rail. The site in the Caucasus was not suitable because it was in the USSR.

That left Lake Eyre, located 450 miles north of Adelaide, South Australia, an area which few white men had explored.

It offered 3700 miles of salt flats. And just as important, it hadn't rained at Lake Eyre in seven years during the time period Campbell would attempt to set the record.

Several persons, including Campbell, went out to see the salt beds at first hand. He even drove a Jaguar at more than 100 miles an hour across the salt, which was harder than Bonneville's. Then the team of British companies backing the venture weighed the first-hand evidence.

Campbell's backers decided that Lake Eyre would be the site for several reasons: a longer raceway, which meant that acceleration and braking could be more gradual, and better traction because the salt bed was so hard and dry.

In addition, the danger of crosswinds would be greatly reduced, provided the attempt was made in April or May, because studies conducted over a thirty year period showed the calmest conditions had been recorded then.

Campbell and his team felt they had the perfect speedway for the perfect car. Since his spectacular '60 crash, Bluebird had been meticulously rebuilt and a lofty tail added for stability.

But little did Campbell, or his team, realize how difficult a job it would be. Heavy floods between mid-April and mid-May forced the team to safety at Lake Eyre.

On May 12, 1963, the sky was cloudy again but Campbell drove his jet at a respectable 240 miles an hour and said the car "behaved magnificently".

Six days later, however, he finally had to concede defeat. All Donald Campbell could do was wait until 1964.

Meanwhile, back at Bonneville the speed season was not yet over.

In 1960, Zeldine Graham vowed to rebuild the ill-fated City of Salt Lake. She believed her late husband's car had a 420 speed potential.

On October 12, the flame-red racer went out of control and slid 1000 feet on its top before coming to a halt. Harry Muhlbach escaped without injury.

There was no fire and most of the outside aluminum was still intact, although considerably bent. The Allison aircraft engine appeared undamaged.

The car was on its first run of the day. Muhlbach had just passed the measured mile when the four-wheeler went into a half-mile long slide, rolled over twice and landed upside down.

The slightly stunned driver said the tachometer was on about 4250 or 4300 r.p.m. and figured he was doing "above 395 miles an hour" when he crashed.

However, chief steward Joe Petrali said the timers calculated he was "doing 240 sideways" during the wild gyration.

Reason for the crash: the braking chute popped out, sending the car careening out of control. It was the same problem that had haunted Muhlbach for four days.

"I just about lost it twice Friday [October 11] because the chute was out," he said.

He dragged the parachute for ten miles down the track during a preliminary run and was unable to get above 200. As with the crash, he was unaware the safety chute was out. The City of Salt Lake was using a new parachute for the record runs.

"Awfully disappointed" about the crash, Zeldine Graham said she would delay her decision about rebuilding the car for a few weeks. "I'm not thinking right now."

Early in November 1963, she reached her decision. She would go racing in 1964.

Why?

"To try and retrieve some of the money I've spent on it. I don't know what it will mean by way of money if we beat the mark. But it should bring some of it back.

"It will take money. Unless we can find someone to help by way of parts, it will be my expense. Two of the [Firestone] tires are gone. We figured that some piece of wire cut up one of the tires on the last run and caused our defeat. Another was also cut. Where the wire came from I don't know.

"We may get some financial help on the body. Otherwise, we don't have much to do to put the racer back on the run. We expect to have it ready to go in the spring."

There had been considerable opposition in Salt Lake City to her plans to rebuild the car. People feared someone else might be killed in it.

"We have thought about it for a long time," she replied. "But we'll try again. We came so close last time."

In September 1963, Dr. Ostich was back with a modified jet.

The suspension, made up of modified standard truck parts, was junked and replaced with aircraft components. The steering wheel ratio was slowed for better high speed control and a new steering shock absorption unit added to front steering arms.

In addition, tires on the streamliner were modified to provide more tread and traction.

It had been reported that the project had cost Ostich more than $100,000 and involved 10,000 man hours. The doctor would not confirm this.

Despite the changes, his luck didn't improve.

On September 21, Flying Caduceus spun out of control during a practice run. Moments before, Ostich had been clocked at 322 and was slowing down when the machine began to spin. His estimated speed at the time was seventy-five miles an hour.

Members of the crew said Ostich apparently applied the brakes too hard. Damage was minor.

"Gee, I didn't realize it was so slippery down there," he said as he climbed out of the cockpit.

On September 27, 1963, Dr. Nathan Ostich made runs of 354 and 351 miles an hour as Caduceus showed signs of engine trouble. Two days later he dejectedly called off further attempts after a 359 run.

"The experts have done all they can here. We just can't get that last ten percent of power."

It was his last ride.

Maybe Ostich thought it was time to leave the daredevil driving to the youngsters. After all, he was fifty-five years old.

To build a faster jet car would take a lot more capital, and he had spent enough to fulfill his dream.

It had become too obvious after repeated effort that his needle-nosed Flying Caduceus would not crack the 400 mile an hour barrier. The options were clear: start from scratch or reluctantly retire.

Dr. Nathan Ostich did the latter.

Former motorcycle speed-king Don Vesco and his 425mph streamliner.
Vesco drove the car with the turbine engine in 1996.
Photograph courtesy of Don Vesco.

The Burkland family's 425mph wheel-driven car. The son, Tom
Burkland, is the driver. The car made its first appearance at Bonneville
Salt Flats, Utah in 1996.
Photograph courtesy of the Burkland Family.

Alexander Winton *(above)* and Ranson E. Olds, both pioneer automobile manufacturers, were the first to race on Ormond Beach, Florida. In 1902, they clocked identical speeds of 57mph in a wheel-to-wheel duel.
Photograph courtesy of the *Birthplace of Speed Association*.

HENRY FORD IN HIS SPECIAL RACER WITH WHICH HE COVERED THE MILE, FLYING START, IN 40 SECONDS

In 1904, Henry Ford powered his hand-built, six cylinder *Arrow* across a frozen lake outside Detroit, reaching a top speed of 91.370mph.
Photograph courtesy of the *Birthplace of Speed Association*.

Barney Oldfield in the *Blitzen Benz,* March 1910 at Ormond Beach, Florida. He set a world record of 131.724mph. The car had a four cylinder, 200 horsepower motor and 112 inch wheel base.
Photograph courtesy of the *Birthplace of Speed Association.*

Henry Segrave of England with the *Sunbeam,* 1927. He was the first man to travel at a speed of 200mph.
Photograph courtesy of the *Birthplace of Speed Association.*

Sir Malcom Campbell sits in the cockpit of the *Bluebird*. During his lifetime he set seven land speed records.
Photograph courtesy of Clayton L. Gontmer.

Sir Malcom Campbell drives his *Bluebird* to a new land speed record of 276.816mph at Ormond Beach, Florida, March 1935.
Photograph courtesy of Robin Richardson.

George Eyston of England, holder of the world land speed record. He battled with fellow countryman, John Cobb, for the title during 1938 and 1939 at Bonneville Salt Flats, Utah. Eyston's massive *Thunderbolt* reached a top speed of 350mph.
Photograph courtesy of Clayton L. Gontner.

John Cobb sits in the *Railton Special*. The car set a land speed record of 394mph in 1947 which wasn't broken for 16 years until 1963.
Photograph courtesy of David Tremayne.

John Cobb's *Railton Special* at Bonneville Salt Flats, Utah, during the record run in 1947 of 394mph – a world record which lasted for sixteen years.
Photograph courtesy of the *Deseret News Publishing Company*.

Ab Jenkins' famed *Mormon Meteor*. He set numerous record marathon-runs on Bonneville Salt Flats, Utah.
Photograph courtesy of the *Firestone Tire and Rubber Company*.

The *Green Monster 6*. This was the first dragster to reach a top speed of 150mph in 1956.
Photograph courtesy of Art Arfons.

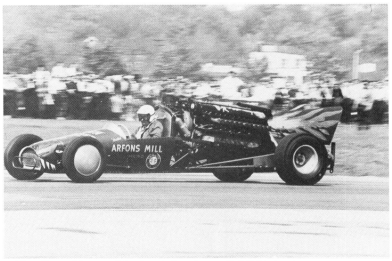

The *Green Monster 11*. Art Arfons has called it his best car.
Photograph courtesy of Art Arfons.

Don Garlits' *Swamp Rat*. He and Art Arfons were drag race rivals during the early days of drag racing.
Photograph courtesy of Don Garlits.

Left: Art Arfons with the *Anteater*. *Right:* 'Doc' Nathan Ostich with the *Flying Caduceus*, Bonneville Salt Flats, Utah 1960.
Photograph courtesy of the *Firestone Tire and Rubber Company*.

Chapter Fourteen

Craig Breedlove... the Spirit of America

If a driver gets in over his head then he's not a good driver. Craig Breedlove is a very good driver. During his first year at Bonneville [1962] with his three-wheeler, the car never handled. It took him all over the place. As I recall, one of his sponsors wanted him to stay and work out the problems, but he said he wouldn't do it and took his car home. He said he'd be back when the car was ready to make a run for the record.

That took guts. Now that's a good driver. He had a fixed wheel and at about 300 his car would sorta mosey around, get off course and he couldn't bring it back. That sponsor had a lot of money invested in the car, but Craig knew running it harder wouldn't suddenly fix the problem. He knew his equipment. He knew wishing didn't make it so. The guy came back in 1963 with a modified car. He and his team did their homework, and he set his first of five land speed records.

Art Arfons

Flashback!

Return with us now to the early 1970s when the 'hot' topic was the mysterious sound barrier. Which driver was going to drive faster than the speed of sound? Reigning king Gary Gabelich? Former kings Craig Breedlove or Art Arfons?

Breedlove, who set five records between 1963 and 1965, put it this way:

"I'm thirty-six now [he was born in March 1937], and I'm sure I don't want to be doing this when I'm fifty. There are too many other things. My son is sixteen and building a dragster.

"I want to help him all I can. After the sound barrier, I'm going to hang it up. I guess I'd rather be remembered as a designer than a builder."

Fast forward, some twenty years.

Gabelich loses his record in 1983, and his life in a highway accident a year later. His plans for a rocket car, powered by four engines, die with him.

Arfons, at age sixty-four, tried a 1989 comeback in a radical two-wheeler. The 'bike' went airborne at 350. He came back to Bonneville in 1990 and 1991 with a 'legitimate' four-wheeler, but couldn't capture the glory days of the 60s.

But those who know him realize this isn't the end of this fairy tale story.

But what of a much older Craig Breedlove?

The man with other things to do with his life simply wanted to take care of 'unfinished business' with Spirit of America – Sonic Arrow, an 850 mph creation scheduled to be unleashed at Black Rock Desert, Nevada, in 1996.

Prior to his Black Rock adventure he said:

"At that time, I would have liked to have gotten my car sponsored, got on with it. But reality wasn't to be. I just took a lot longer. And besides, as far as I'm concerned, no one has broken the barrier.

"I know I haven't been in one of these cars for a long time, so I guess it remains to be seen whether I can still do it. I think I can.

"I'm still a very active guy. I'm very much interested in the land speed record. Another thing is I frankly feel I have a lot of talent and would like to express it in that area.

"Unfortunately, I didn't do it back when I was thirty-five. But the record really hasn't moved all that much since I went 600.601 in 1965. That seems in my mind easily within my grasp to do."

Then he pauses a moment and laughs.

"What else would an old guy like me do?"

Craig Breedlove has kept himself in excellent shape through the years.

"I'm like everybody else. I get on a jag and get in real good shape. Then I get bored with it and slack off. I'm a periodic physical fitness enthusiast.

"Basically, I've done things that many people do. I watch my consumption of fat. I don't smoke and I haven't had a drink in more than five years. I don't say I'll never have one, but I don't seem to have the desire anymore.

"Back in 1965, I probably weighed 150 to 155. Now, I probably weigh between 155 and 160. I'm probably five pounds heavier than I was thirty years ago.

"As the time gets closer to actually getting in the car, I'll probably jog and do light workouts. I don't think that even at my age, the 'fine-tuning' will be that extensive."

Chasing the dream has always been in the back of his mind.

"I've been wanting to go back for years, but for various reasons, as you go through stages in your life, you reach places where you need to do things financially and businesswise.

"You have to take a sabbatical away from chasing a land speed record. I'm in the best financial shape ever. My biggest problem was getting my life into a situation where I can personally focus most of my attention to this. This is not a part-time thing. This is total concentration on only one thing."

Breedlove was prepared to not only start the project, but finish it without any major sponsorship. As it turned out, such giants as Chevrolet, General Electric and Shell Oil, jumped on the 'Breedlove Bandwagon'.

"My motivation has absolutely nothing to do with money," he says. "I think there was a time in my life when I hoped I would make money with land speed racing. I don't have many of those illusions anymore."

Craig Breedlove's fascination with speed dates back to his childhood. He was born on March 23, 1937 in Los Angeles, California.

"At first, I was more fascinated by the mechanical end of cars," he recalls. "The way I got started on them was that the older kids in the neighborhood had a club called 'The Igniters'. I used to hang around with them. I was about twelve and most of them were sixteen or seventeen.

"They took a liking to me. They'd take me to drag races on weekends. I got real interested. I talked my mom into letting me get a car for my thirteenth birthday. I had a little money myself. At Christmas time, I asked for money instead of presents so I could save up for a car.

"I got a 1934 Ford for $75. I had about $45 and my mom and stepdad gave me the other $30 for my birthday. Of course, I was too young to drive. I couldn't drive for three years. I had to promise I'd just work on the car.

"Well, I took that car completely apart, every piece. It was all over the place. I bought hot rod magazines and read all about hopping up cars. I bought special gears for the rear end and installed them. I cleaned the frame and repainted it. I got a super-charged '48 flathead Marc engine.

"About all I did was work on that car, but I didn't have any idea at all of driving."

When he was sixteen, Breedlove brought his hot rod to a race course at El Mirage Dry Lake – but not to drive it. Since 1938, the Southern California Timing Association (SCTA) had used El Mirage for speed trials.

Not long before showing up at El Mirage, Breedlove had driven a car in a race at Bonneville and finished eighth.

"It scared me a little. The car kinda slipped around a lot. I thought it was kinda dangerous.

"El Mirage sort of scared me too. Everybody said it was a tricky course, so I lined up a guy to drive for me. But he was already driving some other cars and the association told me he couldn't take another one. I gave it a try myself."

The reluctant driver calmly went out and set a class record of 142 miles an hour.

Breedlove graduated from Venice High School, majoring in drafting and machine shop, "so I could build parts for my racing cars."

While still in high school, he spent his time around drag strips, working long hours on cars and performing a variety of mechanical jobs.

He worked for two years at a Santa Monica firm that specialized in building race cars. Breedlove added to his store of skills by becoming an expert welder and learned many of the basic principles of speed-car building and design.

Later, he installed air conditioners, then worked in a parts department at an auto agency. From there he went to Douglas Aircraft as a structural technician.

In 1960 he joined the Costa Mesa fire department.

Why a fireman?

"To make more money. It was a good job. Nice pay, nice guys. It was what I wanted to do with my life.

"I didn't think I was accomplishing anything of significance where I was. I wanted to do something more historical. I began thinking that a lot of young Americans were just as good at designing and building cars and souping up engines as were the racing teams of Europe.

"I became convinced that we could build a car that would capture the unlimited record for the measured mile. After all, we lacked only money. These ideas gradually jelled into the Spirit of America project."

He was twenty-two years old, with no college education. Just a dream.

Until Craig Breedlove came along, a string of British drivers had dominated the land speed picture. Segrave... Campbell... Eyston... Cobb.

Ray Keech had been the last American to set the record, and that was back in 1927.

"As a youngster," recalls Breedlove, "Charles Lindbergh was my hero, my role model. I put together models of his plane. I saw his movie starring Jimmy Stewart.

"I loved the name of Lindbergh's plane, Spirit of St. Louis, so when I seriously began to think about a land speed project, the name came easy. I stole 'Spirit of' from the plane and added America. I felt as if I was really racing for my country."

Married at seventeen, he was divorced at twenty-two, the father of three children.

"My wife didn't understand what was inside me to do these things. Everybody wants to do something. People who haven't any drive never get things done."

However, Breedlove's second wife, Lee (they were divorced in 1968) understood what he wanted. She had two children by a previous marriage and shared a love of speed. She was just the kind of encouragement Breedlove needed to launch his seemingly impossible dream.

His first thoughts were of a piston-powered, conventional streamliner. But he soon found out he could buy lots more power for the same price in a jet engine. Further, a jet car would be simpler and far more efficient.

Breedlove drew up plans for such a car, but realizing his limitations as a designer, he turned to experts for help. Through his enthusiasm, he enlisted the aid of an aerodynamicist, a propulsion engineer and a model builder. More than one hundred wind tunnel tests were run for design improvement.

At this point, two years into the project, Breedlove's meager resources ran out.

During this time, the Breedloves learned to live with two air duct molds, ten feet long and weighing one thousand pounds, lying on the living room floor. Breedlove jacked up the rear wall of his garage, moved it back twenty-one feet and extended the roof to cover it. The garage now measured forty-one feet by twenty feet and made the attached five-room house look like an appendage.

Rod Shapel, an automobile designer and project engineer at Task Corporation, drew up the first blueprints.

Art Russell, a model builder for Revell, carved a model out of pine to be used in wind-tunnel tests.

Walt Sheehan, a Lockheed engineer, concocted the air ducts that led from the nose to the rear section and fed air to the jet engine.

The original J–47 engine came from Ed Perkins, a Los Angeles machine shop owner and a bishop in the Mormon church. The J–47, taken off scrapped B–36 and B–52 bombers, produced 5000 pounds of thrust, or 10,000 horsepower.

Breedlove tried to interest major companies in his project, but met with no success until October 1961. Casting about for sponsorship he walked into the Santa Monica district office of Shell Oil and asked to see the manager.

Under one arm he carried a brochure, under the other was a box containing a model of his unique racer. Thinking he was a Shell dealer with the same name, the manager agreed to see Breedlove. When he learned of his error, the manager asked Breedlove to limit his call to ten minutes.

Two hours later, Craig Breedlove was still talking and the manager, fascinated by the prospects and the young man's enthusiasm, was hooked.

Within three months, Shell had agreed to become a sponsor. Goodyear Tire and Rubber agreed to design and build the forty-eight inch tires, as well as machine the wheels and make the brakes.

Breedlove's partly completed machine was moved from the garage behind his home to the shop of Quinn Epperly, a leading builder of racing cars. For months the work went on.

In August 1962, the $250,000 Spirit of America was loaded on a trailer and brought to Bonneville. Accompanying it was an expert crew of more than twenty men, equipped with everything from a complete machine shop to spare parts.

"It was handmade, I mean made with hand tools, a little file and a screwdriver," says Breedlove, proudly. "The car was the equivalent of a prototype fighter plane that would take an aircraft company millions of dollars, twenty thousand men and all their machinery to build."

Breedlove had incorporated theories in the building of the car that had yet to be proven on the salt. The car weighed nearly three tons, stood six foot high, thirty-five foot long and eleven feet wide. It was quite an awesome-looking piece of machinery.

It was supported by only three wheels: one forward and two on a semi-rigid outrigger set up aft. None of these wheels was steerable.

He planned to steer by braking the two rear wheels independently from floor-mounted pedals up to about 150. From then on, a canard fin under the nose was expected to have enough bite in the slipstream to provide control via a conventionally mounted steering wheel. All braking was by parachute.

While Breedlove drove the three-wheeler at speeds estimated at 300 miles an hour, numerous 'bugs' hampered the car's performance. Light crosswinds caused it to veer from the marked course.

The differential braking on the rear wheels, used instead of a steerable front wheel to maintain the car on course, was unable to correct the veering.

The only recourse was to quit running in 1962 and return to the drawing board. New engineering talents were called in. The car was modified in several ways.

The front wheel was made steerable through four degrees. A six foot high vertical tail fin was added to increase stability and move the center of pressure to the rear.

The aircraft-type disc brakes were rigged to work from a single brake pedal. The throttle linkage was arranged for either hand or foot operation, where formally it was operated only by hand.

Late in July 1963, Breedlove was back on the Salt Flats. He reached a speed of 276 miles an hour and reported no problems.

Five days later – August 5 – the twenty-five year old Californian climbed into the cockpit, pushed the throttle to a setting that represented ninety percent of the power, and moved down the track.

At that point, Breedlove had driven Spirit of America less than two hundred miles in a total of twenty-two test runs.

Speed for the first run: 388.47. Quickly the car was turned around, refueled and ready for the crucial return trip. This time Breedlove set the throttle at ninety-five percent power and roared through the measured mile at 427.37. Average for the runs, calculated from the elapsed time, was 407.45 mph.

Craig Breedlove had broken the world land speed record set by John Cobb of England sixteen years before. He was the fastest man on wheels.

But he wanted to go faster. "I don't think the limit has been reached yet. I think I can go faster. The course was bumpy, but the car held up well under the punishment."

Breedlove decided to return to the salt the next day. Then it was announced he would fly instead to New York for personal appearances. Shell and Goodyear wanted to take full advantage of the publicity.

Meanwhile, in Paris, the FIA said Spirit of America was not an automobile and referred all questions concerning recognition of the record to the Federation Internationale Motocycliste (FIM) in Geneva, Switzerland, which welcomed the sudden attention.

In New York, Breedlove said: "I call it a car, because I built it as a car. As far as automobiles go, John Cobb's record still stands."

Late in 1963, after the furor of his achievement had subsided, the team of experts went back to work on Breedlove's car. The Spirit was given a new J–47 engine with 5700 pounds of thrust. The nose was given a more streamlined configuration.

A new set of wheels and tires were installed, but not because of wear. They were taken out of service for historical and exhibition purposes.

By the time the great jet shoot-out between Breedlove and Art Arfons, the Akron, Ohio, drag racer, had ended in 1965, the friendly rivals had set seven land speed records. The speed had risen from 407 to 600.601.

Breedlove's worst moment on the salt took place on October 15, 1964. Two days previous, he had regained the record from Arfons with a two-way average of 468.72. But neither he nor his crew was satisfied.

"I knew I had the record by the way the car performed. It ran beautifully and I managed to miss the rough spot on the course. I'm confident I can hit 500 miles an hour on land and I plan to stay until the job is done."

Breedlove had a sense of imminent danger. "I awakened more scared than usual that morning and the feeling stayed with me. It was usually gone by the time I was completely awake. But this day it lingered, this feeling of fear, or something unexplained."

He managed to crack a faint smile as he climbed into the cockpit. "I shivered again as I sat down. In the mornings, the seat is always ice cold. The cockpit was stark and uncomfortable. The whole thing seemed unsure. I was very apprehensive.

"But for some reason, I don't really know for sure, I stayed with it. Maybe it was because I honestly felt that this was going to be the best ride anybody ever had."

His gloved hand was steady as it held the steering wheel. His knees weren't shaking, but somehow the gnawing fear was still there.

"I took a deep breath and I felt a little better."

The car drove straight and true. Breedlove hit 513.33 mph on his first run. Usually cooperative with the press, Breedlove wouldn't talk.

"I told them to wait until after the second run."

As Breedlove streaked towards the start of the measured mile at speeds approaching 500 miles an hour, "I heard a loud snap and the car began pulling badly to the right.

"Frantically, I turned the wheel to the left. The car came back on course, but I had the steering wheel turned completely upside down. I didn't know whether to abort the run or stay with it and hope for the best.

"I dimly realized that I must have lost one of the suspension bolts and that the front wheel was beginning to camber over. I was steering the car like it was a motorcycle, and it was starting to lean more."

Breedlove was approaching the measured mile.

"All I could do was hang on and see if I could hack it through the timing lights. The front wheel was leaning more and more and was straying off course again.

"I feared I would hit one of the timing lights. I had to back off the throttle. When I did, the car immediately seemed to right itself. It was as if some torque had been released allowing it to go straight again.

"Then it hit me that I could get through the second set of lights without hitting anything. I smashed down again on the throttle and the engine caught and relit. With a big burst of speed, the car cleared the last marker under full power."

The air speed indicator hit 550. Apparently, the danger had passed.

Breedlove began reducing the power and hit the first chute button.

"The first chute came out of its can and I felt a slight tug. I knew I had lost my chute."

He waited for two miles before firing the emergency chute gun.

"The dynamite charge went off and there was nothing. The emergency chute must have come out with the first one. It, too, had been ripped away. I punched the button again and again."

He looked at his brake pedal, then the air speed indicator. Just a tick under 500 miles an hour. The decision wasn't difficult.

"I knew if I didn't use the brakes then, there wouldn't be any later.

"So, I pressed the pedal and it smashed right to the floor. I pumped it again and again, and I could hear the sickening thud of the pedal hitting the metal floor. I had absolutely no brakes."

Soon, he was at the end of the course. Ahead was rough salt, a row of telephone poles, a shallow lake and a ten foot high salt dike. Beyond the dike was a deep lake.

"There was nothing else to look for outside. The markers were gone, I would have to ride it out. The engine was shut down and I could hear only the slamming and banging of the suspension as the car sped over the rough salt surface beneath it."

Straight ahead was the row of telephone poles. "I steered to the right and the car moved over a little. Then I put my head down, ready for the impact."

Divine luck must have been riding with him that day.

Spirit of America hit and splintered one pole, shot up an incline, soared over the dike and finally nosed down, three miles off course, in the canal of salt water eighteen feet deep.

He hit the embankment at about 200 miles an hour, sideways. An outrigger caught the embankment and swung the flying jet car level and straight.

"Just like an airplane. I could see the reservoir water ahead and thought I'd better get the canopy latches open. The canopy hatch had four guide pins and any misalignment when I hit would jam the hatch."

He released the canopy while airborne before the car skipped across the water and then settled. He was climbing out of the cockpit when crew and rescue workers reached him.

Almost hysterically he shouted, "'For my next act, I'll set myself on fire'. I was all in one piece. I just rolled over and started laughing."

When Bill Neely of Goodyear reached the scene, Breedlove told him, "I'm okay, baby, what's my speed?"

He was timed at 539.89 through the mile for a two-way average of 526.26. Breedlove had to be coaxed into an ambulance. At nearby Wendover it took him thirty minutes to convince the doctors he was okay.

By nightfall, the once proud Spirit Of America was finally pulled out of the lake. It marked the last ride for the sleek three-wheeler that had thrilled the racing world and turned a hot rodder from California into an international hero.

During his 'glory' years, Breedlove earned as much as $300,000 per year from endorsements, public appearances and a lucrative contract from Goodyear, as well as a sweet deal with American Motors.

But a divorce took half of everything he had. His shop buildings at Torrance, California, were flooded out, virtually wiping out his livelihood.

"We had prepared two AMX cars and set endurance records with them," recalls Breedlove. "I made Lee an integral part of the program. The two of us, plus a third driver, broke something like 114 Chevrolet records that were set by Smokey Yunick.

"I really loved that type of racing. We averaged 175 miles an hour at Goodyear's five mile circular track at San Angelo, Texas. I'm quite proud of that achievement considering we had only eight weeks to put that entire program together.

"Actually I went to both Ford and Chevrolet with the same proposal. Ford was kinda lukewarm and I had no reason to believe they would go for it.

"So I went to Chevrolet. I talked about using Camaros to set an assortment of endurance records. They liked the program, but they'd been working with Smokey Yunick and they didn't want to switch horses in midstream. They gave Smokey my program and he set more than 100 records."

Breedlove didn't have time to work up a new proposal, so he took what he had – the Ford and Chevy proposals – and tried to interest AMC in the program.

"American Motors called me in December 1965 [one week before Christmas], and wanted to know if I could prepare cars for the seemingly impossible task. We did a crash program in eight weeks, put the cars together and broke all of Smokey's records.

"I think it was a significant achievement from the standpoint that Chevrolet and Smokey Yunick had years and years of background in developing the Chevy racing engine and all of the cars. We had to develop and build the whole program with engines that had never been on the track before, or rear ends, transmissions, anything. To go out and take on Chevrolet head-to-head and beat them... WOW! American Motors were impressed."

In addition to the endurance cars, Breedlove had built The American Spirit, a wheel-driven streamliner geared to break Bobby Summers' 1965 wheel-driven record of 409 mph.

"We actually took the car to Bonneville in the summer of 1968 but no sooner did we start unloading the car and equipment than one of those sudden storms hit us. You know how quickly the Salt Flats flood out. We were standing around in eighteen inches of water."

Thus, Breedlove never had the chance to attack the wheel-driven record.

Breedlove had also built a fuel Chrysler dragster. He also had a Goodyear tire dealership. Things were looking good... for a while.

At about that time, Breedlove's thoughts turned to Indianapolis and the famed 500 race. He actually designed and started building two turbine-powered cars.

"I very much wanted to go to Indy, not just as a designer/builder but as a driver of one of the cars. Danny Ongais was going to drive the second car. He had been a drag racer and had made the successful transition to Indy cars.

"Heck, I was only twenty-eight years old. It wasn't like you'd be trying to teach an old dog new tricks. I was going 175 miles an hour, full out around a banked test track at the time Indy cars were going 160. I knew I could do it.

"Obviously, it takes practice and skill to do that. Racing in general is a repetitive thing. You do it and do it. You get better at it. I didn't have any reservations.

"I felt if I could be afforded the practice time I could learn the track. In my mind, I thought I had a really good chance. That's why I was doing it."

Unfortunately, Breedlove's Indy deal never materialized. Another dream unfulfilled.

During this time period, his marriage with Lee was falling apart.

"When she filed the divorce thing it was pretty devastating. I don't think it would be anywhere as damaging today. And when the flood came, they said that's that.

"Automobile sponsors are basically conservative companies and what you are for those companies is a representative to the public. They spend millions of dollars to make sure that all of the condensation beads on a beer can look just perfect. They'll spend that kind of money just to present that thirty-second image,

"Whoever represents their company must enhance that company, and anything associated that can possibly be construed as detrimental or negative in any way shape or form, they want to cut their losses and run. They must totally disassociate with you.

"In the 1960s, the moral climate and attitude of this country was quite different than it is today. It wasn't nearly as liberal."

Craig Breedlove was at the Kingdome in Seattle when he got the phone call.

"Buster called. He was Keely Smith's brother and was helping me with some business problems. He was in the shop when it happened.

"He called and said we had a real problem. I said, 'What problem?' He said, 'We've had a flood'.

"I thought, 'What is he talking about?' I couldn't even comprehend and didn't really ask any details. I asked if he wanted me to come right home. He said it really wasn't necessary, that I should fulfill my contract at the Kingdome, then take the first flight home.

"When I came home and saw the damage it was inconceivable that could have happened. I had two buildings with over 15,000 square feet. At the time I probably had forty employees... but you can't conduct business with almost everything ruined and forty-eight inches of water turning your buildings into swimming pools.

"The torrential rains occurred about three or four o'clock on a Sunday morning. There were no workers from the City of Torrance on the job.

"They had a system of large sumps that collect water to help out the drain system so that they can actually store water and pump it out later on after the rain subsides. It's a kinda stop-gap system.

"We had had extremely heavy rains and all of the sumps were full. These sumps have a float mechanism in 'em so they won't overflow. What happens when they get right to the brim, then the float automatically turns the pumps on and delivers the water from the sump system back into the storm drain system.

"All of the sumps filled to capacity, the pumps came on and so it pumped all of that water into the storm system when it was already peaked out. That caused the area where my industrial buildings were located to flood."

Breedlove estimated the total loss at $750,000.

"I lost the J–79 engine from the Spirit of America – Sonic I car, all of the engines for the wheel-driven streamliner, all of our supplies, our equipment."

Breedlove had to lay off all his workers. He had no choice.

He lost his sponsorship from AMC, his Goodyear store. He was in heavy debt.

"It took years to pay everybody," he says with pride. "I didn't want to declare bankruptcy. I didn't want to go out owing anybody a penny because that's just not my nature. I paid everybody off every cent that I owed. It took me years to dig out of debt.

"It was a difficult time. It was draining emotionally. But I guess from the worst of times you learn the most, you grow the most. I'm stronger, a better person."

Breedlove tried to recover through his racing, but ultimately he turned to real estate and as a super salesman started bailing himself out and putting his life back on the proper track.

He also learned about true friendship.

"Ted Halibrand was one of the few guys in that whole ordeal that didn't disassociate himself from me. Fortunately, the streamliner I built for the wheel-driven record wasn't damaged in the flood.

"I took all of the running gear, all of the transmission, the differentials that Ted had built for me. I went to him and said, 'Look, I'm really in a terrible financial bind. I want to give you back all of the materials. I'll pay you whatever... If you can't sell it, I'll make good on it.'

"He just put his arm around me and said, 'Look Craig, you've got enough problems. Don't even think about this stuff. You don't even owe me a penny. You'll make it back. There will be other days.'"

Breedlove built a rocket system for the streamliner and would eventually run the dragster at speeds approaching 400 miles an hour in the quarter-mile.

By 1970, a team in Wisconsin had built a rocket-powered land speed car called Blue Flame. Craig Breedlove was asked to drive that machine.

"But at the time," he recalls, "I was trying to put through my program, my own design.

"I had some reservations about the design of that car with respect to the rear struts. I didn't like the rigid strut design in the back. I had concern that with these outboard struts there was the danger of developing a harmonic frequency.

"It could reach a certain frequency and become excited. That would create a problem in the car. The rear end could come off the ground, or spin out of control. You could be killed in it.

"I told them if I got involved I would want to have final say in all engineering aspects of the car. Of course, Blue Flame was their baby. They didn't want it to be a Craig Breedlove creation.

"They were quite convinced that all of the wind tunnel tests on the car were very reliable. I didn't believe it was gospel, the last word.

"They wanted to pay $10,000 total to drive the car and I told them I would be better off if they broke my record so that I'd have something to shoot for.

"I thought the $10,000 figure was inadequate for the risk involved. I told them it would not add to my fame or publicity, that they really needed to find someone who could derive great benefit from the record, not just from a money standpoint, but what the land speed record could do.

"They said, 'Dan Garlits will drive it', and I said, 'Well, God, if you can get Garlits to drive it for $10,000, that would be great'. They told me I was their first choice and I was certainly flattered, but it just wasn't for me."

A short time later, Breedlove received a phone call.

"The Garlits thing didn't pan out and they wanted to know who else I would recommend. I said Gary Gabelich. He was at a place in his career where he could benefit tremendously as the result of setting a land speed record.

"Gary certainly had the credentials as a drag race and drag boat driver. He was a good-looking guy and was quite personable. Besides, I thought he'd probably be willing to do it for that kind of money.

"At that point I hadn't even talked about it with Gary. That wasn't my job to do so. They called me back and wanted more information about Gary. Then they contacted Gary and I figured everything was fine.

"Then I got a call from Gary. He said, 'I don't know what to do with these guys. I signed all these contracts and now they're telling me they don't even know if I'm gonna drive the car or not. I don't know how to handle this'."

So, Craig Breedlove accompanied Gary Gabelich to the Astrodome in Houston, Texas, to meet with officials of the sponsoring American Gas Association, as well as the car builders of Blue Flame.

"I told them they'd better make up their minds as to which driver they wanted to drive the car, Gary or the other driver. I told them I was going to recommend to Gary that he just drop the whole thing and walk away.

"That was enough to firm the deal. They said, 'We don't want that. We like him better.' In October 1970, Gary Gabelich broke my five year old record, and I was glad that he did."

By the mid-1970s, Craig Breedlove was starting to turn around his life. But through all these years, he'd never lost interest in the sport that made him a living legend.

He built a mock-up of a supersonic rocket car, but that deal fizzled.

He talked of an assault on the world water speed record, but it was not to be.

The timing wasn't right. Promises weren't kept.

Time passed, more time than Craig Breedlove had wanted, but he's still young enough to fulfill the dream.

Breedlove considers his first car his best, his first record the most memorable.

Spirit of America, a radical three-wheeler which resembled an exotic fighter plane, established records of 407, 468 and 526 miles an hour between 1963 and 1964.

Spirit of America – Sonic I went 555 and 601.601 a year later.

"Let's try to get the record straight," he says concerning his three-wheeler. "Almost every book on land speed racing I've read lists the 407 record as unofficial.

"That's really a misstatement because it was fully sanctioned by the FIM and timed by USAC. FIM sanctions one, two, three-wheel records. USAC is the official timing body in our country.

"Until my three-wheeler came along, every car had run under FIA sanction, but technically Spirit of America wasn't a car. It was a motorcycle.

"It was the first time in land speed racing history that the FIA found itself in the strange position of no longer having the prestige of sanctioning the world land speed record. FIA sanctions cars, meaning four or more wheels.

"So FIA put out a statement that they didn't sanction the run. That in itself was correct but somehow that got misinterpreted to mean if FIA didn't sanction it, it was therefore unofficial.

"What's really funny, in just about every book, my 468 and 526 records are classified as unofficial, but not the 407. It's the same car, a three-wheeler. All were sanctioned by FIM and, as I said, timed by USAC."

Speaking fondly of that first car which 'resides' in the Peterson Museum in Los Angeles, Breedlove says, "The aerodynamics as far as the ground effect was better in the first car. It's negative aspects were that the single nose wheel tended to tram in every kind of rut or groove that was on the course.

"There was some inherent handling problems with the three-wheel configuration. But that could have been designed out of it. Setting that first record was realizing the impossible dream."

In cementing his 526 record, Breedlove went on a wild ride, splintering telephone poles and landing nose first in a salt pond.

Spirit of America – Sonic I literally wanted to fly.

He averaged 600.601 just eight days after rival Art Arfons had regained the land speed record with a 576 sortie.

He pushed Spirit of America – Sonic I to the absolute max.

Prior to his 600 performance, the four-wheeler lifted off the ground.

"After my near aerial act," says Breedlove, "we knew we had an inherent problem underneath the car. But all we could do at the time was make the nose wings [canards] larger to create downforce to push against the air pressure under the car. [They also put lead in the nose.]

"We increased the area of the nose fins about two and a half times and we had them at their maximum angle of downforce. We knew how to solve the problem, but Goodyear said there was no reason to do so until Art came back and actually broke my record.

"As it turned out, Art crashed at 610 miles an hour in 1966. His car was destroyed. There was no longer a threat to my record. But for the sake of 'what if', I would have built a new nose configuration.

"We needed aluminum formers and things like that, that were in Southern California, in order to complete the work. I would also have had to camber the front wheel fairings, sorta banana-shape 'em so that the air would not accelerate between the wheels.

"I had the car up to 640 when it lifted the first time. We still hadn't tweaked the engine. That car was probably good for 675 with a new nose."

On his run that cemented the 600.601 – 608 mph – "the car was on the verge of doing it again. Would I have been disappointed if say I averaged 599 instead of 600? You betcha.

"My goal was to go 600. We had the speed indicator at 600 marked with a red line. We barely squeezed out the 600. I was sweating bullets because I'd already had one experience of doing a wheelie."

Since Breedlove's 600 mile an hour performance, only a handful of brave men have taken aim at the land speed record. Gabelich's standard lasted thirteen years when Noble went 633.4 in 1983. That remained untouched for more than a decade.

"I'm not really surprised at the lack of activity," says Breedlove. "It's extremely difficult to do. Many people underestimate how hard it is."

Breedlove had nothing but admiration for Noble's record-setting performance.

"I think Richard Noble is an incredibly talented and very unique individual. Not too many people in the United States know much about him. He's a remarkable human being.

"He has uncanny business abilities, a singleness of purpose. His quest for the land speed record lasted nine years. He has a marvelous personality, and very, very good verbal skills.

"And quite frankly he was able to do back then what I could not do and that's put together a significant sponsorship program to go for the record. I give him all the credit in the world because I certainly know it's not easy. If it were anyone else but Richard Noble the British probably wouldn't have the record."

And naturally, Craig Breedlove has the highest of respect for his old land speed rival, Art Arfons.

"We had totally opposite approaches. Art would like to come up, just get in the car, boom and get it over with. He used to say, 'I don't know how you keep running that thing up and down. Why don't you get it over with and get outta here?'

"I would say, 'I want to be really familiar with this car and the course. I want to understand it, have a good feel for it and feel like I'm part of the machine.'"

Bill Neely, the former Goodyear racing spokesman, isn't surprised at anything Craig Breedlove sets his mind to doing.

As Neely, now a highly respected author of seventeen books, puts it: "He could still be doing this stuff when he's sixty-five. Even when he had his bad years, he never lost his positive attitude, his youthful enthusiasm. He still has it.

"I was involved with Goodyear and racing for seven years – Indy, NASCAR, Formula One, land speed racing. A lot of great drivers.

"The only other person who had that same fierce competitive nature was A.J. Foyt. Sure, their personalities were the exact opposite, but there are parallels between Craig and Foyt.

"Craig was a winner. A.J. was a winner. Neither one of them liked to lose. Both approached their tasks in similar manners with very good equipment, perfectly maintained. They were both highly mechanically skilled. They knew what the car was doing at all times, what forces were working against the car.

"Both were keenly aware of their place in racing history. Foyt wanted to be the first to win four Indy 500s, and he did that in 1977. Craig wasn't interested in the number of records. He was interested in the big stuff, the benchmark records.

"He wanted to be known as the man who brought the land speed record back to the United States, and he did that in 1963. He wanted to be the first to average 400... 500... 600... and he realized those goals. I'm sure he wants to be the first to average 650... 700... the first to break the sound barrier as well."

Neely, who considers Craig Breedlove, "one of my closest friends", never saw him scared. "I never saw any fear. I saw some apprehension with the four-wheel car as Craig approached speeds of 600 miles an hour when the panels started buckling and the car was getting very, very light. There was an apprehension.

"He was a little tense before his final runs, but I never saw him pace up and down like you see a lot of race drivers do before a race. He was always jovial. When he averaged the 600.601, he was greatly relieved... and you couldn't blame the guy. That car was ready to fly."

Goodyear's first involvement with land speed racing was sponsoring the late Mickey Thompson's four-engine Challenger I in 1960.

"Mickey went 406 one way," recalls Neely, "but the car broke during the second run. It looked like Mickey would never get the job done, so we switched our attention to a young hot rodder from California.

"He came to Goodyear in Akron with a model of his car under his arm. He ended up in the office of Russell Young, chairman of the board for one of the nation's largest corporations, and proceeded to charm all of us.

"He came with the model, a romantic story about how he wanted to bring the record back to America, this enthusiasm and believability. We believed if anyone could do it, it would probably be Craig.

"He coaxed $10,000 each out of Goodyear and Shell to build the car. And some $200,000 later," Neely says, with a chuckle, "the three-wheeler was finished.

"When I first saw the car, I was impressed with the massiveness of that car, thirty-eight feet long. But more than that, I was impressed by the workmanship, the quality of construction. It was absolutely perfectly finished. It looked great and I said to myself, 'If it runs half as good as it looks, we've got the record'.

"Craig's first year on the salt [1962] was a disappointment. He tried like hell, but couldn't control the car. We knew very well he was going to come back in '63 and do it. But nobody wanted to wait another year. We still had a great deal of faith in him.

"When he went 407 to break John Cobb's sixteen year old record, I took Craig on his first cross-country press junket. We hit something like forty-two cities in forty-seven days. When we started he was a kid from Los Angeles who spent most of his life underneath a car.

"The only things he knew to order from a menu were spaghetti or steak, but by the time we finished the tour, he was a connoisseur of fine wines. He grew up real fast.

"He was always a great interview because of his sincerity and his charm. A lot of people referred to Craig as 'Jack Armstrong, the All-American Boy'. He was clean-cut, good-looking."

Neely's most fearful moment came when Breedlove's three-wheeler went out of control, splintered telephone poles and crashed into a pond.

"I was down at mile zero with the press corp where Craig would normally come coasting to a stop, open the canopy and jump out. But he went by at 500 miles an hour. I jumped in my rental car to chase him, which was absurd, of course.

"I lost sight of him because he ran off course into shallow water. All I could see was a spray. By the time it settled down, I could see the tracks going over the dirt dike. I got up on top and I could just see the tail fin of the three-wheeler sticking out of the drainage ditch.

"About this time Craig had bobbed to the surface and swum to the shore. He was on an absolute emotional high. He was giddy. If there's any humor in a 500 mile an hour crash, it was when they finally loaded Craig in an ambulance which was at the Salt Flats just in case. They were going to take him eleven miles away to a hospital in Wendover.

"But the driver was so excited, he was careering across the flats and Craig was scared to death. The guy had just survived a 500 mile an hour escape and he was afraid he was going to be killed on the way to the hospital. He kept screaming, 'You guys are gonna kill me'."

The great jet battle between Breedlove and Arfons was a PR man's delight.

"And even when Art broke Craig's record, our press releases were always upbeat, pointing out that Craig was ready to come back for the record.

"We had the greatest respect for Art Arfons. He was always ready. Craig was always ready. In fact, after Craig survived the crash, Goodyear still had time reserved on the salt.

"You buy the time from the State of Utah, but you just can't stay home. You have to keep running. Breedlove had gone as fast as he could. Art was waiting in the wings.

"The weather forecast called for rain to move in and probably end the racing season. That's what we were hoping for, so we borrowed two Cobra Daytons from Caroll Shelby and Craig and Bobby Tatroe, one of Walt Arfons' drivers, ran for circular track endurance records. It was total boredom.

"They ran hour after hour, day after day, just to keep Arfons off the salt. But wouldn't you know it, the bad weather held off long enough. Arfons went out, averaged 536 in his Green Monster. We had nothing to come back with. The strategy was good, it would be a long winter waiting to renew the greatest duel in land speed racing history."

By the end of the 1965 speed season, Craig Breedlove would get the last laugh, grabbing the record away from Arfons and becoming the first to break the 600 mph barrier.

Chapter Fifteen

Britannia Versus the Colonies

The battle between me and Craig in 1964–65 was great. I always knew he was my chief competition, the top threat. He was always there, ready and waiting to do me one better. I always had the utmost respect for him. But I don't think he was ever impressed with my Green Monster. He told somebody it was as streamlined as a barn door.

His first Spirit of America was about the most beautiful car in land speed history. It was a piece of art. It was so efficient. It was limited by horsepower. It had no afterburner. He could have put on a burner and gone a lot faster.

Art Arfons

In 1963, Craig Breedlove increased the world land speed record by thirteen miles an hour... from 394 to 407. A rather modest boost.

During that historic speed season, Art Arfons was back in Akron, Ohio consumed by a passion that would take more than 5000 man hours to turn a dream into the most powerful beast Bonneville had ever seen... his 17,500 horsepower Green Monster.

Between 1964 and 1965, Arfons and Breedlove waged 'The Great Jet Battle'. During that blistering period, the record soared to 600.601 miles an hour!

In the end, the handsome Californian would prevail.

Now let's start from the beginning.

Breedlove knew he had a winner in his three-wheeled Spirit of America. All the bugs had been worked out from its disastrous 1962 debut.

Walt Arfons' jet-powered Wingfoot Express proved a dud in 1963. But this was another speed season... a season of renewed hope.

England's Donald Campbell, flooded out in 1963, would return to Lake Eyre, Australia, in 1964 with his turbine-powered Bluebird.

It would be the battle of the jets. Britannia versus the Colonies.

The memorable speed season began with the record at 407.45. It would end with the land speed increased to 536.71 mph... a jump of more than 120 miles an hour!

Campbell, son of the legendary Sir Malcolm Campbell, was first on the firing line. After almost three weeks of waiting, he was ready for his first practice run. On May 5, Campbell clocked an uncomfortable 170. The salt was so soft, the four ton car chopped ruts three inches deep. Campbell knew he couldn't make a record run under these circumstances. He searched hundred of square miles, both by air and from the ground, for a harder running surface, finally settling on a new track north of the existing course.

With the aid of tractors pulling steel girders, a new speedway was carved out. The next step was to test the surface. Campbell gave the surface bursts up to thirty percent of full power. It was hard enough to warrant extending the track to thirteen miles.

At least the track had been found, but now a new danger suddenly developed. Hitting speeds around 300, Campbell experienced violent vibrations. However, when the wheels and tires were changed, the vibrations stopped as suddenly as they had started.

The solution had been found – or so it was thought. Salt sticking to the insides of the wheels had put them out of balance, so the wheels were to be thoroughly cleaned before each run.

His best clocking was a respectable 389 on July 1. Seven days later, Campbell announced that his present series of attempts would be postponed for the time being. The surface of salt had become too dangerous.

He returned to Lake Eyre in mid-July and said he planned to make four runs, no more. All he needed was a dry surface and no wind.

On July 16 he received word that Breedlove had announced intentions of returning to Bonneville in September to boost his record. Campbell knew he had to act fact, but the following day was Friday.

It was a Friday in 1960 that Donald Campbell escaped death on another salt track thousands of miles away. But determined to duplicate the feat of his father as the fastest man on both land and water, Campbell pushed his fears aside for a run at the record.

His battle cry: "Friday be damned!"

On July 17, 1964, the course was dry and the breezes subsided to a barely safe two miles an hour. He fired the jet engine and Bluebird streaked across the salt.

But immediately the car seemed to be weaving and cutting ruts on the surface. The rear tire began throwing rubber. Somehow, Campbell held on and raced through the measured mile at 403.1 and 388.7 for the kilo.

Almost an hour later, he started the crucial return run. The vibrations shook the car, but Campbell just gripped the steering wheel harder and managed to complete the run.

Again his speed was 403.1 through the mile, and a slightly quicker 400.5 through the kilo. When Campbell stopped the car, the right rear tire tread was completely gone. Chunks of his Dunlop tires were scattered over seven miles. Again, he said, he saw visions of his father.

"I nearly killed myself. I was so near going out of control that it wasn't even funny. And when I was sitting in the cockpit at the end of the run I really thought I had had it. For I knew the second run would be worse. I saw no hope at all.

"It was then that it was so extraordinary. You know how the canopy lifts up with the windscreen in front of the cockpit? Well, I suddenly looked up into it and there was my father reflected in the windscreen. I even recognized the white shirt and flannels he used to wear.

"For a few seconds he just looked at me, smiling, then he said, 'Well boy. Now you know how I felt that time at Bonneville in 1935 when the front tires burst at 300. But don't worry. You'll be all right, boy.' Then he faded away."

Campbell's big disappointment was not traveling faster than Breedlove. He had to be content with the wheel-driven record.

That same year, Donald Campbell gunned his jet-powered boat, Bluebird to a two-way water record of 260.32, thus becoming the first man in the annals of speed to set both the land and water records during the same year.

Back at Bonneville, Walt Arfons' Wingfoot Express, with Tom Green at the wheel, was the first on the salt. Arfons was confident.

"Barring an unforeseen accident or car failure," he said, "I feel we can better Breedlove's record. My car has more thrust – 7000 pounds compared to 5200 – therefore more power and more speed."

In 1963, Wingfoot Express was sidelined when salt was sucked into the J–46 engine. Specially constructed guards, designed to deflect the salt spray, were expected to turn the jet car into a winner.

On October 1, the thirty-four year old Green raced into history, by setting a land speed record of 413.31 mph on runs of 406.55 and 420.07. But it wasn't easy.

In fact, it wouldn't have come at all had it not been for Art Arfons.

It had been a long, frustrating week for Walt Arfons, the forty-seven year old grandfather, and Green, a businessman from Wheaton, Illinois.

"Even when I made my first run Monday [he set the record four days later], I was getting pressure in the cockpit. There was indication around the windshield. Too much pressure would have ripped off the seven foot Plexiglas cockpit canopy.

"There was also engine-pulsating the first day. The whole car felt like it was shaking. There was also power surging. I just couldn't control the car. It would have sluggish movement, then unexpectedly start surging.

"Walt thought the engine was bad, so we replaced it with a spare. We finally tried a new engine Thursday night... but it wasn't running right. Things were looking plain miserable.

"That night we removed the 450 screws holding up the engine panel and checked it over. We also found out the fuel line was okay but the car wasn't getting enough fuel."

Key adjustment was widening the exhaust opening from seventeen to nineteen inches.

"By Friday morning we had an engine we could trust even though the horsepower was reduced. With full power I was only able to get up to 299. It was rather frustrating. Walt then decided to try the afterburner which I had never tried before."

Pulling the lever three times produced an additional 4000 horsepower. Green averaged 406.

"I used it in bursts, using the burner three times while the car was in motion. The power burst was terrific."

Because of what he thought was a fuel shortage, Green started the return run only two miles from the measured mile. One half mile from the timing lights Green pulled the burner lever, "but it didn't hit hard at all... about one-third of the previous power.

"I just kept the lever down through the mile. The needle vibrated at 400 and I thought we missed the record. I was tickled pink to find out the car averaged 420. Going 400 miles an hour was quite a thrill, like falling through the sky."

The record shows, Wingfoot Express made fourteen futile runs before claiming the jet title. As it turned out, time was running out. Green cemented the record with less than an hour of daylight remaining.

It was the last day that Walt Arfons had use of the salt. Next up was his younger brother, thirty-eight year old Art Arfons and his Green Monster. Following Arfons, was Craig Breedlove and his record-setting Spirit of America.

Walt Arfons would have had to wait two weeks for another chance, had not some friendly advice turned frustration to joy.

And that advice came from none other than Art Arfons.

Art was already at Bonneville, watching his older brother's car fail time after time. He decided to pass on his remedy to Tom Green who admitted, "It was a significant contribution."

"At seventeen inches", said Green "the engine pressure became too great and the fuel metering system automatically cut off the fuel supply." And although the engine lost horsepower with the bigger cone, it functioned properly for the first time.

"Walter had struggled in 1963, and '64 looked like a real bummer," recalled Art Arfons. "All I did was pass on a suggestion. Even though Walter was my rival, he was still my brother."

Arthur Eugene Arfons came to Bonneville with the most powerful engine in land speed record history, a GE J-79 jet engine with four-stage afterburner. It powered military aircraft to speeds exceeding Mach 2. So why couldn't it push a land-bound vehicle to speeds exceeding 500 miles an hour?

Arfons had been to Bonneville twice before in an Allison-powered car which hit only 313 mph because of mechanical problems and a jet, an open-cockpit jet dragster which didn't have the fuel capacity to run through the measured mile... not at 400 miles an hour, that is.

The key to any success he might enjoy was obtaining a classified J–79.

Therein lies the story.

"I was looking specifically for the J–79. I had a J–47 in my Cyclops and I knew it wasn't enough. Breedlove's Spirit of America went 526 with a J–47, but I knew I couldn't build something as streamlined as he had. I didn't have the money. So I had to have enough horsepower to push what I had."

He needed a car small enough to fit into a school bus he turned into a transporter.

"Every junk yard I went to said, 'If you ever get a 79 gimme a call', and I left my card at each place. I knew the J–79 was considered classified, but a funny thing about that. Sometimes you can get an engine you're not supposed to have because the military is junking them.

"I was running at a dragstrip in Denver and I got a call from a guy in Florida. He dealt in scrap only. He had a damaged J–79. It was taken out of commission for FOD – Foreign Object Damage. It had something run through the engine.

"How did the guy get his hands on the engine? You always bid on it. He must have been a high bidder. Usually you bid on a binful of stuff, and the 79 must have been included in what he bought."

So far, so good. Art Arfons' long shot search was over.

"I called my friend Charlie Mayenschein who lived in Dayton and asked him if he wanted to go down to Florida with me and pick up the engine. He said, 'Sure', so I stopped by and picked him up and we left. I had the bus I used to haul Cyclops in to transport the engine back to Ohio.

"When I saw the 79, it looked pretty good to me. Sure, I looked inside and saw all those bent blades, but I wanted the engine. He wanted $600 and it was a done deal. I didn't try to chisel down the price.

"I never said nothing, just gave him the $600 in cash and we put it in the bus. Of course, I didn't even know at that point whether or not the engine would run.

"There was no sense in trying to straighten out the blades, so I just pulled them out. I figured the engine had more than enough power without them.

"A few days after I got back home, I called General Electric, told them I had a J-79 and asked them to send a manual.

The guy said, 'You don't have that engine. You can't have that engine.' And I said, 'Well, I sure do'. The next day or the day after that, a colonel from Washington showed up at the shop and said that's a classified engine and I can't have it. I said I bought it and showed him my sales receipt.

"The colonel stomped out. Then I got a legal letter from GE, a real nasty letter saying the J-79 was made for marine and aircraft use and it should never be put in a race car."

Art Arfons ignored the officer. He ignored the letter.

The battle plan was relatively simple.

"I hung the engine up and built the car around it. It took a good year to build"... some 5000 man hours. Seven days a week. No let-up.

Because Arfons was limited by the length of his old school bus, he couldn't put the cockpit in front. So, he decided on twin cockpits. He drove from the left side. The dummy right cockpit was for aerodynamic purposes.

It cost more than $4 million to build Donald Campbell's Bluebird, some $250,000 for Breedlove's Spirit of America. Excluding the special tires and wheels designed by Firestone Tire and Rubber at an estimated cost of $50,000, Arfons' investment in his Green Monster was about $10,000.

The government spent $1000 at the time to build an ejection system capable of parachuting astronauts safely back to earth. Arfons paid $3 for a sawed-off gun which he fired to eject his two chutes.

An intricate metal-forming machine sold for $10,000. Arfons built one for $36.

The tailpipe was made of titanium, an unusually tough metal. Arfons constructed a huge grinding wheel to cut and shape the tailpipe.

The only blueprints for the Green Monster were in Art Arfons' head. When Firestone's engineers requested blueprints to design the wheel and tires, all Art could come up with was a hubcap. Firestone then built the tires to conform to the hub.

Arfons built the jet car in his own garage on Pickle Road. Garage dimensions: forty-two feet long, thirty-two feet wide. He built the car twenty-one feet long.

Arfons knew he had something special the first time he fired the J-79.

"I was standing beside the engine. I ran it in a frame on the ground before I ever got the car built. It was awesome.

"There were a whole bunch of guys standing around when it started. It ran so fast up to idle everybody started running. They ran across the road and up the hill. They thought it was gonna explode. I turned around and I was all by myself.

"That engine had so much power. It didn't make a difference if it was missing sixty blades. I never did open it up full power. Firestone took pictures of that test firing. It was quite a sight!"

Afterwards, Arfons would chain his Green Monster down between two trees, and let 'er rip with full afterburner. The engine shrieked, windows rattled and neighbors knew it was just that crazy character on Pickle Road playing his own kind of music.

A man and his dreams headed West, to Bonneville. A junkman with a junk car.

Three days after watching Walt Arfons' Wingfoot Express break the land speed record, Art Arfons took his first ride on his Green Monster. He clocked an easy 350.

Afterwards, Arfons said, "...the car felt good. I was using only half power."

This was supposed to be a 'breaking in' period, man getting used to the machine. No high speed stuff.

H.A. 'Humpy' Wheeler was back in Akron. He was Firestone's racing PR honcho. Wheeler knew Arfons wouldn't do anything crazy like take dead aim, on the land speed record, not with him 15,000 miles away from Utah.

But Wheeler didn't know this guy.

On October 5, 1964, Art Arfons slipped into the left-side cockpit.

"I was just going out the first time and try for 375, but the car felt so good, I nudged it a little more."

Official speed was 396.34 for the mile, a quicker 401.68 in the kilometer. Arfons was within striking distance of the land speed record.

USAC chief steward, Joe Petrali, informed Arfons that he had to average 438 on his return run to break the record. Arfons decided to go for it.

"I turned it loose, but didn't use all the power. In fact, I didn't even turn on the afterburner. It was a tremendous sensation. Everything went by so fast that it was almost over before I got started good."

Arfons' second run was a blistering 479.62 mph for a two-way average of 434.02. Walt Arfons and his driver, Tom Green, had basked in the glory for seventy-two hours.

It would be the third shortest reign in a sport that began back in 1898!

Firestone engineers estimated Arfons utilized about 10,000 of the available 17,500 horsepower on the record-sealing 479 run. There was plenty of kick left in the $600 engine.

Despite the record, Arfons wasn't ready to return home, not with Breedlove lurking in the shadows.

"I'll make a decision tomorrow on whether or not we will try for the record this week," he said. "If we do decide, we will be prepared for a much further increase in speed.

"With a few adjustments we think the car is capable of breaking 500 without a lot of trouble."

He had spent less than five minutes of riding time in the cockpit in total practice time and in making his successful two-way run.

How does it feel to travel close to the ground at that kind of speed?

Close you eyes! Use a little imagination!

Let's take a ride in Art Arfons' Green Monster.

You're sitting in the right cockpit. Arfons drives from the left cockpit.

You're strapped in tight.

The Monster is started externally.

"Ed [Snyder] runs the Buick engines that we set up direct drive to the front shaft. The engine comes to life. I turn on the fuel, set the throttle and hit ignition. When we get a fire, I crank up the power to sixty-seven percent which is idle.

"I let the crew know I'm ready. They shut down the engines and pull it out of the nose. I never had any radio contact. It's all done with hand signals. The engine noise is deafening.

"My pedals are just like in a car, right foot for gas and left foot for brake. The air speed indicator is set out about eight feet in front of the body, right in front of me. I don't have to look for it. It's in my sight.

"I'm sitting right against a red-hot section of the engine. The heat gets unbearable. By the time the twenty-second run is over, it feels like an inferno.

"I know the engine's got oil pressure, fuel pressure, everything's running fine. I've increased the power to ninety-two percent. Time to let it rip.

"I look out the cockpit window and see the air speed indicator, the long black line. Every mile on the course is marked. I know I'm into the measured mile. My huge green and black checkerboard marker is easy to spot, even at 500 miles an hour. Leaving the mile, the markers are colored with black and red florescent crosses.

"The first time I was out at Bonneville, I had smaller markers without bright colors, and darned if I didn't miss the shut-off sign and drive out in the soft salt. So Bud [Arfons' crew member Bud Groff] came up with the monster signs.

"About halfway through the measured mile I start backing out of the throttle so that I won't have a terminal speed way too fast for my tires. I go in full power, stay in for about three seconds, then start slowing down. About a mile later, I put the main chute out.

"You feel like you've got the chutes out the minute you get out of full power. You're on your seat belt, hanging on. You're slowing down real rapid. When you put the first chute out, it really grabs you, like you've run into something. A brick wall. The straps pull so hard they bruise my chest.

"I hit the first chute at about 500 miles an hour. If the main chute doesn't open, there's a back-up chute. And if the second chute doesn't work, you're up the creek. Then you're gonna go for a long ride.

"When you try to make a correction it seems like it's in slow motion. It's like if you had the wheels mired down in the mud and you tried to turn and it won't turn. You're putting all of your force into turning the steering wheel, and it takes forever to bring it back just five feet.

"It takes about twenty seconds to get up to peak speed, six second through the mile. So the whole thing lasts less than a minute. What's forever is when you put the chutes out. You're seven to eight miles from the starting line.

"I get out of the car, walk around. I'm lookin' at the horizon and I can't see nobody coming. I think, 'What happened? Did I hit something?' No one's coming. It takes a car at a hundred miles an hour a long time to get down there to you."

Arfons always carried a variety of good luck charms with him on each run, gifts from friends as well as strangers.

"My mom gave me a little medal, a St. Christopher medal. I always took that one with me. I always had the feeling my dad was driving with me. It was just a feeling I always had."

Two days after setting his first land speed record, Art Arfons decided to shoot for the 500 mile an hour barrier.

He would make several practice runs before taking dead aim on a speed once thought unattainable on land.

But little did Art Arfons realize that a plot had been hatched. A stowaway would sneak into the unoccupied right-side cockpit with a tape recorder to chronicle the ride of his life. The perpetrator: Arfons' close friend, Charlie Mayenschein.

H.A. 'Humpy' Wheeler, at that time Firestone's PR representative, but now the man who runs Charlotte Motor Speedway, recalls that incident.

"First of all, Chuck had more than a passing interest in Art's car. He not only made the wooden scale model of the Green Monster but did a lot of the car's body work.

"About two months before the incident, he asked me if he could ride in the car and I said, 'Absolutely not'. But the guy wouldn't take no for an answer.

"The first day Art took the car out, Chuck again asked to take a ride. Since Art wasn't planning to go over 250, I said okay. Art went 225 in his first run and Chuck must have gotten the bug.

"He stayed in the background when Art broke the record. Apparently nothing happened the next day when Art went out for a few trial runs. That day, however, Chuck laid his plans to hitchhike a ride."

Arfons met Mayenschein during the 1960s when he was campaigning his jet-dragster Cyclops. Mayenschein was a jet engineer working at Wright-Paterson Air Force Base in Dayton, Ohio.

"I met Charlie at a car show and we got to be friends. When I started building the big car, Charlie came around as often as he could to help. When it was time to go to Bonneville, he wanted to make the trip, so he went with me.

"When I was strapped in, I couldn't see the other side. As soon as I got the engine running, Bud [Groff] opened the canopy and Charlie jumped in with his helmet."

Arfons clocked an easy 413 on that run.

When the car came to a halt, Arfons climbed out of his cockpit and went around the other side to confer with Firestone engineers and his crew.

That's when he saw Mayenschein, still strapped in the cockpit and wearing a mile-wide smile. All Art Arfons could say to his friend was, "You crazy son of a gun." Mayenschein was killed in a 1966 motorcycle accident.

After that 413 stroll, Arfons made several more bursts, including a 468 clocking. Then he gently brought his Green Monster to 400... 430... 470... 490, with still a half-mile separating him from the timing zone.

Suddenly, Arfons felt an overpowering jerk on the right side of the car. The pull was so strong he thought the axle had broken and that he had lost the entire right wheel.

"It would have been a 530 run," said Arfons after examining the right-side damage. The right rear tire had exploded. There was damage to the panel.

Firestone engineers searched the area and found a three inch bolt which had been imbedded under the earth's crust, but shot back like a bullet when Arfons' car ran over it. That was the explanation.

Dejectedly, Arfons would have to return to Ohio to make repairs on the car. He had survived a two and a half mile ride after the blowout none the worse for wear.

"I really don't know if I ran over the bolt, or what," says Arfons. "But it makes a good story. All I know is that I left the door wide open for Breedlove and he took full advantage of the opportunity. He became the first to average 530."

On Monday, October 12, Breedlove turned a quick lap of 452, but hit a rough spot on the return trip, pitching his three-wheeler sideways. He hit the chute, and that ended the record bid.

A day late, Breedlove averaged 468.72 mph with runs of 442.59 and 498.13.

The return run, however, was not without incident.

"I shut down too late coming out of the measured mile and hit the wet salt. My head hit the canopy and broke the glass at around 480.

There's a big gash in my helmet, but I hardly felt it... I heard it more than anything when the glass exploded."

He hoped to make repairs before Art Arfons was back at Bonneville, trying to lift the record further away from his rival's reach.

Breedlove pushed the record to 526.26 mph twenty-four hours later, surviving a six mile runaway ride on the return run. Spirit of America splintered telephone poles and landed nose first in a pond. Breedlove swam to safety.

He suffered only bruises in the crash. He could have drowned.

That was the end of his beautiful car. He felt it would take two years to build another land speed contender. Or so he said.

Breedlove was in the middle of a Detroit news conference on October 27, when he learned that Arfons had shattered his record.

His comment: "Boy, isn't that something!" He meant it.

At 9:30 a.m. (Utah time) on October 27, 1964, Art Arfons clocked off a 466 south to north run.

At 1:07 in the afternoon, he went north to south and began the history-making journey... 515.98 through the measured mile.

Forty-three minutes later, using a two and a quarter run-up to the mile, he clocked an even faster 559.179 for a new two-way mark of 536.71 mph.

The car was accelerating rapidly as it left the mile. Then, the right rear tire blew again. Waiting one and a half miles after the left chute had ripped off, Arfons pulled the right chute. It popped, then almost shredded but held long enough to slow down the car.

Art Arfons emerged from the left-side cockpit with a smile on his face.

"My biggest mistake today, if I made one, was running too darned fast," he said.

"The tires [Firestone] did a great job. I had agreed not to run over 350 on the air speed indicator but my foot just got too darned heavy. I figured something would go but I wanted the record."

How did Arfons feel during the runs?

"It scared the hell out of me! The rough salt really bounced me around... but it was worth the bouncing.

"On my return run I entered the mile not as fast as I wanted, so I hit the afterburner for the full mile. When the tire blew, it felt like an explosion. The whole car shook.

"The first chute held a bit, then shredded. It felt like I was freewheeling. I waited until the car had slowed down to 400, then released the second chute. About sixty per cent of it ripped away, but there was enough left to slow me down three miles later.

"When I climbed out of the cockpit I knew I had the record. The car handled beautifully. I'd like to try 600 next. The sound barrier will present a big problem after that but I know the car will go over 650."

Arfons' immediate plans were to go to Chicago and New York over the next few days for press appearances, then return to Akron.

At home, June Arfons was besieged by phone calls. She "...was glad it was finally over".

Their oldest son, Ron, then sixteen, was working on two 1938 Ford hot rods when he heard about his father's record. He thought the feat was "Terrific! I'd love to go that fast some day".

This time a jubilant Arfons returned home with the knowledge that Breedlove was no immediate threat. He could breathe a big sigh of relief.

Well, not exactly. He wasn't counting on his brother, Walter, returning to Bonneville with his Wingfoot Express, the same car that held the record briefly at 413 mph.

While Walt Arfons always maintained the car had 500 mile an hour capability, he brought with him an insurance policy in the form of three JATO (jet assist take-off) rockets.

The plan was to attach the bombs on the car, one in the back of the cockpit and two at the rear of the jet car. However, USAC, the official sanctioning body, nipped that plan in the bud. As did the FIA, the international ruling body for automobiles.

Said USAC: "A car shall be moved only by its own power during a record attempt." The JATOs served as auxiliary power.

The FIA "...will study applications for recognition of records made or beaten by other manned vehicles than those corresponding to the definition of the word automobile as it appears in the international sporting code.

"These vehicles will have to run only on the surface of the ground or on at least four wheels, two of which must be steering wheels. The propelling will probably be assured by other means than the wheels, but propelling and steering will, however, have to be completely controlled by a person onboard the car."

With one door closed, Walt Arfons gained a slight measure of satisfaction when twenty-nine year old Paula Murphy of San Fernando Valley, drove Arfons' jet dragster Avenger to a new women's land speed record, averaging 226.37 mph.

It was the first time a woman had driven a jet car.

In 1963, Murphy averaged 161.20 in a piston-powered car.

Later, Murphy would drive the rocket-powered Pollution Packer to speeds excelling 300 miles an hour on the dragstrip. Quite a lady!

By the end of the 1965 speed season, the women's land speed record would be lifted to 307 miles an hour, first by Betty Skelton in Art Arfons' Cyclops, then by Lee Breedlove in her husband's Spirit of America – Sonic I.

Skelton's drive in the open cockpit dragster was the more impressive. Breedlove went the 307 in a car that would crash the 600 mile an hour barrier.

"It was like a Sunday cruise in that car," says Skelton, a legendary figure in aviation as well as high-speed racing for women.

It would take a book to do Betty Skelton justice. On an international basis, she became the first woman in the world to:
– establish more aviation and automotive records combined than any other person in history
– undergo NASA's physical and psychological tests given to the original seven astronauts before any manned flights
Her accomplishments were featured in *LOOK* magazine cover story, 1960:

- Win Feminine International Aerobatics Championship three times

- Break world land speed record for women four times

- Drive a jet (car) more than 300 mph

- Drive an Indy race car, Chrysler Proving Grounds, Michigan, 1954

- Establish NASCAR records on the sands of Daytona Beach, 1954

- ♠ Break the sex barrier in U.S. closed course air racing, 1968

- ♠ Become a test driver in the auto industry, Chrysler/Dodge, 1954–55

- ♠ Solo pilot an airplane at the age of twelve

- ♠ Receive CAA pilot's license on her sixteenth birthday

- ♠ Fly upside down cutting a ribbon ten feet above the ground

- ♠ Receive race driver's AAA License, 1954

- ♠ Become a member of International Aerobic Hall of Fame

- ♠ Become a member of NASCAR International Automotive Hall of Fame

Betty Skelton was born on June 28, 1926, at Pensacola Florida. And even today she still cherishes the hope of once again climbing into the cockpit of a high-speed race car and setting a woman's two-way record.

"If Art Arfons, or anyone for that matter, would give me a call today, that a car was ready, I'd be out the door by the time he hangs up. For years I've kept in touch with Art, first because he's such a dear man for giving me the chance to run his little car.

"But I've always let him know I'm interested in running, if he has a car for me. But I don't really think he wants to go through that experience again, watching helplessly while someone else pulls away in his car.

"I think Art has had enough worrying without putting a girl in the car. He really was quite uneasy and quite uncomfortable with my driving, which I can understand.

"Art's a great guy, a fine, fine person, very sensitive, very caring of other people. I have a tremendous amount of admiration for him for even allowing me to drive the little car because nobody else would take a chance with me.

"Today, as it was back then, it's very difficult for a woman to get a good ride, whether it be in an Indy-type car or a land speed car. The Breedlove girl got it because her husband owned the car."

Betty Skelton first met Art Arfons when he was at Daytona International Speedway, running his wheel-driven car, Anteater, around the high banks at speeds approaching 200 miles an hour.

"I met him at Daytona and we became friends. I started talking with Art about the possibility of driving one of his cars. Actually, I wanted so much to drive his big Monster at Bonneville, but of course, he wouldn't consider it. I drove the small Cyclops, the open-cockpit car."

Art Arfons knew of her reputation, both in planes (she went 425 mph in a World War II Mustang) and wheel-driven cars.

"I started in 1954 with NASCAR at Daytona, driving for Chrysler Corporation, the Dodge division. I set a class record in a Dodge. Then in '56, I drove the Corvette to a women's land speed record on the beach at Daytona.

"It was sponsored by NASCAR. It was a little rough. A couple of cars went into the water that year. Several other women also ran. I remember Ford had a woman in one of their new cars and evidently in shifting gears something went wrong."

In 1965, Betty Skelton was at Bonneville.

"Art pretty much explained the panel to me, but there wasn't a great deal to explain. He told me what to expect. If you're an acrobatic pilot accustomed to flying upside down ten feet above the ground in an airplane, getting into a car and taking that responsibility isn't really that much different. It's a matter of being a part of the machine and doing what is required to operate the machine.

"I had flown in jets, so the acceleration didn't mean a great deal to me. I flew the T-33. Chuck Yeager took me up for my first jet ride at the Cleveland Air Show in the late 40s. I had also flown some with the Thunderbirds, not as a pilot, but as a passenger. They would take me up with them.

"It was almost impossible at that time to fly a jet because women weren't allowed in the military. The only way you could get any time was if you were rich and could buy your own jet. I wasn't, I couldn't."

Betty Skelton was familiar with the brutish power of the Allison aircraft engine. The Allison propels the P–51 Mustang fighter plane, the fastest prop in World War II.

"I hit a speed of 426 plus in a Mustang, so I knew the feeling of power. You open the power full throttle if you're going for a record, and that's that. Unfortunately, the engine blew and caught on fire as I was finishing the run. I had to make an emergency landing.

"I had gone to Bonneville with the thought that I wanted to average over 300 miles an hour on the two timed runs. I made my first run and I was quite disappointed.

"As we were ready to go back for the return run I said I wasn't interested in making that run if I couldn't go faster. Art had turned the power down. He did some temporary work on the tailpipe which did jump the speed up considerably.

"Going back, the top speed was 315. The average was 277.52. Yet I was not a happy camper even though I was not only the first woman to exceed 300 miles an hour in the measured mile [315.72], but had set the land speed record.

"I felt the record could have been and should have been a great deal higher, but I knew that Art wouldn't want to go through it again. I didn't hit the afterburner. Art held me down on what I could do.

"He only fixed the car where it could go so fast. I would start off and full throttle it and that was it. You can only go so fast. No matter what I've done I've always felt I could do better.

"The only thing I did notice in driving the jet car was that as I got over 300 it took more strength to steer. That's the only thing I really noticed.

"That and the salt flying around. It was an open cockpit car. My plane was open cockpit. Going over 250 at Bonneville, the salt flies in your mouth, in your face. And your fanny is only six inches off the ground."

Betty Skelton called Cyclops a "...nice car, a very good handling car, even when I did get airborne. There wasn't any question of it getting out of shape, but nothing catastrophic happened. Actually, it's a great, great compliment to Art. The car was very stable."

Four years later, Betty Skelton learned about a rocket car being built in Milwaukee.

"I tried to get that ride. I tried very hard. I flew my little experimental plane from Detroit to Milwaukee, went to the garage where they were building the car and spoke to the people.

"I didn't get the ride. They gave it to Gary Gabelich. So then I said I'd sure like to go for a women's record, and that didn't work either."

That was Blue Flame which Gabelich drove to a two-way record of 622.407 in October 1970.

Art Arfons vividly remembers Betty Skelton's Cyclops adventure.

"Betty's a real sweetheart, but she probably made me age ten years that day. I had drag chutes on it. I said, 'Betty, don't pull the chute out until you slow down the car to 250'. She said, 'Okay, okay'. But as soon as she got through the damn clocks, she put the chute out and it picked the car right up.

"That car must have been ten feet high hanging on to the chute. As luck would have it, it just came right down and she said all she could see was sky. It never shook her.

"She said, 'Let me have more throttle. I want to go faster on the way back.' She scared the hell out of me. When Betty took off, I jumped in a plane. We took off together. Betty went out to the two mile marker.

"From the plane I saw the car come up off the ground. The chute raised a lot of salt dust and it looked like she crashed. I was beside myself. I tried to get out of the plane. We were flying about two hundred feet. The pilot got a hold of me. At the time we landed I could see the car was all right. Betty's something else. Absolutely no fear."

How did Betty Skelton get the ride in Cyclops?

"Paula Murphy had run Walter's car and set the record, so Firestone was interested in taking it away. Walter was sponsored by Goodyear. Firestone knew Betty was interested, Betty was a friend and I knew she was capable, so I took two cars out to Bonneville.

"Betty couldn't reach the pedal so we strapped a bunch of pillows behind her and moved her up so she could reach the pedal. I told her once how to run everything. She clicked it off and went.

"When Paula set her piston-powered records, she did it in Andy Granatelli's cars. When he found out that Betty was going to Bonneville to break Paula's jet record, he was angry with me for giving her the ride.

"He really irritated me. He said, 'You know, I don't want you to let her drive it. Paula's got it [the record].' And I said, 'What do you mean?' And he said, 'Just don't let her drive the car'. If that was meant to intimidate me, it didn't. It was meant to scare me, it didn't. I put her in it anyway."

'The Great Jet Duel' resumed in 1965 with Breedlove ultimately winning the shoot-off. Yes, the same Breedlove who said it would take two years to return to Bonneville.

But first to take the salt was the ever-innovative Walt Arfons, not with his jet-powered Wingfoot Express but with an exotic-looking rocket car propelled by fifteen JATOs.

Even with all fifteen bombs firing, average speed for the measured mile, from a standing start, was only 247.59 mph. Average for the last 2000 feet was a quicker 406.40.

Driver Bob Tatroe, twenty-eight, from Grand Rapids, Michigan, said the air speed indicator read 485 at one time. A dejected Walt Arfons promised to return, with more horsepower.

On September 29, Art Arfons drove his Green Monster to a world's quarter-mile drag racing record of 258.42 mph at Bonneville. The run, timed by the American Hot Rod Association and certified by USAC, was over in 6.9 seconds. It marked the first time Arfons had applied full power to the jet car.

"Well, I'm not worried now," he said. "I just never knew how the engine would react when the full juice was on. It ran as smooth as silk."

The run was one of the most spectacular ever witnessed on the historic race course. A sheet of flame more than one hundred feet long shot out of the rear of the massive engine all the way down the course.

"We learned a lot of new things about the car this week," said Harry Davis, Firestone's land speed project engineer. "We feel this has prepared Art very well for a possible run of over 600 this fall."

Arfons planned to return to Akron and wait for Breedlove and Tatroe to make their attempts.

"I can't predict what they'll do but we'll be prepared to go back immediately if they break our record."

He was thrilled with his quarter-mile record.

"This meant an awful lot to me because I was brought up on the drag strips. Everyone has said that you couldn't run over 250 no matter what power you had because of the short space. Actually, it surprised me a little when they told me the time."

Breedlove returned with a new car, Spirit of America – Sonic I, a four-wheeler with a coke-shaped nose and a J–79 engine with three-stage afterburner.

On October 12, Breedlove made three runs exceeding 500 miles an hour. He even thought he had bettered Arfons' record, but the twenty-eight year old Californian was wrong.

He said his airspeed indicator registered between 580 and 590 "...and it reads low". However, official timing devices clocked him at 516.203. That followed a first run of 518.769.

While the car sustained heavy body stress during those runs, Breedlove said the cowling would be reinforced and he would be running within forty-eight hours.

Breedlove was puzzled by the discrepancy between his onboard instruments and USAC's timer.

"It can't be... something's wrong with the timing lights. I used a higher power setting on the second and third runs, but went slower. I can't explain it."

While Breedlove's team was repairing body panels, Walt Arfons was back on the firing line, this time with twenty-five JATO rockets, each packing 1000 pounds of thrust.

Breedlove gave Arfons the go-ahead for his test runs. However, rain and snow halted all speed runs for several days.

When the weather cleared, Arfons hooked up only ten JATO, and from a standing start, Bobby Tatroe hit top speed of 317 mph in nine seconds.

His speed through the measured mile: 212 mph.

And when Arfons' Wingfoot Express was fitted with full power, two of those rockets fell from the car and a third retrofired, singeing the metal skin, wiring and part of a firewall protecting Tatroe.

Official clocking was a more respectable 433.65 mph.

Walt Arfons decided to regroup, relinquishing the remainder of his track time to Breedlove, who was also sponsored by Goodyear Tire & Rubber.

On October 20, Breedlove flirted with disaster as his Sonic I went out of control at 600 miles an hour, finally stopping one and a half miles beyond the end of the track and one hundred feet short of a salt-water pond. Almost a repeat of his 1964 swim.

The car started to veer to the right. Breedlove twisted the steering wheel, trying to bring the car back on course, but nothing happened. He released his braking chutes but it ripped off.

The racer careened out of the official timing area, off the track, across wet salt, through an opening in a line of telephone poles and finally rolled to a stop in front of a pond, nine miles from where he left the track.

Breedlove said the team would set up temporary residence at an Air National Guard hangar at Salt Lake City, some 125 miles away, to hopefully solve the runaway problem.

Two days later, Tatroe roared across the salt at 470.53 mph. He first fired fourteen of the twenty-five rockets, then tripped the remaining eleven. Tatroe said the car handled beautifully, although one rocket on the right side failed to ignite.

Walt Arfons figured the car reached its peak speed just before it entered the measured mile. The car started out less than a mile before the timing lights.

He felt more work had to be done on the rocket system before a serious assault on his brother's record of 536.71 could take place. He had the rockets and the patience.

On November 1, Craig Breedlove set his fourth land speed record, averaging 555.127 mph on runs of 544.382 and 566.304.

Afterwards he said, "I never had to work so hard for a record in my life." He said both runs were made using the first stage of the three-stage burner.

"It's taken all year to build a new car and get the record back, so we intend to stay around. We'll run later this week for the 600 mark to make it tough for Art.

"I was sure he had the record today. I'm wearing my lucky shirt— the one I wore when he set his last record," said Norman Breedlove, Craig's jubilant father.

Breedlove's car was equipped with two canard wings in front to hold the nose down. The device worked to perfection.

But no sooner was Craig Breedlove basking in the glow of his record than Art Arfons and his Green Monster took to the salt and once again proved equal to the challenge.

Arfons survived another right-rear-tire blowout and a crash into a course marker in sealing the two-way land speed record. He was clocked at 575.724 in his opening burst and 577.386 on the ill-fated return run.

"I hit the timing clocks at over 500. The air speed indicator jumped and kept going until it was up to about 625. I was only in the mile about six seconds, and pushed down harder. Then it happened.

"The right rear tire blew and I started leaving the track. Then smoke poured into the cockpit and I lost sight of the guideline for a moment. That's when I began to feel uneasy.

"For a moment I couldn't see a thing, but suddenly everything cleared. I gripped the steering wheel tight and tried to straighten it out, but before I could I crashed into the steel marker.

"Pieces started flying, including my canopy. I finally stopped, got out and looked at the car. It was a mess but I knew I had the record. A lot of things went through my mind when I climbed into the cockpit. I was the loneliest guy in the world.

"My crew and the racing engineers from Firestone had asked me to make a few practice runs and then go for the record. I thought about it, and realized that it had been a year since I had run at record speeds.

"My wife, June, was back in Akron, expecting our third child and I didn't want to cause her any more worry. I just wanted to get it over with. I guess I sound like a guy who was getting ready for a duel, but that really wasn't the case.

"Sure, I had butterflies... king size, too, but I knew my car was ready and there was no use waiting. So I told my crew I was going full blast.

"I closed the hatch and took off. I had only about two miles to get up speed because the course had gotten so rough from all the activity this fall. Breedlove had more than twice this distance before he hit the clocks.

"The first run, despite the bumpy track, was great. I nosed the car up and held my speed between 560 and 590. I only went into minimum afterburner."

Forty minutes later the two braking parachutes were repacked and Arfons was ready for the return trip. On the return run, he used only a mile and three-quarter approach.

"When Ed told me I had to use a shorter approach because of the rough salt, this really shook me up.

"It meant going into afterburner full blast and accelerating as rapidly as possible. We pulled the car into position and I said goodbye to the world again.

"The crew fired the engine and I crept forward, then blasted off. The acceleration was so great, I thought I was going through the back of the car.

"I kept going faster, faster and faster, realizing this was my chance and I'd better do it now."

How did Art Arfons feel when it was all over?

"Great but tired and relieved," he said. "It isn't something I'd want to go through every day. I wasn't in the car but a minute, but it seemed like an eternity."

On Monday, November 15, Craig Breedlove won his duel with Art Arfons, and in the process became the first man in land speed history to hit 600 miles an hour.

Breedlove was clocked at 593.178 mph for his first run and an even quicker 608.201 on the return trip. His two-way average: 600.601. Both he and Arfons knew the season was over.

Arfons was back in Ohio, working on his badly damaged car when word came of Breedlove's shenanigans.

"The repairs will take thirty to forty days to complete. The most time-consuming task will be to check out the engine damage. I think I can repair it. I have spare parts from four other J–79s. The whole right side of the car will also have to be rebuilt.

"Even if I didn't get a cent I'd try to get back to Utah and regain the title. I like Craig... but I also like competition."

The track, softened by overnight rain, was a little rough during Breedlove's record sorties.

"It made driving tough because at 600 miles an hour steering is touchy."

On his first run, Breedlove's braking chute filled with water and salt and collapsed. He was unable to halt the speed jet at the end of the track.

Coming back forty minutes later, he veered to the left after leaving the measured mile and there was momentary fear he was in trouble. But his chute popped open and Craig Breedlove stopped beside his trailer-van headquarters.

"I wanted to park my car right in the garage," he laughed.

It was the Californian's fifth land speed record in three years. He became the first to break the 400... 500... 600 mph barrier!

"But don't talk about the sound barrier. That's a long way off."

While he claimed Spirit of America – Sonic I's speed potential "is in the high 600s", he never set foot in that car again.

That car had more than done its job.

King Craig was sitting high on the throne. Ex-king Arthur was nursing his wounds. It would be a long, long winter.

Chapter Sixteen
The 'Other' Arfons

There's supposed to be a long-standing feud between me and my brother. There have never been words said between us. We keep in touch. I call him quite often, once a month or so. I think the women bitching back and forth caused most of the trouble... my wife and his wife.

Certainly, Walter was an innovator. He had the first jet dragster, the first land speed rocket car, even a steam-powered dragster. His jet car set a record of 413 in 1964 with Tom Green at the wheel. I think my brother has gotten his full credit. I've always been a driver and I think the driver is gonna get more recognition than the guy who builds the cars and has others drove 'em.

Art Arfons

That sparkle is gone in Walt Arfons' eyes.

Now, there is a look of sadness... and it will never go away. "There's not a day that goes by that I don't cry for that boy," he says.

His voice starts cracking, his eyes well up with tears.

"I was holding the microphone and I really wanted him to retire, to forget about it, to call the whole thing off. But I didn't. Even though I know it wouldn't have made a difference, somehow I blame myself.

On July 9, 1989, Walt Arfons, his wife Gertie and his family stood on the shoreline to watch his thirty-nine year old son, Craig, take dead aim on the world's water speed record in his modified hydroplane.

In 1978, Australian Ken Warby pushed his home-built jet boat to a new record of 317 miles an hour. He was the fastest man on water.

"I was scared to death about that boat, but I knew Craig wouldn't quit. He was too involved with sponsors. He had to go through with it.

"Before he made his run he told me, 'I'm gonna break it real good because the boat handles so well. I'm gonna push it so hard, and move that record so far out of reach no one is gonna come back and break my record like they did yours.'

"I knew how Craig felt but I said, 'That's not the way to feel about it. Just barely break it. You can always go back again.'"

Back in 1964, Walt Arfons' jet-powered Wingfoot Express, with Tom Green in the cockpit, set a world land speed record of 413 mph, beating Craig Breedlove's '63 standard by six miles an hour.

But seventy-two hours later, Art Arfons, Walt's younger brother, pushed his 17,500 horsepower Green Monster into the record books with a two-way run of 434.

Walt Arfons tried with that car, and a year later with land speed racing's first rocket-powered creation, but failed in his mission. Craig Arfons grew up with that bitter memory.

Craig's ultimate dream was the land speed record, but that would have to wait.

"Craig had the design, an engine that he put together, and the financial backing for a supersonic jet car," says his father. "He was going to break the sound barrier, and once that car would have been built, he would have done it. He was a genius. There's nothing he couldn't do."

First Craig Arfons purchased a nineteen foot long hydroplane, then fashioned it into the image of a bullet on water. By the time he reworked the boat, it had been lengthened to twenty-five feet.

It was powered by a General Electric turbine engine generating some 4000 horsepower. During an August 1988 shakedown across Lake Jackson in Sebring, Florida, Arfons made three runs, hitting an estimated 220 on his second burst.

When water conditions became rough, he had to call it quits.

"We're not disappointed at all in the boat," he said. "I'm just disappointed we couldn't make another run. It was definitely rough out there.

"I feel like it's time to set a new record. Ten years at 320 mph is long enough. After today, I think 400 is possible. After getting that, I'd like to try for the land speed record."

By Sunday, July 9, 1989, all systems were 'GO' for a record run.

"It was one of the most beautiful runs you've ever seen in your life," recalls his father. "He started out at 125... 150... 175... 250... 275. And then he got over three and a half and..." His voice trails off.

"I could see everything. He was coming right at me. I don't like to talk about it."

Lake Jackson is a tiny lake, barely three miles long. Craig Arfons hit full power about 2000 feet from the start of the flying kilo, then hit afterburner. The speed quickly reached 300 mph.

At an estimated 370 miles an hour the right side of the boat suddenly lifted out of the water. Its left side sliced into the water and the craft cartwheeled and tore apart.

He died some ninety minutes after the crash at a nearby hospital. Craig Arfons left a wife and two children. It marked the second time in as many attempts that a driver had been killed in pursuit of the water speed record.

Californian Lee Taylor, who led the record at 285 but lost it to Warby, was killed in 1980 in his $5 million rocket boat.

Because of the short length of the lake, Arfons tried the same kind of tactic that his uncle, Art, had used in setting three land speed records. He would accelerate like a drag racer from a shorter distance, enter the kilometer at a slower-than-record speed but leave it at a higher velocity. The average speeds he hoped, would be good enough for a record.

"He called it his uncle's approach," said one-time unlimited hydroplane driver, Gene Whipp, the official time trial observer for the Union of International Motorboating (UIM), the world sanctioning body.

Craig Arfons' plan was to reach 375 with the burner, decelerate to about 350. At the end of the kilo, he would deploy a small chute to further slow down the hydroplane, then release a larger chute to stop it.

"It makes a lot of sense," said Whipp. "It minimizes the exposure at top speed. Also, in jet-powered boats, they're more stable under power. It's when you cut the power that you have problems, and with most of them it means you'd be off power for a longer time after the flying kilo."

Ron Hicks, American Power Boat Association (APBA) referee, who was monitoring the record attempt, agreed with Whipp.

"Arfons' idea of how it was going to be done and his feeling on how he approached it were very, very good.

"It's obvious they [Arfons and his crew] had done their homework on air forces and water forces and mathematical interpretations. This wasn't seat-of-the-pants boating."

Arfons' jet boat began to twist off-center at the afterburner/shutdown point, when the small parachute came out.

"It may have been too late," said Whipp, "but we're talking tenths of a second. It didn't open properly.

"Had it billowed, that may have kept the boat from going over... the angle of the boat may have caused the chute to fail. The fuselage could have blocked the flow of air to it."

Whipp said he and Craig Arfons "...had become very close in the past three or four days, working together on this event. It takes you back dramatically when something like this happens, no matter how many friends you have lost before.

"Every one of them hurts you, but you always understand what you're doing and why you're doing it. Craig knew all too well the dangers involved."

The conditions for a run were perfect. The water was mirror-smooth. There was no wind.

Two weeks after the fatal accident, results of an informal investigation were announced. The conclusion: Craig Arfons was simply going too fast for the design of the boat.

Veteran jet-powered funny car driver Roger Gustin tried, but unsuccessfully, to talk his friend out of the water speed attempt.

"Craig was like family," says Gustin. "He'd been building our engines for a year. He'd been driving for us the year he was killed, up to a week before the accident.

"I begged and pleaded with him every week to stay out of that damned boat. He wouldn't do it. There's five of the last six guys who tried to break the water speed record that died in that attempt.

"I knew in the beginning Craig wasn't supposed to drive that boat. When they first started working on the project, Craig was supposed to design and build it and they were gonna get one of those hot-shot drag boat drivers who understood water. Craig never knew anything about water.

"He just felt like he could go out and put his life on the line for one day. No question about it, the boat was obviously plenty capable of doing it. It ran 380 and the record is only 317.

"He told me a few days before that, when he'd been testing it, that there was no way he could read the air speed indicator. He said you could never tell how fast you're going until the run was over.

"He also had an on-board computer in the boat and he could have worked it so the thing would shut off at 350 miles an hour, but he said he didn't have the time.

"I said, 'Man, take the time'. And he said, 'No. I'm just gonna go out there and if it goes real fast on the first run I'm just gonna shut it off early on the second run, just break the record.'

"He said he didn't want to break it [the record] by a few miles an hour. He put it this way, 'If I break it by twenty miles an hour, I'll be satisfied'."

Gustin insists, "Craig was plenty scared of the thing. He knew how dangerous it was. He just got himself to the point where he was just going to get the record and go on with his life.

"That's all he kept saying. I really don't know why he drove it. He was really more interested in building a car for the land speed record. I begged him not to drive it. I didn't even want him to test the boat. He was like a brother to us and his death really tore up our family. Craig was an amazing guy. He could get in anything and drive it. He drove everybody's race cars. As far as engines, fuel controls, he was a genius. There wasn't anything he couldn't rip apart.

"He had an unbelievable talent when it came to designing things. You know, he never had a day of [engineering] school. His kind doesn't come around too often, that's for darned sure."

And to this day, Roger Gustin still doesn't know how a sportswriter called him to let him know about the fatal crash.

"I had raced that week and was in a motel in Atlanta. A sportswriter named Bill Robinson from the *Atlanta Journal* somehow tracked me down. I was so shocked when he told me.

"I don't know to this day how he ever found me at that motel. There was nobody at my office, well, anyway, we started talking. He said he was putting together a story for the paper and asked if I'd give him some comments about Craig. Then my heart just sank."

Gustin flew to Florida for the memorial service.

"Walt was unbelievably strong for his family. I spent a lot of time talking to Art. He was going to Bonneville the next week with his car, and he really didn't want to go. But he knew he had to."

Walt Arfons is long retired from the speed game. He and his wife, Gertie, spend half of the year in Florida, half back in Ohio.

"We were married in 1937," he says proudly, "when I was still in the navy.

"We do everything together. Except for one day I wish I could forget about, it's been a beautiful life. I have no regrets. Gertie used to help me when I ran the jet dragsters."

As a youngster growing up in rural northeast Ohio, Walt worked in his father's feed mill until he joined the navy in 1935.

"As a youngster, I wanted to be a doctor. But back in those days we didn't have the advantages they have today. We didn't have the money to go to college. I graduated high school."

At nineteen, he joined the navy and served until 1939. He was a gunner's mate, serving on a destroyer and cruiser. After his hitch, he returned to Ohio, to Arfons' mill.

Walt and Gertie Arfons would have a daughter and two sons.

"When war broke out in 1941," he says, "I wanted to go, but by then I had a family. But Arthur enlisted in the navy in '43. All our prayers went with him. He came home safe and sound."

In 1952, Art, nine years younger than Walt, saw his first drag race. When he came home, he told his older brother, and their lives would be changed forever.

By the late 1950s, Art was virtually unbeatable in his No. 11, powered by an Allison aircraft engine, but Walt Arfons was thinking of another power source.

"It got to a point where you had to go faster and faster on the dragstrips," says Walt. "And I thought the way to go would be by jet propulsion. But Arthur wasn't interested. It took him until 1962 to drive his first jet.

"I wanted Arthur to go with me, but at that point he didn't want any part of a jet, so we split up. He went his way and I went mine. In 1958, I went down to Jacksonville, Florida, and bought my first jet engine.

"I bought it in a basket for something like $300 or $400. After that I was buying 'em for $400, brand new engines in a can. Never been used, brand new. I must have bought dozens and dozens.

"I bought the first one at a junkyard where they took 'em apart and scraped 'em. I bought the whole thing, the basic engine, all the cams, the afterburner, everything.

"There was no manual. It took me about a year to put it all together, install it in a car, fire it up and actually run it. By then, I had some help. You have to hire somebody to help you.

"It was basically trial and error, but the first time I ran, the car ran pretty good. Mickey Thompson had his drag strip in California and he wanted to be the first promoter to run a jet.

"On the way to California, I stopped over at Milwaukee and ran it for the first time. Oh, my goodness, it scared the hell out of me. I couldn't believe the horsepower.

"I was turning about 6000 pounds of thrust with full burner. The car weighed about 2800 pounds. At first, I ran without burner, because everyone told me when I'd go into burner the car would go into a flat spin and I couldn't control it. They said it wouldn't work. By they, I mean the engineers who should have known better.

"I went as fast as the engine would take me without burner. I had to do something. I punched it at the line once for a split second. I'd do it in short little bursts until I got kinda used to it. It took a while, but I made runs using full burner.

"What's it like to drive a jet? It's like you bend over and take a twenty foot two-by-four and someone smacks you in the butt. It's quite a sensation, believe me."

Walt Arfons' jet-powered Green Monster, the first of its kind, was an instant hit on the drag racing circuit. From that beginning he built five jets, all of them campaigning coast to coast.

Walt drove until 1964.

"I had a heart problem, nothing major. I still have it and still take medication, but by '64, it was time to get out of the cockpit."

He made an estimated 4000 runs in his jet dragsters, hitting top speed of 285 miles an hour.

"It was a good life. I was making money hand-over-fist, as the expression goes. They were all good boys, and when I got out of the business I sold all of the stuff to the drivers."

The worst accident involving a Walt Arfons-built jet car involved Doug Rose who lost both legs in a track mishap.

"It was strictly his fault because he was running in the rain, trying to please the track promoter.

"He was running in West Virginia. He slid under a guardrail. I wasn't there. I was with the other cars. They kept after Doug to run, just go into burner for 300 or 500 feet, and finally he did. It was too much. The track was just too wet. He couldn't control it.

"I've always tried to teach all the drivers, if things don't feel right, turn around and go home. You can always drive again, but you can't do it if you have an accident. Thank goodness, he wasn't killed."

By 1963, Walt Arfons entered the land speed game with his 5000 horsepower Wingfoot Express. Tom Green, in his early thirties, was the driver.

"Boy, I really wanted to drive that car," says Walt.

"Tom was with Sturdivant Tool. They were one of our sponsors. We just liked each other so well. He wanted to do it. Tom helped me design the car. We had problems in '63, but I think if Tom had used the afterburner, we could have done it.

"But he wouldn't use the burner all the way. He'd just give it a little spurt and shut it off. Doug Rose [this was prior to his drag strip accident] came on out to Bonneville because he was bringing one of my dragsters from the West Coast.

"Doug begged me to run that car. He could have popped it off, but I just couldn't pull Tom, it wouldn't have been right. The next year, Tom set the record at 413 miles an hour. It was the happiest day of my life."

Three days later, however, Walt's younger brother went 434 in his 17,500 horsepower Green Monster. Contrary to popular belief, Walt Arfons was happy for Art.

"I knew what he was building. Our shops were only yards apart. I knew if that massive engine worked the way it was supposed to work, Art's car would really go fast.

"I had no ill feelings towards him when he broke the record. I was happy for him. It was what he wanted. I was glad when he done it. There's no feuding like that. It makes for good ink, and that's what they [the writers] did."

Lou Wolf, sister of Walt and Art Arfons, has never seen any ill feeling between her brothers.

"They certainly keep in touch. Very definitely [the feud] has been blown out of proportion. When Craig was killed it was terrible. The [Akron] *Beacon Journal* put it out like they were fighting and everything.

"Arthur got on a plane. He was down there and he stayed with Walter. They just said all of these mean things. That's not so. It really isn't.

"Walter spends a few months of the summer in Ohio. He's got himself a trailer. Then he goes back to Florida. Arthur's been over to see him. He [Walter] stops over at Arthur's a couple times a week, whenever Arthur's home. The three of us are very close."

If his jet-powered Wingfoot Express had lived up to its full potential, the car could have reached 500 miles an hour. But Walt Arfons knew it would ultimately take more to be competitive in the speed race.

"I thought about rocket power for several years before I actually started building the car. Originally, I had hoped to use liquid fuel, but I was told [by the officials] that it wasn't allowed. Funny thing, in 1970, Blue Flame broke the record and that rocket car was liquid fueled.

"My only alternative was solid fuel, so I went with the JATO [jet assist take-off]."

The five ton Wingfoot Express resembled an Atlas missile on its side. It was impressive-looking.

"I was trying to make it like an arrow, shoot it through the air, it has to go. Looking back, which is always easy to do, if I had to do it all over again I'd make it a lot smaller, a lot lighter. But I wanted to build a safe car. There were too many bad cars out there."

Initially, the rocket car was 'armed' with fifteen JATOs, but that wasn't enough, so ten more were added to the rear end rack. But the car failed to break the land speed record.

"The car done 585 in the kilometer, but it couldn't sustain it through the mile. It was underpowered part-way. The car was just too heavy."

So Walt Arfons dejectedly called it quits.

"The Smithsonian Institute wanted that rocket car. They wrote me a letter and wanted that car, but I had just started to cut it up I didn't want to mess with it no more. I just didn't want any more to do with it.

"I didn't want to go back to Bonneville. I was about done then. I thought I had enough money. I was getting older. I wanted to stop."

Before he retired, sold his cars, Walt Arfons built a steam-powered dragster. Bobby Tatroe, who drove the rocket car, also drove the little steam machine.

"I thought it would be different," says Walt Arfons. "You know me. I had no intention of using the dragster as a prototype, then build a bigger land speed version. It was just an idea I had. Like going forward by really going backward in time. Some of the early passenger cars, land speed record cars were steam driven."

Walt openly wonders why it was his son who was killed, not himself or his brother.

"Arthur and I had so many close calls, especially Arthur. It's like he was the cat with nine lives.

"I guess my worst accident was the first time I tried parachutes on my jet in 1961. I was running at Erie, Pennsylvania. I went down to an air base at Athens, Georgia, and watched those jets come in with parachutes billowing. I thought if a chute can stop an eighteen ton aircraft it could surely stop a one ton car.

"I knew you could buy some of these things [chutes] surplus, so that's what I done. But it didn't exactly work as planned. The first chute ripped off. The second chute did the same thing. They just wouldn't hold.

"I went into the woods. Gertie and Craig picked me up. I was hurt pretty bad. Broken ankle. Broken leg. I got beat up quite a bit.

"Rebuilt the car, went down to Florida and ran it. I ran for a long time with that cast up to my hip."

Craig Arfons was packing his father's parachutes "...when he was ten or twelve. When he got older, he built his own car and ran it. His basic talent was everywhere. Anything that you wanna name he was a master of it.

"My other son, Terry, drove a dragster once down the strip, just to see how it felt. But he didn't want to do that. For years he was a tire engineer with Goodyear."

As Walt Arfons reflects back on a long racing career, "I'm so proud of it because I was Number One. I pioneered that stuff. We always put on a good show at the drag strip.

"All that flame, nose, afterburners, parachutes. The fans loved it. But I wouldn't want to go through it again. No sir, one time around the block is enough for me!"

Chapter Seventeen

The Dream Becomes a Nightmare

I had hoped to become the first driver to average 500 miles an hour. Breedlove beat me to it. I wanted to be the first to crack 600, but that son of a gun pulled a 600.601 out of his pocket. That was the Last Hurrah for his Spirit of America – Sonic I. All he could do was wait and see if my Green Monster was up to the task.

My nature doesn't tolerate second best too well. I was confident that 1966 would be my year, and there was nothing Craig could do about it. I had a car that could do it, he was a pedestrian. I was determined to be the fastest man on wheels again.

Art Arfons

Activity was feverish on Pickle Road during the winter of 1965.

Art Arfons was repairing his badly battered Green Monster, victim of another high-speed blowout. Just yards away, in a nearby garage, Walter Arfons, Art's older brother and land speed rival, was streamlining his rocket car, Wingfoot Express for another assault.

Art's jet car was a mess. The frame of the 17,500 horsepower car was broken in four places on the return run that cemented his 576 mph record. The entire right side was mangled. The left side looked like Swiss cheese after ramming into a steel marker.

"It will take thirty to forty days to get the car ready," he said.

Arfons skipped a trip to London and Paris in order to stay home and fix his car. The damage resulted when the right rear tire blew and smoked filled the cockpit, forcing the three-time land speed king to career off the course and slam into the marker.

Day One (Monday, November 14)

Art Arfons made runs of 376.254, 474.934 and 554.017 miles an hour. Despite persistent trouble with the parachute releasing devices Arfons was satisfied with the day's progressively faster runs.

On the first run, both chutes failed to open. Then it was a premature release which required almost three hours of painstaking hand-stitching to repair the shredded nylon chute.

The same right chute was charred by the full blast of the Green Monster's afterburner during Arfons' third run. But he shook off the problem as minor. All it required was tracing the wiring to find the short. He had three chutes available instead of four.

His plan was to reach 350 and 500 mph on his two warm-ups and if enough daylight remained, he would take a crack at Craig Breedlove's year old record of 600.601.

At 4:05 (Utah time), the 17,500 horsepower jet car inched within two and a half miles of the flying mile.

"I just entered the mile too slow," he said afterwards. He entered at about 550. "The car accelerated so quickly it jumped my foot off the gas pedal. When I got back on it and hit the burner, it didn't light at first. Then it caught – but too late."

If Arfons had clocked a faster speed, he would have made the return run.

The crew worked late into the night to fix the chute malfunction. They also reinforced Arfons' unique airfoil, or wing, battered by air pressure underneath the 7800 pound jet.

The dual rear tires were designed to lighten the extreme load, an estimated 6000 pounds, on the right rear tire which had exploded during three previous high-speed and record-shattering bursts.

Day Two (Tuesday, November 15)

By the end of the second day, Arfons had already made six runs. Quite out of character for the Ohio hot rodder who would take the Green Monster out of the bus, make back-to-back runs, set a record, then wait for Breedlove to come back.

He took three more rides across the Salt Flats. The first at 10:39 was a 436.07 warm-up for what Arfons hoped would set the stage for faster speeds to come.

While the chute problem had been solved, other unforeseen developments popped up.

His 524 mph second sortie was made with little help from the Monster's four-stage afterburner, which fired, momentarily went out, then sputtered and died.

"I was getting fuel but I wasn't getting any burner," said a dejected and puzzled Arfons following the run.

The afterburner adds raw jet fuel into the airstream, thereby increasing the engine's thrust by as much as fifty per cent.

That problem was solved by cleaning a clogged fuel line.

At 1:07 p.m., Arfons had the racer pointed for a north-to-south run. It too fell short of the goal. Speed: 541.924.

"I just ran out of power and shut down in the middle of the mile. I'll have to go to a higher power setting."

The weather was perfect, the wind negligible and the salt surface firm.

His plan was simple. Prepare the machine for a second-stage burner and start three miles from the flying mile. He had only utilized the first stage since he began his 17,500 horsepower assault back in 1964. He had never used more than two and a half miles of running room entering the mile.

Day Three (Wednesday, November 16)

It was a long day of waiting for the gusting winds to die down and hoping a chartered plane would arrive in time to deliver specially made firing caps to trigger the parachutes.

While Arfons watched, two-time United States Auto Club (USAC) national champion, Mario Andretti, flew in from Los Angeles early in the day, departed shortly after sunset with two Class C speed marks.

Driving a 1967 Mustang housing a 560 horsepower Indianapolis-type engine, Andretti streaked across the Flats for five-mile and five-kilometer records from a standing start.

In averaging 150.134 (mile) and 136.645 (kilo), he erased the four year old standards of Andy Granatelli, set in a Studebaker. Granatelli averaged 139.69 and 126.39 in August 1962.

Andretti's two runs in his five mile record burst were 146.451, followed by a sizzling 154.008. Andretti said he "had a ball".

Winds gusted up to seventeen miles an hour, far too dangerous for Arfons to take a chance. By the time the plane finally arrived, it was too late as darkness had set in.

The plane had to return to Long Beach, California, on an earlier flight, because of a broken propeller seal. Then the pilot had to find another craft for the 600 mile flight. Although the trip lasted only three hours, two more hours had been wasted through the unscheduled delay.

Actually, there was no other way to deliver the firing caps as any commercial flight would have refused to carry explosives.

Arfons had been prepared to install a manual parachute release if the plane had failed to arrive. That plan called for detonating one cap on the first run, the second and last on the final trip.

If chute trouble had developed, the emergency chute would have been released manually. Arfons had previously rigged up manual release devices in his 8000 horsepower jet dragster, Cyclops.

However, he had never used the manual release to halt the record-setting Green Monster.

Day Four (Thursday, November 17)

A grim and determined Art Arfons stepped into the cockpit of his jet car at 8:03 a.m. He said softly but firmly, "I'm going to stand on the accelerator through the mile."

The Monster whined and screamed as it started, and left a brilliant trail of orange flames as it roared out of sight. Newsmen covering the event said it was one of the fastest starts they had ever witnessed.

Official records showed Arfons averaged 585.366 mph in the measured mile, 589.366 in the kilo, which indicated the jet car was still accelerating as it left the timing traps.

Shortly after streaking past the final timing lights, the car veered to the left of the black guide line. Arfons turned the steering wheel hard right, trying to get back on course. The car pitched violently on its right side, then hit nose first.

The car became airborne at least twice and skidded for long distances on its right side, finally settling on its belly, almost one mile past the traps, some one hundred yards off course.

Parts of the car were strewn all over the Flats. Huge chunks were torn out of the salt, some as deep as twelve inches. The left cockpit was splattered with blood, the instrument panel smashed.

It marked his seventh run at Bonneville in 1966. Unlucky No. 7!

Arfons' Green Monster, the car he affectionately called "my baby", was a mass of twisted metal. The wheels and tires were ripped off as well as the front wing atop the Green Monster.

Arfons was pinned in the wreckage for about five minutes before rescuers could free him. "I'm all right. Take your time getting me out of here," he said.

He was immediately placed on a stretcher and flown in a private plane to Salt Lake City, 125 miles away.

Utah Highway State Patrol officer, Lamar Melville, was on duty at Bonneville that day. "He'll [Arfons] be back. Maybe not next year, but in two years."

The veteran lawman made his prediction following Ted Gillette's on-the-spot diagnosis. Gillette owned a local ambulance service, and was also at the Flats.

"If there's a broken bone, Ted will find it," said Melville, "and he said there were none."

Melville talked about the speed king.

"Everybody loves and respects Art. He talks to people and they all wait for him to come to town."

Only a few visitors were allowed to see him in Room 464. One visitor was his older brother and land speed rival, Walt Arfons, who flew from Ohio when he learned of his brother's crash.

"Racing is his life," philosophized his brother. "Arthur's let the quest of speed possess him. He has to be on top and won't stop until he gets there, is mangled or killed. He certainly was fortunate. Someone had to be riding with him."

Arfons' eyes were covered with gauze, the skin around his eyes and cheekbones raw from salt burns and from flying glass, his body aching.

But no broken bones. Doctors said he would not suffer any permanent cornea damage, although they advised him to wear gauze patches over his eyes for a few days.

Although under sedation he talked about the crash.

"I couldn't really tell what happened. I suddenly noticed I was left of the black line, tried to correct it and lost control." He said he released his braking chutes, "but before I could tell whether they worked, I was upside down."

The right rear tire had blown three times in thirteen months, primarily because of a basic design of the car.

Arfons claimed the sudden torque applied when he cut in the afterburner of his J–79 engine placed a sharp load on the right rear tire. Firestone Tire had tested the tires for fifty seconds at 650 mph with a 2000 pound tire load... but nothing violent happened. Further tests would have to be conducted. The results would prove frightening!

To absorb the sudden shock, Arfons planned to add suspension to the rear of the vehicle which had springs only in front. "In this way, the torque can be carried by both tires instead of the one.

"The most time-consuming tasks," he added, "will be to check out the engine damage. I think I can repair it. I have spare parts from four other J–79s. The whole right side of the car will also have to be rebuilt."

In addition to those major repairs, Arfons planned to modify his specially designed air intake probe. This bulb-shaped device served two functions.

First, it controlled the flow of air into the jet engine, thereby preventing a sputtering or choking of the massive power plant.

Second, it would provide Arfons with data for a sound barrier attempt.

On such a run, the probe would penetrate the powerful shock waves created at supersonic speed.

"I'm going to redesign the probe for the limit of the car, up to 680 miles per hour... if I'm forced to go that fast."

Arfons came up with the novel idea after visiting Bunker Hill Air Force Base in Indiana. The probe was used on the B–58 bombers which reached sound barrier speed at extremely low altitude.

Therein lies a story.

"I don't know how they heard about me, but they called and wanted me to give a talk at an officer's luncheon at Bunker Hill. They heard I had some J–79s, and they wondered how I got them.

"The Colonel took me out to the runway and showed me how the B–58 supersonic bombers flew. They took off, reached a very low altitude and went supersonic. It was awesome.

"They let me measure the intake of the probe. I got all the measurements, and that's how I made my probe. The probe would move the shock wave out of the intake. The engine can't swallow a shock wave 'cause it would set up harmonic vibrations and the blades would come off. The military designed it so the shock wave would go around the engine. It was a great visit."

Money was not the motivation is returning to Utah.

"Even if I didn't get a cent I'd try to get back and regain the record. I like Craig... but I also like competition."

Walt Arfons had arrived at Bonneville earlier in the fall of '65 with the world's first rocket-powered racer, Wingfoot Express. He thought twenty-five JATO rockets would provide more than enough power to claim his second land speed title.

"The power was there [25,000 pounds of thrust]," he said, "but it didn't last long enough. When Bob Tatroe averaged 470 he ran out of power halfway through the mile. He entered the mile at 580, but it's the average of the full run that counts, not the peak speed."

"There are two alternatives. Either bigger JATO rockets of 10,000 pounds each [the others weighed 1100 pounds per engine]. I'd rather have the liquid fuel engine than all of those solid fuel JATO rockets.

"Instead of having rockets that last only fifteen seconds, the man-tested missile engine has enough fuel for sixty-seven seconds and with 19,000 pounds of thrust, the record can be ours."

The particular rocket Walt Arfons hoped to land was fourteen feet long and thirty inches in diameter. Liquid fuel is composed of refined kerosene and acid. He planned to install the rocket... if he could get it... in either his new car or his four year old jet, holder of the land speed record at 413 mph.

"Sure I was disappointed in not getting the record," he said. "If one of the twenty-five rockets hadn't misfired and if we started two hundred feet closer in, I'm sure we'd have claimed the record. But I was delighted with the way the car handled. Bobby didn't have a bit of trouble."

How did Tatroe feel when a short in the electrical wiring system caused the rockets to fire in two directions during an early practice run?

"I didn't know there was any problem until after I stepped out of the car. Then I saw that a lot of the skin had been burned. The next time I'm gonna put air conditioning in the cockpit. It was hot as hell in there," he chuckled.

Walt Arfons' plans for a triumphant return to Bonneville, however, never materialized.

Art Arfons, on the other hand, was scheduled for two weeks, August 7–19, 1966. Arfons' plans were to make test runs with the electronic equipment installed before taking a serious assault at Breedlove's record.

However, delays in securing and installing the equipment on the wheels of Green Monster forced a postponement until mid-September.

Arfons was well aware of the task ahead.

"In order to break Breedlove's record, I'll have to go through the mile in less than six seconds. That means I'll be maintaining top speed for only ten seconds... but it seems like ten years when you're waiting for those markers to come by.

"It will probably be a spooky ride this year. We're getting closer and closer to the sound barrier. It's not knowing what will happen when we reach that speed [720–750] at Bonneville that's scary.

"If I can get to 600 without any problems I'll turn around and shoot for the record. I'd like to go faster. I'll try to level out around 620 and hold it through the mile. I'd like to get 650 on the return run.

"If I can average 630 or better I'll quit right there. I'm greedy but not foolish."

Less than twenty-four hours before Arfons was to return to Utah, a rainstorm swept across the Great Lake Desert, flooding the Bonneville Speedway and threatening his attempt.

Wendover mayor, Johnny Susich, a member of the Speedway Association, said there was one inch of water on portions of the track, making it "impossible" for any runs within the immediate future.

As it turned out, Arfons would have to wait until November 1966. Firestone would conduct static load tests to prevent another blowout. The results were startling. Some 6000 pounds of pressure were exerted on the right rear tire when Arfons kicked in the burner.

With that kind of force, it was no wonder the tire would blow... and blow and blow. But you can't run record speeds without a burner. The solution: run dual tires in the rear, thus absorbing the enormous load. Thus the Green Monster had two wheels up front, four in back.

It worked perfectly at Bonneville.

But Arfons left for Utah with a feeling he couldn't shake... that he would crash. He saw it all in a dream, the first time about a month before his departure. The second time, the night before his ill-fated run.

"Before he left for Bonneville", recalls his wife, June, "Art was fixing everything around the house, even Tim's tree house. Art finally told me he had a premonition about the car crashing.

"Just as any other wife would do I begged him to forget the record and stay home, but he insisted again and again, 'It's only a dream'."

Arfons, likewise, vividly remembers those days so many years ago.

"June really raised a ruckus. I can still hear her saying, 'You can't go. Stay home. Allison is your baby, too. You have to help me raise her.' But when it came time for me to leave, June had my gear packed. She knew I was going."

Arfons didn't usually rest well the night before a record attempt. But he had a miserable time of it Wednesday, November 16.

"I think it might have been the longest night of my life. The dream came back and I just knew I was gonna have a crash. It never happened to me like that before and it's not happened since."

Had Art Arfons been killed, he would have left his wife and family with a roof over their heads, little else. "I had no medical insurance and no life insurance. At that time I had $2000 that I kept in a tin. Military insurance, that's all I had.

"They [insurance companies] wouldn't sell it to me because they knew I was drag racing. I wasn't worried about it. I had taken out mortgage cancellation on everything I owned. On the house, the car, the truck. A bank will sell you mortgage cancellation. If you get killed before you finish paying on it, it's all paid up."

Ever since 1959, a Petrali has been the man in charge of the United States Auto Clubs (USAC) timing team. Title: chief steward.

The late Joe Petrali was hooked on motorcycles as a hill climber, a short tracker. In 1937, he raced across the sand of Ormond Beach, Florida, on a motorcycle at 137 miles an hour.

In 1959, he replaced Art Pillsbury as head man for land speed racing.

The elder Petrali died in 1973. He was succeeded by his son, David, who first went to Bonneville in 1960. He was a member of the USAC timing team when Art Arfons crashed at 610 miles an hour.

"When Arfons was running, the mile long timing wire was laid down between Mile Five and Mile Six. We had our trailer right in the middle," says Petrali, of Upland, California.

"The wire is just on one side of the course. The photo light source is on one side and the photo receiver on the other side. When the car enters the measured mile, it passes the light beam and triggers the electronic timing.

"The day that Arfons crashed I was an observer. He crashed coming towards me. He was just coming out of the mile, and he looked good. I can't tell you how fast he was going, but it was pretty quick.

"He was at an angle to me – ten o'clock. He hadn't passed in front of me. I was quite a way from the track, in excess of 1000 feet. I was following him through the lens of my camera. I had a 500 zoom.

"Suddenly, Art went into the air and it seemed like an eternity until he came down. When he hit, he hit on the belly and slid along the belly for quite a while.

"Then something like this happens, it's probably in a ten to fifteen second time span, but it seems like forever when you're seeing it happen. It's kinda like an earthquake. It seems like forever but it isn't all that long.

"Almost at the time I first saw Art's car take off, I had a flashback. It was almost 1962 all over again when Glenn Leasher was killed.

"The thing that struck me was that both cars were at about the same angle to me when they crashed. But I was much closer to Leasher. Arfons was coming towards me. Leasher's jet car had just gone by me.

"Leasher shut his engine off right in front of me. In fact, I took a picture of the afterburner in full burn. Then he was about in front of me, he turned it off. That's when the thing let go. That's when he lost it.

"Arfons' car, while it did go in the air and there was a tremendous amount of salt and car parts flying around, it didn't tumble like Leasher's car.

"Leasher's car wasn't constructed nearly as well as Arfons' Green Monster. He also had a very serious disadvantage in that he sat in the nose. The whole front end of Leasher's car broke off because he tumbled so violently."

As quickly as he could, Dave Petrali got into his car and raced across the salt flats. "I got there about the same time the ambulance arrived. But I was on the opposite side of his cockpit. I didn't know what to expect as I started walking around the car.

"The top wing was gone, the tail fin was all beat up, but the car didn't look to be in all that bad a condition. I was surprised. I got to the car and he was moving. I couldn't believe it.

"Can you imagine the tremendous forces involved? He survived a 600 mile an hour crash with very little damage. You can talk about how strong the car was built, about the right side sustaining most of the damage, but that's just part of the answer. It just wasn't his time!

"When the day began, we all thought Arfons would break Breedlove's record [600.601]. After all, the car was certainly capable of reaching that kind of record speed, and hadn't they traded back and forth for two years?

"No matter who's going for the record, you hope he gets it, primarily because of the risk involved. These are unusual, intriguing people, just as interesting as their machines... different exercises in engineering."

ART ARFONS' GREEN MONSTER

Owner and Driver	Art Arfons, Akron, Ohio
Attempts	Bonneville, Utah
Record Runs	October 5, 1964 – 434 mph October 27, 1964 – 536.71 mph November 7, 1965 – 576.553 mph
Construction Time	12 months
Estimated Cost	Arfons' cost: approximately $15,000; tires and wheels by Firestone in excess of $50,000

Project Engineer	Art Arfons
Project Associate	Ed Snyder
Engine	J–79 turbo jet with multi-state afterburner
Fuel	Kerosene, 110 gallon capacity
Horsepower	17,500 at sea level with afterburner
Weight	6,500 pounds *
Dimensions	21 feet long, 74 inches wide
Frame	Chromemoly steel tubing, spaced tubed frame
Tires	Firestone 7.00–18 'Bonneville' tires, 200+ pounds pressure
Wheels	Forged aluminum made by Firestone Steel Products Company
Brakes	Disc brakes, two parachutes for added drag at braking point
Suspension	Air over oil on front
Track	65 inches front, 68 inches rear, 170 inch wheel base
Speed Potential	650 mph + with afterburner

* Weight before dual tires added for November 1966 attempt.

Chapter Eighteen

The Sky's the Limit... What About the Earth?

I said a lot of things back in the sixties about shooting for the sound barrier, but it was all hype. Firestone artists drew sketches of sound barrier cars, but they didn't have an 800 mile an hour tire. They just wanted the ink.

You can talk about 800, 900, 1000 miles an hour, but surviving that kind of ride is another thing. You could hit the shock wave anywhere from 680 to 750 miles an hour, depending on the barometric pressure and how dense the air is.

Art Arfons

Webster's New Collegiate Dictionary defines 'Mach' this way: 'high speed expressed by a Mach number'.

It is a word that has become part of our space-age language. Mach... Speed of Sound... interchangeable!

Back in 1887, Dr. Ernest Mach, an Austrian scientist, wrote a paper entitled *Photographic Registration of the Phenomena in the Air Produced by a Projectile*.

This paper described experiments with military shells traveling at speeds faster than sound (supersonic). With the help of his son, Ludwig, a physician, Mach built the world's first wind tunnel. The photographic system he developed was called a 'Schieren' apparatus. *Schieren* in German means shadow.

Seventy years after its discovery, this apparatus which permits photographing of all sorts of shock waves and other flow phenomena involving variations of density, is now an integral part of the equipment of every transonic and supersonic tunnel.

The advent of transonic tunnels paved the way for the study of supersonic planes which could not safely be flown through the sound barrier without definite knowledge of their drag and control characteristics.

On October 14, 1947, U.S. Air Force Captain Charles B. Yeager established aviation history by piloting his rocket-powered Bell X-1 through the previously impenetrable barrier. More than forty years later, Yeager would play a role in another sound barrier adventure. But that's another story.

Dropped from the belly of a B-29 bomber at 35,000 feet, Yeager relied on his four rocket engines developing 6000 pounds of thrust to push X-1 to a speed of 1200 miles an hour.

Twenty years later, William J. 'Pete' Knight, another Air Force test pilot, rode his X-15 through the rarefied atmosphere at 4,543 miles an hour, or Mach 6.72. It was the fastest aircraft flight ever!

While rocket-powered missiles were blasting to unheard of speeds, piston-powered land speed cars were crawling by comparison. In 1947, the land speed record was 394.4. But with the advent of jet power, the record would soar into the 600 mph range within three short years (1963–1965).

And only until Craig Breedlove averaged 600.601 in his Spirit of America – Sonic I did man openly dream about crashing the sound barrier on land.

Rocket sleds, secured to a rail, had already surpassed the speed of sound. On March 19, 1954, Air Force Colonel John Paul Stapp, a veteran of aviation medical research, rode Sonic Wind, a rocket sled, to the speed of 632 miles an hour. Although seriously injured, Stapp lived to tell the tale.

And what a scary tale!

The 2000 pound sled, propelled by nine rockets unleashing 40,000 pounds of thrust, required just seconds on its run down the 2350 foot long track at Holloman Air Force Base in Alamogordo, New Mexico.

It wasn't the tremendous G forces on his body as much as the instantaneous stop that almost killed Stapp.

"That guy must have been the bravest s.o.b. that ever lived," says Arfons.

Three years later, a driverless sled hit 2075 mph over a two mile track. A monorail vehicle has reached 2850 miles an hour. "But," adds Arfons, "those sleds were put on a rail four feet off the ground.

"So, the bottom part of the shock wave would move under the sled. It's a different thing with a car which is riding along the surface of the ground. I think that wave will lift the car. Anyway, I'm too damned old to ever find out.

"When I was a lot younger and bullet-proof, I really wanted no part of that adventure. My record-setting Green Monster was built with a speed potential of 500. It far exceeded that potential.

"And the Monster I built after that, the one I wish I hadn't sold to Slick Gardner, was built for 700. That's just under supersonic. I know I said they were both supersonic cars. What can I say? It was part of the game."

Now let us return to the mid-1960s when the race to the sound barrier was the name of the high-speed game.

To break the sound barrier on land, a driver had to go 720–750 miles an hour. Arfons, Craig Breedlove, Walt Arfons and Donald Campbell all threw their helmets into the ring.

Arfons, who set records of 434, 536 and 576 in 1964–65, announced a sensible approach. He would first rig his Green Monster with a remote control and 'drive' it through the barrier. "The worst that can happen is I lose a car."

He approached the task ahead with caution.

"Very few airplanes that the government has today are allowed to go through [the barrier] at that altitude – 4,000 feet at Bonneville – because of the density of the air. Most can't go supersonic below 5,000 feet."

He felt it would take brute force rather than aerodynamics to get the job done.

"If you had twenty miles of salt, it would take less power and a good design. But with ten to eleven miles of running room, it will take nothing but power."

His thoughts were contained in a bylined article, in July 1965, in a men's interest magazine, under the heading, 'How I'll Drive Faster Than Sound'.

For one thing, he noted, his Green Monster had the power in the form of a 17,500 horsepower GE J–79 jet engine which pushed air force fighters to Mach 2 – twice the speed of sound.

Said the author:

"The J–79 produces 10,000 horsepower at 375 mph [using the formula that in a gas turbine one pound of thrust equals one horsepower at that speed]. It has four stages of afterburner for even more power."

He knew he had the device to keep the front wheels on the ground.

"I used a small hinged wing – a true inverted airfoil – of my own design and construction to keep the proper pressure on those wheels.

"If the Monster began getting anxious to get airborne, a hydraulic cylinder behind the chassis and the front axle sensed it, and instantly transmitted an order to another hydraulic cylinder, between the trailing edge of my wing and the top of the engine cowling, to depress.

"The inverted airfoil, with the 'lift' on its lower side, naturally tended to put pressure on the front wheels. When it was tilted downward, of course, it added more pressure."

The first stage of his sound barrier assault was 650 miles an hour.

"Although I'll use full power from the four-stage afterburner, I don't plan to keep full power for more than eighteen seconds. That should be enough to reach 650.

"I could run on all four stages longer, but I'm not about to be a hero. I don't know what will happen to a car once it reaches supersonic speed... no one really does.

"All it will cost me is one car if it doesn't make it through the barrier. And I don't want to be in the cockpit to find out."

Once he successfully reached the '650 mph plateau', it was then that Art Arfons planned to make a test run via remote control.

By 1965, Craig Breedlove was ready to resume his jet duel with Arfons in a coke-shaped four-wheeler with a more powerful three-stage J–79 with afterburner. Strictly supersonic stuff this Spirit of America – Sonic I.

Breedlove also challenged Arfons as an author. The eye-catching headline on his September 1965 piece said: *750 MPH... HERE I COME*".

In that magazine article, he considered "...transonic speed the real problem, but I think the car can get through safely. A driver just can't charge at the sound barrier. It has to be approached gradually.

"If you increase speed one hundred miles at a crack, you run into behavioral patterns you weren't expecting. If you increase the speed in lesser increments, you can get a good idea each time of the problem you'll encounter at the next stage."

Transonic is the turbulent speed range preceding supersonic. A car could go from calm subsonic to, hopefully, calm supersonic when the air once again would be 'clean'.

"No one ever dreamed of a supersonic automobile a few years ago," he continued. "I expect Spirit to become one. One thing is certain. Some day, someone will drive a car at Mach I or faster."

Breedlove then outlined, in detail, several other major problem areas:

(1) *Local Sonic Flow.* "When the new Spirit is approaching Mach I, there will be sonic or even supersonic air flows at places like the curve of the nose and the curved cockpit canopy. One reason why local sonic flows are dangerous is because they can change a vehicle's center of pressure, making it unstable.

"The car could yaw or try to roll. The front tires might squash into the salt, or the front end could lighten and let the nose lift. Sonic flows can suddenly reverse a car's stability.

"That is, I may find that at a certain speed the car starts drifting to the left, and I'll correct for this. But a couple of seconds later and 100 mph faster, the car may start the same left drift and then reverse its drift. If I had started to correct, I'll be over-correcting. I'd be in big trouble. I'll have to wait part of a second to see what the car is really going to do.

"Local sonic flows create local shock waves, and the timers halfway down the course will hear a boom when the car hurtles past. But observers at the far end of the course won't hear one unless the whole car reaches Mach I. They could use the boom, or lack of it, as an unofficial speed indicator.

"True sonic boom will be generated by several parts of the car at Mach I or faster, and these pressure waves will hit the ground and bounce back against the vehicle. But at the 'low' supersonic speeds I eventually hope to reach, these over-pressures shouldn't cause trouble."

(2) *Skin Temperature.* "The new car can go so fast that aerodynamic heating becomes a problem. Even though we'll

run during the coolest part of the day, right after dawn, the skin temperature will climb to about 160 degrees at Mach I. The transparent canopy has been designed so it won't warp or come apart at high temperature.

"Too, the hot skin heats up the air in the intake duct, expanding and thinning it. This could cause a flame-out by upsetting the critical air-fuel ratio. Furthermore, the inflowing air is blocked and some of it spills back out of the duct intake. The car becomes unstable and hard to control.

"A heat stall isn't as likely in high speed aircraft because they travel in colder air, often as cold as fifty-five below zero. And if an aircraft's engine does flame out, the plane can wander from a straight path without harm. On land there's only one, ultimate penalty for not steering straight at Mach I."

(3) *Tires*. "Goodyear, my main sponsor, have solved that problem. The new tires [pressurized to 250 p.s.i.] have been tested successfully at 850. Goodyear's engineers estimate that at this speed the centrifugal pull on the tires amounts to two million pounds, about a thousand times the centrifugal force exerted on a passenger car tire at 60 mph.

"The rear tires measure 8.00 x 39, on thirty-nine inch forged aluminum wheels, and the front tires are 8.00 x 25s, on twenty-five inch forged aluminum wheels. The tires have a footprint five and a half inches wide, very thin tread, and an extremely low angle in the fabric restrictor belts. We have the tires to go beyond Mach I."

(4) *Braking*. "I'm going to depend again on drag chutes, this time especially strengthened against high opening shock. If necessary, we'll use a reefed chute that 'grows with time'. The chute is small when it hits the air, then a timer is set off which cuts the reef points, allowing the chute to open full size. This insures a gentler opening without a terrific initial impact.

"For final slowing to a stop we are using aircraft-type disc brakes, possibly using liquid nitrogen sprayed as a gas to keep the brake pucks cool."

(5)   *Power.*   "The J–79 develops more than 10,000 pounds of thrusts over 15,000 pounds with afterburner. Power is no problem."

The coke-bottle shape in front of the thirty-five foot long car was no accident.

"This helps balance the area of local sonic flow when Mach I is being approached. This insures the best stability. The shape also helps diminish any problem from ground effect.

"Our first design had a tall, thin, swept-back tail. This has been shortened and made longer for more stability. If the tail should flutter at high speed, it could tear apart and put the car out of control.

"The air intake is placed on top of the car where it can't sweep up foreign objects – even salt could be a problem – from the course. It's located pretty far forward to allow space in the duct for good air distribution before the air enters the engine."

Breedlove had hoped to sit further back instead of up close, just ahead of the duct intake.

"It's the same reason we changed the original long, narrow cockpit canopy to a wide wrap-around canopy that follows the curvature of the air inlet over the top of the car.

"Walt Sheehan [chief designer] explains that the new canopy will create a shock wave at Mach I and that one is needed at this location to slow down the air flowing into the duct. With velocity reduced, the air pressure goes up. This insures engine performance and reduces the risk of a heat stall.

"Walt designed the duct so that the air flowing through it will generate a minimum of noise. Otherwise the loud, shrill scream of the rushing air would be too painful for me to tolerate. He put a slot just below the duct inlet to bleed off boundary layer air for engine cooling."

But ultimately, he felt his main protection "...will be the same careful speed build-up that I've used before checking out every part of the car and the way it handles.

"The next run will be about fifty miles an hour faster if no trouble develops, finally building up to the fastest speed. This method allows us to detect, analyze and correct any trouble before it becomes dangerous"

In 1964, Walt Arfons' jet-powered Wingfoot Express held the spotlight for seventy-two hours when Tom Green set a record of 413 mph. Three days later, Art Arfons went 434.

But in 1965, the older Arfons conceived and built the most intriguing sound barrier candidate in his radical, space-age missile, Wingfoot Express. The massive, three and a half ton, four-wheeler resembled an Atlas missile on its side, ushered in the rocket age to land speed racing. Bobby Tatroe was named 'test pilot'.

"Once the sound barrier is broken", said Walt Arfons, "it will be the end of land speed racing attempts. From then on, it will only be a matter of going faster.

"How many persons know who followed [Charles] Lindberg across the Atlantic and [Roger] Bannister under the four-minute mile?

"There will be a slight shudder as the car goes through the barrier, perhaps not enough to notice. If the car doesn't blast through, the shock waves will tear it apart."

Arfons, who built the first jet-powered dragsters, maintained rocket power was far superior to jet thrust at supersonic speed.

"A rocket has no intakes, so it can have a clean, streamlined body to break air and shock waves. A jet intake has to reach out ahead of the car to suck air. This causes turbulence quite ahead of the car and more turbulence as the air goes into the intake. When the jet is shut off, the air in front packs.

"Before, the car was cutting a hole through the wall of air. Suddenly, there's no hole. The rear of the car would go all over.

"With the rockets the resistance is behind instead of ahead. This keeps the car straight, on the same principle as a flying arrow. The car slips through cleanly."

Arfons' rocket racer was powered by JATO (jet assist take-off) bombs, costing $700 each. The original design, called for fifteen JATOs – each thirty inches long, ten inches wide, weighing 1000 pounds.

When the car made its impressive media run in September 1965, Walt Arfons mapped out his plan as the Wingfoot Express rumbled down the airport runway at about 100 mph, powered by just one stick of dynamite.

Tatroe would release the rockets every two seconds. Five bursts (fifteen rockets) and about 17.8 seconds later, the Wingfoot Express would enter the measured mile at 714 miles an hour.

"The run through the measured mile should last 4.87 seconds. That's 739 miles an hour! And at 4.9 seconds, the speed will be 726.

"Before we shoot for that speed, we'll make a run into the 300s, a run in the 400s, followed by several runs at 600. Since nobody knows what happens when a car approaches sound barrier speed, we'll work up to that gradually.

"By the end of the first week, Bob may nudge 700 if the shock waves aren't too great. Then in October, we'll shoot for the barrier."

England's Donald Campbell completed the mid-1960s sound barrier cast when he announced plans to go supersonic in a 840 mile an hour rocket car named Bluebird, naturally.

Kenneth Norris, designer of Campbell's jet boats and land speed car, felt "...the length of the course available demands high acceleration and heavy braking.

"The primary requirements, therefore, are for a vehicle having high thrust-to-weight ratio, low resistance-to-weight ratio and a reliable means of reducing speed rapidly.

"From previous experience, even for jet-propelled vehicles, the length of the course may be between eight and twelve miles. Assuming an average course length of ten miles is available and that the measured distance is placed in the optimum position – that is, the middle – then the run in from each distance is restricted to four and a half miles.

"These relatively short distances demand a vehicle capable of accelerating and of being braked at an average of 1 G, approximately, in order to reach a Mach number of 1.1 [840] and complete its mission successfully.

"This means, allowing for the rapid rise in aerodynamic drag through the sound barrier, that the vehicle will require a thrust of one and a half times the weight, a resistance not greater than the weight of 840 and a braking system capable of providing an average retarding force at least equal to the weight of the vehicle less that resistance.

"Under these circumstances, the complete run of ten miles one way from the start will take about one minute, the measured distance of one kilometer and one mile taking but two and a half and four seconds respectively.

"It is implicit in the rules that the stability of the vehicle is such that manual control is possible through the speed range.

"Aerodynamic forces, depending on vehicle shape, can change considerably as the vehicle passes through the sound barrier. The shock wave associated with the speed of sound and shed from the nose may rebound back and forth from the ground so that the vehicle may indeed be 'riding' on its own shock wave.

"These aerodynamic effects may adversely affect the stability of the vehicle both in pitch and yaw, but this deterioration must be limited so that the vehicle maintains load on the ground, and in such a manner that steering is adequate.

"Indeed, if the hazard to the driver is to be at all acceptable, aerodynamic stability must be maintained independent of mechanical [tire-to-ground] stability, the suspension must be extremely stiff to maintain control over the attitude of the vehicle [small changes in incidence can considerably affect aerodynamic forces] and the surface over which the run is made must be flat to fractions of an inch over one hundred yards.

"Model and full-scale wind tunnel tests must be carried out to assure that the above requirements are met. Also, to meet these requirements, the wheels of the vehicle should be relatively small, and housed, as far as possible, within the body.

"That means that, in order to reach the high speed required, the wheels will need to revolve at high speed, and consequently, very high centrifugal forces will be general.

"Although temperature rise due to the speed is unlikely to be a problem, there being a theoretical rise at the very nose of the vehicle at seventy degrees Celsius only at 840, noise may cause some difficulty."

Campbell's supersonic Bluebird was to be twenty-two feet long, weigh about 4000 pounds, and be powered by a pair of Bristol-Siddeley BS RATO (rocket assist take-off) engines, mounted one above the other on the tail. A full-scale mock-up was built in 1965.

Instead of tires, Campbell's Mach 1.1 missile would run on solid metal wheels. He would sit up front, ahead of a single front wheel (it was a three-wheeler), the fuel tanks and engines.

Candidates aplenty, but would anyone succeed?

But first, a study of sound in layman's terms, and what the experts of that day thought were the possibilities of a land-bound car traveling faster than the speed of sound along the surface of the ground.

Although invisible, the air is composed of countless numbers of extremely tiny atoms and molecules of nitrogen, oxygen and other gases. Each atom or molecule is so tiny that some 400 billion of them can be found in every cubic inch of the air at sea level.

In constant motion, they travel in all directions, bumping into each other, and striking any object they encounter. In doing so, they exert pressure. When waves of varying air pressure strike our ears, we 'hear' them as sounds.

Sound waves can be likened to the ripples created by the dropping of a stone into a body of still water. Traveling outward, the sound waves eventually pulsate against the ears, much as water pulsates when agitated.

The speed of sound is the time it takes for sound to travel from its source to the receiver, which, in turn, depends upon the speed at which the gas molecules 'carrying' the pressure waves are moving.

Generally speaking, sound travels at 1000 feet per second, but varies with altitude, air density and temperature. At normal temperature at sea level, sound travels at a speed of about 760 miles an hour. Because of the lower air temperatures at higher altitudes, sound travels slower.

At an altitude of 20,000 feet, for example, the speed of sound is about 700 miles an hour, and at 36,000 feet it's only 660.

At subsonic speeds the air flow ahead of the plane or car is stable. But when the vehicle travels faster than the speed of sound, a different air-flow pattern results, much like a boat tossed in a storm.

At such speeds, the air is compressed into a cone-like pattern called a shock wave. This extreme disturbance accumulates in a narrow region just ahead of the craft.

The shock wave travels to the ground at the speed of sound, follows the path of the plane, and becomes audible as a sonic boom as it slaps against the surface of the earth.

A symmetrically shaped plane, traveling in free air, has fewer problems traveling faster than sound, due to the equalizing of the pressures exerted on all parts.

However, this is not the case with a land-bound vehicle. The shock waves created at supersonic speed are cone-shaped, but because of the land obstruction, the pressure exerted on the car is uneven.

The top half of the car produces a negative or suction-like pressure. The bottom wave creates a positive or lifting pressure. After slamming the ground, the shock wave has only one place to travel – up.

This upward pressure could disintegrate the car or turn it into a wingless plane. Without the proper body design, a car could alternately fly and touch down.

Another major problem is thermal heat. Air flowing around a plane heats to a high temperature. For example, the air temperature in low altitude flights at Mach 3 (three times the speed of sound) would be about 940 degrees Fahrenheit. Heat holds the speed of a plane down and tends to weaken and even melt its parts.

The car must be constructed sturdily enough so that, upon entering the barrier, it can resist the pressure exerted on the front end – 1500 pounds per square foot.

For every expert certain there's really no 'mystery' to the sound barrier, his counterpart labels such an adventure extremely hazardous.

Said Boeing engineer John Swihart: "There's no technical reason why an automobile cannot exceed the speed of sound. The only drawback would be the amount of power required.

"The main problem that faced the aircraft industry was one of designing for the airflow encountered at transonic speed [the turbulent stage just before supersonic] and in providing enough thrust to proceed through the transonic drag rise design. They finally overcame the problem through improved aerodynamic design and better engines."

Countered H.K. Gagos of McDonnell Douglas: "The consensus of our aerodynamicists is that it would be extremely hazardous under present knowledge, highly improbable for an automobile, as currently known, to attain supersonic speed.

"For an automobile, the biggest problems would be lack of stability, control and traction. It would require a shape which not only could penetrate the sound barrier, but could, at the same time, generate strong negative lift.

"The air should force the car downward. It is obvious, then, that wind tunnel testing would be mandatory for a vehicle of this kind. In fact, it would be imprudent not to test any high speed racing car, not only to reduce the tremendous drag but to maintain lateral stability."

Both Breedlove and Arfons belonged to the class of wind tunnel non-believers.

"Airplane designers aren't much help to a man building a land racer," said Breedlove, "because conditions on the ground aren't at all like five miles up.

"It's like comparing walking through air with walking through water. All wind-tunnel data is useless to us, and so is the performance of high-speed sleds. They're locked to their tracks."

According to Arfons, "Donald Campbell's Bluebird was tunnel-tested, yet it flew 800 feet in the air at about 350 miles an hour."

In a nutshell, Dean Richmond of Cornell Aeronautical Lab in Buffalo, New York, supplied the description of a wind tunnel. (Cornell's wind tunnel, one of the most advanced in the world, has been used to test models of virtually every American military and commercial aircraft design developed since 1947.)

"The tunnel is laid out in a rectangular shape so that the air within the tunnel makes a continuous circuit. The rectangle is 180 feet long and 70 feet wide.

"The high-velocity air stream, which moves past a stationary model in the test section of the wind tunnel, is created by forty-eight variable-pitch aluminum fan blades, each seven feet long.

"The fans, arranged in three consecutive groups of sixteen each, are driven by an 11,000 horsepower electric motor. It takes about two minutes of operation for the fans to have the air moving through the tunnel at the speed of sound.

A 13,000 horsepower motor is also used during operation of the tunnel to help maintain a steady flow of air through the test section, where the air would have a tendency to become blocked at the higher speed ranges.

"The test section of the tunnel is a large removable cart which can accommodate a model eight feet long with a wing span up to four feet. Many of the models are made of wood and stainless steel.

"The data gathered during a wind tunnel test is provided by small strain gauges embedded in the model. The gauges respond to the forces applied to them in the wind tunnel by generating electrical pulses.

"The pulses are a measure of the amount of force being experienced by the model and are translated into specific figures on such factors as lift or drag.

"A computerized data-processing system receives the raw pulses and immediately converts them into numerical data, which engineers can analyze to determine the effectiveness or efficiency of the [aircraft] design.

"In addition to strain gauges, commonly used equipment includes pressure transducers, still cameras, high-speed movie cameras and shadowgraph photography."

So much for the theory, what of the heroes of the sixties? Was the sound barrier myth or man-killer?

While Breedlove's Spirit of America – Sonic I became the first car to crash the 600 mph barrier (600.601 in 1965), it fell far short of its goal. In fact, the front wheels left the ground at 600. To correct this dangerous situation, weight was added to the nose to keep the car on the ground.

Walt Arfons' rocket started out with fifteen JATOs, at $700 a pop, but it wasn't enough power, so ten more bombs were added to the 6500 pound car. And while Wingfoot Express hit a peak speed, it ran out of muscle midway through the measured mile. So much for 739 miles an hour.

The always innovative Walt Arfons, first to introduce jets to the drag strip, rocket power to land speed racing, went even one step beyond. He envisioned breaking the barrier with good old-fashioned steam.

In fact, he even built a prototype dragster. Again Bobby Tatroe, who drove the rocket racer, was in the cockpit. During its maiden run, the pocket-sized missile flipped at an estimated 200 miles an hour. Tatroe was not injured.

Arfons, however, never pursued his project, a five ton 'steamroller'.

Until November 1966, Art Arfons had never used more than first stage of the brutish J-79's four-stage afterburner. The only time he went to second stage was on November 17, 1966, when he miraculously survived a 610 mph crash. His cherished Green Monster was demolished.

In January 1967, Donald Campbell was killed during an attempt to recapture the world water speed record.

The sensational sixties would come to a close with the sound barrier still the unclaimed prize in the world of speed.

Art Arfons in his *Anteater* at Daytona International Speedway, 1960. It was Arfons' first land speed creation. The car was powered by an Allison Aircraft, World War Two engine.
Photograph courtesy of of Art Arfons.

Art Arfons in his first jet-powered, open cock-pit car, *Cyclops*. He reached a top speed of 360mph in a land speed attempt in 1962.
Photograph courtesy of the *Firestone Tire and Rubber Company*.

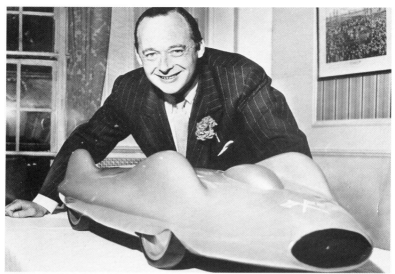

Donald Campbell with a model of the *Bluebird*. He crashed it at
Bonneville Salt Flats, Utah in 1960.
Photograph courtesy of the *Dunlop Tire Company*.

American hot rodder, Mickey Thompson, made a one-way run reaching a
top speed of 406mph in 1960, but the car, *Challenger I*, broke down on
the return trip. He was the first American to hit 400mph.
Photograph courtesy of Mickey Thompson.

Dr. Nathan Ostich and his *Flying Caduceus*, the first jet-powered car in land speed racing. The car made its debut at Bonneville Salt Flats, Utah in 1960.
Photograph courtesy of the *Firestone Tire and Rubber Company*.

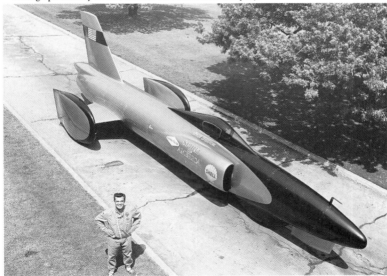

Craig Breedlove stands alongside his three-wheeled *Spirit of America*. He set three land speed records in this jet-powered car during 1963 to 1964.
Photograph courtesy of the *Goodyear Tire and Rubber Company*.

Craig Breedlove in his *Spirit of America* – "an aeroplane on wheels". It set land speed records of 407mph, 468mph and 526mph during 1963 and 1964.

The *Spirit of America* crashes after a run into a salt pond at a speed of 526mph, a land speed record in 1964.

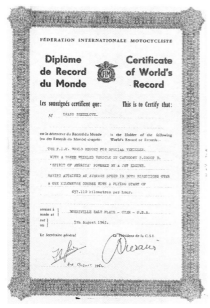

Certificate from FIM (Fédération Internationale Motocycliste). Craig Breedlove's first land speed record of 407mph, 1963.

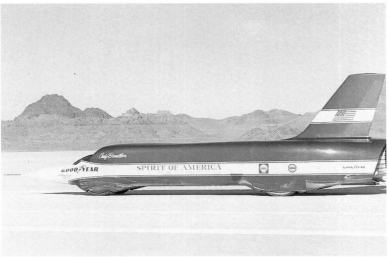

The *Spirit of America – Sonic I,* the first car to average a speed of 600mph. In 1965 it reached a top speed of 600.601mph and in doing so it set two land speed records – Flying Mile, Flying Kilo.

David Campbell set his only land speed record in *Bluebird*. He averaged
a speed of 403mph in his four-wheel driven car, at Lake Eyre, Australia.
Photograph courtesy of the *Mirror Australian Telegraph Publications*.

Betty Skelton set the women's land speed record in Art Arfons' jet-powered
dragster, *Cyclops,* in 1964.
Photograph courtesy of the *Firestone Tire and Rubber Company*.

Tom Green, the driver of the *Wingfoot Express,* receives instructions from Walt Arfons. The car set a land speed record of 413mph in 1964.
Photograph courtesy of the *Goodyear Tire and Rubber Company.*

The *Wingfoot Express* during its record run of 413mph in 1964, with Tom Green in the cockpit. He held the land speed record for three days.
Photograph courtesy of the *Goodyear Tire and Rubber Company.*

The *Wingfoot Express* 'armed' with its JATO rockets. It was built in 1965
by Walt Arfons and resembled an Atlas missile.
Photograph courtesy of the *Goodyear Tire and Rubber Company.*

The *Wingfoot Express* driven by Bob Tatrol was the first rocket-powered
land speed car in 1965. It reached a top speed of 550mph aided by
twenty-five JATO rockets.
Photograph courtesy of the *Goodyear Tire and Rubber Company.*

Chapter Nineteen

622 Miles an Hour on Half Power... the Blue Flame

In its time, the Blue Flame was by far the best car out there. It was a good, clean, stable car. But they sure had trouble getting the record. They stuck it out and prevailed. They had to push the car to a hundred mile an hour speed so they could have enough fuel to carry it through the measured mile. That's the big problem with rocket cars, not enough fuel capacity.

Gary [Gabelich] would run out of power before he'd get through the mile. The speed would drop off. The truck would push the car, then back off and he'd fire the rocket. I met Gary when he was in Akron on a tour after setting the record. He was a real nice guy.

Art Arfons

Once upon a time, as the legend goes, three friends joined forces on a glorious quest:
– to set a new land speed record
– to break the sound barrier.

On October 27, 1970, Gabelich set a new two-way average of 622.407 mph in the rocket-powered Blue Flame. It was more than twenty miles an hour faster than Craig Breedlove's 600.601 standard, set five years previously.

Those three amigos – Dick Keller, Pete Farnsworth, Ray Dausman – were right on target. Break the record in 1970, penetrate through the mysterious barrier in '71. However, they failed to fulfill that dream. Call it small print in a contract.

To finance the ambitious project, they turned to the American Gas Association. AGA was delighted to get involved. What better way to promote Liquified Natural Gas (LNG), the so-called fuel of the future. LNG would be used as the propellant for the needle-nosed rocket car.

But according to the contract the car had to be completed for a 1969 run at the record. However, completion was two months behind schedule. The earliest attempt wouldn't come until 1970.

But delays equal money. More funding to keep the project going.

And once Gabelich broke Breedlove's record, AGA was no longer interested in continuing the project, even it meant breaking the sound barrier.

As per the contract, ownership of the car reverted from the three men and Reaction Dynamics, the company they formed, to American Gas Association. And as the story goes, Blue Flame was sold to a businessman in Holland for a paltry $25,000. The record-breaking car now resides in a museum in West Germany.

Dick Keller, who lives in Plover, Wisconsin, fondly recalls those good old days and what might have been.

"The car was probably the most stable land speed car that ever ran on the salt flats," he says proudly.

"We made twenty-nine runs with the same set of tires. No tread-wear. They were the same Goodyear tires that Breedlove ran in 1963, and according to what the late Joe Petrali [USAC's former land speed division chief steward] had told me, they had to pull the tires off Craig's car after only three or four runs.

"They were supersonic tires. They were tested up to a thousand miles an hour at Goodyear's test facility."

Hypothetically speaking, how does Keller think Blue Flame would fare today in the much publicized battle for the sound barrier.

"We know what Blue Flame did and is still capable of doing. Let's see what Breedlove's and [Richard] Noble's new supersonic jets can do. If I were a betting man, I'd go with the proven product.

"Gary averaged 622, with a peak speed of about 650, in a broken motor. If I had my hands on Blue Flame today, I'd only make minor changes. That's how good that car was.

"We'd make repairs to the engine. We would put in a larger LNG tank.

"The most difficult aspect of going through the sound barrier is going from transonic to supersonic because you have shock waves attaching and detaching at various parts of the vehicle.

"If you look at the front view of the car, it's sorta 'V' shaped. It's not cylindrical. With the V shape, the bottom shock waves would deflect around the car. Shock waves bouncing around under the car can create lift.

"Initially, we designed the car with wheel fairings and more of a wing arrangement, similar to Craig's first Spirit of America. But the wind tunnel tests at Ohio State University, suggested that the shock waves would interact with those parts, so we decided to go with no fairings on the wheels.

"Rather than using a faired strut, or a wing-type thing, we decided to hold the two wheels out there with tubes which would create no lift.

"Wind tunnel tests showed to us the car was capable of exceeding 900 miles an hour. We simulated a ground-effect in the tunnel as much as possible. We just weren't whistling Dixie."

Would Keller ever consider getting involved in another high-speed endeavor?

"If someone shows me $2 million and puts up half of it, I could get very interested very quickly."

Farnsworth, who lives in rural Wisconsin, hopes to return to the land speed hunt one of these days.

"I've had an idea for a wheel-driven car for about twenty years," he says. "I've waited this long, I can wait a little longer. This time I plan to make money on the deal, not just do it for the fun of it.

"It would be a totally different kind of wheel-driven car, but it's just bull until it's done. Aerodynamically, it would be different. It would burn a different kind of fuel. The engine would be unique. It would be a 500 mile an hour machine.

"I've been approached about building a new car for supersonic, but I told 'em the wheel-drive car has gotta come first. I can't wait to prove my concept."

Now, let's start at the beginning of this story!

Back in the early sixties, a young research technician named Ray Dausman wasn't impressed by speeds attained by conventional nitro-burning dragsters. They were clocking 205 in 7.5 seconds.

Dausman was thinking in much faster terms, and discussed the situation with Dick Keller, a co-worker at a the Chicago-based Illinois Institute of Technology Research Center (IIT).

Admittedly, Keller wasn't terribly active in drag racing personally, as a driver.

"I had a car that I raced myself in B Gas Coupe Sedan for two years. Then I was a gopher for Don Garlits for several years.

"I went around with Garlits, helping him with his car. He was probably the best driver I ever saw, and the most intelligent person I've ever met."

Keller and Dausman actually took it well past the idea of just building a top dragster. They were thinking supersonic, but the plan would be implemented by stages:

– build a small prototype rocket motor to demonstrate their ability to design and construct such a power plant

– build a prototype rocket-powered dragster with a larger engine to run on the drag strips

– create a car to smash Craig Breedlove's land speed record, then shoot for the sound barrier, 720 to 750 miles an hour at Bonneville.

"Jet power was readily available," admits Keller, "but we were interested in the speed of sound. Our feeling was that the complications of the aerodynamics with a air-breathing car was significantly higher than with a rocket which doesn't have to have large air inlets and has a much more compact propulsion system.

"The closer you get to the speed of sound, the more the air pressure builds up in front of the vehicle and it gets very complicated. The aerodynamics change drastically as you get into transonic and then into supersonic.

"It's tricky enough doing it with an aircraft, but when you're running on the surface of the ground you have so many other complications. We felt rocket power would simplify the entire equation.

"We could build a different type of car. It would be smaller, lighter and have simpler aerodynamics because you're not worried about air inlets."

Somehow, as Keller reflects back on his life, he always knew he would be involved in building a rocket car.

"As a kid, I had seen a picture of Opel's car in the encyclopedia. He was a German car builder in the 1920s. His cars were called RAK, which stands for Rockets in German. But those are also my initials and it kinda got my attention when I was a little kid. I never forgot about Opel's car."

Keller and Dausman tested their twenty-five pound rocket engine, fueled by hydrogen peroxide, in the fall of 1964. It performed to specifications.

By the end of the 1964 land speed season, the record had been raised from 407 to 536 mph. Art Arfons, an Ohio hot rodder, was 'King of Speed' at 536 mph.

For step two, construction of a rocket-powered dragster, Keller and Dausman, asked the help of Pete Farnsworth, a professional driver and car builder. They formed Reaction Dynamics and, with their own funds, started building the prototype rocket-propelled dragster X-1. The 'pocket rocket' was completed in April 1965.

Farnsworth built his first car when he was fourteen. "And by the time I was twenty-five", he recalls, "I was involved with or had built twenty-five local, national or international record-setting cars.

"I was quite into drag racing at the time, as a builder/driver. I went to Engineering School at both the University of Illinois and Northwestern, but math proved too tough for me. I couldn't complete engineering without the math, so I went toward the cars."

As it turned out, Blue Flame wasn't the first rocket-powered car in land speed history. But when you're No. 2, as the commercial goes, you try harder.

On October 2, 1964, Tom Green drove Walt Arfons' jet-powered Wingfoot Express to a new speed record of 413 mph. Three days later, however, Walt's younger brother, Art, blistered his way across the salt at 434 in his Green Monster.

The older Arfons would return to Bonneville, this time with the first rocket-propelled entry, also named Wingfoot Express. This massive car, which looked like an Atlas missile on its side, would first be propelled by ten JATO (jet assist take-off) rockets, and when that wasn't enough, fifteen more bombs were added.

It looked impressive, but never could sustain high speed through the measured mile.

When Arfons' rocket was in the process of being built, Dick Keller flew to Akron, to see the feuding Arfons Brothers, separately that is.

"I know Art was nervous about Walt's rocket at that time," recalls Keller. "While it was interesting, we really didn't consider it a serious threat for several reasons.

"First, the weight. They were building it with steel plating. We knew the thing was heavier than heck. And we knew there was limited thrust from those JATO units, even with twenty-five firing from the back.

"When we got back to Wisconsin, we made estimations of how fast we thought the car would really go. We were within five miles an hour of what they managed to do. The concept seemed imaginative, but we felt it was the wrong rocket system to use."

The X-1 chassis was completed in the spring of 1966. That summer Dick Keller became the first person to test drive X-1.

"First, we did static testing of the car," says Keller. "We had it chained down. We had a dyno on it. I made the first runs at Union Grove Dragway in Wisconsin.

"I made a couple of half-track runs. We didn't have the chutes hooked up. I ran it up to about 150 and shut it off. It felt like being squirted out of a tube of toothpaste. It was very smooth. You felt the pressure pushing you back, but you didn't have any of the vibrations you'd get from a dragster engine.

"Originally, the plan was that I'd be the driver for X-1, but we decided it wouldn't make any sense for any of the three of us to drive it because we had a partnership going. If one guy drives it, he'd be more of a partner than the others in terms of involvement."

So Dick Keller turned in his helmet.

"We all had regular jobs. We really wouldn't have had the opportunity to take X-1 around the country, but we had a drag racer/builder friend, named Chuck Suba, who was doing this for a living.

"At that time, he owned and drove US 1, and was also building a second jet car from scratch. We asked Chuck if he'd drive the dragster as well as the land speed car and he agreed."

In September 1966, Suba drove X-1, minus the body, to a speed of 203.39. Body work was completed in April 1967, with Farnsworth doing the fabricating.

By 1968, Suba hit an impressive 265.4 at Oklahoma city. Time for the quarter: 5.90 seconds. But what was critically important that day was that several top officials from the natural gas industry were on hand.

That run was the deciding factor in obtaining major sponsorship for a land speed car.

"Through the X-1", recalls Farnsworth, "the gas industry felt we had a good possibility to be successful with a land speed car. Dick [Keller] was mostly involved with selling the concept because he worked at IIT.

"It tied in a number of things that were of interest to the gas industry at the time. One was that the industry had an old stodgy image. They were trying to attract new people, scientists, graduates from engineering schools. They wanted to upgrade their image, to be more youth-oriented.

"The project was very technical, which appealed to the gas industry. But just as crucial, the car was capable of operating with Liquified Natural Gas. That was the point, the safety of LNG."

Keller explains:

"With X-1, we went to hydrogen peroxide because we felt it was extremely reliable and safe. But to set a land speed record, we needed a more powerful chemical system so we could get more power for a longer period of time.

"We needed some sort of system where we could use the hydrogen peroxide more as an oxidizer and have a fuel as well. It could have been gasoline, oil, diesel, whatever, but since I was working for the natural gas industry, LNG seemed the perfect answer."

Completed in the summer of 1970, Blue Flame was 37 feet, 4.6 inches long. Other dimensions: width (overall), 7 feet, 8 inches; height (top of cockpit), 5 feet, 1.5 inches; height (top of tail fin), 8 feet, 8 inches; wheelbase, 306.1 inches.

The designer originally planned to have one front wheel, but then the vehicle would have technically been classified as a three-wheeler or motorcycle. So, they built two front wheels only one inch apart. It was technically an automobile.

The rocket engine, stored in spheres in the car's needle nose, was placed behind the driver. The body and chassis were built as one integral unit, with a lightweight aluminum skin covering the semi-monocoque chassis.

The front wheels were locked in such a way that the steering wheel could be turned only one degree. In addition, a rudder just behind the cockpit was installed to keep the 5500 pound car on line.

Blue Flame was built to accelerate from zero to 750 miles an hour in just 7.5 seconds. The car's rocket engine was designed to deliver 22,000 pounds of thrust – 58,000 horsepower.

Chuck Suba never lived to drive Blue Flame. He was killed on September 13, 1968 while testing a piston-powered dragster for a friend.

"After Chuck died," says Keller, "there were a lot of guys contacted us about driving Blue Flame – Gary Gabelich included. But he really wanted to work out some sort of agreement where he could lease, or rent, X–1, our rocket dragster.

"Gary had sent us a lot of information about himself. He was an interesting guy, but it seemed at that time there would be no relationship. We didn't want to run X–1 and we'd already picked a driver to replace Chuck Suba."

That someone was legendary drag racer Don 'Big Daddy' Garlits.

"I was quite familiar with Garlits. As I said, he was the most intellectual guy I knew, in or out of a race car. He was bright. When I first called him, we talked for quite a while and he was interested.

"We flew him out to New York to meet the gas association PR people, shoot some photos both in New York and Chicago. While Don wanted to drive the car, his wife, Pat, and his mother, had the opposite feeling.

"Obviously, they'd lived with the drag racing. Don had been burned a couple of times and had some close calls. But at least drag racing was something they understood. Land speed racing was something they didn't understand at all.

"They felt that Don wouldn't be in control, so they were very apprehensive about the whole thing. I went out to Tampa to visit Don and I remember driving up the driveway. It was in the evening. There were little signs on the driveway that Pat set out. One said something like 'Speed Kills'.

"But even then, Don still wanted to drive the car. We had a press conference set for the first part of April in 1969 in Beverly Hills, California. Garlits was going to come out for the press conference, so we could unveil the entire package – car, concept and driver.

"We had invited all the motor press. It was something like six in the morning when I got a telegram from Don. He had finally given in. He wasn't going to drive the car.

"The press conference was scheduled for ten o'clock, so we had to virtually rewrite all the press material, to eliminate the driver. I know Don was disappointed, but I think he did the right thing. The family's more important."

Since Gary Gabelich didn't live too far away, Dick Keller called up the veteran drag racer. They had dinner, talked, and Gabelich eventually signed on to drive Blue Flame.

"Gary was good-looking, presented himself well. He was normally very light-hearted, a lot of fun to be around. But you see him change into another person when he got into the car.

"When he started buckling the seat belt and putting on the helmet, it was as if he turned on a switch. He was all business, an excellent driver and a very sharp communicator."

Gabelich worked for North American Rockwell for almost twenty years in various capacities, ranging from mailboy to test astronaut for the Apollo project.

In 1962, he was one of seven test astronauts selected to work in the company's program of environmental control studies. Part of the program called for living in space capsules up to twenty-two days under simulated high-altitude, re-entry and zero gravity conditions.

As a test astronaut, he also jumped from high altitudes with cameras to record the action of parachutes used in the re-entry of outer space capsules.

It was during his time at North American Rockwell that Gabelich was making a name for himself in drag racing – on the strips, on the water.

He started driving at the age of seventeen.

"I know several guys who had an old coupe," he said, "and they let me help. They were four or five years older. I was a donkey, doing all the dirty work.

"One day, out at the old Santa Ana strip, I had the chance to drive the car, but the strip manager said I was too young and needed written permission from my parents.

"I told him I'd be right back. I went to a gas station around the corner, signed my parents' names and then ran 138 miles an hour, the fastest the car had ever turned."

In the next five years, Gabelich drove every exotic piece of racing equipment on the market, ranging from gas and fuel rails to jet-powered cars and dragsters.

At the age of nineteen, he drove Bill Fredrick's jet-powered Valkyrie to speeds in excess of 350 miles an hour. It was Fredrick's first land speed creation, but the car never made an official run.

Gabelich handled the jet dragster Untouchable I, owned by Romeo Palimedes, and later piloted another jet racer owned by Mickey Thompson and Art Malone.

In 1963, Gabelich achieved the goal of all drag racers, beating national champion Dan Garlits in the first United Drag Racing Association meet.

He also piloted high-speed drag boats.

Gabelich was National Drag Boat Association fuel hydro champion in 1965. Three years later, he captured two other prestigious titles – American Power Boat Association nitro fuel and National Drag Boat Association's gasoline hydroplane championships.

By clocking 200.44 in 1969 in Crisis, hydro-powered by a Chrysler hemi engine, he topped Tommy Fultz's quarter-mile record for prop-driven boats.

And now the thirty year old driver, who began as a $1.29 an hour mailboy, was ready to take the ultimate step in racing.

"Even before I signed to drive it," he said, "I discussed it and studied it with several engineers. The wind tunnel tests, though not conclusive, showed the car was stable and the construction sound."

Gabelich knew he had a winner the first time he fired up Blue Flame during static tests.

"We chained her to a post sunk twenty-two feet in the ground and turned the engine on. She felt real good. It was like holding her back when she really wanted to go."

Instruments rigged to the car showed the speed estimated at 700 miles an hour.

LNG, the liquid form of natural gas, chilled to minus 258 degrees Fahrenheit. It served as the fuel, and hydrogen peroxide as the oxidizing agent which cooled the engine to prevent overheating.

In operation, the engine was designed to permit natural gas to be used as a liquid, gas, or both.

Here's how it worked: combustion starts in two stages. First, the oxidizer flow is established. Hydrogen peroxide goes through a catalyst pack which converts it from a liquid to a super-heated gas of 1400 degrees.

Then LNG enters a heat exchanger where it vaporizes and is brought to combustion temperature. The gas is injected into the combustion chamber with the oxygen provided by hydrogen peroxide.

A stable flame front is established and the remaining LNG injected to bring the engine to full power. Hydrogen peroxide alone gives the engine a thrust up to 12,000 pounds. But when LNG is fed into the hot gas, the action almost doubles the thrust.

Engine thrust varies by controlling the flow rates of the propellants with a foot-controlled throttle.

Reaction Dynamics relied on Firestone Tires for the rocket dragster, but after Art Arfons survived a harrowing 610 mph crash in November 1966, Firestone ended its involvement in land speed racing.

"Goodyear entered the picture grudgingly," says Keller. "Because their industrial products were marketed through the natural gas industry, the American Gas Association called in some favors and we ended up getting the tires that were designed for Breedlove's second car [Spirit of America – Sonic I].

"Let's face it, Breedlove ran on Goodyears when he went 600.601, so why get involved in another land speed project? They didn't know us from Adam, and they didn't want us to exceed 700 miles an hour in 1970. They hadn't a clue on how the car was going to perform. They didn't want us going banzai right out of the box."

On September 23, 1970, Gary Gabelich looked over the Bonneville Salt Flats. He walked the course, drove his rental car back and forth over most of the track. The surface was hard. He had thirteen miles of total running room.

Four days later he took his first ride, a leisurely 185 mph stroll.

"The plan was to run initially on lower power," recalls Farnsworth, "just to check out the handling. We didn't even fill the fuel tank for the first half-dozen runs.

"We didn't have the engine fully rated. We were running at about 15,500 pounds of thrust. We used full power on our seventh or eighth run, and we had an explosion inside the engine. It was really caused by a faulty firing procedure.

"We didn't follow what we had done in our test sessions. We changed the procedure. Instead of jamming the throttle wide open, we rolled into the throttle, and at that time we got a hot oxygen back-up into the LNG heat exchanger and it went pop.

"It split the heat exchanger open. It was a very important part of the fuel system. From then on we were handicapped. We just weren't able to up the power to full rating. We had about 12,000 pounds of thrust."

There was really nothing the team could do about the heat exchanger.

"We couldn't replace the part in the engine. It was a handcrafted, precision unit. It would have taken months to reproduce and we didn't have the time."

As far as Pate Farnsworth is concerned, "...the additional 4000 pounds of thrust would have made a tremendous difference on the top end."

It would take thirty-nine long, sometimes agonizing days, but Gary Gabelich would succeed!

"I love her," raved Gabelich. "I've never driven a race car that handles so well. I feel like I'm having an affair with her. It's just unreal."

Moments before the cockpit was sealed on Friday, October 23, 1970, Gary Gabelich knelt by the needle-nose of the car. He caressed the nose and talked to it in a whisper.

"Let's do it together, baby. Give me a good ride. Let's go, baby. You can do it. We can do it together, baby."

At 11:40 a.m. (Utah time), the former test astronaut adjusted his love beads and cradled his St. Christopher medal in his hands. In a split second, it seemed the rocket car disappeared in a stream of white smoke as it streaked to the measured mile almost two miles away.

Blue Flame blasted through the mile in 5.89 seconds. Speed: 617.602 mph. The car was refueled, the safety chutes repacked. And again the veteran driver knelt by the nose, rubbing it fondly, his lips moving.

"That was far out, baby, but we're not through yet. We've got to do it one more time and do it better. We can do it. Just you and me. We can do it. Now, let's go and do our thing together, you and me, baby, you and me."

With twelve minutes remaining in the sixty minute countdown, Blue Flame flashed across the Salt Flats, accelerating through the mile in 5.739 seconds. The even faster 627.287 run cemented a new land speed record of 622.407 miles an hour.

"The mile markers went by real fast and the mountains just sat on the sidelines," bubbled a jubilant Gary Gabelich. "The air speed indicator was showing top speeds between 640 and 660 in the middle of the traps. It was a wild ride. We really got with it. I'm very happy.

"It was smooth, very smooth. It was just a little mushy at the end of the run, but that was probably due to the soft salt. The car handled like a dragster. She's a fantastic machine."

Dick Keller called it "...a dream come true. It got out as quick as a fuel dragster. As far as handling, it was as good as we could have hoped. We never made one chassis adjustment the whole time we were out there."

Even the usually deadpan Joe Petrali, who supervised the seven-man USAC timing crew, was all smiles.

"This in the smoothest handling car I've ever seen. The suspension was built in such a way that there was no buffeting. The car just seemed to glide across the salt."

Moments later, Gary and his father, Mel Gabelich, walked away from the crowd. Gary was smiling. Tears streamed down his father's face. They didn't seem to mind the pelting rain that was turning the salt into mush.

Gary Gabelich had beaten the weather and the record.

"I'll always remember October 23," says Farnsworth, "especially that last run. A storm front came through the pass at the north of the track. There's a mountain pass that comes down between the islands.

"They knew that this storm front was coming and they wanted to get in the runs. Believe me, it was a race against time. We made our second run, and just as Gary hit the high-speed mile, the front came through.

"It blew the car ten feet sideways at 650. He was able to bring it right on the black line at full speed.

"Shortly after he passed out of the timing mile, the USAC timing shack, a quarter of a mile further south of the track, got a wind gust of forty miles an hour, besides direct side gusts.

"We went out and looked at the track. Gary told us it felt like he got blown over a hundred feet. We measured the track. All the tires were down on the ground. The wind had pushed the car over sideways and he steered it right back on to the track."

With the use of a push track and only twenty seconds of fuel on board, the team had to use a slide rule to determine where Blue Flame would reach peak speed in the measured mile.

"We wanted to keep the speed right in the center of the mile," Farnsworth points out, "and achieve the fastest average. Probably enter the mile at 600, peak at 660, coast back down at 600 or just under that leaving the mile. We tried to make the highest average speed in the mile by getting the burn-out point to the center of the mile.

"How did we feel afterwards? Tremendous. It was the culmination of a long effort."

The let-down came when ownership of the car reverted to the American Gas Association.

"There was nothing we could do about it. Life goes on. The following year", says Pete Farnsworth, "we built the world's fastest bike for American Honda. It went 290 miles an hour on a very rough course at Bonneville."

According to Farnsworth, "The Smithsonian Institute was attempting to buy the car for $100,000, but it was sold out of the country. The fellow who bought the car was one of the very first sponsors. He was head of the Dutch national gas industry and had a tremendous amount of power over the North Sea in distribution.

"It was more of a favor to him, I think, than anything else. The car is now at the German National Technical Museum. It's sitting on a platform above Mercedes, Porsches, all those other cars. I was very unhappy about the deal, but there was nothing I could do, any of us could do."

For the next eighteen months following his record-setting ride, Gary Gabelich lived out of a suitcase, making public appearances throughout the United States.

He and Blue Flame not only appeared at auto shows, but the fastest man on wheels also visited numerous junior and senior high schools.

"The kids wanted to know what it really felt like to go that fast. I tried to put them in the driver's seat. I tried to communicate to them what it felt like. A lot of them wanted to know what happened overseas.

"It was an open type of thing. Some wanted to know what I thought about drugs, about this or that. It was a great experience and education."

Gabelich made three USO tours, visiting servicemen in Japan, the Philippines, Okinawa, Hawaii and Vietnam.

"It gave me a good feeling to go over there, talk with the guys and rap with them a little about home."

In the process, he almost became a war zone casualty.

"They kept us away from the demilitarized zone in Vietnam, but we were pretty close. I saw a chopper get shot down, one that we were supposed to catch but missed.

"It was my fault. I was in a hooch with a bunch of guys, just rapping with them. Two people were killed and a couple others injured when the chopper went down. I guess it could have been me."

When Gabelich returned to the United States, he and his associates began building a four-wheel funny car.

"For one thing, it was the first four-wheel drive, monocoque, rear-engine funny car. It was all handmade, even the wheels. It developed 1500–2000 horsepower, depending on how much nitro-methane you were running in the engine."

Speed potential: 225–235 mph.

Gabelich invested heavily in the experimental dragster.

He was in the early stages of testing. On April 7, 1972, his funny car smashed into a guard rail at Orange County International Raceway at Irvine, California, overturned, began disintegrating and burst into flames.

In the violent force of the crash, the car's rear end came off and the wheels flew in all directions. Witnesses said the car rolled two hundred feet.

Gary Gabelich remained conscious during the crash.

"I tried to undo my seat belt and I couldn't get it undone with my left hand, so I pulled down my goggles with my right hand. My left hand was laying down where my left elbow was. It was hanging by a few tendons and some skin, like a dish rag.

"Then I realized my left leg wasn't where it was supposed to be. It was alongside my body, kind of crumbled up in a weird way. I knew I was really messed up."

Part of the guard rail was tangled in his leg, which was partially wrapped around the steering column.

304

Gabelich was on the operating table for six hours. Besides his hand injury, his heel was ripped off, his foot crushed. All told, he underwent six operations.

"At first the doctors told me I might be lucky to regain sixty-five percent use of my hand. But look," he said six months later, "I have more than that, probably eighty-five percent. Some of the nerve endings are gone and I've lost some of the feeling, but it's part of me, not a hook."

The leg, however, was a different story.

"I have a steel pin or rod running into my heel. I almost lost the leg a couple of times when gangrene developed, but they were able to clear it up. It's bent out of shape – mostly to the left – but that means I'll be able to run around left hand corners real fast."

Doctors predicted he wouldn't be well enough to resume racing for eighteen months.

"Maybe the accident was really a blessing in disguise. It's given me plenty of time to think about the sound barrier project, work out presentations to prospective sponsors. You don't raise $500,000 for such a venture overnight. Believe me, it's a lot easier going out and just driving a car."

Despite the near-tragic accident, Gabelich felt confident he would resume his racing career.

"I want to live as much as the next guy, probably more so because I enjoy what I'm doing. But I'd be just a vegetable if I was forced to quit.

"You have to be a driver to understand what I'm talking about. Besides, I've paid my dues now. I've been injured about as badly as one man can and lived. I figure it can't happen twice."

Life went on for Gary Gabelich. He had hopes of building his 800–1000 mph rocket car, American Way, forty-four feet long and powered by a single rocket engine producing a minimum of 50,000 horsepower. Unfortunately, he never lived long enough to fulfill that dream.

On January 26, 1984, Gary Gabelich was fatally injured in a motorcycle/truck accident at San Pedrao, California. He was riding the bike.

The thirty-fourth world land speed record holder was forty-four years old. He left a wife, Rae, and an infant son, Guy. He was the last American to hold the record.

Gabelich's thirteen year reign as speed king ended in 1983, when Richard Noble of Great Britain drove his jet-powered Thrust 2 to a new mark of 633.4 mph.

His record remained on the books through the 1970s, withstanding the assault of several challengers, including a jet from the Soviet Union.

In a sale he would later regret, three-time speed king, Art Arfons, sold his sleek Green Monster to wealthy California rancher, Slick Gardner.

This car was the successor to Arfons' record-setting Monster which set records of 434, 536 and 576 in 1964–65, but was demolished in a horrendous 1966 crash.

Admittedly, the 700 mile an hour machine Arfons sold to Gardner was the best land speed creation he had ever built.

Arfons went along with the deal, not only teaching Gardner about the jet, but taking it for a test ride during the 1978 Labor Day holiday. He clocked an easy 175 in his first Bonneville appearance in twelve years.

"I've got aluminum wheels instead of rubber tires and it was really a rough ride," said Arfons. "The top layer of salt was very thin and it was mud underneath. But it felt great. I wasn't scared one bit."

Gardner was confident. "I'll just do what Art would do. I'll get in it, stand on it and go for the record. Art will be there to help me. He'll actually take some of the power out of the engine. All I want this time is the land speed record."

In October 1978, Gardner squeezed into the cockpit and made two easy runs, including a 250 mile an hour shakedown, before getting serious.

Gardner's Pea Soup Anderson Green Monster swerved off the course at an estimated 500 miles an hour. He was unhurt and brought the car to a safe stop.

"On the runaway ride", recalls Arfons, "he started on the north end of the course where the track was smoother. But when he started into the clocks, the back end started moving over. He didn't catch it soon enough and he was heading in the wrong direction.

"He did a good job in getting the chutes out. He never tried to come back. He just went at the angle he was going at, about one and a half miles off course."

Despite the incident, Arfons was impressed with his former car.

"I couldn't believe the car would accelerate like that. It scared the hell out of me. He had it all."

While Gardner wanted to return the next day, Arfons talked him out of it. "It was just too dangerous," he said, blaming the poor track conditions for the wild ride.

While the Buellton, California rancher talked about running somewhere else, it would be his first and final attempt at the land speed record.

Thousands of miles away, the Russians announced their intentions of joining the fun.

Vladimir K. Nikitin, chief engineer and designer at The Soviet Institute for Automobile and Road at Kharkov, Russia, had long been fascinated by speed.

As a young student attending the same institute, he filled his notebooks with advanced ideas for racing cars. In 1941, he published his first treatise on jet propulsion in land-bound vehicles.

By 1951, Nikitin was appointed 'Master of Sport' and head of the Kharkovsky Automobilno Doroshnik Institut.

All of the Institute's creations would be named HADI (initials of the facility): 1... 2... 3... 4... 5... 6... 7... 8... 9...

In October 1967, he fulfilled his dream of designing and driving a gas turbine-powered car, HADI-7, which reached a terminal speed of 246.09 mph on the Institute's high-speed test track facility at Kyubotin, west of Kharkov.

But he wanted to go faster, not just break the land speed record but exceed the speed of sound.

In an announcement, he said:

"Some of the automobiles have set all-Union or international records of speed. It's but natural that we want to construct a new car to try the luck and compete for the absolute world record.

"Who will drive the car? Well, it will take the first steps with me, under my direction."

Encouraged with his performance, Nikitin enlisted the aid of thirty-three year old Dimitri Filtshin. Filtshin was his most experienced engineer and designer.

By September of 1970, HADI-9 was ready for its initial test run, which was reported to be a disappointing 369.74. Nikitin was convinced the car was too heavy for the available engine. It was decided to completely rebuild the jet.

A month later, Gary Gabelich drove Blue Flame to a new record of 622.407 mph.

However, it wasn't until November 1978 that Nikitin and his car re-surfaced again. The car had been re-modeled. Extensive wind tunnel testing had been used to mold the final shape, a needle-nosed, thirty foot long, three ton creation.

Nikitin sat in an enclosed cockpit at about the midway point. The two front wheels were closely paired, giving a nine inch track. However, the two rear wheels were wide-tracked, seven feet apart, with a wheelbase of 23.5 feet.

The engine was a Tumanskij R-11 gas turbine, developing 11,000 pounds of thrust. It was normally used in the Soviet MIG-21 interceptor.

For this run, Firestone low-pressure, aircraft shock tires were used. "For the sound barrier attempt", said Nikitin, "we plan to use Soviet made all-metal wheels."

His plan called for a series of high speed runs. Like Arfons had announced, the first sound barrier attempt would be made with a driverless car. "Because of the risks involved, we plan to control the vehicle by using radio signals, rather than a human being at the wheel... until we are ready."

On November 7, 1978, according to Soviet reports, Nikitin, Filtshin and their team of automobile design students braved the sub-zero temperature for the attempt. Nikitin started the jet engine and the Tumanskij R-11 whined as he looked down the 50,000 foot long test track.

The run lasted seven seconds. Reported speed: 525.016, certainly a Soviet record. The car reportedly handled straight and true across the frozen surface.

Nikitin had hoped to make a return run. However, he had to call it off due to the severe weather.

Whatever happened to Vladimir Nikitin and his supersonic car?

Apparently 'The Iron Curtain' closed around him and his project. Rumors surfaced concerning a rocket-powered racer... but nothing else.

And assuming a rocket racer had been built and tested, it obviously did not break either Gabelich's record or the sound barrier. The Soviets of those days did not publicize failure... only success.

While California designer/builder Bill Fredrick played just a minor role in the 1960s with his jet-powered Valkyrie I, which never attempted a record run, he was a major player in the seventies.

Early in that decade, he built a rocket-powered dragster, Courage of Australia, which was supposed to serve as the prototype for a fifty foot long supersonic car.

Aussie Vic Wilson campaigned for the dragster throughout the United States and hit 311 mph in a ride that lasted less than six seconds.

Instead, Fredrick built SMI Motivator in the mid-seventies. It was actually a 'rent-a-racer' with two of Hollywood's top stunt greats sharing the cockpit.

Kitty O'Neill set a woman's speed record of 512 mph at Alvord Desert, Oregon, in 1976.

The following year, Hal Needham went off course, at Alvord, at speeds in excess of 500 miles an hour.

In 1979, the 'Fredrick-Needham Connection' re-surfaced with Budweiser Rocket. This time Needham was owner and another stuntman, Stan Barrett, the driver.

This controversial episode in land speed racing history is covered in depth in the next chapter.

Chapter Twenty

Budweiser Rocket... Record or Rip-Off?

When it happened I was really upset, but it don't matter now. That whole Budweiser Rocket deal was all bull as far as I'm concerned. First, they claimed a one-way land speed record. That doesn't exist. Then they claimed they broke the sound barrier. I don't know how fast that car went. They were never clocked through the measured mile is all I said, and from what I've heard I really don't think their timing was right. I'll leave it to the experts to argue about.

Art Arfons

The date: December 17, 1979.

The place: Edwards Air Force Base, California.

The time: seven o'clock in the morning... and counting.

It is cold, twenty degrees Fahrenheit.

A long, pencil-thin missile on wheels is poised. Stan Barrett is bolted securely into the tiny cockpit. The car seat is only twenty inches wide. Barrett is a small man, 5 feet 9 inches, 147 pounds.

It is the eighteenth run for Barrett in his rocket-powered Budweiser Rocket. But the small party assembled knew it had all come down to this moment. This was the run through the sound barrier.

Highly respected television motorsports commentator, Ken Squier, was there, covering *Project S.O.S.* for CBS.

"I was about three hundred feet away from that awesome car," he recalls.

"I was at the start line when Stanley took off. There would be a burn-out. Once he was ready, Stan lit that baby. It was truly awesome, one of the biggest thrills I've ever had.

"All of us were very nervous, but not Stanley. He was calm all the way through the whole thing. I've got to think that's how Stanley did all of his stuff.

"I think that's how he performed in stunts. I think that's the way he did everything. When it came to crunch time he became sorta introverted, quiet, just focused on what he was gonna do and went about doing it.

"I had come down to this last run. We knew it was attainable that this run could get him well over 700 miles an hour. I think everybody was very stressed at this point.

"We'd waited a couple of days for just the right temperature and that doesn't help the nerves. And how much punishment could the car take with the Sidewinder? Nobody knew. There was a lot of anxiety."

Barrett rode the three-wheeled, bright red volcano to about 620 miles an hour, then unleashed the power of the Sidewinder missile. The entire run lasted seventeen seconds.

However, it would be another ten hours before the U.S. Air Force announced that Stan Barrett had unofficially broken the speed of sound: 739.666 mph; Mach 1.0106.

It was the ultimate stunt for one of Hollywood's top stuntmen.

"When I hit the Sidewinder," said Barrett, "I was really accelerating unbelievably. I felt a lot of buffeting, then a period of smooth-out, and then it was like I hit a wall. But it turned pretty smooth again.

"Then came the biggest jolt shortly after. I guess it was the re-entry, going backwards through the sound barrier while slowing down."

Designer/car builder Bill Fredrick was ecstatic and thankful.

"The good Lord must have had His hands over Stan. The periods of 'smooth-out' he told about were his rear wheels lifting off the ground. He drove a thousand feet on the front wheel only, like a wheelbarrow.

"For long stretches we found only one single track in the dirt and our instruments registered no load on the rear suspension for those periods."

In other words, the two rear wheels were off the ground!

Retired Air Force General Chuck Yeager, the first to pilot a plane through the sound barrier in 1947, witnessed the run, and said there was no doubt in his mind that the Budweiser Rocket had indeed surpassed the speed of sound.

"The Guinness official photographer, Franklin Berger, was on hand to witness and photograph the first land vehicle to exceed the speed of sound. Mr. Berger requested that I provide written testimony, describing my judgment on the success of the endeavor.

"It is quite obvious that the Hal Needham Budweiser Rocket Car exceeded the speed of sound because of the rear wheels leaving the ground as the car achieved top speed.

"As the car approaches .9 to .94 Mach number, very strong shock waves will form on the nose, the tail and the wheel struts. When the car goes supersonic the shock waves which formed on the nose at lower speeds will move to the rear of the car.

"Evidently the choking effect of the shock waves under the car as they moved to the rear lifted the car off the ground. I observed the track of the rear wheels on the supersonic run and the rear wheels were off the ground for 650–700 feet.

"A photo taken at the traps shows the rear wheels off the ground about ten inches. Since the rear wheels weigh about one hundred pounds each and were rotating between 7000 and 8000 r.p.m. they acted as gyros to keep the car from turning, directionally or laterally.

"Having been involved in supersonic research since the days of the X–1 rocket plane, which I flew on the first supersonic flight on October 14, 1947, there is no doubt in my mind that the rocket car exceeded the speed of sound on December 17, 1979."

And if that wasn't enough, Pete Knight, who had flown a later model of the experimental rocket plane 4500 miles an hour, sent a telegram to car owner Hal Needham.

Dear Mr. Needham: In cooperation with Speed of Sound engineering personnel, the Air Force has performed a review of the limited accelerometer, photographic, air speed, and radar data taken during the speed of sound land speed attempts on Rogers Dry lake at Edwards Air Force Base in November–December 1979.

AIR FORCE OFC OF PUBLIC AFFAIRS, WEST COAST
11000 WILSHIRE BLVD RM 10114
LOS ANGELES CA 90024

THIS MAILGRAM IS A CONFIRMATION COPY OF THE FOLLOWING MESSAGE:

8O54982206 IORN THOUSAND OAKS CA 118 01-05 1150A EST
PMS HAL NEEDHAM, PRESIDENT, SPEED OF SOUND INC, CARE CBS SPORTS, ASAP,
LR
REMOTE CONTROL BROADCAST BOOTH, STANFORD UNIVERSITY STADIUM
PALO ALTO CA
DEAR MR NEEDHAM
IN COOPERATION WITH SPEED OF SOUND ENGINEERING PERSONNEL, THE AIR
FORCE HAS PERFORMED A REVIEW OF THE LIMITED ACCELLROMETER,
PHOTOGRAPHIC, AIR SPEED, AND RADAR DATA TAKEN DURING THE SPEED OF
SOUND LAND SPEED ATTEMPTS ON ROGERS DRY LAKE AT EDWARDS AIR FORCE
BASE IN NOVEMBER-DECEMBER 1979.
WITHIN THE ACCURACY OF THE SPEED MEASURING DEVICES USED, IT IS OUR
JUDGMENT THAT THE OVER ALL OBJECTIVE OF ATTAINING MACH ONE (THE SPEED
OF SOUND) WITH A LAND VEHICLE WAS ACHIEVED AT 7126 A.M. ON DECEMBER
17, 1979.
THIS TELEGRAM CONCLUDES AIR FORCE PARTICIPATION AND COOPERATION WITH
YOUR SPEED OF SOUND ORGANIZATION. A DETAILED STATEMENT OF CHARGES
WILL BE PROVIDED AS SOON AS POSSIBLE. VERY SINCERELY YOURS
COLONEL PETE KNIGHT
VICE COMMANDER
AIR FORCE FLIGHT TEST CENTER

11:53 EST

MGMCOMP MGM

Telegram from Colonel Pete Knight, Vice Commander
of the Air Force Test Center, to Hal Needham. Dated
January 5, 1980.

> *Within the accuracy of the speed measuring devices used, it is our judgment that the overall objective of attaining Mach One (the speed of sound) with a land vehicle was achieved at 7:26 a.m. on December 17, 1979.*
>
> *This telegram concludes Air Force participation and cooperation with your Speed of Sound organization, a detailed statement of charges will be provided as soon as possible.*

It was signed: "Very Sincerely Yours, Colonel Pete Knight, Vice Commander, Air Force Flight Test Center."

Colonel Knight sent the telegram to Needham on January 5, 1980, or twenty days after Barrett's unofficial 739 mph sortie. Certainly enough time to study all the available data.

That should have ended the issues but it didn't.

In fact, more than a decade after Barrett's thundering rides the controversy still exists. Not just of the sound barrier episode but of the claim of a 'one-way' land speed record as well. But more about that later.

Did the Budweiser Rocket surpass the speed of sound? Was it a record or a rip-off?

Obviously for Needham, Fredrick and Barrett, it is a moot question.

Ken Squier, for one, believes to this day that Stan Barrett did indeed travel 739 miles an hour on land.

"There's no doubt in my mind," he says. "It got up there. The Air Force tracked him from the beginning, from the time the car left the line. So why did it take so long for the announcement that Stanley had unofficially broken the sound barrier? That's typical of the Air Force.

"I think the Air Force got intrigued with it [the project], with the idea of making it work. They turned it into a real exercise. There were mile markers. There was a speed trap down there where they [the team] felt the car would max out.

"But beyond that, I think the Air Force had stuff to check it, to follow the car. They had this incredible camera with one of those gigantic lenses. They used it for measuring rockets when they sent 'em up. They used that to follow it [the car]. That's what's a part of Edwards that no other place has."

Certainly Stan Barrett is as brave as any man who has ever squeezed into the cockpit of a high-speed race car. But he is also human.

Did Ken Squier ever see him express any fear?

"Yeah," recalls Squier. "It was after they made the first run with that Sidewinder missile in the back. He was very, very concerned. They told him it was obtainable but it was at tremendous risk.

"Stanley was concerned as to how much more stress that car could take with that missile load. I think he made four or five runs with a Sidewinder.

"I think it was Yeager who came up with the idea of a Sidewinder. There simply wasn't enough energy produced from the vehicle to get it close to where the barrier was. It would hit about 620 and flatten out. The Sidewinder gave it some 12,000 extra horses.

"I don't know how much Stanley was paid for his sound barrier effort. I know him well enough to know money was not the motivating factor. He's just a nice person. I thought everything he did he did with a real purpose.

"He was a born-again Christian. He was going to use that as a platform for his missionary work. He thought the sound barrier publicity would give him the visibility to talk about some of the things he believed were important. But money was not the bottom line with him, not at all."

Don Namam, Executive Director of the International Sports Hall of Fame at Talladega, Alabama, also believes the Budweiser Rocket broke the sound barrier. An exact replica of the thirty-nine foot long car is on display at that museum.

Namam says: "The Bud Rocket car broke the speed of sound in 1979 as the plaque indicates. We have the original film sanctioned by the U.S. Air Force showing it making the run at Edwards Air Force Base. The Air Force confirmed the record."

The plaque at the Budweiser Rocket display lists the following:

RECORD RUNS

Sept. 9, 1979	Bonneville Salt Flats	638.637 mph
Dec. 3, 1979	Edwards Air Force Base	643.086 mph
Dec. 4, 1979	Edwards Air Force Base	677.328 mph
Dec. 17, 1979	Edwards Air Force Base	739.666 mph

Underneath the four records it reads:
"SPEED OF SOUND... MACH 1.0106."

But surprisingly, the general public does not have the opportunity to see the real car. It is kept in storage at The Smithsonian Institute in Washington, D.C. In fact, it has never been put on public display.

Why is the Budweiser Rocket kept under wraps?

Is it because of the controversy created by a basic philosophy of creating your own criteria, then claiming a record? Certainly there was too much furor created by the so-called 'one-way' land speed record and then by the sound barrier run.

"After the car came here," says Gordon White, Auto Racing Adviser, Smithsonian Institution, "we were inundated with mail about how the Rocket record is a fraud. We cannot say that it is or not, but as of now the Rocket is hidden away with little likelihood of being displayed."

The Smithsonian just didn't want to become the focal point of the endless debate.

But there are those such as land speed king Richard Noble of England, five-time record holder Craig Breedlove, Pete Farnsworth, and Dick Keller of Blue Flame fame, who are highly critical of the entire Budweiser Rocket philosophy, from the claim of a one-way land speed record to the sound barrier run.

Noble, who averaged 633.4 mph during his 1983 assault, says, "Like many people, I am concerned about the Budweiser Rocket. We all know that a one-way run was made and that it went very fast, with Stan Barrett running a horrendous personal risk.

"But there appears to be serious doubt as to what peak speed was actually achieved. Even *The Guinness Book of Records* qualifies the speed. It's an awful position for Stan, the crew and the sponsors to be in and there is only one way to settle it.

"Run the car again with an accepted timing and prove the supersonic claim one way or another. Unless this happens, it's believed the claim is flawed.

"As we found out, there is tremendous difference between the one-way runs and the conventional two-way, sixty minute LSR run. With a one-way run you can take a year to prepare the car, choose exactly the right conditions and temperatures and accelerate over the hardest part of the course.

"If you go the Budweiser route you claim the peak speed. With the conventional record you have to average your speed over the measured mile, which is technically much tougher than a 'firework' run.

"Then, with a two-way run you have the hardest part of all: you have to return through the mile within sixty minutes of entering it the first time. This time you do not really control the situation.

"There is little time to prepare the car; the weather and temperature may suddenly change; the condition of the course may not be the best and the driver is no longer fresh.

"All these variables conspire to make the second run a really hairy event, quite unlike the calm laboratory conditions of the first. That's why we get upset when claims are made for single pass peak speed runs, which are far easier to achieve and bear little resemblance to the sheer achievement of a two-pass distance run."

Breedlove, who has built his forty-two footer for a crack at Noble's record, is outwardly more incensed than his British counterpart.

"It absolutely did not break the sound barrier," he says. "But essentially, it's a non-issue. The run was unsanctioned by an official. The timing instruments were uncalibrated.

"If you look clearly at the photo which supposedly proved the car went supersonic, you'll see the two back wheels are off the ground. I won't argue with that. But you'll also see the timing lights in the picture.

"A man named Earl Flanders timed that run. He owned the timing lights and he told me at Black Rock Desert when I was watching the English car run in 1983 what it was all about.

"I asked him specifically, 'What's the deal with the Budweiser Car?' And Earl Flanders said to me it went 666. I said, 'What do you mean it went 666?'

"He said, 'Well, I timed the car through the run, and through the electronic timer it went 666 in the 52.8 feet that I had the clock set up... that's what it went through my light'.

"I wasn't there. Earl sadly has passed away. He had the clocks on it during the run."

The Budweiser people, however, never disputed that the car was clocked 666 mph through Flanders' speed trap. They say the car had run out of power by then, and that the 739 clocking was attained earlier in the run.

Breedlove continues, "I can think of fifteen reasons why the back wheels would lift off the ground, and that has nothing to do with breaking the sound barrier as Chuck Yeager contended.

"I don't know what deal was made with Yeager. He wrote a letter that said he watched the car run. He went out and personally observed that the rear wheels were off the ground during the run which all the photographs showed.

"He concluded that the reason the wheels were off the ground was because the car was supersonic. And as proof he said that the center of pressure in objects shifts aft as they approach the speed of sound. So this must be the reason the wheels came off the ground. That's just nonsense! That's just one possibility.

"And if you really look at Pete Knight's statement, it sure doesn't sound like a ringing endorsement to me. Knight's telegram said, upon review of the limited exceleramater, radar and whatever data, that they have concluded the car unofficially achieved its objective.

"The whole statement was qualified by 'within the limited score' of the instrumentation that they had. Fredrick barred everybody from going there and seeing that thing. There were only a few people allowed to go there. I wasn't one of them," he says with a chuckle.

"Quite simply they claim they used the NORAD Early Warning Radar System, which I think is a satellite, to project some kind of a radar grid down to the lake bed, and then somehow, picking the movement of the car on the lake bed, transmit that back to telemetry equipment that was at Edwards, and then give a speed of the car.

"When they ran the car, the speed that the radar showed was ridiculously slow... twenty-eight miles an hour or something. It was way off. After a certain amount of scrutiny they came up with the position that there was a water truck, which was a much larger target, moving in the area and they tried to come up with ways to extrapolate the water truck data from the signal so that they would end up with whatever was left over being whatever electronic signal was picked up from the car.

"After about eight hours they came out and announced that the car had reached a speed of 739.89. I'm sorry. It's been doctored and covered up and this and that.

"But you have to understand the nature of the contract that was signed between Needham and Budweiser. Then you understand the method of that madness. The contract was written so that Needham was supposed to get $300,000 to break the existing land speed record and an additional bonus of $700,000 to break the sound barrier.

"Specifically, when the contract was written, the intent of the contract was that they break the sound barrier during the land speed run. However, the way the contract was written it didn't specify that the land speed record had to be broken on the run that it went through the sound barrier.

"So when they were turned down by FIM and by NHRA and the accredited sanctioning people to change the venue from a flying mile two ways to a 52.8 feet speed trap for one way, they then focused on being able to get that $700,000 bonus out of Budweiser.

"Upon the strength of Chuck Yeager's letter it was decided from a promotional or public relations standpoint that Budweiser could say that the car had gone through the sound barrier.

"But you'll note that the ads didn't run long. I think they got a lot of heat and just decided that discretion was the better part of valor. They probably took it for the seven hundred grand and decided to write it off."

Breedlove's first goal is to average 650, more than enough to exceed Noble's record. "Then we'd test the car in an unmanned situation, and if the car was found capable it would be my goal to drive it through the sound barrier, in the course of a run through the measured mile. It's a land speed car with, I hope, supersonic capability."

Like millions of Americans, Dick Keller watched *Project S.O.S.* with fascination on television. He knew creating a supersonic car was feasible. After all, he was project manager for Blue Flame.

While driver Gary Gabelich averaged 622.407 mph through the measured mile and 630 through the kilometer back in October 1970, Blue Flame fell short of its intended target.

The car, the brainchild of Keller, Ray Dausman and Pete Farnsworth, was built to break the sound barrier. It had 900 mile an hour speed potential. It would hold the land speed record for thirteen years.

"At the outset of any record-breaking project," says Keller of Plover, Wisconsin, "you know what you're doing is just for the moment. Just as you have the ambition to set a record, you know someone else is coming at you and eventually is gonna do it. You resign yourself to that right from the start. It's a temporary accomplishment.

"I knew that Fredrick had access to a lot of our data. A lot of stuff was published in articles by the consultants we used at IIT [Illinois Institute of Technology]. It was part of a graduate student project.

"One of the conditions of the project was that IIT would publish any of the technical data. Besides that, when we first got out to the salt flats for the first week or so Fredrick was on Jim Deist's team, which was handling our parachutes."

Keller's initial intention was to contact either Fredrick, who built Budweiser Rocket, or car owner, Hal Needham, and congratulate them for the reported 739 mile an hour adventure.

But it wasn't until he read an article in *Road & Track* magazine that he changed his mind. He wasn't willing to accept the supersonic run on face value, even though it appeared to have the blessing of the U.S. Air Force.

"I read an article by Henry Manney. Henry had been a Formula One reporter for several years in Europe. He was not only a good journalist, he was a very creative writer, probably the best writer the magazine had," recalls Keller.

"He was not only technically accurate but he was also very humorous. He raised a lot of questions in his article. He didn't have the time to research it but he was there when they were running. He was put off by the secretiveness of the group running it. He made no bones about it in the article. I would say his article was filled with sarcasm."

So Keller set out to obtain more detailed information about the 739 mile an hour run.

"I'm not sure if I contacted Fredrick or Needham first. I'd gotten an address somewhere and just asked for the information on the record attempt.

"I believe what I got back was a copy of the telegram that was read on TV during a football game. There was a business card attached to it."

The business card was from Fleishman-Hillard Inc., the St. Louis Firm handling the Budweiser account. The telegram was signed by Colonel Pete Knight, Vice Commander, Air Force Flight Test Center. In part it said:

"In cooperation with Speed of Sound engineering personnel the Air Force has performed a review of the limited accelerometer, photographic, air speed and radar data taken during the Speed of Sound land speed attempts at Rogers Dry Lake at Edwards Air Force Base in November–December, 1979.

"Within the accuracy of the speed measuring devices used it is our judgment that the overall objective of attaining Mach One (the speed of sound) with a land vehicle was achieved at 7:26 a.m. on December 17, 1979..."

But that still wasn't good enough for Dick Keller. He wanted data. As a scientist he would settle for nothing less.

For two years Keller conducted a campaign to see the data, and what he eventually saw created more questions than answers for him.

"Heck, I wasn't some Joe Schmoo sleeping on a park bench. They were claiming something that I had been hoping to attain. They owed me, and Art Arfons, and Craig Breedlove, and the others who were really interested in land speed records, an accurate account of what they did and why it is true."

Keller says he contacted Col. Knight but was referred back to S.O.S., a company owned by Hal Needham. He eventually petitioned his United States Senator, William Proxmire, to intervene on his behalf.

"I had assumed all along," says Keller, "that the runs were being sanctioned by the FIM [international organization which recognizes speed records by a three-wheeled vehicle such as Budweiser Rocket]. Earl Flanders was doing the timing for FIM. But the more I dug into it the more I found out that had nothing to do with it whatsoever.

"I tried to contact [Earl] Flanders because I wanted to find out what timing he did get. Never got in touch with Flanders, but his son called back. He told me, 'Leave the poor old guy alone'. That's as official as it got with me with the FIM timing. They just didn't want to release anything."

Flanders had set up a 52.8 foot speed trap. That was where the three-wheeler was supposed to reach maximum speed. According to Keller it didn't quite work out that way.

"As I understand it the car reached its peak speed outside those traps. On my estimation the only reliable data would have been the data from the FIM one-hundredth of a mile timing trap. That's the data that Earl Flanders had. That was the only data taken from measuring the performance of the car."

After the car's final run it would be some ten hours before word came that Stan Barrett had unofficially smashed the sound barrier.

In a position paper, authored by Ray W. Van Aken of Romatec Research Laboratory of Chatsworth, California, and presented at the Atmosphere Flight Mechanics Session American Institute of Aeronautics and Astronautics 19th Aerospace Sciences Meeting on January, 12–15, 1981:

"The [supersonic] run was made early in the morning to take advantage of the low temperature and hence a low velocity of sound. Temperature at the course was twenty degrees Fahrenheit. A meteorologist verified the temperature and correlated it with readings taken at other locations. Corresponding speed of sound was 731.9 mph.

"All systems performed well and the driver ignited the Sidewinder [missile] at essentially the optimum time. During the highest speed portion of the run the rear wheels were off the ground. Distance traveled in this condition was about 800 feet. Peak speed was reached before the timing trap. Speed at the trap was 666.234 mph. Two approaches were taken to obtain the peak speed.

"Radar information furnished three data points in the flat part of the peak speed. A speed of 739.666 mph represented the average of those points. The speed observed by radar correlated with the speed at the timing trap.

"Another approach was to integrate the measured acceleration over time. This was done from start to timing trap. The accelerometer was then calibrated and agreement of the integrated speed and time trap speed was reached. A peak speed of 741 mph was determined by this method.

"At present a trajectory reconstruction analysis is underway. This analysis will integrate the radar data with the car accelerometer data in order to provide a best estimated trajectory. Variations in peak speed may result, but the level of peak speed confirms that it was supersonic."

During the course of his investigation, Dick Keller received this report. He claims it failed to justify a 739 mph run.

"When I contacted the officer named in the telegram," recalls Keller, "the word I got was that they [the Air Force] were just basically providing services for Romatec. Any conclusions drawn were theirs.

"But Romatec was Bill Fredrick's organization. The reason it was written was to justify their claim that they went supersonic. The paper is filled with ninety-five percent of verifiable facts that don't really say it broke the sound barrier.

"And then it gets down to some very subjective things that says it does. What you have is a combination of a lot of very good facts and a weak conclusion that it went supersonic.

"What I wanted then, and I'd still like, is data supplied by somebody that does not have a vested interest in the thing, so I could indeed agree that the car had broken the sound barrier.

"Maybe the car went 739. I don't know. But they can't determine how fast they went because there's not enough information to say anything. So they shouldn't have said anything."

Then he adds, "As far as I'm concerned, the first person to prove that they broke the sound barrier is yet to be seen."

Radar was claimed to be an integral part in determining that the Budweiser Rocket indeed went supersonic. To be specific, the Air Force's Digital AK Instrumented Radar.

Dick Keller has trouble with that.

"As I said, the car didn't hit peak speed through the FIM speed trap. To me, it seems almost as an afterthought that somebody in the Air Force had this radar dish aimed at the vehicle.

"Again, I'm interpreting this thing because everybody's so closed-mouthed about it. But from what I could read into this it sounds like some technician was sitting out there. He had this radar dish which is aimed by a television camera. It's used for tracking these research aircraft when they're flying over the test range and landing. That sort of thing.

"It's probably mounted on a pole of some sort. It's controlled remotely by some kind of a button, switch, or whatever. The person that had the controls could elevate and rotate the radar dish. The radar dish had this camera on it.

"It looked to me what this guy was doing was getting a nice view of this vehicle riding down the course – by tracking it with the TV cameras just like you might with a hand-held video camera.

"Have you ever operated a camera on a tripod, trying to catch something across? As you try to do this you generally find you're slowing up or slowing down.

"Sometimes the camera rotates rather than the vehicle. Sometimes it's slower and the vehicle moves back and forth across the screen. So this fellow was rotating the antenna and viewing the car that was running.

"Afterwards apparently they found they didn't have any data to support the fact that they went supersonic. Somebody found this guy who was following the run on his TV camera that apparently generates data of some sort that was recorded as to the time and position of this antenna.

"What you can do is measure how fast the antenna rotates. That was one data point that they wanted to use. The only thing that was causing this antenna to rotate wasn't the car. It was the guy who had the controls. It was a measure of how fast he was rotating the antenna.

"What they wanted to do was take the data that they had on the antenna rotation and extrapolate it into the speed of the car. But in order to take the rotation of that antenna and convert that into speed you also have to know other information.

"You have to know how far away the car was at each angle of rotation of the antenna. They didn't have any information on that. So

DEPARTMENT OF THE AIR FORCE
WASHINGTON, D.C. 20330

OFFICE OF THE SECRETARY

Honorable William Proxmire
United States Senate
Washington, D. C. 20510

17 DEC 1981

Dear Senator Proxmire:

Thank you for your recent inquiry in behalf of Mr. Richard Keller, President of Keller Design, Hartland, Wisconsin, concerning Air Force assistance to the Speed of Sound, Incorporated (SOS) rocket car project.

The Air Force agreed to permit use of Edwards AFB, California, for the rocket car project because of the potential recruiting benefit to the Air Force, particularly in view of our urgent need for scientists, engineers, and technical people. Air Force support was provided at no interference to the operational mission at Edwards AFB, and on a reimbursable basis. This support included radar tracking and data reduction, fire and crash services, facilities refurbishment, administrative staffing, office space, utilities, and other related assistance. All support was paid for by the project sponsor at a cost of $24,000. Cooperation with SOS was the same as with other similar organizations. The Air Force did not make any press releases concerning this event.

The test runs were not sponsored by the Air Force and were conducted solely under the auspices of SOS. Data produced by the Air Force Flight Test Center engineering section was provided at commercial rates to SOS. It was the intent of the Air Force that such data be interpreted by that organization. The Air Force never intended to give official sanction to test results, nor to give the appearance of expressing an official view as to the speed attained by the test vehicle. Any such opinion was that of individual Air Force personnel, not of the Air Force.

We regret the misunderstanding that arose from Air Force involvement in this test and trust that this information will assist in clarifying our action.

Sincerely,

MICHAEL S. ALBA, LtCol, USAF
Congressional Inquiry Division
Office of Legislative Liaison

Attachment

Letter from Air Force Lieutenant Colonel Michael S. Alba to Senator William Proxmire. Dated December 17, 1981.

JAKE GARN, UTAH, CHAIRMAN

JOHN TOWER, TEX.   HARRISON A. WILLIAMS, JR., N.J.
JOHN HEINZ, PA.   WILLIAM PROXMIRE, WIS.
WILLIAM L. ARMSTRONG, COLO.   ALAN CRANSTON, CALIF.
RICHARD G. LUGAR, IND.   DONALD W. RIEGLE, JR., MICH.
ALFONSE M. D'AMATO, N.Y.   PAUL S. SARBANES, MD.
JOHN H. CHAFEE, R.I.   CHRISTOPHER J. DODD, CONN.
HARRISON SCHMITT, N. MEX.   ALAN J. DIXON, ILL.

W. DANNY WALL, STAFF DIRECTOR
HOWARD A. MENELL, MINORITY STAFF DIRECTOR AND COUNSEL

United States Senate
COMMITTEE ON BANKING, HOUSING, AND
URBAN AFFAIRS
WASHINGTON, D.C. 20510

December 28, 1981

Mr. Richard Keller
Keller Design Corporation
N52 W30555 Moraine Drive
Hartland, Wisconsin 53029

Dear Richard:

I have just received a response from the Air Force about your inquiry. It seems that the Air Force now agrees with you, after the fact. I know that is not very satisfactory but at least you will now have a statement indicating that they gave no official sanction to the test nor do they confirm test results in any official capacity.

Please review the Air Force letter and let me know what you think.

Sincerely,

William Proxmire, U.S.S.

WP:rtd

Telegram from Senator William Proxmire to Richard
Keller. Dated December 28, 1981.

what they did was use a truck trying to follow the course across the desert and this time they turned on the radar. All this radar does is it's designed to tell you how far away an object is. Period. It's not like a radar gun, used by a cop to determine whether or not you're speeding.

"I called up the guy who designed the radar to find out what it was. He told me and also sent information on it. When they're testing aircraft it allows them to determine how far away it is from the point of the radar site. That's the only information you get. The Air Force can convert that into a lot of data with a lot of other equipment.

"When they tried to make the correction and run the other vehicle down the same road as the car it was iffy at best. The limits of accuracy, both of the measure of rotation versus time and distance, are such that you can't tell within a reasonable amount what the actual speed was.

"I plotted all the available information, but you've got a wide scatter on those data points. What that indicates is that the system overall is not very accurate for the purpose they were trying to use it. It doesn't take much error to significantly affect the calculated speed of the car.

"There's no way of knowing how fast the car went with any accuracy. They may have done it but they can't prove it. If they did go 739 I find it highly unfortunate they really didn't have the proof to back it up."

Finally, Dick Keller contacted U.S. Senator William Proxmire.

On December 11, 1981, Senator Proxmire received a letter from Air Force Lt. Col. Michael S. Alba, Congressional Inquiry Division.

It read in part:

"The Air Force agreed to permit use of Edwards AFB, California, for the rocket car project because of the potential recruiting benefit to the Air Force, particularly in view of our urgent need for scientists, engineers, and technical people.

"Air Force support was provided at no interference to the operational mission at Edwards AFB, and on a reimbursable basis. This support included radar tracking and data reduction, fire and crash services, facilities refurbishment, administrative staffing, office space, utilities, and other related assistance. All support was paid for by the project sponsor at a cost of $24,000. Cooperation with S.O.S. was

GUINNESS SUPERLATIVES LIMITED
2 Cecil Court, London Road
Enfield, Middlesex EN2 6DJ
Telephone : 01 367 4567
Telegrams and cables : MOSTEST ENFIELD
Telex : 23573

GUINNESS BOOKS

PUBLISHERS

A MEMBER OF THE GUINNESS GROUP OF COMPANIES

Richard Keller,
President,
Keller Design Corporation,
N52 W 30555 Morain Drive,
Hartland,
Wisconsin 53029,
USA.

6th May, 1982

Dear Mr. Keller,

I have now had the opportunity of re-reading our correspondence and enclosures over the last month.

We have decided to relegate the events of 17th Decmeber 1979 from the top of the list to footnote status, each accompanied by the two sentences "This published speed of mark 1.010b is not officially sanctioned by the USAF whose Digital Instrumented Radar was not calibrated or certified. The radar information was not generated by the vehicle directly, but by an operator aiming the dish by means of a TV screen. A claim to six significant figures appears to be wholly unjustifiable."

I hope you will keep us in touch with any further developments though it appears that the Department of Defense has now gone deaf - a characteristic of Government Departments the world over.

One could adapt Churchill's phrase by saying "Among public servants with index pensions truth is the first casualty".

With all best wishes.

Yours sincerely,

Norris McWhirter
Editor
Guinness Book of Records

Letter from Norris McWhirter, Editor of *The Guinness Book of Records*, to Richard Keller. Dated May 6, 1982.

the same as with other similar organizations. The Air Force did not make any press releases concerning this event.

"The test runs were not sponsored by the Air Force and were conducted solely under the auspices of S.O.S. Data produced by the Air Force Test Flight Center engineering section was provided at commercial rates to S.O.S. It was the intent of the Air Force that such data be interpreted by that organization.

"The Air Force never intended to give official sanction to test results nor to give the appearance of expressing an official view as to the speed attained by the test vehicle. Any such opinion was that of individual Air Force personnel, not of the Air Force.

"We regret the misunderstanding that arose from Air Force involvement in this test and trust this information will assist in clarifying our action."

But was this really damage control? After Lt. Col. Pete Knight had publicly stated in his telegram to S.O.S. president, Hal Needham, that Budweiser Rocket had become the first vehicle in history to exceed the speed of sound on land.

Dick Keller can understand why Lt. Col. Pete Knight signed the telegram.

"Pete Knight was a test pilot. He was around when they were trying to break the sound barrier. These guys get all excited about that stuff. They're pretty adventurous guys and this was an adventurous project. I don't blame him for getting excited about it. But I think they [Air Force] were used."

The letter from Lt. Col. Alba, however, came as no relief.

"For me it would have been a relief if the Air Force had said, 'We had our best technical guys working on it. We used our best equipment. This is how it works and this is the number we got.' That would have been that. And I would have said, 'Fine'.

"To me what the letter said was, 'What they [S.O.S.] were presenting as evidence was not evidence. They were claiming the Air Force said we broke the sound barrier and the Air Force said, 'No, you didn't'."

Dick Keller, however, wasn't quite finished. For several years he had been in touch with Guinness Books, which publishes a book of world records. It is considered highly reputable.

Keller submitted copies of all his correspondence, whatever material he had, and sent it to Norris McWhirter, editor of Guinness Books in England.

McWhirter replied to Keller on May 6, 1982:

"I have now had the opportunity of re-reading our correspondence and enclosures over the last month.

"We have decided to relegate the events of December 17, 1979 from the top of the list to footnote status, accompanied by the two sentences, 'This published speed of Mach 1.0106 is not officially sanctioned by the USAF, whose Digital Instrumented Radar was not calibrated or certified. The radar information was not generated by the vehicle directly, but by an operator aiming the dish by means of a TV screen. A claim of six significant figures appears to be unjustifiable.'

"I hope you will keep in touch with any further developments, though it appears that the Department of Defense has now gone deaf— a characteristic of Government Departments the world over.

"One could adapt Churchill's phrase by saying, 'Among public servants with index pensions, trust is the first casualty'."

Pete Farnsworth, builder of the rocket-powered Blue Flame, also has his serious doubts about the Budweiser Rocket episode.

"I know people that were there who claimed they never heard a sonic boom. They didn't think it was done. There's no documentation that it really happened. You can't go by telemetry from the car because Fredrick could easily have faked that.

"The whole concept was a publicity stunt in that the car was never built at all to make a one-hour turn-around run. It was made to go one way. As I understand it, it took 'em eight hours to change the carbon nozzle and put a new carbon polypack in it. The engine was so hot, they couldn't have made a turn-around in one hour. The measured mile or the kilometer are internationally recognized distances.

"Bruce Flanders and his dad, Earl, were the timers for the run. The highest speed recorded on the clocks that I know of was 666, and not 739."

According to Farnsworth, Blue Flame served as a model for Fredrick's three-wheeler.

Farnsworth recalls, "Bill Fredrick was out on the Salt Flats when we were running in 1970. We knew him from drag racing. He was basically eye-balling our car. We told him initially what we were going to build before the design expanded considerably.

"He built basically what we were going to build initially, except that ours was going to be a four-wheeler, not a three-wheeler. Ours was going to be much smaller initially, but we couldn't get the tires done for the advertising campaign, so we had to go with bigger, redesigned tires off Breedlove's Sonic I car."

All of Fredrick's adult life had been consumed with racing. At the age of twenty-one, he built the jet-powered Valkyrie, which was considered a genuine land speed threat in 1962.

However, following the death of Glenn Leasher that speed season in another jet-thrust vehicle, Fredrick found it impossible to obtain insurance. So the car never officially entered the land speed game.

He re-emerged on to the racing scene with a twenty-seven foot long, rocket-powered dragster, Courage of Australia I. On November 11, 1971, the Wynn's sponsored car turned in a spectacular 311.41 run in just 5.107 seconds at Orange County International Raceway in Irvine, California.

The driver, Vic Wilson of Australia, "...really enjoyed the ride. I didn't believe the car had gone that fast." The dragster used seventy-five percent of its 12,000 horsepower. "It was really a smooth ride," said the twenty-eight year old driver. "Sometimes when I go fast my eyeballs vibrate, but not this time."

The dragster was to serve as a prototype for Fredrick's sound-barrier car, a sixty foot long creation also called Courage of Australia. Speed potential was 1000 miles an hour, burning hydrogen peroxide. Wilson was to drive the longest car in land speed history.

At that same point in time, Craig Breedlove was campaigning his own rocket-powered dragster. It, too, served as a prototype for his Spirit of America – Sonic II, a missile propelled by a 35,000 pound thrust engine, derived from the descent stage of the Apollo lunar module.

It was touted as a supersonic drag race with both cars starting 150 yards apart. In this scenario, Gary Gabelich would drive Courage of Australia.

The proposed match race made good copy, but that's all. Neither car was ever built.

But this is where the story starts getting interesting.

Bill Fredrick would build a rocket racer, a three-wheeler, thirty-nine feet long, standing ninety-two inches high at the tail, ten feet wide (at the rear wheels) and stretched over a wheelbase measuring 335 inches.

It weighed 4942 pounds wet, ran on solid 3 x 32 inch Cragar metal wheels, and was propelled by a Romatec V–4 hydrogen peroxide rocket system, capable of producing some 48,000 horsepower.

Canon Camera was the first announced sponsor and the car was to be called Aqua Slide 'n' Glide Special.

But the car never ran under that name and that corporate banner. Instead, it would campaign as the SMI Motivator.

The name derived from Paul Meyer's Texas-based company, Success Motivation Institute, dedicated to "motivating people to their full potential".

The driver would be Meyer's twenty year old son, Billy, already a hot-shot funny car driver. Meyer had started drag racing when he was sixteen. That was in 1971.

It was now 1975. Gary Gabelich had held the land speed record for five years. Three-time land speed king Art Arfons, who survived a 610 mph crash in 1966, had built a more streamlined, more powerful Green Monster. He was ready to regain his title.

A proposed match race between Arfons and Meyer was in the offing.

As Billy 'The Kid' put it, "This should be a young man's record; an old man shouldn't be trying anything like this. Only a young man should try it and set it."

The old man, Art Arfons, was forty-nine years old.

But the match race never materialized. Billy Meyer never drove the car.

Meyer says, "The SMI Motivator was originally built by Bill Fredrick. He owned fifty-five percent of the car and we owned forty-five. After the project was delayed on numerous occasions we decided to change directions, which enabled him to put someone else in the car.

"The car was originally supposed to run in July 1975, but he did not run it until late 1976. I returned to drag racing and driving funny cars."

What followed was a 'rent-a-ride' to both Kitty O'Neill and Hal Needham, two of Hollywood's top stunt performers. The price tag: $20,000 each.

It was a scriptwriter's dream. O'Neill would first take dead aim at Lee Breedlove's 1965 women's land speed record of 307 mph, set in her husband's jet car.

Then Needham would take over the controls for an assault on Gabelich's 622.407, set in 1970.

O'Neill, then twenty-eight, was part-Irish, half-Cherokee. She stood five foot three inches and weighed only ninety-seven pounds. Born totally deaf, she learned how to lip-read and speak well enough to attend regular classes before she completed grade school.

Despite being crippled by spinal meningitis, she was a promising diver in the 1960s. In fact, she won the women's ten meter National AAU title in 1964 and finished eighth in the Tokyo Olympics.

She also raced drag boats, top fuel dragsters and production sports cars, tried sky diving and scuba diving.

"I guess I like danger," she said, "and thrills. But mostly I want always to have a goal, some dream that I can try for."

In 1976 she became a licensed stunt woman. It was only fitting she try the ultimate stunts driving a rocket-powered car faster than any other woman had ever done.

In September of that year, Kitty went to El Mirage dry lake in California for a test session and clocked an unofficial 358 miles an hour.

A month later, the team went to Bonneville for an all-out attempt to set the record. Approaching speeds of 300 miles an hour, SMI Motivator began shaking badly over the rough course. "I was fighting for my life out there," she said after the run.

After two months of haggling, the Bureau of Land Management allowed the rocket car to run at Lake Alvord in southeastern Oregon, when it was proven the water vapor emitted by the engine did not pose a threat to life or the environment.

On December 4, 1976, Kitty O'Neill averaged 322 mph for her two runs through the flying kilometer, but she wanted to go even faster. Two days later, on her ninth and tenth runs in the rocket car, Kitty O'Neill blazed to a 512.083 average. Peak speed approached 600 miles an hour.

During her first run, she hit 180 in five seconds and 500 in fifteen. Her recorded speed: 514.120 mph. She was a tick slower on the return trip, blasting through the kilo in 4.375 seconds.

Kitty was the fastest woman on wheels.

But that's as far as that script went. Under the contract, Kitty O'Neill was only supposed to drive SMI Motivator to a new women's record. Tempt breaking the contract and a certain lawsuit.

Marvin Glass and Associates had developed a toy line featuring Needham and sold it to Gabriel Industries. But you can't promote a 'super hero' until he does something super.

Needham lookalikes: the dolls came in two kits which included a launcher that sent them tumbling into the air to land one-handed, one-armed or one-legged to the nearest object.

One kit, with a $15 price tag, included launcher and a couple of one-dimensional cowboy props. The big set, at $25, had a cardboard stage with windows to tumble from, other cowboys to fight, roofs to fall off.

Needham's cut was four percent on the sale of each doll, but the sales figured to sky-rocket if he could break the land speed record, then break the sound barrier.

"What does anyone do anything for?" he asked. "I stand to make a bundle from this. I'll be remembered as the first man who broke the sound barrier on land. Who remembers the second man?

"I'm as well-known in Hollywood as most actors, but this will get me national recognition, and that's not so shabby from a guy who dropped out of a Missouri high school to become a tree topper.

"I don't want to be a stuntman a lot longer. Some of these young hotshots coming up will start crowding me, and I'd rather stop while I'm on top rather than keep going until someone says, 'Look at Needham over there with the extras. He used to be the top stuntman in Hollywood.'"

By the time Kitty O'Neill was running at Bonneville, Needham was busy directing and editing the first movie he had written, *Smokey and the Bandit*. But he claimed he was ready to fly out on short notice. As it turned out, that trip wasn't necessary.

A day after Kitty O'Neill set her record, a strong, cold wind swept across the Alvord Desert. By nightfall, it was snowing.

In November 1976, Needham was at Bonneville, and clocked an unofficial 619 run before driving off course on to the rough salt, damaging the three-wheeler.

In 1977, the scene switched to Lake Alvord in Nevada. Needham made three runs, careening off the course after a 548 clocking. The car became airborne for more than 160 feet before crashing. Surprisingly, neither Needham nor the rocket car was seriously affected. Needham suffered only bruises.

Acid had been splashed on to the SMI Motivator's main chutes. There were charges of sabotage.

It would be the last hurrah for SMI Motivator. Or would it?

In 1979, another Fredrick three-wheeler, this one called Budweiser Rocket, burst on to the speed scene with thirty-seven year old stuntman, Stan Barrett, in the driver's seat.

Barrett, born in St. Louis, was a Golden Gloves lightweight champion. He also earned a black belt in karate. While in the Air Force he tested aerospace escape systems.

Looking for a summer job in 1964, he found work on a film being made in Oregon. That led to meeting Needham and a career as a stuntman.

And now he would drive this pencil-thin car, thirty-nine feet, two inches in length, eight feet, ten inches tall at the tip of the vertical fin at the rear.

The wheels were solid forged aluminum. The hybrid engine combining both liquid and solid propellants, produced 24,000 pounds of thrust or 48,000 horsepower.

Meyer charges that SMI Motivator and Budweiser Rocket were really one and the same car.

"Hal Needham was theoretically sold a project by Bill Fredrick, which was supposed to be a new car. Our car, the SMI Motivator, was sent on a world tour.

"Unfortunately, Mr. Fredrick built a fake car which he sent on the world tour, thus taking the original SMI Motivator and making it into the new car for Hal Needham. At the time, Hal Needham hired Stan Barrett and put together a program with Budweiser to break the land speed record.

"During my investigations, I was able to prove that Bill Fredrick had fraudulently represented the entire program. He had built a fake car to go overseas and had actually sold the rights to our car to Hal

Needham. This is how Hal Needham and I became friends and also partners in our other racing endeavors through NASCAR and Drag Racing."

How did Meyer prove the car sent overseas was an impostor and not the real SMI Motivator?

"He said our car was on display overseas," says Meyer. "By taking pictures of the car overseas, I was able to prove it was not the same car. There were one-third as many screws and fasteners in the fake car.

"I did get an SMI distributor in Germany to take pictures of the fake car on display to prove it. The real car is at The Smithsonian, the fake car is in St. Louis."

Meyer says he did not confront Fredrick with his evidence.

"Bill Fredrick tried a fraudulent idea on me, and, I guess, the public. Needham honored our partnership. Hal was a true gentleman. He's a very honest person. We became partners and he took the car off Fredrick."

Meyer says he became suspicious "...when I heard Fredrick built a new car for Needham in three months. It couldn't be. It took two years to build the real car."

The 'real car' debuted at Bonneville in September 1979. Needham announced his car would go after the land speed record, then try to break the speed of sound.

But this game would be played with an entirely different set of rules. No measured mile, no two runs. Just a speed trap to clock terminal speed.

On Friday, September 7, Barrett clocked 566.535 in a tune up.

Two days later, newspaper headlines across the country read:
– "Please, Read This Fast, Or He Will Zoom Past" *(The Miami Herald)*
– "Land Speed Mark at 638.637" *(The New York Times)*
– "Land Speed mark" *(The Tampa Tribune)*.

United Press International trumpeted the good news. Here are the opening two paragraphs:

> *Stan Barrett, a Hollywood stuntman, drove a 48,000 horsepower rocket car to a world land speed record of 638.637 miles per hour today and then decided that*

Utah's salt flats were too rough for an attempt to exceed the speed of sound.

In a cloud of steam, the car thundered across the crusted salt shortly after dawn, breaking Gary Gabelich's mark of 631.367, set in 1970 on the western Utah desert.

Even the highly regarded auto racing weekly tabloid, *National Speed Sport News*, carried a banner headline:

"Barrett's Rocket Car Sets New World LSR."

It was in print. So, it must be true.

Barrett was glad his Bonneville adventure was over.

"The salt flats were so rough the rocket tricycled. It lifted one rear wheel off the surface and bounced me around so much I could barely see." Then he added, "I want to finish what we set out to do. It's like doing half of a job. Being the fastest man in the world is something to think about, but that wasn't the specific goal. The goal is the sound barrier."

Needham and Fredrick announced the team had received permission from the Air Force to use the Air Force Flight Test Center at Edwards AFB in California.

"When the land speed record was 394 miles an hour I was dreaming about the speed of sound," said Fredrick. "Everybody said, 'You're crazy. No one will ever go 750.'"

Needham oozed enthusiasm.

"When I drove Bill's other car we went from zero to 600 in three runs within four hours. This car is much more sophisticated, so I don't anticipate any problems."

This so-called 'one-way' land speed record was set over a distance of one-hundredth of a mile, and naturally it brought out a barrage of criticism.

Gabelich says, "How can they say he [Barrett] broke my one-way record. I don't hold any one-way record in the first place because there is no such thing. The only land speed record is a two-way run and the two runs cannot be separated.

"I busted my butt for the record. I spent eight weeks out there [Bonneville]. I made fourteen runs over 500 miles an hour and five over 600 and I'm not about to lose a record or part of a record. Not this way. It's not cricket.

"As far as I'm concerned, USAC is the one that conducts land speed records in this country. Think about this for a while. Just suppose those timing clocks were in error by one-hundredth of a second. It would amount to 168 miles an hour.

"Personally, I don't think the car went that fast and I don't feel it has supersonic capabilities. And I don't believe it's the second land speed car that Fredrick has built. It's the same SMI Motivator that Needham and Kitty O'Neill drove. The only thing difference is the paint job."

Arfons, a three-time land speed king, was home in Akron, Ohio, recovering from triple bypass surgery.

"It's bullshit," he said. "It's really got me upset. I'll tell you what the big crime is. Everyone, except maybe a few of us, knows they didn't set a record.

"And even if they went 638, there's no such thing as a one-way record. And they sure as hell didn't do it through a measured mile and it wasn't conducted by USAC.

"When I was running for the records, USAC would even take the temperature of the tapes and make sure it was an accurate mile. If you're off by only a few inches, you could be off by a lot of miles an hour. It's just plain aggravating."

Five-time speed king Craig Breedlove put it this way:

"You do not change the procedure to suit the vehicle. If you wanted to set a new home run record in baseball, you wouldn't move in the center field wall by one hundred feet to accommodate yourself."

The anger has not faded through the years.

"Heck, during one of my 600 mile an hour runs in 1965, I peaked out at 640, but I sure as heck didn't claim a record."

Los Angeles Herald auto racing columnist, Deke Houlgate, followed the entire 'Fredrick-Needham Connection' and came to this conclusion:

"It's just the sort of hokum that keeps the sport of motor racing in the Dark Ages. Television would rather cover a non-existent 'terminal velocity' record attempt than a 500 mile stock car race. Why? Because it's showbiz, baby, and to hell with integrity."

On September 15, millions of television viewers were treated to Barrett's feat in a one hour special: *PROJECT S.O.S.* (Speed of Sound). Ken Squier was the man on the scene.

Says Squier:

"They knew they weren't going for the traditional record. There was no effort made to go two-way, through the measured mile. It wasn't even an issue because they knew they couldn't refuel fast enough to turn around and come back. All they were trying to do was get up there and get what they were looking for, a one-way run."

The same Earl Flanders was the 'official' timer during that run.

Barrett accelerated for two miles until he hit a triple set of timing lights, set 52.8 feet apart.

Flanders justified the 'one-way record' this way:

"I know it sounds controversial, but there is no need for two-direction runs at speeds at or beyond Mach I. We have such sophisticated aerospace equipment, we can accurately measure top-speed velocity of a vehicle in traps to the hundred-thousandth of a second. It has opened up a whole new world for ground speed measurement."

Then he discussed safety.

"If his parachute failed to open, Stan Barrett would travel fourteen miles before he stopped. That means he would need twenty-eight miles to safely conduct a two-way run. There isn't a place in the free world capable of such a test."

According to Flanders, he used the twenty-eight mile figure for the timing method at Bonneville. If the old method of one-mile timing traps were used, he reasoned the distance would be twenty-nine miles. Barrett had ten miles of available salt.

Flanders' twenty-eight mile theory fascinated Arfons.

"It's pure baloney," he countered. "He's talking about putting the timing lights in the middle of a twenty-eight mile long course. The furthest I ever went through the traps was four miles, and that was without brakes."

Fredrick justified the claim this way:

"If you set a world record in the one hundred yard dash, you don't have to turn around and run back the other way, do you?"

A fact sheet or 'Statement in Response To Questions About Validity On Land Speed Record' was issued. In part it said:

"The first 'land speed record' was set by an electric car in France in 1898 with a clocking of 39.24 miles an hour that was, at the time, termed 'unthinkable'.

"Some scientists believed that the human body could suffer damage if it traveled faster than sixty.

"That was a long time ago.

"The 'official' land speed record is one of tradition dating back to 1898 – a four-wheeled vehicle timed over a running kilometer and a mile with runs in both directions within one hour, all sanctioned by the FIA, the international automobile sanctioning body.

"The entire idea of two-way runs was based on equalizing any advantages or disadvantages one direction might have because of slope or wind. The mile and kilometer distances were used because the first runs were timed with stopwatches and an easily timeable distance was needed.

"At 600 miles an hour, wind isn't a factor – any breeze forces postponement of a run.

"Gary Gabelich's record of 622 is a two-way average; his highest speed was 631.367 in one direction. On his return run the speed was about 619 and he wound up running off the end of the course at Bonneville.

"The point is that at these speeds, approaching Mach I, and with modern timing equipment, the combination of technology and safety indicates it's time to modernize the speed record system and break from old tradition..."

Since the three-wheeled Budweiser Rocket was technically considered a bicycle, the Ohio-based American Motorcycle Association was caught in the middle.

Ed Youngblood, director of government relations for the AMA and the FIM, the international sanctioning body for one, two and three-wheeled records, said:

"Earl Flanders is a referee and timer with us and has credentials as an FIM steward. Earl will file his report with us, including his own recommendations. We will study that report, then submit it to the FIM if we feel it should be considered.

"We don't want to look like fools and I'm sure Earl doesn't want to put his neck in a noose. One thing I'm sure about, FIM will be exceedingly careful in studying this case. They don't want to blow their credibility." From a purely personal standpoint, Youngblood said, "I do not think the FIM will approve the record by suddenly ignoring the accepted procedure.

"I certainly hope Craig Breedlove doesn't believe this record claim has been certified and accepted. I can remember Triumph claiming a record, and capitalizing on that advertising for a year. However, the record was never certified by FIM."

And neither was the Budweiser Rocket's claim of a one-way, 52.8 foot land speed record.

Breedlove felt sure FIM would 'do the right thing'.

"I've run under both [FIA and FIM] and FIM was far more stringent," he pointed out. He had to fly four international observers from Europe to Bonneville to verify each run.

"Two would supervise the loading of the recorder into the car. One observer was stationed at the end of the run. They also had to verify that more than fifty percent of the car's static weight was in touch with the ground."

The speed scene then shifted to Edwards Air Force Base.

Fredrick knew the task ahead was difficult, that the sound barrier was really a barrier. Before reaching supersonic speed, a vehicle must pass through the turbulent transonic speed zone.

"The drag coefficient triples in the transonic region," he said, "so it's almost like hitting a brick wall. It takes twice the power to go 750 as it does 600 miles an hour.

"No automobile has really been transonic; that's the toughest part and we're going to be the first. When the Pitot tube [air speed tube at the tip of the nose] generates a shock wave out in front of the car, we'll be through the sound barrier.

"This shock wave will be weak by the time it reflects back and bounces off the bottom of the car. We've designed the bottom in a triangular shape with the apex at the bottom so it dissipates the shock wave.

"There will probably be a mild sonic boom, like a gunshot off in the distance. Once you've done it, you've done it. We'll be the first."

The rocket engine combined both liquid and solid propellants. Fredrick explained:

"The hydrogen peroxide goes through a catalyst and decomposes, giving you superheated steam and oxygen at temperatures of 1370 degrees. This erodes the solid fuel [polybutadiene] and that automatically ignites as soon as it's gaseous."

"After actuating the proper sequence of switches. Stan Barrett will touch the accelerator with his right foot, starting the rocket and sending him on a ride of about a minute from start to finish," said Fredrick.

The rocket burns about sixteen to twenty seconds, with about another thirty seconds required to stop the car. It was estimated Barrett would be subjected to six Gs of pressure (six times his normal body weight).

Needham added, "I hope people don't compare this to Evil Knievil trying to jump a dump truck. This is a scientific and engineering achievement. Not only did the Air Force allow the team use of its test facility, but it okayed the use of an unarmed Sidewinder missile for additional power boost.

"We asked the Air Force for permission to use Rogers Dry Lake at Edwards because Bonneville wasn't safe for speeds above 650 miles an hour," said Fredrick.

"We are, of course, pleased that the Air Force has given us the go ahead to use their facility, the only safe place in the free world for this effort."

For the purist, it was another example of 'in your face'.

Auxiliary power sources were simply not allowed in any recognized land speed attempt.

Back in 1960, Mickey Thompson turned in a 406 mile an hour run in his four-engine, wheel-driven Challenger I. He then asked permission to use three JATO rockets for added thrust. His request was denied.

Four years later, Tom Green drove Walt Arfons' jet-powered Wingfoot Express to a new land speed record of 413. Less than seventy-two hours later, Art Arfons went 434 and all his older brother had was memories.

Walt Arfons also wanted to use three JATO rockets, one fastened on in the back of the cockpit, two at the rear of the 8000 horsepower car.

USAC said: "A car shall be moved only by its own power during a record attempt."

FIA ruled "...the propelling will possibly be assured by other means than the wheels, but propelling and steering will, however, have to be completely controlled by a person onboard the car."

And naturally, it followed that when Stan Barrett hit the switch to unleash the Sidewinder's 12,000 horses, he had no control over that power source. He was simply along for the wild and scary ride.

On December 1, Barrett was nearing 550 when the three-wheeler veered off the dry landbed course. Barrett regained control and brought it to a safe stop.

The engine problem occurred when the insulation in the rocket engine throat burned out at ignition, melting the nozzle. A new nozzle would have to be built using a different manufacturing technique.

Two days later, Barrett hit 643.086 through the timing traps. "The run really felt good," he said afterwards. "It was a little short of what we anticipated, but that's all part of the game."

On December 4, Barrett hit a speed of 677.323. Supersonic expert Ray Van Aiken, monitoring the test runs, said Barrett may have reached 700.

"The airspeed indicator showed a speed of around 700 and we can reach an estimate by comparing the timing trap speed and the air speed system. We have a history of each of the several runs and based on all this it is reasonable to estimate we reached 700 miles an hour."

On Saturday, December 15, Budweiser Rocket, with the aid of a Sidewinder, was tracked by Air Force radar at a top speed of 702 mph. Moments later, the car was timed by electronic devices at 692.774 mph.

The stage was now set for December 17, 1979.

Seventy-six years before at Kitty Hawk, North Carolina, two obscure bicycle makers from Dayton, Ohio claimed their share of immortality in the first powered flight.

Orville and Wilbur Wright created excitement and unleashed man's imagination with their achievement.

The Budweiser Rocket, however, generated only controversy... and cast a giant shadow on any other sound barrier attempt.

As five-time speed king, Craig Breedlove, who has built a supersonic jet car, put it back then, "If Needham's car goes through the speed of sound and then someone does it with a two-way average over a mile, the first one will always overshadow the legitimate one. I don't like that."

Chapter Twenty-One

A Wild Ride at About Eight Miles an Hour

When you run a dragster, every track is perfect, nice dry pavement. Or you don't run. With a tractor, you get the sand, and clay, and mud and all kinds of conditions. You have to balance your tractor to fit the track. It's a skill you had better acquire, or all you have is a long drive home with empty pockets.

If you don't have the front just off the ground you're not going to make a full pull. Some of these guys can take a screwdriver out, stick it into the track and figure out how much compaction they got. Then they'll go move one weight and they'll beat me. Tractor pulling is an exciting, competitive and highly professional sport. No dumb farmers, that's for sure.

Art Arfons

Twenty-four hours after miraculously surviving his 610 mile an hour crash, Art Arfons was on his way back to Akron, Ohio, his head filled with thoughts of a smaller, more aerodynamic package of dynamite. Another Green Monster.

He was considering a cockpit ejection system that would catapult the driver and cockpit into the air and parachute them to safety from the crash.

Under this system, the cockpit would be inflated with rubber or plastic material and would hold the driver in place and cushion the fall. But as it turned out, Art Arfons never employed this revolutionary system in his land speed car.

He suffered minor cuts near his right eye, salt burns around the eye sockets and scratched corneas caused by flying salt that filled the cockpit during his wild, cartwheeling ride.

His eyes were covered by gauze patches. He would not suffer any permanent cornea damage.

While he was home, his crew was making the long ride home, transporting the remains of the jet racer.

Looking at the demolished Green Monster was painful, but necessary. It was only by examining the remains that Arfons could pinpoint the reason for his crash: the wheel bearing.

"I never figured I'd have a problem 'cause it was packed full of grease. I didn't think it would take grease off at that r.p.m. The bearing froze. We needed oil.

"In my last car, I put oil bearings in all the four wheels. I could have done it with the old Monster. Timken [Timken Ball Bearing Company] told me I'd have a problem if I went past so many r.p.m. on a grease-packed wheel. Then you have to go to a lighter lubricant. I had no problem up until then, so I sorta dismissed it."

At first he stared at his beloved car.

"I didn't see how I got out of it alive. The cockpit was near gone. There was really nothing left. I really had it going on that last run. I think I had the record.

"I looked and I was at 610 and I was halfway through the mile. I knew it would come out a lot more than that. I didn't know I had a problem until the horizon was on the wrong side of the windshield. The car flipped once before I had any inkling I was in any trouble.

"I remember saying, 'Oh, shit', and then the car was going backwards and the chute couldn't come out. I was conscious until it hit. Then I remember hearing voices. I was still in the car.

"I was floating in and out of consciousness. I'd come to a little bit and then I'd go out again. Jim Cook [Firestone's PR representative in 1966] went with me on the plane. I remember talking to him on the way to Salt Lake.

"I remember saying, 'How's my car?' And he said something like, 'There's not much left'."

Shortly after the crash, Arfons did one of the dumbest things in his life.

"I was offered $25,000 to put the car on display at Madison Square Garden. They wanted it as it was, showing I survived the crash. I thought it was gruesome, ghoulish.

"I took it to a junkyard and got $27 for it. I could have made a fortune by letting them show the junk. Now, I'd sure as hell do it. All I kept was the tail."

Arfons' land speed car was gone, but he still had his 8,000 horsepower jet dragster, Cyclops. He could still make a good living, taking it back on the drag race circuit.

Well, not quite!

The money sure would have helped since Arfons didn't receive a penny from Firestone as a result of the 610 mph crash. His contract - a handshake - was simple. Pay me if I set the record.

But he had this crazy kind of idea. Convert the dragster into a boat and shoot for the world water speed record. It didn't matter if Art Arfons couldn't swim. It didn't matter if he had never gone faster than fifteen miles an hour on water.

Just construct two aluminum pontoons, about twenty feet long, fill them with Styrofoam. Make cut-outs for the tires which would remain on the hybrid craft. At speeds of eighty to one hundred mph, the front end would lift out of the water, and the car, uh, boat would roll merrily along at speeds approaching 300.

Elementary, my dear Arfons!

He explains:

"I heard a lot about the boats and John Cobb [killed in a jet-propelled boat in 1952]. When he got up to speed, the vibrations would get so great that a ripple would be like running over a two-by-four.

"I got to thinking, well, if I put tires on there and if you could hydroplane after you get up to a hundred miles an hour or so, you could ride on the water and the tire would absorb these little ripples and make it a lot safer to run. That was my theory behind the whole thing. I thought I could drive on the water.

"It was something I could throw together. Certainly not like building a car from scratch. I couldn't get anybody interested in sponsoring me, and I built it. I honestly thought it would be easy, real easy."

At that time, the late Lee Taylor of Downey, California, held the water speed record at 285.21 mph, set on Lake Guntersville in

Alabama. Taylor would later be killed in his five million dollar rocket-powered boat.

A month after his car crash at Bonneville, Arfons tested his 'Green Submarine', as his wife, June, dubbed it, on a pond behind a Firestone plant. The hybrid watercraft floated. He was ecstatic.

In January 1967, Donald Campbell was killed when his jet-powered boat Bluebird went airborne, flipped and disintegrated just short of completing a return run which would have wrestled the record away from Taylor.

Although Arfons was shaken by the death of his one-time land speed rival, he decided to continue with the water speed project. During the summer of '67, Arfons went to the water twice, then abandoned the project.

First, he took his 'Green Submarine' to Lake Milton, near Youngstown. The front ends however, began to plow into the water.

Afterwards, he attached an aluminum plate to the two pontoons, hoping it would create the necessary lift to ease the four ton beast out of the water.

"I wanted to see if the boat would go up or go down. I hadn't gone very far when it started plowing right under." He considered the problem as minor.

The final appearance took place on a small lake outside of Akron.

Although the boat did not plow on its first of three test runs, the plate did not do the complete job. So, Arfons drilled two holes in the rear pontoons, thereby flooding the rear compartments – another device to create lift.

That maneuver thrust the front of the 8,000 horsepower creation out of the water. Shortly afterwards, the engine was doused with water because of the rough riding conditions.

After a two hour delay for more repair works a sheet of metal was installed in front. It was to act as a shield, keeping the water from being sucked into the intake.

Arfons tried again, but called it a day as wind and rough water conditions worsened. Even at a snail-like fifteen to twenty miles an hour Art Arfons turned in his fastest speed on water.

Arfons was seeking $100,000 to run his unique water craft. He came up empty.

"It's stupid to take a chance for nothing. If I tried to go at it alone, it would cost about $10,000 to run the boat.

"There's the cost of getting to the water [Lake Mead in Nevada], plus keeping a crew. You could sit for a month waiting for the right weather. Donald Campbell waited nine weeks before he could run."

In the years that followed, Arfons would build his 'dream' machine, a 300 mile an hour dragster, switch careers from the fast lane to the dirt, building and driving that sport's first jet-powered tractor.

First, the land speed car.

"I found out I could run a 79 upside down and lower the whole car almost a foot and clean up the front end. This car was so much more streamlined than the old car [record-setting Green Monster]. It would have been the fastest thing I ever built had I got help to run it at Bonneville."

He started building the jet-powered car in 1967 "...and ran that thing all through the sixties and into the seventies on the drag strip.

His fastest speed was 271 in the quarter.

"It's the same car I ran 325 in England, but that was longer than regulation. It was at an airport runway. It was the fastest thing ever run in England.

"Superficially, it looked quite a bit like the old Monster. Both cars had right and left-side cockpits and were powered by the J–79. It was a more forgiving car than my record-setter.

"That car was right from the start. I couldn't get Firestone interested and I couldn't get a sponsor to rent the salt. I was just stubborn, and when Slick [wealthy California rancher, Slick Gardner] wanted to buy it, I sold him the damn thing [for $125,000].

"But the offer came at a time when I needed the money. Maybe if I had to do it all over again, I might have done differently. It was a 700 mile an hour car."

It was also the first Bonneville car equipped with metal wheels.

As part of the deal, Arfons acted as Gardner's tutor when he took the Green Monster to Bonneville in 1978. Gardner renamed the car Andersen's Pea Soup Monster. It was a combination of names of his sponsor and the Green Monster.

Gardner's car suddenly turned hard left at 552 miles an hour. He still owns the jet but has not made another land speed record attempt.

In the early 1970s, Arfons built his Super Cyclops strictly for the drag strips. It was a 300 mile an hour beast. Unfortunately, a tire blew during a '71 exhibition run at Dallas and three people were killed in the mishap.

"It was a ton lighter than the old car. By the time I added dual tires to the old Monster it weighed almost 8000 pounds. The car I sold to Slick weighed only 5000."

For a short while, Art Arfons took the kind of job he hated. The Monday to Friday, 9 a.m. to 5 p.m. job. No racing, mostly PR.

"It was a bad deal as it turned out," he says. "It was a speed shop and parts house. This group of guys said they were going to start a franchise business, Art Arfons Speed Shops, and we'd get rich. Shops all across the country. All I had to do was give my name and be there at the shop in Akron every day. I didn't like the idea, but it sure sounded like financial security. So I agreed.

"After we built the building, they sold out. They sold the building. I think they made money. If I was gonna quit drag racing, I had to do something, so I thought I'll do this. I didn't have a retirement. I had no income."

But that's when another funny thing happened that changed Art Arfons' life, as had happened when he saw his first drag race in 1952.

"A friend of mine who lived up the road, kept telling me about the tractors using Allison aircraft engines. I thought it was a bunch of bull. A bunch of farmers out playing around.

"I finally gave in and went with him to a tractor pull. I was hooked. It was the power, the noise, the whole scene. One guy had four Fords in a tractor. Several of 'em had Allison engines.

"It was intriguing and my life went another direction. My friend and I built the tractor together. We built the first turbine. I said, 'Hey, Bob, I've got a turbine engine. Let's build it with a turbine.

"We didn't have any blueprints. We bought an old farm tractor and used the front end and the rear end. We made a special tubed space frame and put the turbine engine and the transmission in it.

"At that time they didn't have any safety rules. We built it. They inspected it and let us run. And guess what? First time we ran it we won a meet.

"We got the swelled head like we really had something. We run quite a bit. People wanted it 'cause it was different, so we went to a lot of meets."

Naturally, Arfons' jet tractor was dubbed Green Monster.

"Did we really know what we were doing back in those days? Not really. We knew it was a thousand horsepower and that's the equivalent of what an Allison is, so we figured that's all we needed.

"But it doesn't take long for beginner's luck to change. After we got to running a while, we got our plow cleaned. We got beat quite a bit. It sure took the wind out of our sails.

"Back in my early days, we used to race just for a trophy which was worth maybe ten bucks. Now when you race, you can get $2,000 to $3,000 for winning a meet. The sport's come a long way.

"It kept growing and growing. Bob George is the guy that put it in indoor buildings. He's the one who changed the sport. ESPN started televising the meets. People demanded seeing more and more, and that's what they got. Oh yeah, we've got followers.

"As the sport grew, so did the sophistication and the cost of being competitive. I'm running an old, old tractor with two turbines. I've got 3000 horses, and boy, am I underpowered.

"One guy I run against has four jet engines. He's got 12,000 horses. There are guys running 4–5 Arias engines and those cost $35,000 a piece. I could easily build a whole new tractor for that!"

When Art Arfons first began, he competed in the 7000 and 9000 modified classes. "But now they've got away from it. Everybody bitched too much about hauling a ton of weight to add to the next class. Now, we've been running one class. Same show.

"I'd like a three-engine tractor, but I'm getting a little bit old to build another tractor. Years ago, I ran sixty to seventy meets a year. I was gone just about every weekend. You usually don't run the month of December, but you're busy the rest of the year. I've worked from LA to Philadelphia and back to Arkansas."

As holder of the land speed record, Art Arfons was a star attraction, and as such was usually paid appearance money, plus whatever he could earn in his competition. No extravagant sum, but every little bit helped.

He was sponsored by Busch, while Firestone, his old sponsor, kicked in with expensive, oversize tractor tires.

But gradually, Busch withdrew its modest financial support. Firestone quit making those kind of tires. Thus, Arfons was forced to become a true independent.

In recent years, his daughter, Dusty Allison, has joined Arfons on the tractor pulling circuit. She drives her own jet tractor. He enjoys the company. Team Arfons is a real crowd-pleaser.

"This sport is really family," he says. "Everybody helps each other. I was in Detroit coming out of a pull in the middle of the night. It was about three in the morning. I broke an axle. I was on a hill. I couldn't get off the hill.

"Dusty got on the CB and one of our competitors was going by. He backed up, hooked a tow line and pulled us around the corner. He stayed there and he helped me change the axle.

"Yeah, I know it didn't happen during a meet when each competitor wants to win. But it wouldn't have made a difference. I remember one meet. I was next up, it was my time to run, and I couldn't get my engine started. I run my batteries down. Here comes a guy running with a jumper cable and got me going. He was one of the guys competing against me. Everybody wants to win, but they're not gonna win by not helping you."

At the Bonneville Salt Flats, there are few people on hand when Art Arfons seeks the land speed record. Not so at tractor pulling!

"Indoors, we had 72,000 at the Pontiac Superdome. I run every year at Bowling Green, Ohio, which isn't too far up the road. They can probably seat 20,000 and they fill it up five nights in a row.

"Its more fun outdoors 'cause you get going a lot faster. A full pull is 300 feet. Indoors, the distance is variable depending on the size of the arena. But competition is still competition.

"The real thrill of motorsports is in the competition, and that we have all over the place in tractor pulling, where you combine power and technique."

The roots of tractor pulling as a sport go back to the old draught-horse 'pulls' of the nineteenth and early twentieth centuries. It was 1929 when the first recorded motorized tractor pulling competition was held.

It wasn't until 1969 that a group of veteran pullers organized the National Tractor Pullers Association, which sanctioned events and governed the sport. It became a professional big-time sport, a major form of entertainment.

The basic challenge of competition is to move further down a dirt track with a high-powered tractor, pulling an ever-increasing resistance, than can the competition driving machines of similar weight on the same track.

Pulled by these tractors are specially designed sleds built to resemble flat-bed trailers but with a metal skid in place of the front wheels.

A special weight-box on the sled, weighing 40,000 pounds, is located to the rear at the start of the pull, but moves forward as the tractor rolls down the tracks increasing the resistance gradually until the tractor is no longer able to tug at all.

"At that point, says Arfons, "gravity and friction take over and everything comes to a stop. Then, you measure the length of the pull."

The modified class, which Arfons competes in, represents the wildest and most far-out machines on the circuit. There are only two restrictions: these are tractor length and the fact that horsepower must be transmitted to the ground through the rear wheels.

Modified division competitors may use drag racing, marine or aircraft-type engines, developing horsepower ratings as high as 30,000 and producing the fire and smoke, dust-churning event which is the favorite of fans.

Although tractor pulling looks like nothing more than a horsepower contest, there is much more involved. Just because a puller has more horsepower than his competition doesn't necessarily mean he will win.

Balance plays a major role. The tractor must be balanced so that it will try to lift the front wheels. When a tractor tries to lift its front end, all the weight of the tractor will be applied to the rear wheels.

If the front end lifts too much, the tractor will be out of control. If the front is too heavy, the front end will lay on the ground and the pull will be short.

Selecting the right gear is critical. All tracks pull differently. Some tracks take a lot horsepower and require a slower gear. Others take a lot of wheel speed and require a faster gear. If a puller chooses a gear that is too fast, he will run out of horsepower before the pull is over. Too slow a gear and he will not make a competitive pull.

A lot of work is done on tractor tires. It's important that each tire gets an equal amount of bite on the track.

When a tractor is carrying its front end, the only way to steer is with the brakes. When the traction is not equal, either because the air pressure is not the same between the two rear tires or the tires are not 'cut' properly, it is almost impossible to make the tractor go where you want.

A lot of time is spent cutting the tread of the tires so they will bite equally on the clay pulling surface. At any tractor pull you'll see competitors grinding tires in the pit area, hoping that sharp tires will make the winning difference.

Although the pulling track is only thirty to forty feet wide, where a puller starts his run and how he makes his run are as important as how much power he has in his tractor.

Driving could be the most important factor in pulling. A good driver will watch the track long before it's his turn to pull. Keeping a close eye on what is going on during the class will help the puller decide where to spot the sled, what gear to run, what air pressure to run, whether to come out of the hold hard or easy.

Hopefully, all of this preparation will result on the longest pull, the winning run.

"I think tractor pulling is a more complex sport than drag racing. In drag racing, you just hang on for five seconds. In tractor pulling, you take your pull in twelve seconds sometimes and you're almost out of control all the time. It can really be a wild ride.

"You steer with one hand and you have to throttle with the other, and that ain't easy, believe me. Whatever gear you choose you're in that gear for the pull. You can't shift gears.

"And you've really got to know the track. If you've got a real hard track, you can nail it right away. Out least, where they have sand tracks, if you nail it before the sled gets moving, you've just dug a hole.

"It's a real pain. The guy that can go out and read the dirt, stick a screwdriver in, say, 'Well, I need this many weights up front and I'm gonna come out with this much power', he's the guy that gets further and usually wins."

Since Arfons is almost underpowered, how can he be competitive?

"I think it's the air drive, the type of clutch I've got in my tractor. It comes out smoother. You just keep adding power.

"If you don't keep on learning in this sport, and I've been doing it for twenty years now, you're gonna be left behind. Dusty has been doing it about eight years. She's learned a lot, but she's got a lot yet to learn. She's a good pupil.

"It's an intriguing sport to me, even after all these years, even after all these miles. It's funny how things have happened in my life and how my life has changed as a result.

"I've never tried to figure it out, why I accidentally saw my first drag race back in 1952 and why, some twenty years later, I let a friend talk me into seeing a tractor pull.

"I guess it was just meant to be!"

Chapter Twenty-Two

Richard Noble... 'For Britain, For the Hell of It'

Before I went to Bonneville in 1990, Richard Noble called me from England. He wanted to know if it was true that I was going to try to beat his record. When I told him it was; he told me he'd be there if at all possible. We had a nice conversation. He sounded like a real nice guy.

When I was at the salt that first morning, a tall, good-looking man started walking towards me. Somehow, I knew that was Richard. He looked like he sounded. He looked very British. We spent a lot of time together for two days, and he's genuine.

I give him and his team all the credit in the world. They tried for three years, and with time running out, they did it. That's determination. He pushed the car almost to its flying point. He was running clear to the edge. They over-temped it, over-sped it. He was running just as light as he could. That car was in a take-off attitude.

Art Arfons

Buckle up tight. Take a deep breath. Get ready for the ride of your life... a 650 mile an hour blast-off across Black Rock Desert in Nevada. Your tour guide: Richard Noble, the world's fastest man on wheels.

"Our first run through the measured mile was 624.241 miles per hour. Slightly disappointing, but acceptable when you consider the south to north run was on the poor part of the course. Very dusty, very draggy.

"The south end would be much better, much harder and a longer run, almost one mile longer. The massive Avon engine is started by our crew. I'm buckled tight in the seat, running down the checklist.

"As power reached ten percent, I depress my throttle pedal very slightly. That opens up what we called the HT cock. Fuel starts to flow into the engine and into the combustion chambers. It's a tremendous rumble.

"The power reaches forty percent, it's very, very rough. I'm sitting at the end of the runway with the engine idling, waiting for the go-ahead. A plane is dispatched, checking out the course. It's a 'GO' situation.

"I'm holding the car, the brakes are locked and the power level is moving up steadily to ninety-one percent. The temp is fine. My left foot is still strong on the brake.

"I lift the left foot and simultaneously slam-accelerate the engine to 104.5 percent. It's a very, very brutal move. The engine accelerates very rapidly and the afterburner automatically kicks in. We're overcooking the Avon engine. The r.p.m. is about 8000. It's a calculated risk.

"My right foot, controlling the throttle, is flat on the floor. My brake foot rests on a special pedal. The four ton beast starts to move. At 350 miles an hour, the car is very unstable. It swings and it's damn hard to keep the front wheels in front of the back wheels.

"There's not enough airflow going over the car to make it absolutely directional and stable. The steering feels absolutely dead. I'm wearing a fighter pilot's helmet. For some reason, the visor jumps up. I can't see. I hold the steering wheel hard with my right hand, raise my left hand and somehow click the visor back into shape. Scary experience.

"The speed steadily climbs to 400. Between 500 and 550, nothing. Boring. At 550 the engine roars like an enormous organ pipe. Air flow starts to go supersonic over the nose. I can see the condensation. There's also accelerated airflow under the car.

"These shock waves meet under the car and jam up the airflow. We've lost our ground effect. The only thing keeping Thrust 2 on the ground is purely its weight.

"Almost entering the measured mile at 600. I'm driving from the right side and I can't see the left side of the course at all. The six foot square color markers are stationed a mile apart. Big enough to see at slower speeds.

"It comes up over the tick more than two miles away. But at 600, I can't read the big marker. Quite extraordinary. At this speed the tops of the mountain range change quite fast. Quite interesting.

"I'm into the measured mile at 615. My helmet starts to move, backwards and forwards. I'm wearing a protective mask under my helmet. My two eye holes are covered. Quite hairy.

"I flip my head up, as I can't take my hands off the steering wheel. I can suddenly see! I'm going faster than I've ever gone before. It's more than 630 miles an hour. I found out later my peak speed through the mile is 650.88, my average on the return run 642.971.

"I'm out of the measured mile. My parachutes can be deployed at Mach I [speed of sound], but it's not a good idea to do so. The stop would be too sudden, the G forces too severe. Who knows what might happen to the car.

"Slow down gradually. I lift my foot off the throttle ever so slightly. Throttle back to eighty-five percent power. Count ONE... TWO... THREE... press the firing button on the steering wheel.

"Just touch it, a projectile is fired and that instantly releases the main chute on a one hundred foot long line. You're losing speed at 132 miles an hour per second. The Gs are five and a half to six during this rapid deceleration.

"The violent deceleration upsets the inner ear. You feel as if you're driving straight down a cliff. Your head goes straight down too. It more or less hits the steering wheel. Weird, really weird.

"The chute works perfectly, the car slows down, you're going in a straight line. What's most important, you're safe. Just sit back and watch the speed go down to about 400.

"If there's a problem at 400, the back-up parachute system is deployed. If that fails, you say a quick prayer, hang on tight and ride it out. That didn't happen.

"Start applying the brakes about 150. Bring the car to a halt. Take off the mask and helmet. Make sure all systems are shut down. Take out a little notebook and jot down everything about the run. As many little details as possible, including things that went wrong.

"The fire crew is now on the scene, just in case. The cockpit is opened, the parachute firing mechanism disarmed. Let the celebration begin!"

On October 4, 1983, Richard Noble ended his nine year long quest for the world land speed record. He became the seventh Englishman to become the fastest man on wheels in a sport that began on a road in France back in 1898.

During his 1983 assaults Noble exceeded speeds of 600 miles an hour seven times in his massive jet.

With a jubilant crew around him, which included his wife, Sally, a British journalist asked Richard Noble the sixty-four dollar question.

"WHY?"

Without blinking an eye, Noble calmly replied: "For Britain, and for the hell of it." That said it all!

From a dollars and cents standpoint, Noble did not become rich as the result of the record. Not from a monetary standpoint that is.

"We didn't set out to do that. We set out as a team to achieve an objective and that objective was the land speed record. We thought it was too difficult to set out to achieve the record and make a profit. It's gotta be a break-even proposition otherwise you're running a financial risk.

"I've had a lot of fun out of it because I've done an awful lot of lectures all over the world, and that's been very exciting. I know a lot of fascinating people."

After setting the record, the Thrust team, together for three years, disbanded. Noble started his own aviation company.

"A total of twenty-seven planes were built", he says, "and nineteen sold. We had engine problems and therefore our sales dropped off and we had to put it into liquidation.

"I'm never going to retire from anything. I'm gonna go on until I'm senile. The fundamental problem simply boils down to money. When people like Cobb went back to attack their own records they did it with their own finances.

"I'm not a wealthy man. I don't have that sort of resource and therefore we're dependent on sponsorship. Whilst I think it would be forthcoming for the recovery of the record, it wouldn't be forthcoming for an ego trip. .

"Unless my memory is failing, some chap named Richard Noble broke the record in 1983. And no one since has taken it away. I wish someone would. I'd love to do it. I mean I'd really love to do it. It's very much a team thing, but I think that everybody would love to do it.

"It's been, naturally, the highlight of our lives. Given the chance to do it again, to drive Thrust 3, we'd like to take it out a bit further. We've learned so much from our experience. I think we'd all like to push on."

As it turned out, a few years later, Noble would leave the actual driving of his supersonic car for an RAF 'Jet Jockey'.

For nine long years, including three racing seasons at Bonneville and Black Rock, Sally Noble was by her husband's side. When he finally realized his dream in October 1983, she shared in the victory.

"I just felt tremendous relief and joy when he eventually broke the record," she recalls. "It was a beautiful evening – wonderful sunset and peace!"

She knows her husband very well. She knows what is in his heart.

"I am sure Richard would like to do it all again – but over my dead body. I personally couldn't go through all that again. We have a young son [Jack] and I would hate him to turn into another Donald Campbell [meaning son who followed in his famous father's footsteps, and was killed in '67].

"In fact, in October 1991, Richard started talking Thrust 3 and initially I thought 'great', then this feeling of sheer horror filled my whole being."

Sally Noble, wife and mother of three, is bluntly honest.

"I don't think that the land speed racing brought us closer. It was always a pain to me. I did hate that car, but at the same time I did enjoy the excitement of that car starting up. Now, when I see military aircraft or the Concorde take off, I feel, or am reminded of Thrust 2 over again."

When Richard Noble began his land speed quest in 1974 with the building of Thrust 1, a crude jet-powered car, "I felt this was just a passing fancy," recalls Sally Noble.

"When it was destroyed in a crash [March 1977], I sighed with relief that it was all over. But then Thrust 2. For the first couple of years, I felt it wouldn't happen due to lack of sponsorship. About 1980 it might get further. My husband doesn't give up easily."

By 1981, Thrust 2 had been built. Noble and his crew went to Bonneville, but were rained out both that year and 1982. In 1983, the scene shifted to Black Rock Desert in Nevada.

"I had to go to Bonneville and Black Rock," says Sally. "Waiting at home would have been intolerable, especially if he had been hurt in an accident. I needed to be there.

"I never felt brave. I used to feel a lot of anger and frustration. My worst time was watching Thrust 1 crash. I wasn't around when he crashed Thrust 2 at Greenham Common [a British air base where Noble crashed in 1982].

"I was convinced that in 1981 I would either bring him back in a wooden box, or as a hero. And when we were rained off, it wasn't the result I'd prepared for. I was always scared."

'The Richard Noble Story' actually began when he was six years old. Father and son were out for a leisurely drive.

"The UK had been very badly hit economically," Noble recalls. "Everything was very mundane and very drab.

"We suddenly came upon a crowd, and a silver and red, streamlined, gas turbine boat was just fantastic. It was almost unreal. I just got hooked on it."

That boat was John Cobb's Crusader. Cobb was killed in 1952 at speeds exceeding 200 miles an hour. But the sight of that boat unleashed the imagination of a little boy.

"After that, I started reading everything I could on jets, rockets. Later, when I discovered the land speed records that made more sense to me than racing on water.

"Cobb became my hero. He was the greatest. He went out to achieve the maximum speed that he possibly could from these vehicles. He wasn't interested in just acquiring the record, but in achieving the best result he possibly could. He was also a very humble man, and that attracted me enormously.

"I guess I was about fifteen or so when it started to really become very important [setting the land speed record]. Then, as a grown-up, I went into a conventional industrial career. It became even more imperative because I felt I was going to get trapped and I'd never get a chance to do it."

Noble considered driving on water far more perilous than driving on land.

"Running for the water speed records as Cobb and so many others after him proved, is just very, very dangerous. At least when you're dealing with a car, you can control your variables. With water, you can't. That's why my dream always centered on land, not water."

In 1972, Noble placed an ad in the London *Times*, looking for six people to join him in a grand adventure, an overland expedition to Cape Town in a thirteen year old Land Rover he prepared and rebuilt himself. That's how he met Sally Bruford, his future wife.

In 1974, at the age of twenty-eight, Noble set out on his quest. The fastest he had driven a land-bound vehicle was 120 plus in his TR6.

"I knew it was going to be a long battle. I'd have to start with Thrust 1.

"I had no building skills of my own. I'd thought of a series of jet cars, actually three to achieve the land speed record. It was only when we got the wind tunnel test for Thrust 2 that we realized that Thrust 2 could do it."

Seek and ye shall find. Noble sought and found an old Rolls Royce jet engine and talked his way into buying the power plant for only two hundred pounds. He had sold his TR6 to raise his 1000 pound budget.

He completed building of the crude car and cruised down the runway at a British Air Force base at fifty miles an hour. On March 5, 1977, Noble tried to push his car closer to the 200 mile an hour speed range.

During a run at another Royal Air Force Base, a wheel bearing seized at about 140. Thrust 1 went airborne and rolled three times. The car was demolished. Noble was unhurt. Nor was he discouraged.

"The first time I'd run Thrust 1 it was a great moment to know I'd done my jet engine installation correctly and it all seemed to work. I had three alternatives after the crash.

"I could quit, call it a jolly good show. I could build a second version of Thrust 1, or I could seek a professional designer, skilled engineer, and build a wholly new car."

The choice was simple. Start Thrust Cars Ltd., and proceed full speed ahead. Noble sold Thrust 1 for scrap, to start the fund. Next, he began the search for another jet engine.

He found an old government-owned Rolls Royce Avon, boasting 15,000 pounds of thrust. It was twenty-five feet long and weighed almost 3000. The cost: five hundred pounds sterling.

In September 1977, Noble placed a newspaper ad, seeking a designer. John Ackroyd answered that ad and was hired. Someone else shared his 'madness'.

"John and I ran the company. Basically, he did all the engineering and the building of the car. Later on, he was responsible for the run program. I did the money. Basically, I held the organization together, did the PR and the driving.

"When it all began, I hoped it would take about four or five years. I never imagined start to finish would take nine years. I was a complete unknown, with no high-speed skills whatsoever.

"Secondly, all the sponsorship money in the UK was going into things like circuit racing. To actually persuade people to divert their sponsorship funds into land speed racing was completely counter to the industry. It was high risk, very much high risk.

"It was terribly difficult. What we did was start off with small companies. It was the small companies that would advance funds. Then we got a lucky break when we got Initial Services, a laundry, and they started to put in money into the project.

"A most unlikely combination isn't it? A land speed record car and a laundry – but that's basically how we got our break. They didn't give us a large amount of money, but it was twice as much as anybody else had given us before."

The final design work began in May 1978. The first metal was cut in the end of June. In September 1978, low-speed wind tunnel testing involved a one-tenth scale model of Thrust 2. The tests showed record potential.

Noble had the knack of raising funds. Ackroyd had left his job with Porsche to devote himself full-time to the land speed project. Others were also hired.

By March 1979, the Avon engine had been installed. Sixteen months later, Thrust 2 was ready for its first static test. "It's totally awe-inspiring power," says Noble.

"When Thrust 2 is tied down for engine tests, the flame is some forty feet long out the back. The noise level is at 160 decibels. It just shakes the whole ground behind it. It's very, very violent. You look at it and you think, 'God, how am I going to be able to control that?'"

Noble never doubted that he could do the job.

"Like all things in life, if you take it steadily, gradually and sensibly, you get to the point where you can do it. In any kind of really aggressive team, everybody has got to perform. Everybody's got to meet standards. If I didn't meet the standards and requirements that we set, I would have resigned and we'd have had to have found another driver. I wasn't going to let that happen.

"An awful lot of people put a lot of time and money into that particular project. The thing I wanted above all was for the project to succeed with me as driver.

"We were all brand new at the land speed game. We knew the car needed an awful lot of development. We were going very much into the unknown. We had some terrible low spots at times, particularly my crash in 1982. That was probably the low spot, rock bottom. But we climbed out of it."

Bouncing over a bumpy surface, Thrust 2 hit 180 on its maiden run.

But by September 1980, Noble was becoming more and more accustomed to the jet. He set six British speed records during a two day assault, including 259.74 for the quarter mile.

In 1981, the team acquired an even more powerful power plant, an Avon 302 from a Lightning fighter plane. It packed a wallop of 17,000 pounds of thrust.

An air of optimism accompanied the team to Bonneville and a crack at the land speed record. Six long weeks later, heavy rains ended the quest. Thrust 2 proved unstable on the hard salt. The front metal wheels were too narrow. Handling was difficult.

During the winter of '81, the four ton car was completely rebuilt.

On June 16, 1982, Noble was making a practice run at Greenham Common. He blew off the line, reached 230 miles an hour, then hit the main chute release. The chute failed to open.

The back-up chute also failed to deploy. He was in trouble. Noble headed off the runway. At 180, he slammed the brakes. The car skidded with locked wheels for 4000 feet.

Thrust 2 continued across the runway in a four-wheel slide, hit grass at 125, careened across rough terrain in a series of leaps and finally came to rest.

There was chassis and front suspension damage. Repairable.

There had been no roll-over. No fire.

Working virtually round the clock for twelve weeks, the team made the car ready – ready for Bonneville. Ackroyd replaced the four inch wide front wheels with six inch wheels.

Ken Norris, who had designed the late Donald Campbell's jet-powered Bluebird, joined the team as manager.

On September 28, 1982, heavy rains hit Bonneville for the second straight year. There were two choices: pack up and go home, or look for another racing site.

Potential sites included Alvord Desert in Oregon, Edwards Air Force Base in California (formerly known as Muroc Dry Lake), Black Rock Desert in Nevada, White Sands in New Mexico.

The following day, Ackroyd and Noble left for Alvord, then went on to Black Rock. They selected Black Rock, one of the world's largest deserts (8000 square miles). The surface appeared smooth, with a thin mud crust.

While the residents of nearby Gerlach welcomed the 'British Invasion', a group of environmentalists would wage a fierce battle to ban the car and its metal wheels from running for the land speed record.

In the long run, Noble and his team would gain victory and return the record to the UK. But not a total victory. The Bureau of Land Management (BLM) ruled that oil could not be put down as guidelines. Noble would follow the trail left by the team's Jaguar.

By October 9, 1982, Noble hit an easy 320 during an unofficial run. Four days later, the United States Auto Club timing team, headed by Dave Petrali, set up its equipment.

Despite a faulty afterburner which failed to ignite, Noble clocked 349.78 through the measured mile in mid-October. He also had parachute problems.

On October 21, Noble set British records for the mile (463.683) and kilo (468.972). It was a prelude of faster things to come.

Two weeks later, despite a balky burner, Noble hit 596.421 for the measured mile. The speedometer registered a peak speed of 615.

It was good, but not close enough to Gary Gabelich's two-way mark of 622.407, set in 1970. "If we don't get that power", said Noble, "we haven't got a chance in hell."

Sandstorms hit on November 6. A day later, it was snowing. That ended the very promising 1982 speed season. Noble had three runs with peak speeds in the 600 mile an hour range.

In April 1983, Rolls Royce experts went to work on the Avon 302, squeezing out an estimated 3000 more pounds of thrust.

Noble and his team were back at Black Rock. He could tell during a 375 test run that the adjustments had worked. "She's much crisper in response to the throttle," he said.

While he kept clicking off 600-plus runs through the measured mile, the record seemed out of reach. With reigning land speed king Gary Gabelich on hand, Noble clocked 607.9.

Gabelich praised the Englishman. Noble was disappointed.

It appeared something drastic had to be done. That something was cranking up the power from 102 to 104 percent. Noble responded with a blistering run of 622.837 mph. However, the engine failed and the second run was aborted.

On September 30, 1983, Thrust Cars Ltd., was to end its operations. Financial backing from the eleven sponsors would run out on that day.

When the deadline came, seven of the eleven sponsors agreed to gut it out for one more week. Time was running out for Noble and Thrust 2. Almost 1.75 million pounds had gone into the project, or about $4 million in U.S. currency.

At 4:25 p.m., October 4, 1983, Richard Noble roared into the land speed record books. Job well done!

What kind of a person is best suited to set a record? Noble has analyzed that question over the years.

"If you're the sort of person who's doing it for a kick, for real excitement, then you're completely the wrong person to do it. The trouble is you brought that awful emotion into it, it's a killer. You've got to perform like an ice-cold computer. That's what it's all about.

"You've got to know your systems. You've got to know the construction. You've got to be involved all the way through the design and build of the car so you know its limitations.

"Obviously, I can only speak to myself. I've spoken to Art [Arfons] and Craig [Breedlove] about this very thing and they fit the mold as well. We've all been through a hell of an experience. I think if you were an emotional sort of person, most people would kinda freak out under those circumstances."

There's another side to this story though. His name: John Ackroyd.

Noble well knew his own limitations as a car designer. While Thrust 1 had proven its point as a prototype, he wasn't brash enough to think he could create a genuine 650 mile an hour land speed contender.

So, Richard Noble did the logical thing, despite the fact the kitty was virtually bare. He placed an ad in several motorsports magazines:

"WANTED, 650 MPH CAR DESIGNER."

Just the stuff of which dreams are made. Ackroyd, a talented designer at Porsche, answered the ad, set up a personal interview with Noble and passed his test with flying colors.

It mattered not that there was no place to build such a car, no materials, no tools, no team, no experience, no money. But Richard Noble was a super-salesman, a modern-day Pied Piper weaving his special kind of magic with enthusiasm and conviction.

After all, he had talked the British government out of a Rolls Royce Avon engine for virtually peanuts – an old, reliable power plant boasting some 15,000 pounds of thrust.

Ackroyd continued his full-time job at Porsche while planning Thrust 2 on a part-time basis. When Noble started shaking loose corporate dollars, Ackroyd left his secure position and went about trying to restore the glory and honor of what was once Great Britain to the land speed scene.

How does one go about designing a record-setting car? Ackroyd explains.

"The design objective of a Land Speed Record [LSR] car is to achieve sufficient performance as simply and safely as possible, while conforming to the rules in operation. We followed them to the letter so that our record could not be disputed.

"The target was the World Unlimited Flying Start Mile, commonly known as the LSR. The record we had to beat was set for the USA by Gary Gabelich in the rocket car, Blue Flame, in 1970 at 622.407 miles per hour. To better this by one percent we would need to exceed 628.

"Any vehicle is the project of numerous compromises, and due to its extreme nature, the record car is especially so. Performance must be balanced against cost and safety, sophistication against limited facilities, quality against time, stability against frontal area, rigidity against weight, and design theory against build practicality.

"Thrust 2 was to be built on a tight budget, by a handful of dedicated craftsmen, with very limited facilities, in an old boat shed. With these limitations it was decided to go for a conventional rather than radical concept [Thrust 2 closely resembled Art Arfons' record-setting Green Monster in its frontal area and its twin-cockpit concept], using readily available skills, materials and components.

"Terminal speed is reached when the drag builds up to equal the thrust, but the actual speed 'through the lights' is limited by the run-up distance available – about five to six miles on known tracks.

"To increase the speed for a given run-in requires increased acceleration, which is determined by the excess of thrust over drag. To reduce drag, the vehicle is wrapped in a 'slippery' shape with minimum frontal area.

"A lightweight structure is used to keep weight to minimum, but a very powerful engine is still required to provide the necessary acceleration.

"Both jet and rocket engines have been used to provide the power and each has its benefits and drawbacks. The rocket car does not need an air intake, so the front wheels, fuel, driver and engine can be placed in line, achieving a slim, pencil-shaped body, spoiled by having to stick the rear wheels on the end of struts for stability.

"The low drag and high power-to-weight ratio produces rapid acceleration to top speed. However, to enable the car to maintain this speed for a full mile at the colossal drag encountered near Mach I [Speed of Sound] would require a drastic increase in fuel load.

"This means a heavier car and reduced acceleration, requiring a longer run-up and more fuel. This compound effect may be difficult to overcome. Rocket fuel is expensive and difficult to handle, making the one hour turn-around a severe limitation.

"The jet car needs to suck in vast quantities of air and the intake for this pushes the other components aside, making for a greater frontal area and greater drag than the rocket. The result is a bulkier vehicle with lower acceleration.

"However, the fuel weight is not so critical and the performance can be held for the statutory mile. The fuel is readily available, and easily handled, allowing quick refueling for the turn-around. The decision for Thrust 2 was clinched by the availability of the well-proven Rolls Royce Avon.

"Having elected the engine, this, and all other vital components such as driver, fuel tanks, wheels and drag chutes, have to be arranged in the best possible layout to suit interests, such as frontal area, safety, visibility, weight distribution, stability, accessibility and, not least, cost.

"A convenient way to hold these components together can be provided by a space frame of tubular steel. This frame acts as a base from which the rest of the car is built up, providing datums to work from and attachments for all components and the outside skins.

"Primary safety is dependent on structural and mechanical integrity and vehicle stability and control. Stability is produced by a combination of aerodynamic shape, center of gravity and ground adhesion.

"For a 'straight line' car we have followed the 'arrow principle' – weight at the front and fins at the rear. Control of the car is through front-wheel steering. To keep the wheels firmly on the ground there is all-round independent suspension on rubber springs, which build up their resistance progressively and help to keep ride height and angle within strict limits under large load variations.

"This suspension is vital for running on solid wheels without a rubber tire to iron out the surface irregularities. In the event of loss of control, a drag chute can be deployed to straighten up and slow down the car.

"To protect against impact or fire, the driver is isolated in a strong roll car surrounded by firewalls. This cage is located in the center of the car, away from the corner impacts, with the driver firmly harnessed into a form-fitting seat of energy-absorbing foam.

"Fuel tanks are of aircraft rubber bag type, housed in aluminum containers and further protected with anti-implosive foam. Inlets and outlets are guarded by shut-off valves.

"From the melting pot of the preceding considerations, Thrust 2 evolved as a twenty-seven foot long, four ton projectile with wheels, ancillary bays, cockpits and fuel tanks housed in sidebodies either side of the central engine pod.

"The driver sits on the right hand side [Arfons sat on the left side]. His forward visibility is limited, but adequate, and there is enough bonnet to air the car. His controls are basic."

So much for theory. Now for a lesson in anatomy.

Type	World Land Speed Record Special
Class	Category C, Group Jet
Seating	Offset, right-hand drive Occasional passenger on left side
Propulsion	Jet thrust
Transmission	None
Length	27 feet 4 inches
Height	8 feet 4 inches
Height, body	4 feet 3 inches
Height, fins	7 feet 0 inches
Wheelbase	250 inches
Track, front	79 inches
Track, rear	97 inches
Ground clearance	5 inches
Weight, ready to run	4 tons
Distribution	64% front, 36% rear
Engine, type	Rolls Royce Avon 302 with heat (afterburner)
Engine, thrust	16,800 pounds of thrust at sea level Equivalent to 30,000 horsepower
Body/chassis construction	Square tube space frame with riveted aluminum panels
Suspension, type	Four wheels all independent

Suspension, front	Double wishbones
Suspension, rear	Trailing arms
Suspension, springs	Avon rubber, bump and rebound
Suspension, dampers	Spax gas filled, two per wheel
Steering, type	Adwest rack and pinion, manual
Steering, lock	16 degrees lock-to-lock
Steering, turning circle	150 feet
Braking, from 650 mph	Single 7 foot 6 inch diameter drag chute
Braking, from 375 mph	Triple cluster of 7 feet 6 inch diameter drag chutes
Braking, from 100 mph	Wheel brakes
Wheel brakes	Four wheel 15 inch diameter, solid discs
Wheel brakes, front	Two twin pot calipers
Wheel brakes, rear	One twin pot caliper
Wheel brakes, system	Fully powered hydraulic, 900 lbs per square inch
Wheels, type	Solid, forged aluminum alloy
Wheels, diameter	30 inches outside, no tires
Wheels, front	6 inches spherical tread
Wheels, rear	4 inches, V-tread
Fuel, type	Jet AI kerosene

Fuel, tanks	Saddle, rubber bag in aluminum case
Fuel capacity	62 imperial gallons each side
Fuel, supply	Fueldraulic system and turbo-pump
Fuel consumption	60 gallon/minute 6 gallons per mile

PERFORMANCE

Top speed	650 miles per hour (Mach 0.84 at 75 degrees Fahrenheit)
Acceleration	0 to 200 in 9 seconds 0 to 400 in 20 seconds 0 to 600 in 40 seconds 0 to 650 in 59 seconds
Acceleration, start-to-stop	10.1 miles

TRACK

Type	Dry lake bed
Location	Black Rock Desert, Nevada
Length	Up to 13 miles
Width	800 feet, 16 lanes 50 feet wide
Surface	Alkali mud
Altitude	3900 feet

While Ackroyd is proud of a "job well done", he knows his jet car "is not the ultimate record breaker. It is centered around a twenty-two year old engine that had already led a full life, and its design reflects the simple facilities with which it was built.

"The object was to regain the record by an acceptable margin, rather than to make a quantum leap in performance, involving a lot of new technology. Consistency of operation was a prime consideration in our program. Thrust 2 made nine runs at over 600. On all of these the steering, suspension, handling, stability and structure were trouble-free and taken for granted.

"Only the systems required some minor debugging. This was a good return on our investment in robust design, meticulous workmanship and first-class materials. The car must be built to the highest standards of one's conscience. It is no good having nagging doubts or regrets when the car is winding up on the start line with a man inside it.

"It is tempting to surmise that the chassis would have more speed up its sleeve given greater power, a harder surface, or hotter air, but perfect conditions have eluded most competitors and it will be the same for the future contenders attacking our record.

"To Richard Noble must go tribute for starting it all off and keeping the project rolling. It is no mean feat to commute up and down a desert at 600 miles per hour, but this was the tip of the iceberg.

"Funding a project of this magnitude and keeping it afloat through recession and setbacks requires extraordinary determination and drive. His final success was well deserved and hard-earned."

Chapter Twenty-Three
Will it Be a Two-Wheel Monster?

> *I don't know how long I managed to keep it a secret from June. But one day she came into the shop and saw that thing. She knew enough about engines to know how to jam a metal bar into the intake. She had the weapon in her hand and I told her to think it over. 'I'll just have to take out a mortgage on our house and buy another motor'. She may have been mad as hell, but she's far from stupid. She put down that bar.*

> Art Arfons

The year: 1989.

Art Arfons had celebrated his sixty-fourth birthday in February.

The calendar said he was getting older. His own body told him the same thing, but there was no slow-down for this legendary motorsports figure.

He was competing full-time on the lucrative, coast-to-coast tractor pulling circuit, continuing to drive thousands and thousands of miles, rushing home between meets to pursue his obsession...

A six year obsession which took the form of a radical Green Monster, No. 27, a two-wheeler that weighed just 1800 pounds. A 650–700 mile an hour jet which would carry Arfons to his fourth land speed record.

"I'm gettin' too damn old for this kinda stuff. My eyes ain't as good as they used to be. I feel like an old man." A grin spreads across his face. "I don't know why I'm doin' it... I can hardly wait."

Becoming a 'golden ager' had toned down his expectations.

"I figure the fastest this car (oops), bike can go is about 700. It'll sorta flatten out at that speed. That's as close as I want to get to the sound barrier. I think the air should still be smooth."

Arfons would have to average 640 plus for his two runs in order to bring the record back to the United States.

From 1963 to 1983, four Americans held a stranglehold on the world land speed record – Arfons, Breedlove, Tom Green and Gary Gabelich.

The speed increased from Breedlove's 407 in '63 to Gabelich's 622.407 in '70, driving the rocket-powered Blue Flame.

Thirteen years later, Richard Noble finally brought back the speed title to Great Britain, driving his massive jet-powered Thrust 2 to an average speed of 633.4 mph.

"That engine was revved to the max," says Arfons. "He was probably getting 25,000 pounds of thrust." The car weighed four tons.

So why not build a heavyweight instead of a lightweight?

"I certainly could have done it the old way. I sure as heck had enough J-79s around here. [Arfons used a J-79 as the power plant for his three records.] But something a guy told me back around 1970 or 1971 was really responsible for this two-wheeler."

That guy was Tom Green, who set the land speed record of 413 back in 1964, and held it for three days before Art Arfons cranked up his Green Monster for the first time.

The two men were far from strangers. Art was at the Salt Flats when Green, driving Walt Arfons' Wingfoot Express, struggled to get up speed.

Just when it appeared Walt Arfons would fail for the second straight year, Art took Green aside and made a suggestion. Just widen the car's exhaust cone from seventeen to nineteen inches.

Green responded with a two-way run of 413.2 mph.

So, it was only fair, years later, that Green return the favor.

"I met him in Chicago," recalls Arfons. "He'd seen my drag racing rig and came over to say hello. We had lunch together. He said something like, 'You know, the ideal machine would be a two-wheeler so you wouldn't have the ground effect to worry about'.

"That stuck with me through the years. Really, that was his idea and when you think about it, all you've really got on the ground is three inches of a wheel.

"You don't have a big body, an extra set of wheels or anything. It's just gotta be less problems aerodynamically. With one wheel behind the other, there's sure as heck got to be a lot less drag."

From the idea to reality took Art Arfons six years and $100,000 of his own money to build. No financial reward. Just inner satisfaction.

Now for the vital statistics: the super bike was twenty-two feet long, and about two and a half feet wide; the jet engine generated 4500 pounds of thrust; the fuel capacity was twenty-two gallons; the circumference of the metal wheels was twenty-six inches, with specially designed/cut-outs (treads) for traction; the width of the wheels was all of three inches.

"I designed it that way so the wheel won't skid as it's accelerating. If you ever lock up a wheel on a motorcycle, bicycle or truck, you're gonna lose it.

"This wheel's got to accelerate as fast as the bike accelerates, so that's why I designed a tread in it like that, so it'll build up speed."

The space-age jet also had a small tail fin and two up-front wings (canards) to keep the missile from taking off.

The most intriguing feature was a pair of six inch long skis at the end of two V-shaped bars. An onboard computer would release the skis which were recessed in the body, and they would act as balancers to keep the Monster upright until it reached the speed of 125 miles an hour. At that speed, the skis would automatically pull back into the body. The process would be repeated when Arfons slowed down following a high-speed run. Strictly Buck Rogers stuff!

Arfons' record-setting Monster had a four-stage afterburner. During his ill-fated 610 mph crash in 1966, he used second stage for the first time.

What about this 5000 horsepower engine on the mini-Monster?

"You bring the engine up to one hundred percent power. When the engine stabilizes, you just light the burner, like a dragster. You've seen a dragster run. It sits on the starting line for a while. When the Rs are right, you go!"

The most salt Arfons had ever used at Bonneville before hitting the measured mile had been two and a half miles. Then one mile through the clocks, four more miles to come to a safe stop. "I'd like at least two and a half miles before hitting the clocks."

Unlike Breedlove and Gabelich, who made countless test runs, slowly increasing the speed before making a record attempt, Arfons had no such plans.

"I don't plan to make more than five or six total runs. I'd like to make a pass at about 300 or 400 miles an hour and see if it's gonna shimmy or something. If it don't, then go!"

He simply calls the whole thing 'Russian Roulette'.

"The more times you pull the trigger, the greater the chances of blowing your head off."

As the time drew nearer to leave for Utah, Arfons became more excited.

"I think about it, it seems, twenty-four hours a day. In my dreams I see myself in the cockpit, streaking down the salt. I've even woken up from a dream, gone to the shop and made a change in the car, all from a dream."

In the late 1980s, a group called Utah Salt Flats Racing Association was formed. Racers with a common interest with costs equally share among the forty or so members. Art Arfons joined. It was the reasonable way to keep expenses to a sane level.

But shortly before the first meet in 1988, USFRA officials told Arfons to stay at home.

"My car didn't meet their specs and there was no way I could make the changes they wanted."

A year later, he hoped it would be different.

A week before he was scheduled to run at Bonneville, word reached Art that Craig Arfons, his forty year old nephew, had been killed during an ill-fated attempt to set a world water speed record at Sebring, Florida.

Craig Arfons, a veteran jet-powered funny car driver, had plans to build a land speed car. But that would have to wait until he attacked the water mark in a modified unlimited hydroplane. In 1978, Australian, Ken Warby, set a new record averaging 317 mph in a jet boat.

Arfons reached an estimated 380 miles an hour during his first run. Then the boat went violently out of control and broke apart. He died in hospital.

"I was in Wisconsin and I got the call. I knew he was gonna make some tests. I didn't think he was gonna go that fast. After hearing about Craig, I really didn't want to do it.

"But I knew I had to. I'd put six years of my life into building the car. I didn't have a sponsor; the kind of money it takes to rent the salt, I had to run with the group or I wouldn't get to run."

June Arfons, Art's wife of more than forty years, had always been against her husband's land speed obsession. Her fear became almost unbearable after the tragedy.

"Craig's death just ripped everyone apart, and now you're going to go out and do the same to us."

The climate in Utah didn't cool off any for Art Arfons. No sooner did he arrive at Bonneville than his two-wheeler became the center of controversy.

Again, the Green Monster was ruled ineligible to run during the three day USFRA meet. However, he could go it alone the day after the event ended. All it would cost him was $250 an hour for insurance, ambulance, stand-by fire truck, timing officials.

Group vice president Rick Vesco said:

"We don't have any rules for jet-powered vehicles. The inspectors checked the vehicle to see if everything was tight and secure. There is nothing in our rules book that covers Arfons' vehicle. It's a big reason why we were hesitant to let him run with us."

Vesco also questioned the bike's fire system and design.

To that charge, Arfons countered:

"I have a complete fire system and they approved it. I saw cars out there that didn't meet any of the association's specs. So I think this is something they've come up with not to let me run. I've been running into this all my life."

Less than a mile into his first run, Arfons shut down the engine. The bike wasn't stable, even at one hundred miles an hour.

The skis were fully extended when Arfons started his first run.

"The bike was bouncing from side to side. It just wouldn't balance. Before I left, I talked to a guy who had an autopilot. So we stuck a rudder right up on the top. He said this thing will keep you upright because if it leans one way, it'll sense it and correct the lean. The damn thing didn't work."

Arfons would remove it after the second attempt.

The second run was likewise a disaster. Eighty miles an hour, rocking 'n' rolling. Shut down.

That's when veteran Bonneville driver Don Vesco came over and offered some advice.

"I had the skids about an inch off the ground. Don said it would be a good idea to block 'em solid, so I could get a hang of how it felt. It made sense. We sawed off some wood and bolted it on. It felt a lot better on the third run. It didn't wobble from side to side."

Arfons knew that would be his last run, maybe he'd crank it up to 150–200 miles an hour. There was no reason to insert the two small canard fins in the front of the bike. Nice 'n' easy does it.

But then a not-so-funny thing happened.

"Right from the start it felt good. It was running straight, no wiggle, no nothin'. I got a spot in the salt where it was really smooth. I seen the clocks and I wanted to get a timed run.

"I just got on it and stayed on it thinking I could make it to the clocks. Then I seen the horizon fall off the windshield and I knew I was in trouble. The first thing that came to my mind was, 'Oh, shit, not again'. It got up thirty feet, then leveled off and rolled twice."

Arfons' speed was estimated at 350 miles an hour when his Green Monster became airborne. Arfons wiggled out of the cockpit head first.

His son Tim was first on the scene. When the color returned to his face, he said, "He is one lucky man, that's all I can say."

Paramedics on the scene checked him over. Minor thigh and chest injuries. Nothing serious.

The crash had its frightening aspect.

"I was hanging on real tight. My windshield was gone and I didn't want to fall out."

When Arfons' head was exposed, the bike vaulted some three hundred feet through the air, landing on its right side one hundred feet off the track. It had skidded more than a half mile, ripping up large chunks of salt.

Arfons walked around the Monster, trying to assess damage.

"We bent the frame up a bit. We're still hoping to run in September or October, but right now it's hard to tell.

"Tim and I built this vehicle pretty good. It could have sustained even worse damage. I'm not too disappointed."

Moments after the crash, he called home to tell his wife what had happened.

"I have to talk to my family about what we're going to do when I get home. I know she's going to raise hell."

The fury, however, came from USFRA vice president Rick Vesco.

"He was to see if the car would balance at one hundred miles per hour with the skids out. He agreed to do that, but he didn't.

"He was very lucky the vehicle didn't roll. Even though he survived, he violated and showed total disregard for our safety regulations. We'll have a meeting to discuss timing him again. I'm one hundred percent against it.

"If he had done what I said, everything would have been fine. He can come out anytime by himself, but he will have to hire another timing organization.

"I don't know if we can have him back. He's too nice of a guy and I don't want to be the one to pick him up off the track. The thing actually flew, which shows it was poorly designed."

Arfons didn't understand all the fuss.

"I joined the group in the first place so that I'd be timed without having to rent the salt myself. I couldn't afford to do that.

"They wouldn't let me run in '88 because, for one thing, I didn't have an on-board fire extinguisher. I had never even been aware of a rule book for land speed racers. When I got the rule book, I made all the changes that they required. I installed a complete fire system. You had to have the suspension parts magnafluxed, for instance, and I did that.

"When I showed up that Saturday Don Vesco [USFRA president] and another guy came over and inspected the car. There was no problem. But I guess the members had a meeting and decided they didn't want me to run with them. But I could run by myself on Monday if I'd pay for the ambulance and the extra personnel.

"The ruling was really bad. It was either put the bike back in the trailer and go home, or stay over Monday. Talk about being caught between a rock and a hard place."

But even had Arfons inserted the front fins, he feels that "...once I hit the burner, it would have toppled over. It just couldn't have worked.

"You can't sit in front of the wheel, laying down on your back in a motorcycle and have a good feel of the vehicle. It would have been better to sit in the middle, but you can't because that's where the engine is located. So you really couldn't have done it. It couldn't work that way, but the trouble is I had to learn the hard way."

But then he quickly added, "It could have worked as a rocket-powered bike. You could sit back, have a lot of car in front of you, something to aim by and go like hell. You can't sit back with a jet."

As a bike, "It was a son of a gun to build. I had all that stainless steel work to get that pipe going around the tire, and that's what caused the engine screech, having the tire sit up in the middle of the exhaust pipe. I'd have liked to have got paid even a buck an hour for it.

"I had to call Breedlove for help when I was building it. I couldn't figure out the linkage steering. Craig had used it on his three-wheeler. He sent me a diagram. It's his steering in the thing. It worked good. The front end is good."

Prior to returning to Bonneville for the first time in almost twenty-three years, Arfons oozed confidence.

"I wouldn't be making this attempt if I didn't think I could break the record. Ever since I crashed [November 1966], I've wanted to run.

"There is no doubt in my mind that I'll reach 650. I'll just go out and do it. If I don't do it, then I would have designed something that is worthless. But I won't go out and shoot myself if I don't."

His dream had become a nightmare. Would he admit defeat, and just walk away from it all? Or somehow try to change defeat into victory?

Chapter Twenty-Four

He's Sixty-Four... Still Too Young to Quit?

After my '89 aerial act with the two-wheeler, I sure as heck didn't anticipate any real problems in '90. The Green Monster was a four-wheeler, and I was honestly looking for a 650 two-way average. I knew there would be fifty to sixty other cars at the three day meet and my runs would be limited. It wasn't like the good old days when Firestone was my sponsor; they rented the salt for a certain period of time, and I could work out the bugs if necessary.

I didn't go back to Bonneville with thoughts of failure. I was hoping to make two trial runs, and if it handled good, I was hoping to nail it. I thought the third run would be the one.

Art Arfons

Tall, articulate Richard Noble of England wears his crown with style and dignity. He is the fastest man on wheels, holder of the world's land speed record.

However, the man who rumbled across the Nevada desert in 1983, at an average speed of 633 miles an hour in his brutish, four ton, jet-powered Thrust 2, wishes in the worst way he was ex-king Richard.

"I don't want to become a [Bobby] Summers."

Who?

That boyish-looking, crew-cut lad who drove his four-engine Goldenrod across the Bonneville Salt Flats to a wheel-driven record of

409. On the other hand, Noble's growling beast was a projectile, a member of the thrust-unlimited breed.

Remember golden oldie time when Summers did his thing?

President Lyndon Johnson envisioned his 'Great Society'... Cassius Clay retained his heavyweight title with a twelfth round TKO over former champ, Floyd Patterson... former British prime minister, Winston Churchill, died... Russia's Yuri Gagarin completed the first manned orbit of earth... Petula Clark's rock 'n' roll smash 'Downtown' dominated the music charts.

Ah, nostalgia. That wonderful year: 1965.

No thick, hard-to-understand accent. Every once in a while a 'jolly good...' Every once in a while a titillating 'bloody...' Truly a Noble Englishman. A man with an admitted addiction to speed. A man who grows restless. But a man who knows the cart does not go before the horse. Meaning, no British company or companies in 1990 would invest in another land speed project until Noble's record was broken. It cost an estimated four million dollars to finance his three year (1981–83) effort.

Land speed assaults have come few and far between since the mid-1960s when Arfons and Breedlove staged their memorable shoot-outs.

But since those glory days, only the late Gary Gabelich in 1970, another Californian, Slick Gardner (1978), and Noble picked up the gauntlet and accepted the challenge. Gabelich averaged 622.407 in his rocket-propelled Blue Flame and held that record for thirteen years until Noble finally prevailed. Gardner's jet car went out of control at 550 mph in his only land speed record attempt.

But with a rare attempt came a gathering of legends. Noble, Breedlove, Arfons and Gardner, a shadowy figure.

It was unseasonably mild for late October 1990 at Bonneville, with temperatures in the mid to high seventies. The total length of the speedway measured ten miles, with the measured mile located at the midway point.

The three day event, attracting some fifty to sixty exotic machines, was dubbed First Annual Bonneville World Finals, but the spotlight clearly shone on a sixty-four year old grandfather. The godfather of American drag racing. Arthur Eugene Arfons.

Back in those glory days, Arfons was sponsored by Firestone, Breedlove by tire rival, Goodyear. It was somebody else's money.

But this is another time. Never a rich man, Arfons spent $100,000 of his own money on his latest Green Monster.

From a dollars and cents standpoint, it was pure insanity. No way to get the money back. An ego trip that few could understand. His wife and his children included.

Originally Green Monster No. 27 was built as a two-wheeler, a super bike. But after a 350 mile an hour aerial ride during a practice session in July 1989, Arfons knew the idea would never work. No stability.

"Maybe someone else could drive it, but not me. I never had a feeling sitting in front of the front wheel. It screwed up my equilibrium."

So, the two-wheeler became a conventional four-wheeler. Two small metal wheels in front, bolted together. Two rear wheels. No more ski skids.

A $100,000 dream machine? Or a $100,000 nightmare?

When word reached Noble in London that Arfons was ready to go, he called Ohio to confirm the dates.

"I discovered it was true. I thought, 'Great'. This is a serious attempt on our record. Excellent, I must get out if I possibly can. We said as long as we held the thing for twenty-four hours, that would be good enough. We've held it over seven years now. Nobody's made an attempt."

Breedlove, who had been away from the speed game for two decades but still dreamed of returning to Bonneville in a jet creation, wanted to see an old friend.

"Sure, it was an intense rivalry, but not a bitter rivalry. It was exciting, like two wild bulls charging at each other. I really admire what he's doing, building another car and still trying. I think it's great."

Way back in 1978, Gardner, a wealthy rancher from Buellton, California, bought an Arfons Green Monster for $125,000. Arfons has called it the best car he's ever built.

During his one official land speed appearance in '78, Gardner's jet suddenly veered left at a forty-five degree angle, just short of the timing traps. He was hitting an unofficial 550 and still accelerating.

He was at Bonneville, not only out of curiosity, but with a plan in mind. A proposal.

All the elements were in place. Let the drama begin.

Never a patient man, Arfons took few runs. The first time he drove his Monster in 1964, he took two warm-up runs, then turned up the power. The result: a 434 record, including a return trip of 479 mph.

Breedlove, on the other hand, made countless runs, increasing his speed slowly, taking his time to get used to the salt, the car. A man of caution.

During his two day, three run appearance at Bonneville, Art Arfons poised his tiny jet just outside the three mile marker. That meant he had two miles of running room before hitting the timing clocks, the measured mile.

"I thought it would be easy," said Arfons. "Just take it out of the trailer, fire it up, hit 300 or 400 the first time. No problems, no nothin'."

Not exactly!

Trouble just seconds after the twenty-two foot long car started to move. Violent cockpit vibrations. Arfons' head banged against the roll bar. He couldn't read the speedometer. He couldn't see. Speed: 177 mph through the measured mile.

Run No. 2 the next day, October 28, a satisfactory 306.

"It felt a hundred percent, better than yesterday," he commented after that dash. "All we did was add a couple hundred pounds of air in the front wheel. I think it might have been pounding on the bottom."

During that run, Arfons tapped the afterburner.

"I just wanted to feel it. I just went out a little way and jumped it."

Noble, his new-found friend, came over to congratulate the land speed legend.

Noble:
Good, great. It looked bloody good from the start. Stability looked good. I like the way you hit the burner... bang!
Arfons:
There was a lot of vibration. It really beat my head around. I think it's because of the solid wheels, and the rough salt. I slowed in the middle of it [the measured mile]. I thought I was through it. But it's starting to feel a little more comfortable.

Breedlove, however, saw a different side of Art Arfons after that 306 sortie, one he had never seen before. He went over and talked to his one-time rival.

"It wasn't necessary twenty years ago," said Breedlove. "Art knew what he wanted to do and it would have been presumptuous. But I saw an old friend who was visibly shaken. It's the first time I'd ever seen him without an air of confidence about what he was doing. I thought about it before I did it and I told him what I thought. That's all."

Arfons admitted the talk with Craig Breedlove helped.

"Craig just told me to feel out the car, take it easy, don't do anything foolish. He said I'd been away from this kind of stuff for a long time, get accustomed to it, don't get discouraged. I really appreciated his advice."

Run No. 3.

Noble watched intently as Arfons was strapped into the cockpit. A few seconds later, the Green Monster started its run. A short burst of the afterburner, an orange flame out of the rear. Dust kicking up behind the jet. Then a series of booms.

Official clocking through the measured mile: 338.4 mph.

Arfons was calm as he unbuckled the safety belt and slowly removed his helmet. A small crowd huddled around him, including his son, Tim.

"I couldn't read the speedometer," he told his son. "The vibrations were so bad I didn't know where I was on the track. That scared me. I thought I was through the mile when I shut off, and I was only halfway through.

"I'm not gonna run no more. I think it's time. I owe it to June [Art's wife]."

Tim Arfons smiled.

Art continued, "Maybe I'll bring it back next year and let someone else run it. I don't know."

Thus, Art Arfons quietly, unceremoniously announced his retirement from a land speed racing career that began in 1960 with his Allison-powered Anteater.

By now, Richard Noble had heard the news. He put his hands on Arfons' shoulders.

Noble:

So you're doing something stupid like stopping.

Arfons:

Yeah, yeah.

Noble:

Tomorrow's another day, huh?

Arfons:

I know that. Without a speedometer, I really can't tell how fast I'm going. I thought I was going better than 400. When I was in the clocks, I couldn't see the last clock and I shut off early.

Noble:

You looked good to me.

Arfons:

I need to build another [tail] pipe. See, my wheel well is still in that pipe.

Noble:

Yeah, I could see that.

Arfons:

It's got a bad screech when I get into burner. I can fix it, and put in a big speedometer or an air speed indicator like I had on my old car. If I was a lot younger, I'd probably go back home, work on the damn thing and bring it back next year. But my wife has put up with so much from me. I owe it to her to give it up.

Noble:

I remember seeing that [air speed indicator]. It was outside the cockpit, right?

Arfons:

Yeah.

Noble:

That's right, so you don't have to refocus. Very neat.

Arfons:

It was always in the line of vision. As soon as the needle got up, you'd level off.

Noble:

I got to the point where I never watched it [speedometer].

Arfons:

You just gave it all you had.

Noble:

That's right, exactly. Oh, gee.

Arfons:
When are you leaving?
Noble:
Probably Monday [in two days], I think.
Arfons:
I'll be out here tomorrow [Sunday].
Noble:
Great, great.
Arfons:
It was a pleasure meeting you, keep in touch.
Noble:
Yeah, sure.

Stunned by Arfons' unexpected retirement, Noble tried to put his thoughts together.

"The man I spoke to on the phone and the man I met are exactly the same. Total out-and-out racer. Absolutely fantastic. I don't know what it's like to grow old. I guess there comes a point where you've had enough.

"Art's one of the very, very top. Anybody who can actually design, build and run his own cars – this is a hell of a combination. I'm just a guy who drove a car. Art did it all. Financed it, designed it, built it, drove it. You can't do better than that."

Did Green monster No. 27 have the potential to set a land speed record?

"Well, it's certainly got the directional stability. The vertical stability seems a bit of a problem because fundamentally I suspect it may be because the wheels are positioned directly behind the cockpit.

"This means, therefore, that any vertical motion that can come up through the wheels is amplified by the time it gets to the cockpit because you know the thing is oscillating around its rear wheels.

"He can't see because he's getting this very rough vertical acceleration. It's a very scary situation, even at fifty miles an hour, if you can't see."

Noble, whose Thrust 2 resembled the record-setting Green Monster in its frontal shape and the position of the driver (dual cockpits with the driver in the left side), said from the time he would receive enough money to finance another land speed car, it would take two to three years at the earliest to build and test that machine.

Breedlove's one million dollar jet, powered by a J–79 engine (17,000 horsepower) would take a year at the earliest, once his project is 'GO'. It would be a five-wheeler, another massive creation.

"Art's approach was interesting," he said of the 1800 pound jet, "but I would favor a much larger vehicle, primarily because of the mass. It's my preference. The magnitude of the forces at that speed [600 mph plus] are so high that it has to do with mass, density and how it's affected aerodynamically.

"At 600, the forces are much higher than most people think they are. They bend big steel parts of the car, stuff like that.

"If you had a little tornado going right here and you had two balls, one in each hand, one a steel ball bearing and the other a ping-pong ball. There were the same size. You throw the ping-pong ball into the tornado and God knows where it's gonna be. If you throw the ball bearing, it's gonna go right through it, right out the other side."

Breedlove was "...very happy he's made this decision [to retire]. I just think it was a real good decision. I'm glad he got to build his car, bring it out. He found out something. Now he can retire knowing that he came out and gave it a try. I think that's fine. I'm very happy that he's safe. I love the guy and don't want to see him get hurt."

Breedlove enjoyed those glory days of yesterday, the fabled Arfons-versus-Breedlove jet duel.

"I think the public was captivated by it. We competed because that's how we earned our living, basically. The name of the game was survive and win. There was a battle between Firestone [Arfons' sponsor] and Goodyear [Breedlove's tire company] at one time when they viewed the land speed record as very beneficial to their marketing strategies, especially in the case of Goodyear.

"When they [Goodyear] first started, Firestone dominated Indianapolis and all other phases of racing, and they were looking for a foothold and a reputation in the industry. The land speed program at that time was very important to them because it was really the only success they had.

"I had a strong obligation to come out and do the job and have the record for a year so they could promote it. I knew that if I didn't do the job, I'd be down the street. So I guess it's like any form of competitive athletics. If you can't win, you're out of a job."

Slick Gardner, on the other hand, came to Bonneville on a buying mission.

If he could purchase one Green Monster from Arfons in 1973, why not a second?

Gardner's obsession isn't the land speed record, but a 600 mile an hour drag race, winner takes all!

"I want to match-race a guy as fast as he wants to go. It doesn't make any difference if it's way faster than the land speed record. I just wanna have the world's fastest race. Let's line 'em up, two cars, three, I don't care, and let's have a real race. Whatever distance it takes to go 600, 650. I've got a car I know can go 700.

"I can't see myself running up and down the salt flats, or anywhere else, by myself. That's not competition, and I'm a competitor. I don't care if nobody's around, but if some promoter wants to pay big money for the show, that's fine by me."

Gardner made an offer to Arfons, $50,000 cash and ownership changes hands rights then and there. Arfons was looking for at least $100,000, what he'd put into the car, so it was no deal.

With two cars, according to Gardner, he could then have a match race.

"Maybe Art's car can hit 600, I don't know. It's not my type of car. It would have been a lot easier that way. Now when I find the time, I'll have to build one. That's a real pain."

In June 1990, Gardner placed his Green Monster on the auction block. He turned down 1.2 million for his jet car.

"I wanted 1.5 million dollars," he said, matter-of-factly.

Arfons campaigned that jet car in the late 1960s and campaigned it on the drag strip for three seasons, reaching 280 in the quarter-mile. But he was short on cash, and reluctantly sold the car to Gardner.

"I'm ready to rock 'n' roll right now," said Gardner. "I spent a lot of money on the thing. As much as I offered Arfons for that other car, I had three guys working all summer.

"It's basically brand new, except for the J-79 [engine]. I've changed the burner design and some other stuff that doesn't make it quite like it was. I've fired the engine.

"After I bought the car from Art, I'd go to Bonneville or El Mirage [California dry lake] almost every weekend for months, sneak on with my crew, pack the chutes, let her rip.

"I didn't run it for a mile at 650, just get it up to velocity, pop the chutes. I was just looking to see what it could do, I took it up to 500 a dozen times, probably ten times at 600.

"That car accelerated so hard. It went 329 in the quarter. There isn't a jet in the country that'll outrun it. A drag car would outrun it for about the first 500–600 feet, but after that it's all over. I thought it would be a piece of cake, show up at Bonneville, make two runs and set a land speed record. Never had one problem with that car. That's why I was so astounded when it turned on me."

Why? Gardner explained:

"A couple of different things, but the main thing is that it was packing air in the back wheel wells. It actually lifted enough weight off the back of the car. It blew itself around is what it did. I'll fix that problem. It was catching air and it wasn't unloading fast enough.

"That thing is a projectile. They just clocked me at 500 and I was another 700–800 feet away from the traps. It was going at least 550 and it turned itself forty-five degrees in a matter of two hundred to three hundred feet."

Art Arfons, who acted as Gardner's adviser back in 1978, blamed the poor salt conditions for Gardner's spin-out.

Two days on the salt, three runs in a radically designed car, and Arfons returned home a failure. His dream unfulfilled. No proper ending to his storybook career.

But once back in his Pickle Road workshop, Arfons' mood quickly changed. He kinda unretired. "Everybody knows I'm a liar."

However, he really wasn't lying at Bonneville.

"I thought it was all me, that I was getting too old for this nonsense. I couldn't believe how much my body had deteriorated. I was disgusted with myself because I couldn't see. I thought if I were twenty years younger I could have hung on to it, drove it anyway."

He worked on his car, and kept his intentions hidden from his wife. It would be only a matter of time before she would know, but by then, he hoped, the car would be ready for a Bonneville return.

"I thought I could just climb in the car and it would go that fast. But the vibrations shook the heck out of me. I couldn't see the traps, so I just couldn't do it.

"The screech, or violent cockpit vibrations, was caused by an uneven burn," he said. "We tore the engine down and we're redesigning the tailpipe. It's flames in the tailpipe, erratic flames. It jumps around. It burns in the front and the back. I had to put the fuel in behind the wheel well and that made a real short burner. The flame only had to go behind it.

"The wheel set up inside the exhaust pipe, and if you look in you can see the housing where the wheel was in there. I've cut all that out. It's gonna be like a regular pipe now. Same pipe without the wheel well. It's gonna be a long, even burn all the way back. It shouldn't do it anymore."

According to Arfons, the screech problems seemed to be inherent in the J–85 engine which is also used on the drag strips. "I never had that problem with the J–79. Hit the burner and blast off." Before leaving for Utah in October 1990, Arfons made one static test. No screech.

To soften the ride, Arfons planned to add some suspension to the rigid, rear bars which were attached to the metal wheels.

His third problem, however, he admitted, wouldn't be that easy to solve. In all of his dragsters, and his Green Monster which set three land speed records, he sat upright in the cockpit. But in his mini-jet, Arfons assumed a reclining position.

Goldenrod in action – it set a wheel driven record of 409mph in 1965 using only three gears as it never had enough room for a fourth gear to be employed. It was powered by four engines.
Photograph courtesy of *Chrysler-Plymouth Performance Publicity.*

Brothers, Bobby Summers *(left)* and Billy Summers *(right),* set the wheel driven record of 409mph in 1965 in *Goldenrod.* Bobby was the driver.
Photograph courtesy of *Chrysler-Plymouth Performance Publicity.*

Art Arfons *(left)* and Harvey Shapiro *(right)* stand in front of Arfons' jet-powered car at the formal unveiling of the *Green Monster* in 1964. Photograph courtesy of Art Arfons.

Art Arfons sitting in the cockpit of the *Green Monster* at its formal unveiling at Akron City Airport in 1964.
Photograph courtesy of the *Firestone Tire and Rubber Company.*

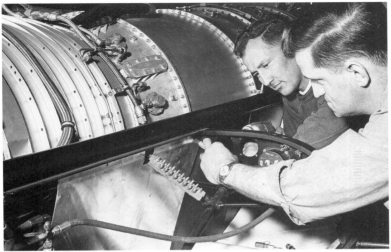

Art Arfons *(left)* and Ed Snyder *(right)* check the wiring in the first jet-powered *Green Monster*.
Photograph courtesy of the *Firestone Tire and Rubber Company*.

The *Green Monster's* first public appearance at Akron City Airport, 1964. Art Arfons is in the cockpit firing the engine. *Note:* the car is chained down.
Photograph courtesy of Art Arfons.

Art Arfons set land speed records of 434mph, 536mph, and 576mph, during 1964 and 1965 in his *Green Monster,* shown above travelling at speed in 1964.
Photograph courtesy of the *Firestone Tire and Rubber Company.*

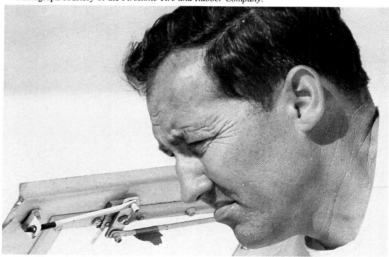

A very serious Art Arfons makes last minute adjustments within the cockpit of the *Green Monster* before driving it to a new quarter mile drag record of 258.62mph, Bonneville Salt Flats, Utah 1965.
Photograph courtesy of the *Firestone Tire and Rubber Company.*

Frontal view of Art Arfons' streamlined *Green Monster* showing the
supersonic probe that was added in 1966.
Photograph by Harvey Shapiro.

The same car as above, demolished on 17th November 1966, Bonneville
Salt Flats, Utah.
Photograph courtesy of *Deseret News Publishing Company*.

Rear right side of wrecked *Green Monster* demolished on 17th November 1966. *Note:* wheels and tires ripped from car.
Photograph courtesy of the *Firestone Tire and Rubber Company.*

Gary Gabelich celebrating after setting a new land speed record of 622.40mph in his rocket-powered *Blue Flame* on 23rd October 1970.
Photograph courtesy of the *Goodyear Tire and Rubber Company.*

The *Blue Flame* setting the land speed record of 622.407mph in 1970. The rocket car was powered by liquified nitrogen gas and hydrogen peroxide.
Photograph courtesy of the *Institute of Gas Technology*.

Stan Barret driving the *Budweiser Rocket* ignites the Sidewinder missile unleashing the extra power which caused it to unofficially break the speed of sound at 739.666mph, Edwards Airforce Base, California 1979.
Photograph courtesy of *Long Photography Inc.*

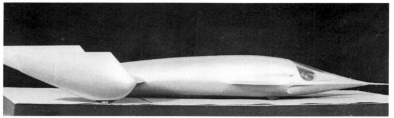

Scale model of a Russian jet car – *HADI-9*, built by the Kharkovsky Automobilno Doroshnik Institute. It was ninth in a series of cars designed by Dr. Vladimir Nikitin in 1970.
Photograph courtesy of Dr. Vladimir Nikitin.

The *Budweiser Rocket* during the time trials, Edwards Air Force Base, 17th December 1979. Note: the rear wheels are off the ground.
Photograph courtesy of *Long Photography Inc.*

The *Thrust 2* set the land speed record of 633.4mph in 1983.
Photograph courtesy of Richard Noble.

Chapter Twenty-Five
Once More For His Old Friend

I've known Ed since the fourth or fifth grade. He's my best friend. The last couple of years I asked him to come to Bonneville, but he refused. I was really surprised when he said he'd be there in 1991. It really surprised me. He thought he'd bring me some luck because I'd go faster. He knew me. I'm glad he was there.

Art Arfons

Ed Snyder was part of it all. A part of the excitement, a part of the glory, a part of the legend.

He helped Art and Art's older brother, Walt, build the first Green Monster. He worked side by side with his best friend through those drag racing days of the 1950s, the land speed days of the 1960s, the record-setting runs, the crashes.

It seemed the boyhood friends would go on forever, but in 1967 Ed Snyder wanted no part in the high-speed game. So, he handed in his 'resignation'. No hard feelings. Still pals.

Snyder would take that short drive up the road, watch Art build his jet cars, then his tractors, and finally his 1800 pound Green Monster in the hope of claiming a fourth land speed record.

Arfons failed in 1989 when the Monster was a two-wheeler. He went back again in 1990 when the bike was changed into a conventional four-wheeled car. And once again, Art Arfons failed.

"I just didn't like that car," recalls Snyder. "I thought it was too small and too dangerous. I'd seen enough crashes and I was fearful. I told Art that. I didn't mince any words."

But he knew his friend's talents and he got caught up in Art Arfons' enthusiasm. Or maybe Ed thought time was running out.

Snyder's health had been failing for years, a victim of emphysema. He'd worked too many years for an Akron company, inhaling too much asbestos. Retirement had been forced on him.

Once upon a time, during those racing heydays, Ed would work full-time during the day, come home, eat supper and work on Arfons' record-setting Monster. On weekends, he'd be at his buddy's Pickle Road shop for endless hours.

But Art Arfons was no longer thirty-eight, strong enough to wrestle a bear. He had celebrated his sixty-fifth birthday in February 1991. He was the oldest man in land speed racing history to seek a speed title. Arfons had survived a triple bypass ten years before and never slowed down a beat.

Obviously, the biological clock was working against him.

So, in the summer of '91, Arfons again asked his best friend if he'd like to go to Bonneville.

"And when I told him I thought I'd go out, Art didn't say anything. He kinda grinned."

The grin said it all.

But let's start at the beginning of this story. Let's go back to rural Ohio in the late 1930s.

"I've known Art since about the fifth grade. It was 1936, I think. It was mainly farms back then. I was a farmer and Art's dad ran a feed mill. When we got home from school, he'd have work to do and so did I. I'd take a team of horses and go into the field and plow. We were the first ones in the neighborhood to have a tractor and a baler. We'd go around and bale all the hay around those fields.

"There were actually three feed mills in the area, including the Arfons mill. They ground the feed and supplied those chicken houses, rabbit places. You know, where you go to buy chickens and rabbits. They sold a lot of feed to those poultry houses.

"In fact, after I got married, I worked for them, driving a delivery truck. I worked nights at the rubber factory and three days a week I'd run deliveries.

"I can't remember a time when Art didn't work on building something. He always had an erector set and we'd play with that. At the end of the evening, after we'd both done our chores, we'd play around back by the chicken coop, building cars. And before we got involved in drag racing, Art and Walter were building planes.

"I always did fool around with cars, starting when I was about eight. My dad would take me and we'd put clutches in the cars, brakes, whatever."

It seemed only natural that the Arfons brothers would turn their attention to drag racing.

"It started getting serious about 1954 or '55," says Snyder. "We were running a Rolls engine. We were at Moline, Illinois, the first time Art met [Don] Garlits.

"The shaft broke. We drove back home to Akron and in three days replaced the Rolls with an Allison and went back to Oklahoma City for the Nationals. Talk about not getting much sleep. We must have been crazy back then.

"At Great Bend, Kansas, in 1956, Art became the first to hit 150. That was really a big thrill. The best drag car was No. 11. He ran it four years, I guess. They wouldn't let us run it no more. They retired it undefeated."

By 1960, Arfons made his land speed debut in an odd-shaped, Allison-powered car, Anteater.

"That car would have set a record all right," insists Snyder, "but we had trouble with the transmission.

"I think we ran 313 in low gear. When we got it shifted to high gear, the mechanism just failed. Just getting to Bonneville is a story in itself.

"We went there from California. We had to come through the low Sierras and it was scary to me. There were no interstates then and there were signs that said 'gas up', but no gas stations for a hundred miles.

"We had a couple of those old five gallon cans, those old army cans. We'd carry gas in it. There was one place about halfway across the desert and the truck [pulling the car] started getting hot. I pulled into this station to get some water.

"There were these great big water tanks out back and I started drawing some water when this guy came out cussin' and carrying on something awful. I told him I'd pay for the water. He wouldn't sell us a drop. He said it was our problem.

"So, we ended up putting motor oil in the radiator. We blew a head gasket, but we made it to Bonneville. Talk about an adventure. We had it before we even got to the Salt Flats."

Despite the appearance of Mickey Thompson's Challenger and Donald Campbell's jet-powered Bluebird, the underdog Ohioans weren't there just for experience.

"Art and I were both real confident. I don't know if we were cocky or not but we were sure we could do it. Campbell's car was fabulous. They had to put two to three million dollars into it, but it would never do nothing. It would just never perform.

"And that other jet, driven by Doc Ostich, was a loser from the beginning. He was having trouble because of those great big wheels."

Arfons failed in both 1960 and 1961 with Anteater, then returned to Bonneville in 1962 with his jet-powered Cyclops which was really his dragster.

"Cyclops was really a good car," says Snyder. "Art ran that open-cockpit jet for years on the strip and I'm sure if we had more fuel capacity it would have been a record-setter."

Ed Snyder still holds a warm spot in his heart for the 17,500 horsepower Green Monster which set three land speed records (434, 536, 576) in 1964–1965.

"It took a year to build. We worked seven days a week. I don't know why some people think it was an ugly car. To me it was beautiful. The car done what it was supposed to do. I was real proud of it.

"It was probably our most trouble-free car. Somehow we kept on blowin' a tire. We had to keep bringing it home and rebuilding it, the whole back end. I don't know what caused it.

"One time we'd blow a tire at one speed and then we'd run a hundred miles an hour faster and then blow a tire. It was a puzzlement figuring out what was wrong with it."

Help also came from Charlie Mayehschein and Bud Groff.

"Charlie worked at Wright-Paterson Air Force Base in Dayton, and he'd come up on weekends to give us a hand, to do what he could.

"Old Bud was a retired painter, and a good one. One day he dropped by the shop, told Art he'd do anything for a chance to go with us. Art put him to work, doing everything and anything. He helped Art, I guess, for about ten years."

The Green Monster was powered by a J–79 (GE) with four-stage afterburner, at that time the most powerful engine in land speed history. And, therein lies another story.

"If I remember right, Art went down to Florida to get that engine. It was supposed to be a salvage engine. He brought it back, but we needed some manuals. General Electric informed us that it was a classified engine, and how did we get it in the first place?

"It was a long, drawn-out thing. Finally, they agreed that since it wasn't going into a commercial aircraft it was okay for us to use it. Then they started to cooperate with us. They gave us manuals, and even repaired a fuel control valve for us. I think it took about two weeks to do it. They did it in their spare time.

"Once, when we tore the engine apart, we needed a device called a Pogo stick. Since Charlie worked there, he made sure it was sent to us, and since they had to have it back the next day, he took it back with him.

"And after we finally got it running, a couple of engineers from GE came down to help us the first time we started it. After that, we had no problems."

Some 5000 man hours after the little band began, the Green Monster was ready for the 1964 speed season. Ed Snyder remained with his pal through two high-speed blowouts, three records and a nightmarish 610 mile an hour crash in 1966.

"I was in the car following, going down the track. I started out when Art did. The start looked normal. He was really on it. He just went down the salt perfect.

"I was in the passenger seat. As we continued to follow it looked like something bad had happened. There was a chunk in the salt in several different places. That was a sign of tires losing their shape.

"I seen a couple of them and the next thing I seen were body parts [of the car]. I thought he blew a tire again. It wasn't too far and there was a crater in the salt, and a series of parts. That's where he came down and landed. It was a sick feeling.

"When I got there, Art was still in the car, kinda pinned in. They had to take pliers to get him out. I didn't think he had a chance of surviving the crash in that car. Even the frame was mangled. I thought it was all over. It was tough to take.

"I got up almost to him and I think he kept hollering at me. Finally he said, 'Ed, I'm okay. I can wriggle my toes.' He kept slipping in and out of consciousness. We got him on an airplane which took him to Salt Lake."

Snyder hitched an airplane ride with noted motorsports journalist Don Francisco, but not until he supervised removal of the battered car.

"They picked it up and put it on what looked like a tow truck. The plane ride seemed forever. They had a state patrol car right there waiting for us at the Salt Lake airport. On our way to the hospital, we heard on the radio that Art had died.

"When we got to the hospital they told me he was all right, just a few bruises. I went into his room, but the bed was empty. I thought somebody was a liar, so I went out of the room yelling, 'There's nobody in this room'. But the nurse insisted he was in there. Someone was sure nuts, and it wasn't me."

So, Snyder returned to the room with the nurse. "She said he was taking a shower. There was a shower right off the room. Outside of being a little sandblasted he was all right. I sat there and talked to Art for quite a bit. I think we stayed the whole night because we were still pretty shook up."

High-speed crashes somehow went with the territory. So did surviving!

"He had some nasty drag race accidents, like the one at Lancaster, Pennsylvania, with No. 11. Took us about a week to get it to go again. We had to replace the engine. It rolled on its top.

"The one he had in 1957 or '58 in that Baloney Slicer. I think it was really his worst accident. That messed up his finger for life. That was in the Carolinas.

"Believe it or not, he had a wicked one, and he couldn't have been going more than fifty miles an hour. We went to the Nationals with two cars. One was No. 11, the other a brand new car, and Art was going to let me drive it. The only place it had ever been run was down the road, down Pickle Road.

"When we got to the Nationals, we unloaded the cars. Art says to me he'd better drive the new car first 'cause it's never been run at any kind of speed. A test run. So he got in it. We got it started and he went down the strip.

"For some reason they had a road crossing there and they didn't have it closed off. Somebody came across, right in front of Art, and it was either hit him or wreck the car. So he swerved and started rolling. I think it was a push car that went across.

"I was going down the track behind him in a car. I said to myself, 'That was supposed to be me'. And I never got in it. But out at Bonneville, I took a ride in the Green Monster, in the right cockpit, at about 350. We had a lot of time to play around. It was a good time to take that ride. I wore a helmet, was all buckled in. There was a lot of noise, a certain amount of vibration."

Not longer after the demise of that Monster in November 1966, Art Arfons and his long-time friend began building another jet-thrust car.

Snyder agreed to help, based on Arfons' promise to leave the driving to someone else.

"When he said he was gonna drive it, I thought it was the best time, so I just left. I didn't want any part of it anymore."

Arfons left Bonneville in October 1990 with a lousy taste in his mouth. The bitter taste of frustration and failure. He had unexpectedly announced his retirement at the Flats.

"I meant it when I said it," he recalls, "but after I got home I changed my mind. If Richard [Noble] had stopped after failure in 1981 and 1982, he wouldn't have gotten it in '83. You have to keep trying. What the hell."

When Art wasn't on the tractor pulling circuit to earn a living, he was working on the Green Monster. He felt the problems had been solved. The car was ready to go. What about the man?

"Back in 1964, I was drag racing. Certainly, I was a lot younger, but my body was used to the speed, the acceleration. I can remember when I sold my land speed car to Slick Gardner in the 1970s. I used to look down at him then when he kept telling me to '...back that engine down. It's accelerating too hard. I can't stand it.'

"So, I'd back it down. He took another ride, said it was still too hard and I'd back it down where it could hardly stay in burner. I thought to myself, 'My God, anybody can drive this thing'. But now I think back. He wasn't accustomed to that acceleration and I just now understood what he was talking about."

How could Art Arfons overcome the red-out, the helpless feeling of being blind?

"It hit me instantly when I hit the burner, and it faded just as quickly when I got out of it. Real scary."

There were two possible solutions.

"Timmy [Art's son] said just build a dragster, go run free somewhere and get used to it again. I thought about it a bit, and rejected that idea. I thought I was better off with a centrifuge, so we stopped at an Air Force base and talked to the guys about it.

"The one guy got on the phone and he called several others. The bottom line: they wanted something like $10,000 an hour for me to rent one. So I went home and called Franklin [technical writer Franklin Ratliff] and told him what I had in mind."

Ratliff, a student of land speed racing, called back "...and gave me all the dimensions and how to go about building one. That guy can get his hands on more information than anyone I know.

"We went through a junkyard and picked up some beams. The arm is thirty feet long. It's got a capsule, a balance arm which goes the other way so you can put weights on it and balance whatever weight the driver has."

Arfons duplicated the position of his driver's seat in the Green Monster, a reclining position. Cranking up the capsule to a top speed of sixty miles an hour produced a pull of three Gs (the force of gravity) on Arfons' body.

"The first time we had it geared too slow. It was only one and a half Gs. Then we changed the gears and we got two Gs. It's a slow process, no thirty minute oil change and lube job. Finally, we got the three Gs. The first time in that thing, it was a rough ride. But after a while the body gets used to it."

All told, Art Arfons took two dozen rides in the centrifuge.

"I could feel the improvement each time I'd take that wild ride. And there was no red-out!"

In those good, old days Firestone would rent the salt for a week, giving Arfons unlimited excess to the saline speedway. No long lines to run. Just ready, set, go.

"With that kind of set-up there's practically no problem you couldn't work out. It's according to how much help you've got and if you've got equipment.

"Breedlove went to Salt Lake and got an armory and they completely reworked the car's body. Campbell [Donald] went to Wendover – 11 miles away – and got a hangar. That's where they worked on his car. There's places you could work on it."

When Arfons was at Bonneville in 1964-65-66, a huge tent covered the jet. It was the team's workshop.

But in 1989, 1990 and 1991, Arfons returned to Utah unsponsored. Every penny spent came from his pocket.

In 1989, he was supposed to run with a club to help defray the cost of running his two-wheeler. "But as it turned out, they wouldn't let me run with the boys. They didn't want a thrust-powered car running with them. They ran their meet, and they let me run by myself on a Monday after it was all over.

"But I had to pay for my own insurance, pay for the ambulance, pay for the stand-by fire truck. This cost me $250 an hour. I made two passes and thought I'd make a last one, hit it hard and then go home. That's when I flipped at about 350."

In 1990, Arfons returned to Bonneville, changed the bike into a four-wheeler and was one of sixty entries in the first annual SCTA-sponsored (Southern California Timing Association) Bonneville World Finals.

His entry fee was minimal. Arfons made three runs, experienced violent cockpit vibration and unexpectedly announced his retirement. Ten months later, however, he was on hand for Speed Week, a tradition for more than three decades.

To accommodate the faster cars, a second course was prepared.

Arfons was confident of faster things to come.

"I was hoping to make two trial runs and if it handled good, I was planning to nail it. I thought the third ran would be THE ONE. I had no reason to think otherwise. I thought I had solved all the problems."

Even during hard times in 1990, Arfons was clocked at 338 through the measured mile. It was his fastest of three attempts. Tim Arfons, crew chief and son, also felt confident.

"There was no doubt in my mind he was gonna go 500 miles an hour the first time out. I thought the car would do it. Last year it went 338 without a burner. It went straight as an arrow."

And if Art Arfons needed any more luck, Ed Snyder was there to provide it for him. "I wanted to see him set a record because that's what Art wanted."

On his first '91 run, Arfons eased along the salt at about 100 miles an hour, then tapped the afterburner.

"As soon as I lit the burner it took a hard right turn. It went right off the track. I didn't think it would happen because it never did it before. I only had three degrees of steering and I couldn't bring it back. It took a good forty-five degree turn."

He would make just one more run, then park his fickle Green Monster.

"On the second run, I started out slow and when I was moving pretty good, I lit the burner and it took a hard right again. It was like two wheels are tied together in front and it just made it turn right. There was no sense in continuing. I said the hell with it."

While Arfons' second run was posted at 268 miles an hour, Tim can't figure it out.

"Dad never made it into the timing clocks. They must have picked him up somewhere on the course."

To call it disappointment would be an understatement. Shock would be more like it.

"I think he wanted it just as bad as ever," says Snyder. "But you've got to understand. With the other car the first run we made in 1964, we ran almost 400 miles an hour. There was no problem. This new car had never run right. There's a lot of difference.

"In the last four or five years I've talked to Art and told him he really should not be out there. After he made that last run, we went in back to the trailer. Art walked up to me, shook my hand and said, 'I should have listened to you'."

Tim Arfons recalls: "I went out in 1989, 1990 and 1991 and I don't think I've ever been disappointed as much until after those last two runs. It was just unbelievable."

As for Art Arfons, he fluctuated between giving it up as a lost cause, or trying to work out the bugs and return to Bonneville.

"Maybe it is Dud No. 2," he says. Dud No. 1 was a dragster he built. "I kept rebuilding and rebuilding. I rebuilt it three or four times before I got it right. I ran it for about five years and sold it."

When Arfons came home after the '91 failure, "I took it apart, took the salt off of it." It would sit for a year until the urge to try again resurfaced.

On the flip side, "...this car has the potential. It's the quickest accelerating land speed car I've ever built. The get-up-and-go is really unbelievable.

"Can I walk away? I honestly can't answer that question. I know there's a point when it doesn't make any sense to continue. Right now, I'm frustrated as hell. But I feel like it's unfinished business."

The puzzle is solvable, he insisted.

"For one thing, I'd take the suspension out of it. I'd move the wheel up front so I have a little more length on the wheelbase. That means lengthening the car about five feet. It's twenty-two feet long.

"By adding length to the car, you're also adding weight. With the 1800 pound, twenty-two foot long car, potential was 650 miles an hour. The existing land speed record is 633, but you've got to better that by one full percent, meaning 640. By making those major changes, that would be cutting it very, very close.

"The solution would be to add a second engine, a little jet, the kind that Tim runs on his jump car. That engine puts out about a thousand horses. It would hang on the tail."

And if Art Arfons decided to make those changes, his son would "help all I can. I'd go back to Bonneville with him. I've never been against him trying it. I just don't want to see him get hurt.

"I think Bart Starr [Green Bay Packers quarterback] would give anything in the world to win a Super Bowl again, but he can't do it. But going for the land speed record is different, it's ageless. Dad can still do it."

But would he?

That is THE QUESTION!

Art Arfons reworked Green Monster No. 27. He was ready in 1994 and 1995 to return to Bonneville. It did not work out.

He was ready in July 1996 to compete in a four day meet, but six to eight inches of rain turned the saline speedway into a lake.

He still waits and hopes...

Chapter Twenty-Six
The Brave Can Only Wait and Pray

I hate doing it to her. It's something I didn't do on purpose. It's just something I had to do. What can I say? I feel sorry for her. I know I'm putting her through hell. I told her next time around she can get someone better.

Art Arfons

Art Arfons didn't set out to become a drag racing legend. It just kinda happened.

Although, as a boy growing up in rural Ohio, he read books about John Cobb, George Eyston and Sir Malcolm Campbell, he never dreamed that his name would be etched alongside theirs in the annals of land speed racing.

As a youngster, he was fascinated with cars, but there aren't too many Americans who aren't. He enlisted in the navy during World War II. He was seventeen.

When he returned home, he went to work at his father's feed mill, began dating the young woman he had met before the war, got married, and started raising a family.

That was to be his lot in life, or so he thought.

But then Art Arfons went to his first drag race (1952) and everything changed after that. He was destined not only to build machines, but to drive faster and faster. Speed became his obsession.

"When I started drag racing," he recalls, "it was a step up in making money. She [his wife June] put up with it because we were getting the house paid for. We could get better cars. It was worth the worry.

"She probably went with me half the time while I was drag racing. I'd go to the track and she'd go shopping. She never did watch me race. I asked her to go to the tracks but she wouldn't do it. I don't think she wanted to see me get hurt.

"I was doing good at drag racing and she said there was no need for me to go into land speed racing. When I took Cyclops out [his jet-powered dragster] in 1962 and went so fast [344 in an open-cockpit car], she knew I got serious about it.

"She don't pout. She just screams and carries on. I don't argue too much. I hear it. I go ahead and do what I want to do anyway. But when it's time for me to leave she's got my bag packed."

Lou Wolf, Art's older sister, sympathizes with her sister-in-law.

"Like any other woman, June's worried sick whenever Arthur is doing his thing.

"All these years, every time he goes out, we get real worried. He has to do his thing and you might as well forget about it and let him do what he feels he has to do.

"I don't understand it. I never will. We've often wondered why Arthur and Walter turned to racing. Daddy had a business going. They had an airplane first. They both had licenses. And then the cars..."

Lou Wolf was standing on the shoreline in July 1989 when Craig Arfons, Art's nephew, was killed during an attempt to set a world water speed record. His boat crashed at an estimated 380 miles an hour.

"We stood there and watched. It was a horrible thing. There isn't a day goes by that we all don't cry over Craig. Walter didn't like for him to go on water. Water is too dangerous. It just makes me ill when I think about it.

"Maybe we never thought it would happen. After all, didn't Arthur survive all those horrible crashes?"

Art Arfons is well aware of his wife's pain.

"First thing I do when I get back off from the salt flats every night is to call my wife. And every night, first thing she says to me is, 'Don't go fast and come on home'."

In 1966, Art Arfons' jet-powered Green Monster went out of control at 610 miles an hour. Firestone racing PR man, Jim Cook, helps carry the stretcher to the ambulance plane. He is sure his friend is dead.

"What do you think?" Cook asks the doctor.

From under the mummy-like wrappings of blankets Arfons says, "I think I'm all right"; then, "Will you call June and tell her I'm okay. She didn't want me to go fast."

Cook, stunned, replies, "Uh, yes."

Back in about 1988 June Arfons finally discovered her husband's secret and she exploded.

"She found out I was building a car. I'd worked on it about five years before she found out about it. She grabs hold of a bar. She knows a little bit about engines. She was gonna jam it in the intake. I said, 'Boy, don't do that. If you hurt the engine I'll have to sell your house to buy another engine.' That was the end of that.

"Every year I go out [1989–90–91] it gets worse. She knows there's no money involved. She knows I'm not gonna make a penny on this deal. To her it's really foolish. She said, 'You've done it, you don't have to prove anything. Why are you doing it?' I don't have an answer for her, not really."

If he had his way, none of Art Arfons' children would ever see him run for the land speed record.

"I didn't want to take any of my kids because after [Glenn] Leasher got killed [1962], it was a mess picking him up. I didn't want them to see that if I had an accident."

Tim Arfons was a member of his father's crew in 1989 when Art Arfons went to Bonneville with his two-wheeled jet.

"And even when I did take Tim I thought it really wouldn't bother him if I crashed. He comes off as sorta callous. But when I did roll the two-wheeler and he come running up to see if I was all right, he had a lot of fright on his face and I thought to myself, 'The kid does worry a little bit'.

"He's a grown man now, he can take anything; but I wouldn't have taken him when he was a child."

As a sixteen year old, Tim Arfons went 214 miles an hour in his father's turbine dragster.

"Timmy was always wanting to drive a dragster," recalls his father.

"When I seen the burner, he got off and then back on the track. He just scared me to death. When we come home I said, 'Timmy, I think tractors would be more your speed'. So I cut the thing up and built the tractor. He campaigned a jet tractor for two or three years. He was very successful."

Tim then graduated to a jet-powered quads and most recently ten cars. "*My* goal is to jump twenty," he says. "I'll do it, too."

He's taking it one small leap at a time.

"We started out with six. Then it's ten... fifteen... and eventually twenty. It's rougher to do it with a car because you don't have any control in the air. A motorcycle when it lands, you can use your legs and everything.

"But you're landing flat on your back in this thing. I'm landing on four tires. The ramp is twenty foot long and almost eight foot tall at the end with an angle of elevation of thirteen degrees. I'm probably going to keep the same angle and increase my speed.

"It's a small missile engine. It's all custom made by myself. The engine on the car is only one hundred pounds of thrust, but the ramp itself is a catapult. There's another turbine engine in the ramp.

"It's a different way to earn a living, to make money. I can't see doing it for nothing. I guess I'm not like my dad in that respect."

Tim's love of machines dates back to his childhood.

"I was about eleven years old when I got interested in cars. Maybe because they were always around. My dad has taught me everything I know, or most everything. The rest I learned from reading books.

"He taught me about common sense first. That's something that most people, even people going to colleges, are lacking. If you've got a little bit of common sense you can figure out most things, how things operate.

"As a kid, he let me know when I did something stupid. And now, as an adult [late thirties], he still lets me know when I do something dumb. But he praises me for doing right. It doesn't come in the form of a pat on the shoulder. It's a little smile that says it all."

Tim Arfons admits he kept on hounding his father until he got his way.

"When I was fourteen, he took me for a ride in his twin-cockpit jet car, Super Cyclops. He was clocked going 267 in an exhibition run. It was at drag strip U.S. 30 at York, Pennsylvania.

"When I was sixteen he let me drive the wheel-driven turbine car. Believe me, I begged for that one, too. Teddy Austin drove the car before me. As a kid, I wanted to be an Indy car driver. Dad basically left it up to me.

"I had a choice of what I wanted to do... if I wanted to go to college or get into this business. I was a good student in high school and was president of the student council.

"I'd say I got serious about it when I invested my own money and built my own funny car. You can't say you're serious until you put everything you've got into it. Before that I was driving stuff that Dad had made.

"As a kid, it was a neat feeling having a father who was the fastest guy on wheels. To me, he'll always be No. 1, whether or not he ever gets back in the cockpit with No. 27. He doesn't have to prove anything to me.

"I've worked with my father for some twenty years. I've had my cars down at his shop since I was seventeen or eighteen. I took a few years and tried to work at a regular job, but it didn't work out.

"When Dad first built the Green Monster it was a two-wheeler and I didn't like two wheels. When he went back to Bonneville he was sixty-four, but his age had nothing against me not wanting him to do it.

"He doesn't need it. I helped him on the project. I helped him all the way. It's what he wanted to do. When that bike went airborne in '89, it scared the hell out of me.

"I was following him in a car. We were far behind, but we were still the first ones to reach him. The car was already over the horizon when we saw it coming back. I helped him out. He didn't have a scratch on him.

"After the second year [1990], I was convinced the car would do it. There was no doubt in my mind he was gonna go 500 miles an hour the first time out, the first pass [1991]."

If anything, Tim Arfons shows interest in building and driving a wheel-driven car.

"I would like to go out there and teach those guys a lesson, if there were tires available.

"Maybe some day I'd like to go out there [Bonneville] and break the motorcycle record. That's the only record I'd be interested in right now. But first of all, my thing is about making money."

For almost a decade, Art's buddy on the professional tractor pulling circuit has been his daughter, Dusty Allison.

"Dusty was eighteen when she drove her first tractor," says her proud father.

"She wanted to drive. It was Timmy's tractor, but it became her first tractor when Timmy went to funny cars. It must have sat two to three years. I put a new paint job on it and let her drive it.

"Dusty's sorta a natural. She's always been a feminine, pretty little thing. I got her a two-wheel motorcycle when she was five. I put training wheels on it. She drove that thing and I took the wheels off. She ran it straight.

"She started around the house and I couldn't keep up with her. She went clear around the house, scared me to death. I thought she'd go out on the road.

"We took CDL license tests. If you drive a rig that weighs more than 25,000 pounds, you've got to have a CDL license. When I got mine, I missed a question. She got hers and got one hundred on all three tests. She got a perfect score.

"Dusty is pretty darned good. She's still learning. She gets better every year. Some people can catch on quicker than others. You learn. There are corners to cut and how to do it.

"I've never worried about my kids getting hurt. Take Tim's little jet jumpers for instance. He's built a good cage to protect himself as much as possible. Even if he's T-boned in this car by another car, he's got enough protection.

"You notice Dusty's tractor [Dragon Lady]. I built her a roll cage and I stuck her in it. Dusty's down at the shop every day. She helps me build these engines, maintains all the stuff and keeps the office clean.

"Dusty never expressed an interest in going fast. Tim really didn't either. It's something I wouldn't push on anybody. I've always had a friendly relationship with my three kids. I wasn't stand-offish at all.

"One thing I was very strict on was be as good as your word. Be home on time. I always knew where my kids were. Come midnight they'd better be in the house.

"They were all good. When my boys wouldn't come in at midnight that was the time they had to find their own place. I wasn't gonna stay up and worry about where they were.

"Rules were rules and it applied to Dusty when she was home and was twenty-three or twenty-four. She was still home before midnight.

If she was gonna be five minutes later, she'd call up and say, 'I'm gonna be late'."

Art Arfons was at the Bonneville Salt Flats in November 1965 to try to regain the land speed record.

He was hoping he'd be able to set the record, return home and be there for the birth of his third child. He went 576 on November 7, crashed on the return run, but he was once again world's fastest man on wheels.

"She was born while I was busting my buns to get back to Ohio. I was in Wyoming. The state patrol was out looking for me. I drove straight home."

Now about the name, Dusty Allison.

Art Arfons explains:

"When my first kid was born [Ron], I was gonna name him or her Dusty. The name had been on my mind even before I got married. I was writing 'Dusty' on the mixers in the feed mill. Years later, I'd seen where I wrote the name in paint.

"I somehow lost out when both of my boys were born, but not with my daughter. The name Allison comes from those old Allison aircraft engines.

"That's why she's got two 'L's in her name."

In the course of her tractor pulling career, Dusty has won only a handful of championships, and she's beaten her father along the way.

"There's other guys I'd much rather beat than my dad," she admits. "The modified class is so competitive. All you can do is your best. I'm learning every day. Ask my dad and he'll tell you he's still learning, even after all these years.

"What happened the first time I beat him?" she asks with a giggle. "There was a big old grin on his face. He's a real competitor. He goes out to win, but if he doesn't it's okay. I'm happy if he wins and I finish second."

For more than a year, Dusty Arfons knew her father was building a jet car. However, she didn't tell her mother.

"Dusty's a bright kid," says Art Arfons. "She can put two and two together. When she found out, and she had to sooner or later, I asked her not to say anything about it."

Dusty admits she didn't want her father to return to Bonneville in 1989.

"I tried to express my feelings to him, but I just shut up. About the time I found out he was building the car, I was going through all the boxes of clippings he'd accumulated over the years. I was starting to file them.

"You can't but read the articles. When he set his land speed records I hadn't even been born, so that stuff really wasn't part of my life. I went through all the clippings and for about twenty years he was talking about going back.

"I love an article written in 1982 [by the author, incidentally], when he talked about his next vehicle, what it would be like. It ended up being within pounds and inches of what he said. That kinda makes you understand why he wants to go back.

"We certainly weren't thrilled about it, but I came to realize how much going back meant to him. I knew he was gonna do it. I knew both times [1990 and 1991] he was going back because he would come home from Bonneville and immediately start getting the car ready to go back again.

"I do know when he goes, it's very rough on my mother. She's crying every day and I have to take her to the mall. Every day!

"Dad's just very special to all of us. I spend an awful lot of time with him, and for that I'm very grateful. He's not only my father, he's my friend.

"When I was eighteen he gave me a choice. He told me I could go to college or I could have a tractor. I picked the tractor. Tim quit driving the tractor, so the ride was available.

"I really had very little practice for my first meet. I fired up the tractor a few times, then they had me back up to a chain and tighten the chain. That's the only kind of practice I had."

Dusty has been driving a jet-powered tractor with two engines about five years.

"I'm nowhere as good a driver as my dad. Believe me, it's not easy, driving with one hand and controlling the throttle with the other. Dad's made it easier for me by installing power steering. He doesn't have it.

"I can remember another father-daughter team on the circuit. It might have been her first meet, but she didn't do well. Her father wasn't anything like mine. He chewed her out in front of everyone.

"When I do well, Dad says so, but when I make a mistake, he just takes me to one side and quietly, calmly, he tells me what I did wrong. He always has patience. He's never yelled at me."

While injuries, even fatalities, can take place in professional tractor pulling, Art Arfons considers it far less dangerous than drag racing.

Ron Arfons, the oldest of the three children, is the only one not involved in motorsports. Not that he didn't want to, but more about that a bit later.

Ron, now in his forties, lives near his parents, in Uniontown, Ohio, with his wife, Pattie, and sons, Ron and Steve.

Ron was a junior in high school when his father crashed at 610 miles an hour. That was November 17, 1966.

"It was right at noon. I was in art class. I snuck out to go down and get some baked goods for the kids in class. One of the guys who had graduated the year before was in the cafeteria.

"He said, 'Oh, man, I didn't think you'd be in school today'. I said, 'What do you mean?' He told me, 'I heard your dad got killed today'. WHLO radio first announced it, that my dad had been killed. I called Mom and she said, 'Don't believe what you hear on the radio'. She said he was okay.

"I thought she was lying to me. I drove to school that day but I was so upset that I left the car sitting in the Springfield High School lot and walked home.

"It all started with the pilot from *Sports Illustrated* who was at Bonneville when Dad crashed. He's the one who pulled him out of the wreckage. He said the guy there thought my father was dead, and that's what they reported right after the crash. Later, the story changed."

When Ron Arfons left the service in 1972, he had hoped to join his father as a drag racer. "But it wasn't long before I got out that Garth [Hardacre] was killed in one of Dad's dragsters. He was like a third son to Dad, like a brother to me.

"I spent a lot of time with Garth on the road, traveling with him. To this day, Dad doesn't believe that I talked Garth into letting me drive that dragster. I drove it once at a nowhere track called Pony Express Dragway near St. Joseph, Missouri. It was a car my dad called The Dud.

"I was married [at the age of twenty] when I asked Dad if I could drive for him. He didn't want to have it on his conscience if something happened to me. I used my best logic like, 'But you were married when you started drag racing'. It didn't work."

So, Ron Arfons got a real job at a gas station. Then he worked at monarch Rubber Company as a quality control inspector. Now he's a mechanic at a hospital.

"Dad was real easygoing, real mild-mannered, but boy, you don't ever want to tick him off. He only spanked me three times when I was a kid and I remember every damn one of them. Two I deserved, one I didn't.

"My cousin, Tommy, and my brother, Timmy, were playing with a can of gasoline. They had a bucket of water and were setting these little plastic boats on fire, then watching 'em sink.

"I'm next door at my neighbor's house. They're at my grandmother's apartment. I see this flame going up against the gas can. Everything was like in slow motion. I took off running, knocked my cousin down, grabbed the gas can and pitched it into the air.

"Unfortunately, it went towards my grandmother's apartment. Her oil tank exploded. No one got hurt. Then I proceeded to try to put the fire out.

"Timmy was too young to know better, so they said. Tommy's Mom wouldn't let my dad spank him. So Dad took out all the aggression on me. I remember that one well. He used a nice belt off of a lathe."

But Ron Arfons says, "My dad is probably my biggest hero. He's a man who's doing what he really enjoys in life and making money at it. None of us wanted him to go back to Bonneville, but we're not gonna go against his wishes. He's gonna do it anyway, come hell and high water."

Ron, his wife, and sons, were at the induction ceremonies when his father was added to the Motorsports Hall of Fame list of racing legends. "It was the proudest moment of my life.

"He didn't make a long speech, but he made a good one. It was a night I'll always remember. I've always considered him a genius when it comes to mechanical stuff and making something out of literally nothing but junks, without blueprints, without plans. It's total genius.

"Why did Dad go back to Bonneville in 1989–90–91? Why might he still go back? On the street he drives like an old lady, but on a land speed car he's a speedaholic.

"But maybe he has to show himself that he can still do it, that he's not too old."

Will Art Arfons return to Bonneville for a final shot at 650 miles an hour? A last hurrah?

"Oh, I know he wants to go back," says his wife, June. "He's not the type who can really retire. He can't sit too long. He does stay home a little bit more when he's home. We'll go out on a Sunday. He'll go over to the shop on a Sunday morning and piddle around a little bit. Then we'll go out for a drive, or go somewhere for dinner or something."

Art met June before he enlisted in the navy (1943) during World War II.

"I thought he was darned good-looking," she says. "There was another boy I was going with at the time I met Art, and another boy I wrote to who was killed. I had just gotten a letter from him. You know how they cut it all out, how it was censored. The next thing I read in the paper he was killed. I'd known him since high school."

When Art Arfons began drag racing in 1952, it was more as a hobby. But as he built faster and faster dragsters, it became an obsession. By the late fifties, it was a career.

"Every time he went racing, you have it in the back of your mind that he's going to get hurt. You just wait for the phone to ring. Art tells everyone that I'm a shopaholic. It's true that I like to shop. I go shopping a lot.

"I don't like to be around the track because I feel like something happens when I'm there. When I'm far away it doesn't seem to happen as much."

On that fateful Thursday in 1966 when Art Arfons crashed, June was at home feeding her infant daughter, Dusty. "I was listening to WAKR and they said the car was disintegrated. I thought that when they said the car was disintegrated that he was gone, too.

"I was giving Dusty a bottle. I was sitting in the dining room and I got up. I remember going down the hall like I was falling. I thought, 'Why doesn't the phone ring? Why doesn't somebody call me?'

"And then Jim Cook [Firestone racing PR rep] called and said Art was all right, that he was hurt. They were in the hospital. They tried to wash his wounds and Jim said Art would have none of that. He was taking a shower.

"And I said, 'God, if he can take a shower, he can call me'. He said, 'I'll get him on the phone'. But until that phone call, I thought he was gone."

For almost five years, Art Arfons managed to keep his secret from his wife, that he was building a two-wheeled, jet-powered Green Monster. Then one day in 1989, June found out and threatened to destroy the engine.

"I would have liked to have smashed it," she readily admits. "But he's got a temper. I was afraid he would have gotten so mad and maybe he'd have a heart attack. I figured it was better not to try it."

On a July night in 1991, Art Arfons was assured racing immortality by being inducted into the Motorsports Hall of Fame.

"I felt he belonged, but my husband didn't. With so many big names and everything, it just kinda floored him. That's just Arthur. He's real humble."

In June 1996, Art and June Arfons celebrated their forty-ninth wedding anniversary. What is the secret of this long marriage?

Says June:

"He's not a star at home. He's just my husband. We're each other's best friends. And even after all these years, we're in love with one another."

Chapter Twenty-Seven
Tale of Five Champions

If there was seventeen to eighteen total miles of salt at Bonneville, there's no doubt in my mind that a wheel-driven car would hit 500 miles an hour. But lack of running room has hurt. Look at Al Teague. He went 432 on his first run, but the speed dropped way off on the return because he couldn't get the same distance.

There's probably a half dozen wheel-driven cars today with 400 or better potential. I think that's great. The public doesn't really appreciate how much engineering goes into these cars. It's the big numbers the jets and rocket cars have turned that makes 400 look like a Sunday stroll.

Art Arfons

By his own admission, fifty-ish Al Teague of California has spent $150,000 to $200,000 over the past dozen years to do his thing. "It's been about $10,000 a year. Some years less, some years more. It all depends on the salt."

In August of 1991, during Speed Week, Teague pushed his streamliner to a two-way speed of 409 mph to set a new world land speed record for wheel-driven cars.

But wait a minute! Doesn't a driver have to exceed the existing record by one percent in order to erase the old standard?

Yes.

And didn't Bobby Summers, another Californian, average 409.2 way back in 1965 to better the late Donald Campbell's effort of 403.1 set one year previous?

Yes.

So doesn't that mean that Al Teague came close, but not close enough?

No.

Let Al Teague explain:

"Technically speaking," he says, "we're in two different classes. We're Unlimited Supercharged or Blown. Summers was Unlimited, Normally Aspirated, or Unblown."

That differentiation was made by the ruling body in automobile (four or more wheels) land speed attempts, Federation Internationale l'Automobile (FIA).

Previously, both supercharged and non-supercharged cars computed against each other in one class. The Summers brothers used four unblown Chrysler engines to power their pencil-thin Goldenrod. Teague used a supercharged Keith Black aluminum block engine burning equal amounts of methanol and nitro-methane.

While Teague's name was placed in the record books, it was a shallow victory.

"My goal was to break Bobby's record by the required one percent. I'm not really disappointed.

"Goldenrod was the ultimate wheel-driven car. It didn't have enough room to get into fourth gear. Bobby ran 425 in the measured mile. Powerwise, they ran it on alcohol. They didn't build injected engines. They could run nitro in 'em. They could run a lot better."

This chapter focuses on the giants of wheel-driven 'mania'. Three are alive today to continue their love affair with Bonneville which began decades ago.

Teague and former motorcycle king, Don Vesco, are in their fifties, and not ready to take up building model cars. Nolan White, the third Californian in the 'old, familiar gang', celebrated his sixty-sixth birthday in January, 1997. He was the first to exceed 400 mph since Summers (401 in 1990).

Summers, a jogging 'freak' who kept himself in excellent shape, died of a massive heart attack in December 1992 while taking a morning run. He was fifty-three.

Mickey Thompson, holder of hundreds of speed records and the first American to exceed 400 mph on land (406 in 1960), was murdered in the driveway of his home, along with his wife. The double homicide, dating back to 1988, still hasn't been solved. He was fifty-nine.

Art Arfons agrees with Al Teague.

"Bobby Summers' car was the cleanest wheel-driven car ever built. It had the lowest drag coefficient. It had a lower frontal area than any other car out there.

"But I don't know if he could have gone much faster. He was running on twenty-two inch tires. That leaves a smaller footprint on the salt. He was close to what he could do.

"I don't think there was a whole lot left in that car. The engineering had to be perfect. The car had four engines. He did everything right because he never had gearing problems. He built that thing to stay together."

Arfons and Summers were both sponsored by Firestone. Art shared some of his salt time in 1965 when Summers set the wheel-driven mark.

"Bobby was very quiet. You couldn't got much out of him, but [his brother] Billy was a lot more talkative."

The three-time land speed king appreciates the effort that goes into building a wheel-driven car.

"These cars are not computer built. You have to figure out the air drag, friction, so everything is right. Summers had four engines, same as Thompson. There's no reason why you couldn't put seven engines in a streamliner. They do that now in a fourteen foot long tractor. Power is no problem."

This chapter is the story of five champions.

Al Teague

For Al Teague, competing at Bonneville has been a love affair with speed that began more than twenty-five years ago.

By 1976, he made the mold for an open-wheel lakester.

"The car was originally built from the mold of a motorcycle liner. I used the mold to build the initial shape around the driver.

"Over the years, the car has been lengthened quite a bit. It started out nineteen feet long. It's now twenty-eight feet. In 1981, I set a Bonneville Nationals 'B' lakester record of 308. It became a streamliner the next year.

"In 1985, the speed went up to 354. By then I was pretty sure I could approach the 409."

Back then, Teague's machine was powered by a 370 cubic inch Chrysler. It would be replaced with muscle, the kind of muscle that a 496 Keith Black would provide.

Teague reached 384 in 1988, a quicker 392 the following speed season.

"For about two years", he recalls, "we were stuck in the 390s. It was a little discouraging. Nolan White hit 401 in 1990. He was the first to break 400 with a single-engine car, and it seemed he had the definite edge.

"No matter how long you're at it, you're always learning. It was really a matter of some minor adjustments to get back on track. When White went up a notch to 402, I finally reached 400. We were pretty close. We were nip and tuck."

That is until 1991 when Al Teague moved to the head of the wheel-driven class.

Teague didn't realize he had reached 432 during his first run through the timing clocks.

"I knew I was moving but I didn't know I was going quite that fast. The car handled extremely well. The salt was in good shape."

He had a five mile approach into the measured mile. First speed is about the first mile. That's 200 miles an hour. Second speed is the second mile. It's roughly 280. Third is another mile and that puts Teague at 370 miles an hour.

"Fourth gear is from 370 on up to whatever. Our average from three to four was 408.121. Then we made the kilo time [five-eighths of a mile] of 422.438. We were at 425.230 from mile four to five and right at the end of the trap at 432.692.

"We tried to get more room on the return run. We graded it another half mile. But as soon as the car started to go down at the ends it sank right in mud. We had to pull it out. Good salt just wasn't available.

"Coming back the first mile was 394.602. That's to be averaged with the 425. Then also the second mile coming back was a 411.852. That's the mile they used. They used the 408 and 411. If you average 'em both out, we actually averaged 409 over a distance of two miles in each direction.

"Instead of doing it in one mile, we did it in two. I'm pretty confident I can go faster. It's not only the length of the course, but, until recently, the tires.

"Until M&H began making tires for Mickey Thompson again about a year or so ago, it was survival of the smartest. When I went the 432, I'd already worn through one core. They were eight-ply tires."

In fact the search for new rubber became so desperate, that Teague's journey took him to Salt Lake City, for tires built for Athol Graham's home-made car in 1960. Graham was fatally injured that year.

As he put it back then:

"We were going to run tires that were on Athol Graham's car. I got 'em from a fella that had 'em up in Salt Lake City. They're Firestones, and I've had the best luck with tires from Firestones.

"Art [Arfons] himself told me that at about 450 you'll start having trouble. I think they'll go faster but being that they've sat for almost thirty years and they're cracked and really not in the best shape, I've got to be careful with them. But they're better than what I've got!"

In March 1995, he used one set of Mickey Thompsons during his 370 mph effort in soggy Australia, and reported no problems with the new tires.

But three years before that, on those same thirty year old tires, his racing days almost ended tragically,

It was July 24–26 at the USFRA meet.

"My first run was 416 through the measured mile," he recalls, "and it was surprising because the car only felt so-so. It was right off the trailer. My approach into the measured mile was five and a half miles, same as I did in 1991. I actually shut it off midway through the mile."

It was during his attempt on the second day that trouble came at 400 miles an hour.

"We made a few adjustments for what I thought would be several runs that Saturday. I was four miles into the run when I started smelling burning rubber. The car felt good. There were no vibrations. About three seconds later, KABOOM, like a stick of dynamite. It was an awful jolt, a big explosion.

"My front tires are slightly staggered and it was a front tire that went. It blew a hole in the canopy fiberglass. The window was covered with salt. Once the initial shock wore off, and that didn't take long, believe me, I knew I didn't want to do anything stupid.

"The front end of the car was veering off course and I was hoping it wouldn't roll over. I could barely steer it, but I was slowing down. When I let go of the first chute I began to feel a little better.

"The car was still sliding, the course was rough and very bumpy. Once I got below 300, I hit the big chute. I basically had to let the car go where it wanted to. You don't jerk the steering wheel.

"What's crazy about the whole thing is that about twenty minutes before I did my thing, Nolan White had a similar experience as I did. His car came to a stop, off course left. Our cars were almost across from each other. One of his aircraft tires came off at almost 400."

Teague called it "my worst accident in this car". Fortunately, he wasn't hurt. What caused the accident? He's not sure.

"If the axle broke first I don't think I would have smelt rubber. But on the other hand, I'm not totally convinced it was tire failure."

Three weeks later, after round-the-clock repairs, Teague and his car were ready for Speed Week. When activity was resumed, following a heavy storm which shut down the course for four days, he did 407 through the measured mile. Exit speed: 416.

That was the last time he exceeded 400 miles an hour.

Don Vesco

Don Vesco has had a love affair with Bonneville since the mid-fifties. At the age of sixteen, he ran a bike for the first time on the salt. In 1963, he became a member of the Bonneville 200 Mph Club, in both a car and a motorcycle.

On September 17, 1970, the Californian became the first man to ride a bike at more than 250, with a two-way average speed of 251.924 through the measured mile. He drove a streamliner, powered by twin Yamaha 350 cc engines.

Four years later, he set a new AMA record of 281.702 with twin Yamaha TZ road-racing power plants. In 1975, he was the first motorcyclist to exceed 300 mph, hitting 303.928 in the mile and 302.657 in the kilo.

Three years later, Vesco went 315.892, then bettered that a month later at 318.598. Vesco built that record-setting missile. It was twenty-one feet long, weighed 1100 pounds and was driven by two 11,000 Kawasaki power plants.

"I was trying to run 360," he recalls.

"I was paid about $80,000 and I had to live and race on that amount."

Actually, Vesco built another Kawasaki-powered streamliner for the sole purpose of exceeding the wheel-driven automobile record of 409.

"It was possible", he says, "with that bike and it's just as possible today. It had more horsepower than my 318 machine. I designed it to go that speed. I actually made three runs with metal wheels, but couldn't hook up. The salt was real wet."

Don Vesco will drive anything on wheels... two, three, four, five. Be it bike or car.

Once he set the bike record at 318, Vesco's attention turned in earnest to get the automobile wheel-driven record. He built a streamliner and used several different kinds of engines.

First it was a small-block 536 Chevy, the same kind that NASCAR stockers once utilized. "I hit 351 on gasoline, but there wasn't enough power."

By 1984, Vesco switched to the proven power of a four cylinder Drake-Offy, the same kind of engine that dominated the Indianapolis 500 for so many years.

During the '84 Speed Week extravaganza at Bonneville, he hit an easy 235. Then, the rains came and washed out the meet.

By 1985, Don Vesco had nudged past the 300 mark, at 318. Things were looking up for the ex-motorcycle speed king and his new five-wheel creation.

But little did he realize the worst was yet to come.

"I was going 350 when a tire blew. I went end over end for almost a mile, suffered a broken vertebra in my neck, and other injuries. The wheels, the tires, the body, totally disintegrated."

Vesco knew "...it was a squirrely car, but I felt I could handle it. When the right rear went flat, and at the time I didn't know that had happened, I suddenly had no control.

"I tried to steer it like a car, but it had become a bike, a two-wheeled vehicle that was out of track, probably nine inches. I should have counter-steered but I didn't."

Vesco released the chutes, but that didn't help.

Witnesses said the car soared straight up about sixty feet, flipped and crashed down on its nose.

"I remember it coming down, and I remember the canopy coming off. I saw that.

"I was conscious. It happened so quickly, but it all seemed like slow motion. It really knocked me dingy."

Vesco's helmet was shattered by the crash. He also suffered a broken foot.

"My legs weren't restrained. They hit the inside of the chassis so bad that one of them popped open. It felt like someone shot me with a .38."

The tough man wasn't even hospitalized.

That was the end of that car, but not the end of Don Vesco's pursuit of the wheel-driven record.

Seems his brother, Rick, had worked five years building a machine for just that purpose. Thirty-one feet in length, three feet wide, thirty-two inches high, powered by a pair of Drake-Offy engines. Speed potential: 475 mph.

In its first runs (1988), Vesco reached 285. By the following year, he upped the speed to 350. In 1991, Vesco reached 377 for the measured mile.

"I was hitting 394 when I shut it off. I could feel it slowing down. One engine quit running. A coil wire came loose.

"There's no reason why this car can't hit the high 400s," he says. "Bonneville is like a big drag strip. You don't do it in the first quarter-mile. This car is real sluggish at the start, but really starts accelerating in the last two miles."

In theory, Vesco had a winner. In reality, not so. But when he made a deal with Tim Arfons to purchase a 4000 horsepower gas turbine engine in 1995, Vesco finally had the power to do the job.

Until recent years, it seems Mickey Thompson had little or no company in pursuit of the wheel-driven record. Now there's a half a dozen legitimate threats, including the Rick/Don Vesco entry.

Despite Teague's 409 effort in 1991, Vesco considers the Chet Herbert four-engine creation as his biggest threat.

"Once they get the bugs ironed out in that monster, it could run 500."

"In theory," says Vesco "there's no reason why a wheel-driven car can't exceed the 633 unlimited record by England's Richard Noble in his jet car. Just as I believe there's no reason why a bike can't go faster than Summers' 409."

Don Vesco won't be satisfied with just the wheel-driven record.

"I'd like to own the jet record some day. There's definitely a difference between 300 and 390. Can you imagine what it will feel like at 650? Sounds good to me."

Nolan White

I was born in Texas, but my family moved to San Diego when I was a youngster. I've lived there fifty-five years of my life, so that makes me practically a native.

Nolan White

White began running at El Mirage Dry Lake in California more than thirty years ago.

"I was in high school when I started," he recalls. "But then I took a few years off. In the early sixties, I was points champion in SCTA [Southern California Timing Association] three years in a row. Up until a few years ago, I was the only person who ever did that."

White was running a modified sportster at the time, "...the same thing that guys like Ak Miller and Dean Moon were racing in those days. Fortunately, I didn't have to look at their tail lights. They were always looking at mine."

White built the cars and used a variety of fiberglass bodies.

"I was the first to run over 200 miles an hour on gas at the lakebed," he says proudly. "That was back around 1961. It took another fifteen or twenty years before anybody else went 200 on gas.

"El Mirage was a short course. We ran through a speed trap, like they do at a drag race."

Back in the early sixties, Nolan White used a Chevy power plant. Some thirty years later, he's still hooked on Chevies.

"Before they came around, I was running flatheads. But since Chevy's been around, I've always run a Chevy."

When White took his sabbatical from El Mirage, he tried other forms of racing.

"I did some drag racing for a while, but I didn't get hooked on that. I did a little bit of SCCA sports car racing, as well, but I just kinda settled in on Bonneville."

He competed at his first Bonneville Nationals in 1958, and has been running ever since.

"That particular year, I had an old '32 car. They kinda called 'em all sporty cars, so I made my '32 look like it would fit in one of those classes. They put me in Modified Sports.

"It was just a '32 rail with a body. It had a radical nose. I ended up in Modified Sports because it couldn't fit in Roadster. At Bonneville in the early sixties, I was probably running twenty-five miles an hour faster than my competition. I was clocking about 225 to 230 in 1961, 1962. The car was powered by a 327. The sports cars were gas classes.

"Bonneville sure must have been intriguing to me because I've sure spent a lot of my life at that damn place. Guess I'm a little weak in the brain. Anytime meets are scheduled, I'm there.

"In the mid-seventies they eliminated what they called sports racing, and that moved me to the streamliner class. I was also the first car to go over 200 miles an hour on gas at Bonneville. I was the first over 200, 300 and 400 with a Chevy.

"I was running about 320 with a little 327, so I told myself if I built a big block and got a smaller car, I'm gonna step up to 400 miles an hour. But I honestly didn't know it would be this hard. If I had, I probably wouldn't have done it.

"Getting to 300 was the easy part. I set my goal at 400, and I did that. Actually, I set my goal for the wheel-driven land speed record and I've kinda hit a wall. But I was the first at 400 in a single-engine car."

The record book states Nolan White clocked 401 in 1990, but he claims, "I actually did it the first time in 1989. It was the tail end of a USFRTA meet. But the year I got credit for the one-way run was 1990.

"At that time I was running a 454. Now I'm up to a 488. But I have a whole bunch of engines. I've got 427s, 488s, 510s and even 550s. With enough room entering the measured mile, I'm sure the 488 will do the trick.

"In 1990, I was just starting to make the thing run. I think I finally have it right now. We really haven't had any good salt for a while.

"Back in 1990, we had ten or eleven miles. Probably 1990–91 was the last good salt we had. We haven't had any salt conducive for wheel-driven cars going any faster."

Nolan White's car is small, some twenty-four feet long, and weighs 4850 pounds. He calls the streamliner which first campaigned way back in 1980, The Spirit of Autopower.

"That's my business. My son's in it too.

"I used to have a pretty good-sized tail, but I've reduced it quite a bit in size, and I can't feel any difference in handling. I've had two, three different people drive it and no one has had a problem with it. It's a real stable car."

White is currently using a four-speed transmission.

"Right now, I'm having the best luck I've ever had, and believe me, I've tried a lot of different set-ups."

He's hoping for a minimum ten miles of running room for a serious assault at the wheel-driven record.

"Ideally," he says, "I'd like five miles into the measured mile.

"I'd probably be going 225 to 240 in first gear, about 300 in second, up to 380 in third, before I'd shift into top gear. I'd like to be about halfway through the mile at peak speed.

"With ten miles, I'd go the necessary one percent to break Al Teague's record. With 11 to 11.5 miles, I'd be over 425. Under ideal conditions, it'll run 450... but that's if I get the maximum amount of salt."

Until recently, tires have been a major problem, not with Nolan White but with just about every 400 mile an hour competitor. Now he's running on brand new Mickey Thompsons.

"I run eighteen inch tires on the back and sixteen-inchers on the front. I tried some aircraft tires in 1992. We hadn't been able to have any tires and I blew an aircraft tire about two hundred feet in the air, took part of the body section off. I was probably going around 380 when I blew that tire."

After all these years, Nolan White knows exactly how fast he's going.

"I just look at my tach and I can tell within two or three miles an hour how fast I'm going. The tach works real well."

White and Teague have 'banged heads' for years, but it's a friendly rivalry.

"I like Al a whole lot. He's a nice guy. We've basically run heads up for a long time, even though we're technically in different classes.

"He runs a little bigger engine, but we're both after the same thing. I use very little nitro, Al uses a lot of nitro. I only use about fifteen percent. I mix it with methanol. I have enough power with only fifteen percent. It's a little less expensive!"

Then he adds, "It wouldn't have mattered if I used ninety percent nitro. The conditions haven't been good enough, regardless of the power."

Nolan White is a burly man, standing six feet tall and weighing two hundred pounds. "I've been two hundred for the last forty-five years."

Over the years, he has became a bit fatalistic.

"If it's meant to be, it will. A friend of mine is an excellent pilot. He's been flying for more than twenty-five years. He flies up to Bonneville just about every time I've been there.

"Well, he crashed his plane on the landing strip when he came home, and he hasn't been the same since. He never had any problem before that.

"I'll keep on running until I get the wheel-driven records, even if I'm seventy, like old Art [Arfons], I give that man all the credit in the world.

"I sure hope he gets that fourth unlimited thrust record. What do I most admire about Arfons? He's done his own thing all of his life and supported himself real well at that.

"What more can you ask out of life than to do what you want to do? He's really done that. He's been his own man. I haven't been quite able to do that. I've had to make a living elsewhere.

"Once I got my record, I'm gonna stop and help my son. Rick [in his mid-forties] also drives the car and does a real good job. I'll let him do his own thing."

Few people realize that Nolan White took a shot at the wheel-driven in 1982–83 while England's Richard Noble was shooting for the unlimited mark at Black Rock Desert, Nevada.

"I was up there both years when Noble was running his big jet," says White. "Guess if I'd have broken the record back then," he says, tongue-in-cheek, "somebody would have remembered that little bit of trivia.

"Actually, I'm the only guy to go for the wheel-driven record at Black Rock, and considering the conditions I didn't do too bad. I ran about 350 in 1983.

"The place is just too soft for a wheel-driven car. It's not a hard surface. When you've got a thrust car, it doesn't know the difference. You don't have to hook up on the ground, in other words.

"All I can say is that it was an interesting experience. It certainly didn't discourage me. I just found out that when Bonneville is right, the record will fall. The grass sure wasn't greener in Nevada."

Mickey Thompson

When Art Arfons and his Allison-powered Anteater entered the land speed game in 1960, he considered the late Doc (Nathan) Ostich's jet-powered Flying Caduceus as the car to beat, and not Thompson's Challenger I.

"I knew Mickey went about 360 in 1959," recalls Arfons, "but I considered Ostich and his jet as the one to be beat, that is until I saw it run.

"Mickey's car was streamlined and he sure had the power, but he had drive-line problems. That's why he never could back up to run. He had no suspension. The salt would just shake it apart. But I give him plenty of credit for his 406 run."

In the late 1960s, Thompson returned to Bonneville with his Autolite Special, but failed to snare the wheel-driven record.

"After he got that 406", says Arfons, "Thompson was consumed with his business and his other ventures. I don't think he really put all his effort into that Ford car. It probably could have set a record."

During his lifetime, California-born Mickey Thompson set almost five hundred speed records. After his land speed career, he pioneered the off-road racing circuit, promoting it into a big-time sport.

On May 16, 1988, Thompson and his wife, Trudy (forty-one), were murdered in the driveway of their Bradbury, California, home, gunned down 'assassination style'. It was shortly after six in the morning that shots shattered the calm, and two men reportedly fled the scene on bicycles.

Responding to a series of 911 emergency calls, Los Angeles County Sheriff's deputies found the two. They had been shot "several times in the upper torso", according to the Sheriff Department's official statement.

Robbery was ruled out as a possible motive. There was no attempt to enter the house. According to Deke Houlgate, a respected California motorsports consultant who worked with Thompson, "Mickey told us about his death threats".

Authorities explored several different possible motives for the crimes but nothing to implicate anyone. To this day, the deaths of Mickey and Trudy Thompson remain an unsolved mystery.

By his own count, Thompson participated in more than 10,000 races and drove more than a million miles. He won at least one championship each in midgets, sprints, off-road vehicles, stock cars, drags and sports cars.

Five-time land speed king, Craig Breedlove, remembered Thompson as a friend in need.

"Back in 1968, when my shop was flooded and I really hit the skids, Mickey used to call me all the time to see if I was okay... if I needed anything. He really cared."

He was born Marion Lee Thompson Jr., on December 7, 1928, in San Fernando, California. By the time he was twelve, Mickey had assembled a coaster that ran uphill on junk batteries he picked up for twelve cents each.

Two years later, Thompson found a 127 Chevy coupe. He paid $7.50 for the junker, put it together from bits and pieces and later resold the same car for $125.

Afterwards, he bought a model A roadster for nine dollars. It was his first hot rod. Thompson's fascination with speed dated back to 1937. His boyhood hero was Frank Lockhart, who was killed during a land speed attempt at Ormond Beach, Florida, in the 1920s. Lockhart was twenty-six.

Before he was old enough for a driver's license, Mickey Thompson gunned the Model A to a speed of 79 mph at El Mirage Dry Lake. His patched-up machine had farm implement tires in front that were guaranteed to be safe at five miles an hour.

To support his 'habit', Mickey mowed lawns, sold papers and worked on other people's cars. Mechanics came easy to him.

By 1949, he was hitting 90 at the Santa Ana drag strip. Three years later, he pushed his tandem-engine hot rod to a national speed record of 194.34 mph.

Never satisfied, Thompson sought other challenges. In 1954 and 1955 he entered the grueling Pan Am, a 1900 mile test of man and machine across Mexico. Both races ended in crashes.

He also tried his hand at closed-circuit sports car driving. A 1957 crash at treacherous Riverside in California resulted in a broken kneecap. By his own count, Thompson had been hospitalized twenty-seven times because of racing – for reasons ranging from exhaustion to a shattered vertebra which left him briefly paralyzed.

During those hectic early years, Thompson made three hundred to four hundred dollars a week, but he did it the hard way. He worked as a pressman at the *Los Angeles Times*, ran the Lions Club drag strip in Long Beach and also had his own garage.

All this time he was thinking of Bonneville and the land speed record. As early as 1952, Thompson made sketches of a streamliner, with two engines driving the four wheels.

Six years later a few lines on a drawing pad came to life in the form of a snarling, twin-engine slingshot dragster. Mickey's target was the 266.2 clocking, set by Bill Kenz in 1957.

Kenz's reign as the fastest American on wheels was about to come to an end.

Using gasoline as a propellent, Thompson hit an easy 159 in a mile run that lasted 9.72 seconds. Methodically he upped the speed to 241... 251. Then, Thompson bettered Kenz's effort with a two-way 266.866 average.

But that wasn't fast enough.

Adding thirty percent nitro, Mickey Thompson startled American speed enthusiasts by driving his 800 horsepower creations to a speed of 290 miles an hour. He was getting close to his goal.

Since 1927, the world's land speed record had been broken fifteen times, all on American soil – first in Ormond Beach and then at Bonneville.

But during that time only one American had held the record. That was in 1927 when Ray Keech hit 207.55 in his three-engine Triplex. His mark stood for only one year.

Thompson was shooting at the late John Cobb's record of 394.20, set in 1947. England ruled the world of speed.

Thompson called his car Challenger I. It was small by land speed standards, being eight feet shorter and three feet narrower than Cobb's Railton Special. His hot rod weighed less than 5000 pounds.

Powered by four 450 horsepower Pontiac engines, Challenger I was publicly unveiled in August 1959. Thompson made no boasts that day. He didn't promise any miracles.

"I don't promise to break the land speed record. No one can make such a promise. But I think I can promise you that I will go faster than any American ever has; that means breaking my own record."

Thompson kept his word, hitting a top average of 330.51 mph. Before rain prevented any more record attempts, he powered Challenger I to a new American flying mile record of 363.67.

In 1960, Thompson added four blowers to increase his horsepower. He also brought along JATO rockets for additional thrust. However, the governing bodies of auto racing ruled the rockets illegal.

For three weeks, everything had gone wrong for Mickey Thompson. Then things began looking up. On September 4, he clocked 372.67. But when a driveshaft broke three days later, he should have realized it was an omen of things to come.

On September 9, Thompson and Challenger roared across the Flats at 406.60. It marked the first time an American had cracked the 400 barrier. It was a good run from the start.

At the end of the track, mechanics swarmed all over the homemade car. The streamliner looked perfect. Mickey Thompson walked around making personal checks and shaking hands with reporters. His hands were steady.

"I'm not nervous, look at that," he commented. "I never felt better."

Within minutes, Thompson began his return run to cement the record. But it soon became apparent the car was in trouble as it just coasted into the timing zone.

Thompson had come so close, only to be stymied by a driveshaft that snapped when he shifted into second gear at about 210 miles an hour.

Dejectedly he vowed, "We'll be back in a week. I guess we just stressed everything in the car. The whole crew needs a rest and I want to see my kids again."

It was Challenger's last hurrah.

Despite the failure, Thompson was convinced the car never reached its speed potential.

"This car would have run considerably faster if we had not been continually plagued with drive-gear problem – and taking into consideration the particular design of the car, it was almost impossible to patch."

And even when the jets pushed the piston-powered cars into the background, Mickey Thompson refused to go along with the times.

"I've built and driven a jet to a new strip record the first time out. I find it takes no skill to drive the car and really no mechanical knowledge to make it go fast."

As he put it: "My goal is to hit 425 miles an hour on the Flats. Then I'll quit."

Thompson returned to Bonneville in both 1968 and 1969 with his Autolite Special, a twin-engine streamliner powered by a pair of Ford engines boasting 2000 horses.

On October 30, 1969, the thirty foot car skidded out of control at speeds exceeding 400 miles an hour. Thompson was clocked at 303 in a two mile stretch and was still accelerating when he went into a slide.

During one point he was heading straight for the USAC timing shack, but managed to steer the 5400 pound runaway away from the building. He missed it by only seventy-five yards.

Thompson estimated he would have driven through the timing traps at 435 mph had he remained on course.

Undaunted by his failure to set the record, he returned in 1969.

"We ran the car on two occasions that year, attaining 360 the first week. The instrumentation inside the car checked out exactly with the official clocking speed."

He returned to Utah a few weeks later, but the water season was closing in fast.

"The morning of our attempt it rained on three sections of the course for about three miles. However, I made a run which was recorded at 411 in one direction.

"Due to the wet salt the car went out of control and off the course for about one mile. Consequently, we missed the last timing light and were not officially timed for the run."

While Ford experts said the car had a speed potential of 500 miles an hour, it never ran again.

In 1969, the State of California honored its native son with a Senate Resolution. In part it said:

Whereas Mickey Thompson was the first man to travel on the ground at a speed in excess of 400 miles per hour and is the holder of 485 national and international speed and endurance records; and...

Whereas his record of accomplishments has helped to enhance American prestige in international automobile racing and his exceptional endurance, sportsmanship and competitiveness have proved a fine example for the youth of the nation...

Bobby Summers

Bobby Summers was born April 4, 1937, in Omaha, Nebraska. As a child he and his brother, Bill, moved to California with their parents.

As an industrial arts major in high school, Bobby spent most of his spare time around cars and hot rodding. His skills as a machinist and welder would serve him well in the major construction of Goldenrod.

From a model A Ford which Bobby Summers acquired as a youngster, the brothers collaborated on their first serious hot rod, a 1936 Ford with a Chrysler engine, which they ran at Bonneville in 1954.

With Bobby at the wheel, the Summers brothers set a string of records at local drag strips, El Mirage Dry Lake and Bonneville. He joined the exclusive 200 Miles an Hour Club with a two-way clocking of 221.06 at Bonneville.

In 1962, at the Bonneville National Speed Trials, Summers drove their single-engine streamliner 322.79 mph. The following year, he established national and international Class C records with the same car. His speeds were 283.71 (kilometer), 279.74 (mile).

Two years later, the handsome Californian smashed the land speed mark for wheel-driven cars.

The Goldenrod was four years in the planning stage and took fifty-three weeks to build from the ground up.

By 1964, Bobby had quit his job as a mechanic. Bill was supporting both of them from his earnings as a truck driver, so that his younger brother could devote himself full-time to launching the car's construction.

They had a written presentation to solicit sponsorship. Engineering studies had been made, a scale model built and some preliminary work on the car completed.

On paper the project appeared feasible, but it was totally impractical without major financial backing. For several months Bobby Summers made the rounds of potential sponsors. Just when it appeared that the project would have to be scrapped, George Hurst heard about it.

Hurst, who sold many of his products to hot rodders, believed the car could be successful. He listened to the proposal and liked it, but time was running out. It was August 1964 and unless the project was pushed to full-time status at once, it would be too late to complete the car to run in 1965.

Hurst took the gamble. He agreed to furnish a special transmission shifter and forged aluminum wheels, and he told Bill Summers to quit his job so that both brothers could concentrate on building Goldenrod.

Hurst said if other sponsorship failed to materialize, he would carry the entire financial load himself. With George Hurst's endorsement, three additional primary sponsors were quickly brought into the picture – Chrysler Corporation, Firestone Tire and Rubber Company and Mobil Oil.

Bobby Summers designed and engineered the car, utilizing a unique drive system. He arranged the Chrysler V–8 hemi-engines in pairs, the front two driving the front wheels and the rear pair operating the rear wheels.

A common driveline along the left side of the car kept all four engines turning at the same speed. Except for dry sump, lubrication and fuel injection – required for low overall height – the engines were stock specifications throughout. The 426 cubic inch power plants generated a combined 2400 horsepower.

Firestone supplied special 600 mph nylon tubeless tires. Mobil developed special lubricants to withstand gear heat and pressure and prepared the super premium racing gasoline.

Hurst developed the intricate two-unit transmission system which was placed between Summers' knees. By what engineers called a 'series hook-up', he was able to shift two transmissions through an 'H' pattern simultaneously with each gear change.

Long and lean, Goldenrod was thirty-two feet overall, forty-eight inches wide at the front wheels and only twenty-eight inches off the ground at the hood, The highest point was forty-two inches at the tail fin.

The frame was constructed of steel, the body material of aluminum. Total weight was 5500 to 6000 pounds.

By working round the clock, the Summers brothers had Goldenrod ready for the wheel-driven assault in 1965.

However, the record didn't come easy.

In early September, a smooth practice run was made at 220 with only six miles of usable salt. Bobby really needed twice that much for maximum acceleration.

Then problems began to develop. Minor fuel injection adjustments, a wiring short, a potential failure in the drive-line coupler that required redesign and a trip to Salt Lake City, a sticky shifting cable, a broken hydraulic steering line.

Summers even made a run on three engines when someone forgot to connect a coil wire to the fourth power plant.

It seemed that each time the car was ready, the weather turned sour. One afternoon during the first week, the wind kicked up to forty miles an hour just before a practice run.

In mid-September, with twelve miles of usable salt, strong gusts blew water over the first four miles of the course.

But little by little, the speed went up. During an easy 244.9 ride, Bobby pronounced that stability was good and it appeared that the bugs had been worked out.

On September 27, Summers was clocked at 373.5. It was essentially a practice run since the car was still in third gear. In spite of the wet salt and poor traction, Summers felt the record was attainable the next morning. However, heavy winds that night drove standing water across the track.

So, the Summers brothers, dejected, returned home with Goldenrod to wait for another attempt. Back in their shop, the car was stripped, cleaned, thoroughly checked over and repairs were made.

Back at the Flats in late October, the string of bad luck continued after two practice runs, one at more than 400 miles an hour. After the runs, a worn wheel bearing and a damaged transfer case gear were discovered, forcing the brothers to once again return to California for repairs.

Yet on that day – October 25 – Bobby Summers proved that his four-engine creation had the capability of bringing back the wheel-driven mark to America after an absence of thirty-seven years. His two-way average through the measured mile was 383.959, including a 405.095 clocking through the kilo.

Seventeen long days later all systems were 'GO'.

Summers roared through the measured mile at 412.702 and 409.243 in the kilo during his north-to-south run. Fifty-five minutes later, Goldenrod was refueled and the parachutes repacked. Bobby Summers was securely strapped into the cockpit.

While his south-to-north return run (405.908) was almost five miles an hour slower than his first burst, it was still fast enough to assure Summers the world land speed record for wheel-driven automobiles.

"In fact, it started to rain the very last part of the return run", Summers told the author just months before his untimely death.

The following day – November 13 – Summers and Goldenrod returned to the wet, soft track.

"We changed air scoops and we thought maybe these air scoops might have more potential, and they did. They worked much better."

Summers stormed through the flying mile at a faster 425 miles an hour. However, a return run was not to be, and Bobby Summers accepted that call.

"The sponsors thought it wouldn't be a good idea to do that [raise the record]. All the news had been put out the previous day, so that was the last run for Goldenrod."

Twenty-four hours later, heavy rains turned the Bonneville Salt Flats into a pool. The speed season was over.

Summers set the record using third gear.

"We tried fourth gear only once. I shifted in the middle of the traps and there was no gain to it because the distance was so short, the total amount of salt available. I think I probably used three, maybe three and a half miles before the measured mile.

"Goldenrod wasn't a dragster. The car weighed four tons, which was really a lot heavier than we wanted, so it took a while to reach peak speed... which I never did. We never had a long enough track to allow Goldenrod to reach its maximum potential."

What would that potential be?

"From the data that wind tunnel testing provided us," said Bobby Summers, "and from one of the Chrysler engineers, we were told the car would run easily 465 miles an hour if it had ten miles of salt. We had nine miles, maybe even less."

Summers made a total of nine runs in the thirty-two foot long dart.

"The chassis design was pretty straight forward," he pointed out. "We did that initially. The aerodynamic design had quite a few changes because of the wind tunnel testing at Cal Tech.

"We made a model and did a lot of testing. Wind tunnel testing is extremely expensive and you can only afford it with major financial backing. I made the model out of wood. It took me a lot of time to make that thing."

The long, bullet-like shape "...was predicated by the fact we wanted all of these [four] engines in line in order to minimize frontal area. We wanted the driver in the back, so that basically determined the shape. It wasn't something that we'd seen before. Simply the shape was determined on the layout of all the machinery."

Mickey Thompson's four-engine Challenger, which hit 406 mph in 1960, influenced Bobby Summers' decisions for a four-engine vehicle.

"We knew Mickey quite well. He was a friend of ours. I'd seen him run at Bonneville in 1960. I was big-time impressed. The car really wasn't built well nor well-designed, but for the time it was quite advanced."

All told, Bobby and his brother, Billy, built about a dozen speed machines. All were single engines, except Goldenrod.

"If you look back over our years of racing," says Billy Summers, "every car was an advancement. We knew how the single-motor car worked and we knew what it would take to get the job done."

When the Summers brothers began their assault on the wheel-driven record, it was 394 miles an hour, set by the late John Cobb of England in 1947. But by the time Goldenrod was wheeled on to the salt, they were shooting for Donald Campbell's 403.1, established in 1964 in a jet car.

"All of the power of Campbell's Bluebird", said Bobby Summers, "went directly through the wheels. It was not a thrust vehicle, unlike the jets of Arfons, Breedlove, Ostich, Leasher.

"Building a thrust-powered car never entered our minds. That did not provide any kind of a challenge to me at all. I would not even consider that. I was not interested, nor would I ever be interested in that kind of car."

What kind of a driver was Bobby Summers?

Says his older brother:

"He's brave. He's got a lead foot. He would never let up. One time, before we had the record-setting car, Bobby was driving our single engine, front-wheel drive streamliner.

"He went to the Salt Flats and the car really wasn't handling. I think he went 327. One time he made a run and all of a sudden the car turned right. He simply turned left, came back on that course and proceeded to hustle down the track. We had a roadster that he ran in '57 and he flipped it, going about 240. Didn't shake him up one bit."

The most complex part of building Goldenrod was to harness the potential 2500 horsepower of the four Chrysler engines.

"There was a lot of work to get it all tied together," said Bobby Summers. "We had to make special gear boxes. All four engines were in line and it's four-wheel drive.

"The front wheels were connected to the rear wheels. It was designed so that we couldn't have any overspeed on any engine. It's pretty complex.

"We had one shifter, two gear boxes. The shifting mechanism was built by the Hurst people. Boy, that was their specialty and they did a good job on it."

Summers considered driving from the rear a definite advantage.

"You're much more sensitive to the attitude of the vehicle when you sit that far back, much more sensitive. The rear end couldn't break loose because we had the front and rear end tied together. It had to break loose with all four wheels at the same time. We intentionally made it that way.

"I had fairly good straight-ahead vision. We had the two hood scoops in the car offset so I could look down the middle. However, peripheral vision was not very good because the canopy opening is not very wide.

"It was an extremely heavy car, but it was easy to drive. Our plan was to build up speed slowly, to be sure we had no mechanical or safety problems.

"Make some runs in the high 200s, a few in the low 300s, a few in the high 300s and then shoot for the 400 range. The car worked relatively good right from the start.

"In fact, I hit 300 on about the third run. The fact that we could get up to that speed so quickly kind of built a lot of enthusiasm and confidence in what we had done."

Once inside the cockpit, Bobby Summers admitted "...your concentration is so great, your ears are kinda shut off. You can't remember noise. You can't remember temperature. You're concerned so much in keeping the car going down the salt in a straight line. All your other senses are shut off."

Not a holler-type guy, Bobby felt an inner exhilaration after setting the wheel-driven mark.

"I'm yelling and screaming to myself, 'Atta boy', but I'm not the type who shows wild emotion.

"I try to make sure that people understand that he [Billy] was very much an integral part of the whole thing. Still, the driver always gets the lion's share of the glory."

Following the record, Billy Summers took the car on an extensive tour.

"Goldenrod has been to Europe four times, across the country numerous times, to Canada."

On several occasions, the car was on display at a Wendover, Utah, speed museum. It is now back with Billy Summers.

"From time to time we kicked around the idea of selling it, but nothing materialized. Strictly off the top of my head, I'd place the selling price at $250,000."

Goldenrod, after extensive fine-tuning which could take from six to twelve months, could be available for a wheel-driven land speed attempt with another driver behind the wheel.

Anyone with about $3 million can contact him at Ontario, California.

In any case, both Bobby and Billy Summers were delighted that Al Teague, their long-time friend, went a tick faster in his single-engine streamliner in 1992.

"When we had our twenty-fifth anniversary to celebrate the setting of our record," pointed out Billy Summers, "I told Al if anyone breaks our record, I hope it's him. Me and my brother sent him a telegram after he set his record."

Said Bobby Summers:

"Al is a super guy. He's paid his dues to the sport. He's a low-buck guy. He's done it all on his own. He's had no major financial sponsorship, so the guy has done an amazing job. We're happy for him.

"I think Al is limited by two factors. First, tires. Plus the fact he's got only two-wheel drive. If he had four-wheel drive, he'd be going a lot faster.

"You could make the conversion, but I think it would be very difficult. You'd almost have to build a new car. When you're going at this speed, that four-wheel drive becomes important.

"We had a lot of people put up a lot of money and put a lot of effort in our effort. There was a lot of feeling of responsibility on our shoulders. We didn't want to let people down. It's a great feeling to know that didn't happen."

Major sponsors kicked in about $250,000 in the wheel-driven assault.

"I spent a lot of time in Detroit," said Bobby Summers, "knocking on people's doors. It took almost a year before we got somebody to give us a commitment."

Added Billy Summers:

"We started the project with $108,000, but had to go back to the sponsors and ask for more. We'd been at Bonneville for about a month, made some runs, had some problems and had to return to California.

"But we'd already spent the money we'd asked for. Only Firestone was a little hesitant, but other than that, we had no problems. And if we'd been rained out in 1965, I'm sure those same sponsors would have backed our return in '66. Fortunately, we beat the weather and the record."

Only a year separated Billy and Bobby Summers. They always were very close. It was always 'the Summers brothers', a team, except for one incident that still gnaws at Billy Summers, more than twenty-five years after it occurred.

"I really don't like to talk about it," said Billy. "When the day was finally over, the day we set the record, we went back to the little restaurant we usually ate at. We all got there at about the same time.

"Peter Damson, who was a Chrysler engineer, toasted Bob Summers for setting this record. It hurt me because he didn't toast Billy and Bobby. I'm very much aware that the driver gets all the gravy, all the glory. But in our own little bunch, that hurt me because my brother, who is kinda dense at times didn't say, 'Well, don't forget Bill'."

Decades later, Bobby Summers still regretted his mistake.

"I should have said something, and I didn't. You can't set a record by yourself and I think there's always that problem when there's two people involved.

"The driver almost invariably gets ninety percent of the glory and the other partner feels left out... and it's unfortunate."

Bobby Summers wanted to get behind the wheel of a land speed car once again, but he was realistic enough to know it wouldn't happen.

"I'd really like to do that", he said shortly before his fatal heart attack. "My business is really my race car. I have twenty-five employees who rely heavily on me. I have a family of two kids and a wife and I have a banker who would flip out if he found out I was racing again."

The Summers brothers began their business on the heels of their land speed success. It started out with two people, and has employed as many as thirty-eight during peak business periods.

"We manufacture basic engine and drive-line components for all types of race cars," pointed out Bobby Summers, "ranging from off-road, to oval track, to street rods, to boats."

"Bill and I always liked to race, and when we built our race cars back in the late fifties and early sixties you couldn't buy any speed equipment. You pretty much had to make everything yourself. We made a lot of stuff ourselves. A lot of other guys who wanted to race came to us and wanted us to start making parts for them. That's how it started.

"We design it and manufacture it and in a lot of cases we have to have special equipment to allow us to efficiently manufacture the product."

In 1989, Billy sold his half of the business to his brother. He now has his own business, Summers Exhibits/Services.

"I transport trade show exhibits. What it really boils down to is that I'm in the trucking business."

In recent years, Billy Summers has not only become a car owner, but is getting faster in his lakester.

"The primary driver is the sponsor's wife [Pat Zimmerman]. She's already gone 202. I've gotten it up to 194. I'm finding out the more I drive it, the more I like it. Sure would like to hit 200.

"The Smithsonian had asked us about the car, but nothing came of it. I think Goldenrod, even by today's standards, is heads and shoulders above the field as far as engineering potential to go faster is concerned. It's surprised me that Al [Teague] has run as fast as he has.

"While it seems like there's been a sudden proliferation of 400 mile an hour wheel-driven cars, it's not really so. Most have been around for years and now a few of 'em are inching up to record potential.

"I've always told people through the years, when I see a brand new car come out of the trailer, and within a few runs, or very quickly, run 375 at Bonneville, then it's a potential record-setter. But nobody's done that, including Al.

"Eventually, I can see a wheel-driven car go 450. I think it would take a very small, lightweight car with a lot of horsepower. It would take a lot of traction, like four-wheel drive."

Hypothetically speaking, of course, Bobby Summers knew what he would do to improve Goldenrod's speed potential.

"Assuming I was racing, and assuming I had the necessary capital, the easy thing would be to go to Keith Black's place [famed racing engine builder], write out the check and shortly thereafter you've got what it takes...

"But if I had a choice, I'd go for a jet helicopter turbine engine, the same kind that powered Andy Granatelli's dynamite race cars at the Indianapolis 500."

Bobby Summers realized his days of dreaming were over. Let others reach for the brass ring.

Chapter Twenty-Eight
Is He 'Skating' on Thin Ice?

I like Waldo. He's personable and intense. The guy eats and sleeps land speed racing. I think his project is intriguing. But it's too far out for me, and too dangerous. Honestly, I think it's too light and I don't think he can keep it on the ground.

But he's definitely got the power. I don't care if it's a jet or rocket car with metal wheels or, in this case, a rocket sled on runners. If he did it according to the rules, held his speed through the measured mile, left his marks on the ground, and bettered the existing land speed record, there's no reason why it wouldn't be official. As far as I'm concerned it would be a record. You betcha.

Art Arfons

Many have sought the title as 'Fastest Man On Wheels'. However, only a few have gained admittance into this exclusive and prestigious club.

The sport began in 1898 and since then, a total of thirty-four brave young men in their marvelous racing machines have set sixty-three land speed records.

It's easy to announce plans for a mind-boggling contraption. Building that creation is far more difficult; setting a record, tougher than that.

The road to land speed racing immortality is strewn with the blueprints of dreams unfulfilled and with the carcasses of cars unfinished, of contenders not quite fast enough.

A few examples will illustrate the point.

Herbert Austin's twelve-cylinder engines dominated the water speed scene in the early 1900s. In fact, the twin-engined Maple Leaf IV captured the prestigious British International Trophy, in 1912.

The twin engines generated 380 blown horsepower, quite impressive for its day. By 1920, Austin started thinking of a land speed car, powered by the same powerful twelve cylinder engine. However, nothing came of that project.

The late Harlen Fengler, best known as the long-time starter for the Indianapolis 500, tried to create support in 1931 for his America I car, to be powered by two Miller engines. Legendary driver Peter de Paolo was to sit in the cockpit. Fengler never could raise the funds.

By 1939, Germany was ready to assault the land speed record. The Daimler-Benz T80 was actually built, powered by an aircraft engine. Projected speed: 450 miles an hour. Famed Grand Prix driver Hans Stuck was given the ride. The car never ran. It is on display at the Daimler-Benz Museum at Stuttgart-Unterurkeim, Germany.

Back in 1961, America's Bob Knapp had visions of a massive beast, weighing almost three tons and powered by a pair of J-47 jet engines. He began construction, but never finished building the car.

Australians Jack MacDonald and Terry O'Hare built a three-wheeled jet, powered by a Rolls Royce engine. Their 1970 goal was to establish an Australian speed record, then turn the car into a twin-jet creation to attack Donald Campbell's wheel-driven mark of 403.1. The MacDonald-O'Hare Special never turned a wheel.

By 1973 Johnny Conway, another Aussie, announced plans not only to shatter the wheel-driven record, but the sound barrier as well, in his thirty-six engine, sixteen-wheeler he called Mach I. End of that tale.

In the early 1970s, Minnesota business tycoon Tony Fox had entered drag racing in a big way, with his rocket-powered dragster, Pollution Packer. In 1974, however, driver Dave Anderson was killed. An impressive forty-five foot long mock-up of his sound barrier car, Proud American, made the rounds across the country's drag strips.

But by 1977, Fox had abandoned plans for a supersonic car. Instead, he devoted his efforts to building a small jet plane.

In the early 1980s, Coloradan Bill Gaynor talked about the big picture. He called it Project 1000. He would build a forty-two foot rocket car, powered by seven engines. He envisioned a top speed of 1450 miles an hour for his City of Sterling. Construction began on Gaynor's dream machine with a 1986 target date. End of that story.

Five-time land speed king Craig Breedlove actually built a mock-up model of his rocket-powered Spirit of America – Sonic II in 1982. The thirty-nine foot long missile originally would utilize four rocket engines. Later, the concept was changed to a one-rocket power plant generating 30,000 pounds of thrust.

The financial backing appeared in place, but the deal fell through. And by then the cost of rocket fuel had already become prohibitive.

Art Arfons, Breedlove's arch-rival in the 1960s, took three strikes in 1989, 1990 and 1991. First, his lightweight Green Monster was a two-wheeler. It took off at 350. In 1990, Arfons converted it into a conventional four-wheeler. However, the 1800 pound jet sputtered in both '90 and '91, which proves that success is never guaranteed, no matter the reputation, the aura of the legend-maker.

While Breedlove and Arfons were doing their thing in the 1960s, a youngster was dreaming his dreams, hoping to add his name and his feats into the land speed record book.

Waldo Stakes is now in his late thirties and can't wait for his lonely trip in an intriguing vehicle straight out of a Buck Rogers or Flash Gordon movie.

His creation, Sonic Wind, is an 800 pound rocket – sled, fuel, driver – powered by a twenty-seven pound rocket engine with a legendary history. It is an X–1 engine, the same kind that propelled Chuck Yeager through the sound barrier in 1947. Yeager's missile had four rockets.

Stakes will proceed in stages. His first major goal is breaking the speed record on ice, 247 miles an hour, set by Sammy Miller. That will be followed by an assault on Richard Noble's two-way land speed record of 633.4 mph, and ultimately Stakes will gun for the sound barrier... and beyond.

The conventional tires, and now metal wheels, have been replaced by runners. While the Californian says he could run his rocket at Bonneville, or Black Rock Desert, he plans to do his thing on ice.

Back in 1904, Henry Ford drove his Arrow to a new land speed record of 91.37 mph across frozen Lake St. Clair near Detroit. It is on this same lake that Stakes hopes one day to duplicate that feat in his space-age 'pocket rocket'.

Is Stakes a fool? Or a visionary? Only time will tell. Draw your own conclusion.

Question:
Who is Waldo Stakes? What is your background as a driver, as a builder?

Answer:
I'm a proud product of the Chicago-Ghetto. As a teenager, I built hot rods and played 'rat race', which is a game of high-speed tag through the streets of Chicago and suburbs. It was played with a group of other hot rodders. It wasn't uncommon to hit speeds well in excess of 100 mph on city surface streets. After that, I built high-speed motorcycles. One 400 cc street racer could hit 130. It was equipped with airfoils to keep it stable, as I could commute to work every day at over one hundred miles an hour.

I've spent thousands of hours in libraries. I have held as many as eight different library cards. I researched land speed racing history and collected just about every word printed on any LSR contender in history. During the 1970s, I helped a Texas-based rocket dragster group design the first rocket-altered body. They called it Instant Insanity Concept I. Owned by Brent Fanning and driven by Bostik. Later, I worked as crew chief on the BMW streamliner motorcycle of Kenny Lyons. It now holds five world speed records in various classes.

Question:
How long have you been interested in LSR? Why the fascination?

Answer:
I was ten years old when someone gave me a Cracker Jack toy of the Railton Special. On the bottom were the statistics stamped into the plastic. I thought it was beautiful and that its shape was so different. I read the 394 mph speed and thought it had to be a mistake. Nothing goes that fast on the ground. I was hooked.

Question:
Do you have one hero above all?

Answer:
Retired Air Force Colonel John Paul Stapp, a pioneer in aerospace medicine is my all-time favorite. I made a pilgrimage to New

Mexico to meet him a few years ago. He rode a rocket sled, sitting strapped to a chair at 632 mph, one year before I was born [1954].

Question:

Why do you want to do 900 mph across a frozen lake?

Answer:

I chose ice to run on because it's a large flat surface near populated areas. Exposure is what I'm after. Then, I can generate an interest in what I do and perpetuate it. Besides, a runner on ice has virtually no measurable friction, so I don't have bearing or rolling friction to contend with. I need less overall power to do what I want. Also, the temperature will be much lower, so the speed of sound will be at a lower speed, again, taking less power to do it.

Question:

How do you plan to assault the sound barrier?

Answer:

I plan to take a progressive step to high speed. Sonic Wind [name of Stakes' sled is same name as Stapp's sled] is a vehicle designed to be totally convertible. At present, it is equipped to run at a theoretical top speed in excess of 900 mph, but I can lengthen it and double the power at will.

Question:

Do you have the driving experience for such ultimate speed?

Answer:

Did Noble? Did Breedlove? The first time they ran their vehicles they were as green as can be. Even if you took this year's Indy 500 winner and put him in the vehicle, it wouldn't make a difference. This is a learned skill. Everyone is a greenhorn.

It is too different to apply driving skill. It only takes courage, common sense and the will to learn it. Don't let the speed freak you out. It goes along with the falling off a building theory. What does it matter whether you fall two stories or one hundred? Are you scared to death flying in a commercial jet liner at 650 mph? Half a million people do it every day.

Question:

How do you mentally, physically prepare yourself for such speed?

Answer:

Physically, I'm on a workout program just to tighten internal organs that could rip apart in a high G crash. Mentally, I tell myself it will be a piece of cake and I have no fear; I believe you can convince yourself of anything if you want it bad enough.

To answer the big WHY. I love the whole concept of land speed racing. To me it is not racing. It's a perfect art, a blend of unbelievable power, fear in the quest for the unknown. This is perfect fantasy.

I don't care for the press and after I raise the money I need, I won't need to talk to the press. I'm not a glory boy. I don't care about what people who don't care about me think of me. It is my life. I will live or lose it at my choice.

Question:

What is the No. 1 concern in a sound barrier attempt?

Answer:

The greatest risk is at the transonic speed range. Shocks are virtually unpredictable at these speeds. Sonic Wind is not a subsonic vehicle trying to go supersonic. It was designed to perform best at supersonic speeds. It is designed to be stable transonically. It will go easily through the transonic transition because of its shape.

Question:

Can a small and light vehicle handle these tremendous forces?

Answer:

A bullet weighs a few grams and moves at Mach 2–3.

Question:

Tell us about the design of Sonic Wind.

Answer:

This vehicle is designed with the dynamics of a dart or arrow or model rocket in mind. Balance is critical, so the vehicle's center of gravity is in front of its center of pressure. As an example, a dart has a heavy weight at its tip and the fins [for drag aft] at the rear. No matter how a dart is thrown it will flop forward and align itself with its airflow and strike the target nose first. The vehicle has to have a dead man's stability. It must track a straight line without driver aid.

The main body is a cylinder with an ogival nose and boat tail for low drag. The boat tail terminates in another cylinder so all the airflow is directed from the body into the rocket flow.

Sonic Wind stands apart from past land speed record contenders as it has a higher power-to-weight ratio, lower drag coefficient and better aspect ratio. In short, it is a micro-high-impulse rocket-ice-sled.

By eliminating the wheels in a high-speed design vehicle design, many problems are eliminated. The vehicle becomes more efficient and stable. Blowouts, for instance, are eliminated. So is rolling resistance, bearing failure.

Question:

Minus fuel and driver, the sled weighs 380 pounds. Loaded, it's 780. Won't this create a serious situation?

Answer:

As the design now stands, the vehicle should become increasingly more stable as its speed increases. As the rocket expands its propellants, the only weight that won't change is the driver's. Consequently, the center of gravity will actually move forward.

Since the vehicle is extremely light, the weight of the driver and the heaviest fuels are placed forward. The driver is located in the nose, then the LOX tank, the alcohol/water tank, the helium tank and finally the parachute for braking.

Question:

Five-time speed king, Craig Breedlove, believes in mass, meaning a large, heavy car. You're going the opposite direction, aren't you?

Answer:

Both Breedlove's Spirit of America and Spirit of America – Sonic I are what I call 'battle tanks'. I don't care for that approach, simply because of the vast amount of power needed to overcome inertia and kinetic energy effects of large mass.

Question:

Where does the name Sonic Wind derive from? Tell us the story.

Answer:

When I was in high school, I came up with the name for the shock wave a vehicle would make as it passed by. Later, I found out it was the name given to John Paul Stapp's rocket sled by Northrop, it's contractor. I considered this a good omen and kept it.

Question:
By definition, is this a land speed vehicle?
Answer:
Any vehicle that goes fast on the ground is a LSR vehicle. I'm sure that the Land Speed Authority [recently formed sanctioning body] will sanction a serious record attempt if I pay for that service. This is always the key, MONEY... sad but true.

When I'm ready for a serious run at any record, I'll probably use a SCTA [Southern California Timing Association] group of timers affiliated with the BNI [Bonneville Nationals] or USFRA [United States].

These are the people who actually set world records and whose opinions I personally care about and respect. No one else in the world has as much knowledge as the American Hot Rodder. So the opinions of other bodies mean little to me. I'm always surprised at how many LSR experts there are in the world considering that only three or four actual contenders for the unlimited title exist.

Besides, if I were a real jerk I would set up my own clocks, run a couple of hundred miles an hour, have my sponsor flood the media with a supersonic record story and everyone would believe it. It would be my word against the doubters. Don't think it can't happen? I won't go into it.

When the time comes and I have the bugs worked out of this vehicle and feel comfortable enough with it, I will run through the measured mile both ways. Just the way all my predecessors did. It would be an insult not to run as they did, especially to the ones who died trying. I couldn't look myself in the face and claim a 'one-way' record.

One more thing, the public cares about the dynamics of the whole concept, the stunt aspect's the death defier. But the public believes what it is told. Ask any PR man or any politician.

Question:
Will it be easier to run on ice, rather than at Bonneville?
Answer:
An ice course could be prepared quicker than, say, Bonneville. Because I plan to run in heavy-populated areas, major city machine shops and supplies are more available. I plan to survey the course, then plow it with jeeps and then drill the surface and pump water

from underneath on to the course. The water should seek level and freeze. During the winter season there is less competition for TV airtime and fewer events, so a good turnout and exposure is assured.

Question:
Could this rocket sled be run on the salt?

Answer:
Sonic Wind is a slider and could run on the Salt Flats. I have tested runners there, but because of the added drag, the peak speeds would be lower and the abrasive salt would damage the runners.

When a runner is on ice, the pressure of the weight melts a bit of the ice, so the runner is always on water, and thus well-lubricated. The only thing that offers less friction is Teflon against Teflon.

Question:
How much total running surface will you really need?

Answer:
In its present configuration 3.4 miles to 926 mph, but there are no guarantees.

Question:
In how many seconds will you be hitting 100... 200... 300... etc.?

Answer:
Average acceleration rate is 3.6 Gs or about 50 mph per second with a full load of fuel which will last 22-plus seconds.

Question:
How much room will it take to stop?

Answer:
It actually stops faster than it accelerates – about five Gs.

Question:
What happens in case of trouble?

Answer:
The vehicle itself is a capsule because of its construction and its lightness. What hits harder? A bullet or a ballistic missile?

Question:
Of what material is it made?

Answer:
The driver's section and primary chassis is aluminum wrapped with four layers of fiberglass. The rear section is 4130 Chromemoly tubing, aluminum and mild steel.

Question:
In a layman's definition, can you describe how a rocket works?

Answer:
A rocket is a controlled explosion, an engine using its fuel to the most explosive point without destroying itself.

Question:
What kind of propellant? How expensive?

Answer:
Sonic Wind runs on ethanol-water mixture and LOX, or liquid oxygen. It could run on Bacardi 151 and LOX fuel. The cost: about fifty cents a pound.

Question:
Once you turn on the power, is it completely throttleable?

Answer:
The power comes on and the vehicle accelerates because it is getting lighter as it uses fuel. But we decided not to make it throttleable. Throttling a rocket may yield asymmetrical thrust or destabilize the vehicle. It's on and off. My dad always said I was like that... off or wide open!

Question:
How many test firings have you made of the engine?

Answer:
Ken Mason has fired this engine about ten times and is very familiar with its operation. He is one of my partners on this project and handles all the propulsion chores. Another great help has been Larry Hayes who has done a lot of fabrication on this vehicle and helped me overcome many problems.

Question:
What about steering?

Answer:
Steering is accomplished by the front runner, which can change alignment from ten to two degrees. This is done with an adjustment. Lesser directional change will be necessary as speeds increase. The front runner is also an airfoil, so steering is done dynamically by contact and aerodynamically.

I'm researching canards mounted on the front runner fork to keep the nose steady, and if they are mounted at this point, the drag beneath the vehicle will add to the negative lift.

Because rebounding shock waves are a concern, the main body is a cylinder to minimize their effect. There is also a blade running along the underside centerline to the cylinder to split rebounding shocks, at the same time adding to directional stability. There is also a raised hump running along this line to further reduce shock rebound.

Question:

Tell us about the fins.

Answer:

The fins on this rocket and the rocket engine itself are mounted on a boom which can be extended. This means I can extend the vehicle fourteen feet in overall length, which allows me to change where the center of pressure is located.

The rear fins are not mounted horizontally, but rather canted at a forty-five degree angle from the body to each rear runner. This generates negative lift on the nose, and at the same time makes them less susceptible to directional changes caused by side winds blowing across the course.

This vehicle has most of its drag at the rear to counteract yaw. The fins are staggered, left fin mounted forward of the right fin. This is so any shock waves generated by the fins rebounding on the ground would be distributed over a larger footprint, rather than pinioning at one point and possibly causing lift or instability.

Staggering them behind the wider sections of the body also takes into consideration the area rule for easier transonic-range travel.

Question:

How do you plan to stop this 'pocket' rocket?

Answer:

After the propellant is expended, the vehicle uses two parachutes to slow down. The first chute will create about 3000 pounds of drag at about 700 mph; coupled with the 1000-plus pounds of drag already acting on the vehicle this should decelerate the vehicle at about six-plus Gs negative.

At 375 mph the second chute will be deployed. It will generate about 7000 pounds of drag and ten-plus Gs of deceleration. The high-speed chute is on a forty-five foot tow line, and the low-speed chute is on a thirty foot line, so they will pull together. On average, Sonic Wind should slow about 150 mph per second while deployment is underway.

At 100 miles an hour a rake-shaped brake will be rammed into the ice, under the vehicle and behind the center of gravity, braking and stabilizing. This brake will be similar to a bobsled's activated by compressed air on board – either air or helium bled from the pressure tank.

Sonic Wind stands apart from past land speed contenders as it has a higher power-to-weight ratio, lower drag coefficient and better aspect ratio. In short it is a micro-high-impulse rocket-ice-sled. A rocket-powered sports car scaled to the size and weight of the pilot.

This vehicle is a streamliner designed to gracefully and efficiently slip through the air, as opposed to vehicles which are aesthetically styled which bulldog their way to their destination.

Sonic Wind has been a major part of my life since I was eighteen. It's been more than four years in the building and cost me some $60,000.

Now I can't wait to start my great adventure. I built it as a vehicle that will last a lifetime. Not one shot baby and bye-bye, off to some museum or scrap heap.

SONIC WIND

Length	23 feet extendible to 30
Width	21 inches body diameter
Height	29 inches
Rear track	46 inches
Runner base	159.5 inches to left runner 183.5 inches to right runner
Weight	780 pounds loaded – fuel/driver 380 pounds empty

Ground clearance	5 inches front, 12 inches rear
Aspect ratio	11.5 convertible to 15.5
Drag coefficient	.15–.17 estimated
Airframe structure	Aluminum/fiberglass monocoque coupled with a space frame rear load structure
Propulsion	1–RL 11 thrust chamber rating; 2000+ pounds of thrust
Propellants	Aqueous Alcohol/LOX Pressure fed by helium
Duration	22+ seconds
Specific impulse	202 pounds per second
Vehicle performance	Mach I+
Suspension	One-quarter inch thick mild steel runners. Front runner has rubber dampening. Rear runners are bolted to fins of cast 7075 aluminum wrapped with sheet 6061 aluminum riveted to form monocoque structure
Braking	700 mph 29 dia. ring slot chute 3000 pounds drag 375 mph 7 dia. ring slot chute 7000 pounds drag 100 mph pneumatic ice ram

Sonic Wind is accomplished mostly with government surplus aerospace hardware. These components were modified for use in a rocket sled instead of an airplane or spacecraft.

Here's an interesting look at this 'Frankenstein' creation:

COMPONENTS	AIR/SPACECRAFT
LR–11 rocket engine	X–1 rocket plane
Safety equipment	F–4 Phantom
Fuselage and finnage	F–104 Starfighter
Fuel valve	Titan rocket
Fuel tanks	Lockheed satellites
Drag chutes	Subroc rocket torpedo
Drag chutes	Air Force target drones
Switches	Atlas rocket
Brackets	Edwards Air Force Base test track
Bolts	X–15 rocket plane

Chapter Twenty-Nine
The Final Chapter

I've probably known Franklin Ratliff for about eight years. I wouldn't call him a student of land speed racing. More like 'The Professor'. He's a walking encyclopedia, not only as far as the history is concerned, but from a technical standpoint as well. He knows as much about my cars as I do.

But I didn't get to meet him until October 1990 at Bonneville. I had all sorts of problems, not just car problems, but physical problems as well. When I got home, I called Franklin and we talked for quite a while.

He suggested I build a centrifuge to lick the problem of 'red-out'. A few days later, Franklin called me back with the complete details of how to build a centrifuge, which I put up in my backyard. Where he got the information I don't know. All I know is that it worked.

Art Arfons

(AUTHOR'S NOTE: Franklin Ratliff is a technical writer, based in Florida, with a passion for racing. He is presently building a unique car which he will run at Bonneville. The car incorporates a sandwich composite chassis into a piston-engine vehicle driven through a propeller.

He has met or corresponded with many of high-speed racing's most famous names, including Art Arfons, Craig Breedlove, Richard Noble, Walt Arfons, Walt's son, Craig, who was killed in a 1989 world water speed attempt.

It was the construction and subsequent crash of Arfons' Rain-X Record Challenger jet hydroplane that influenced Ratliff to incorporate sandwich composite construction into his Bonneville machine.

Vehicles that Ratliff has personally seen in action include Art Arfons' Green Monster No. 27, Bill Fredrick's [then Fred Sibley's] Valkyrie J-46 jet car, the 300 mile an hour Pollution Packer rocket dragster, Jack McClure's 200 mph rocket go-kart, Craig Arfons' 300 mph J-85 jet dragster, Al Teague's 409 mph B/Fuel Streamliner, Bob Motz's 200 mph J-79 jet truck.)

By Franklin Ratliff

Art Arfons drove a Land Speed Record car at Bonneville on the last day of the 1960 Bonneville Nationals. He made three shakedown runs with a piston-engine streamliner, powered by an Allison aircraft engine. His highest speed was 200 mph.

Arfons returned to Bonneville with his car and crew 9:30 Sunday morning, September 4, 1960. They spent the rest of Sunday getting the car ready to run.

Arfons first fired the car's engine at 7:40 Monday morning. He started his first run for the day at 12:35 p.m., recording a speed of 249. He started another run that afternoon, recording a speed of 235. After experiencing problems with driveshaft bearing and the clutch, he left for home on Wednesday. Arfons would not return with this car until 1961.

The car's welded space frame was fabricated from rectangular steel tubing. The aluminum body panels that gave the car its shape were designed and formed by Lujie Lasovsky, a race car designer and builder based in Los Angeles. A compartment in the tail held a braking parachute.

In the opinion of Robert 'Jocko' Johnson (a pioneer in areas such as downforce-producing streamlined bodies, engine porting, etc.) the body that Lasovsky built for Arfons was a much more sound design than the simple body Athol Graham built for his 344 mph Allison-powered streamliner.

Jocko believes that with further development to its engine and drive-training, Arfons' car had the potential to run 430.

Arfons' car rolled on four 7.00 x 18 Firestone Bonneville tires and Halibrand magnesium wheels. Buick aluminum-drum brakes on each wheel supplemented the braking parachute. All four wheels were driven by a 1,720 cubic inch Allison V–12 with a huge exhaust-driven turbo-supercharger (the same basic engine used in the P–38 Lightning fighter).

Behind the engine was a unit built by Arfons consisting of a fabricated steel case that enclosed a multiple-disc clutch (running in oil) and a two-speed transmission. The car was geared so that it could run speeds as high as 315 mph in low gear. At 4000 r.p.m. the car speed would be 400. On the right side of the clutch/transmission housing was a power take-off unit.

A shaft extended from this unit to a differential in the rear axle assembly. A short stub axle drove the right wheel, and a long axle drove the left wheel. A long shaft extended from the power take-off unit forward to a differential in the front axle assembly. This shaft rotated at speed over 10,000 r.p.m. and ran in two plain bearings mounted on the frame members.

The car had a suspension system that allowed the front and rear axles to move in relation to the frame. Flat steel radius rods held the axles in the correct relationship to the frame.

Arfons had trouble with the car's clutch from his very first run at the Bonneville Nationals. Although it was the same clutch he used in his Allison-powered dragsters, it was not up to driving the Bonneville car.

The difference seemed to be that when drag racing, the rear tires broke loose so much that the clutch didn't have much to do. On the last run Arfons made in 1960, the clutch was completely run out. Another problem the car had was with one of the bearings on the driveshaft for the front axle assembly.

Lack of clearance and adequate lubrication caused the bearing to burn out. When Arfons returned to Bonneville in 1961, he did manage a speed of 313 (the top speed recorded at the 1961 Bonneville Nationals).

In 1962, the year Arfons first brought a jet car to Bonneville, there were only six operable pure jets in existence. These cars were Craig Breedlove's Spirit of America, Walt Arfons' Green Monster 16, Dr. Nathan Ostich's Flying Caduceus, Bill Fredrick's Valkyrie, Romeo Palimedes' Infinity and Art Arfons' Cyclops. All except Green Monster 16 were taken to Bonneville.

Cyclops was a simple car weighing about 5000 pounds, but could run the quarter-mile in 6.96 seconds at 210 mph. Large diameter chassis tubes cradled the engine and formed the cockpit. A fiberglass nose and air-intake ducts enclosed the otherwise open cockpit.

Wheels were Halibrand magnesium with 7.00 x 13 Firestone Bonneville tires. The front axle was a 148 Ford with a reinforcing plate for strength. Front and rear wheels were located by long radius rods with suspension provided by a pair of aircraft tail wheel air-oil shock struts.

Rear suspension was provided by a set of oleo struts from a BT–13 airplane. Brakes were '57 Buick with Grey-Rock ceramic lining plus a pair of twenty-four foot parachutes. The car was twenty-three feet long and forty-one inches high with a one hundred and fourteen inch wheelbase.

Front and rear treads were sixty-five and fifty-seven inches respectively. The Cyclops carried twenty gallons of fuel and five of water (as compared to forty-two of fuel and twenty of water in Breedlove's Spirit). This was sufficient fuel and water for quarter-mile sprints, but not really enough for a 400 mph record.

During the Southern California Timing Association's fourteenth Bonneville National Speed Trials (held August 19–25, 1962), Arfons made a qualifying run of 230.791.

Arfons followed this with a two-way average of 330.013 mph to establish a record for the then new jet class. Like Infinity, Cyclops was powered by an afterburner-equipped General Electric J–47. (Flying Caduceus and Spirit of America were powered by non-afterburning versions of the J–47.)

Although Cyclops did well for a car not built from the outset as a Land Speed Record car, it would have needed changes beyond just larger fuel tanks to set a record over 400 mph. The air ducts alongside the cockpit worked fine on drag strips, but at speeds above 300 were breaking loose and forcing in on him.

Compounding this problem was wind buffeting in the open cockpit. The windshield was not deflecting air up and over as it had done at lower speeds.

A unique feature on Cyclops that Arfons later incorporated into his 500 mph Green Monster was a self-adjusting wing mounted above the cockpit. The wing was arranged to pivot on the action of the struts connected to front radius rods, so that if the front end should lift, the wing would pivot to produce downforce (negative lift) on the front end.

For visual indication a short antenna-like rod at the front of the cockpit was also rigged to the front suspension. Should it begin to drop, Arfons knew his front wheels were lifting off the ground. Over twenty-five years later, Arfons incorporated a variation of his self-adjusting wing concept into his General Electric J-35 powered Green Monster 27.

Arfons sat out the 1963 season building a jet car that was at first intended for 500 mph, but would eventually approach 600. Key to the success of this fearsome new car was its General Electric J-79 engine, a then state-of-the-art engine that represented a ten year advancement beyond the technology of the J-47.

The key to Art Arfons' success would be the J-79 General Electric engine with four-stage afterburner. That classified military engine powered planes to a speed of 1400 miles per hour.

Arfons was appearing at a Denver dragstrip with his jet-powered Cyclops when his big break came in November 1982. A dealer in Florida contacted him and said a J-79 was available.

"I was looking specifically for a J-79," recalls Arfons. "Every junk yard I went to I said, 'If you ever get a 79, give me a call'. I left my card at each place.

"I had a J-47 in my Cyclops and was running it. I knew it wasn't enough. Breedlove had a 47 in his first Spirit of America and that car ultimately went 526.

"I knew I couldn't build something as streamlined as Craig did. I didn't have the money. So I had to have enough horsepower to not only build a car around that engine, but make it short enough to still get it in my bus."

Arfons had been around the block long enough to know that sometimes strange things happen, that classified hardware suddenly becomes available. That's what happened with the J-79 he was seeking.

"The guy from Florida called me. He dealt in scrap only and he got a military engine for scrap. Instead of scrapping it, he called me. As far as the military were concerned it was total junk."

Superficially similar to Romeo Palimedes' Infinity, the J-79 Green Monster had some important differences. Unlike Infinity, it had a vertical stabilizer and it incorporated a self-adjusting wing as Arfons had done with Cyclops.

To lessen the chance of the cockpit being crushed (as happened during the crash of Infinity which took the life of Glenn Leasher), Arfons placed the cockpit between the loft wheels. Arfons completed the new car in the summer of 1964.

In an interview published in the August 1960 issue of *Hot Rod* magazine, Arfons described it as a "...very sturdy, dependable car..." He said, "I went [to Bonneville] four times and set the record three times. The good thing about the car was that I didn't have to take any test runs after the initial two shakedown runs.

"The first time out I set the record in two runs [434.02 mph]. The second time I got the record in three attempts [536.71], and the third time I set the record in two runs [576.533]. The fourth time out with the LSR Green Monster [1966] I crashed.

"At 600 mph the wheels on my jet car were turning 7000 r.p.m., putting quite a strain on the wheel bearings. The bearings in the old LSR car [Arfons built a replacement in 1968] were lubricated with grease, and the right front bearing ran dry, welded itself to the spindle and took the whole wheel assembly right off the car.

"The right front corner dropped down and dug in and the car did a big end-over. It flew 527 feet before it hit the ground the first time."

The J–79 Green Monster rolled on Firestone 7.00 x 18 tires developed specifically for the new car and mounted on aluminum wheels also built by Firestone.

The Buick drum brakes used on the previous cars were replaced by disc brakes. The front suspension consisted of a '37 Lincoln I-beam axle with split wishbones sandwiched between two one and a half ton Dodge truck-ends and tied to the frame via a pair of adjustable over-oil aircraft shock struts.

Attached to the front axle was a hydraulic master cylinder, which when moved by the front axle actuated a hydraulic slave cylinder that changed the angle of self-adjusting wing.

Tie rods and ends, drag link and everything else in the steering was early Dodge truck, except for a steering box taken from a pre-war Packard. The rear suspension consisted of a two ton Ford truck axle mounted solidly to the frame but with a series of positioning holes that gave seven to eight inches vertical adjustment.

The ability to take the car from one and a half inches ground clearance at the front to eight inches ground clearance at the back was essential toward diffusing any air pressure that might build up under the car at high speed.

In the late eighties, Arfons became intrigued with the concept of a small, ultra-light vehicle for the LSR – the opposite extreme from the J–79 car.

By this time the first generation of jet dragsters had been made obsolete by the development of more compact, much lighter cars powered by a General Electric J–85. The J–85 weighs only about 400 pounds, making possible the construction of jet dragsters weighing only 1200 to 1400 pounds.

Use of the J–85 in drag racing was pioneered by Walt Arfons' son, Craig. On afterburner, the J–35–17 engine produces about 4500 pounds of thrust, almost as much as the rated thrust of the J–47 used in Craig Breedlove's 8000 pound Spirit of America.

In theory, a much smaller and lighter vehicle having the same thrust would run much faster than the 526 mph speed attained at Bonneville by Spirit of America. Further advantages of an ultra-light vehicle are increased case of construction (for one or two people) and reduced construction costs.

Arfons took things one step beyond radical by opting to build a J–85 motorcycle streamliner instead of a car. Motorcycle streamliners have a long history of sooner or later ending up on their side.

Proper design of the front suspension and steering is a particularly complex problem. A jet motorcycle streamliner is further complicated by the tendency of the engine to torque over when the throttle setting is changed (such as when the afterburner is fired).

At the time Arfons began construction of his vehicle, Green Monster 27, only one motorcycle streamliner (Don Vesco's) had run over 300 mph. Arfons believed that the decrease in drag from the reduced frontal area of a motorcycle streamliner might outweigh the problems with stability.

As construction on Green Monster 27 neared completion, it was suggested to this author, by designer/builder Arvil Porter, that the only real chance of working a J–85 motorcycle streamliner had, was to be 'flown' from the cockpit using controls connected to the aerodynamic surfaces that could induce a controlled lean into the vehicle.

Porter is a pioneer of hydrogen peroxide rocket vehicles in drag racing and constructed the first hydrogen peroxide rocket motorcycle.

Green Monster 27 was completed in June 1989. A Kevlar/epoxy body shell enclosed the vehicle's relatively conventional 4130 Chromemoly tubing space frame.

Steering was through an unusual system of push-pull levers (one on each side of the cockpit) connected to the front suspension by steel cables. A pair of canard wings were fitted into the tip of the nose and linked to the front suspension.

If the front end of the vehicle began lifting, the rising front suspension increased the angle on the canard wings to push the nose down. Instead of a center hub system usually used in motorcycle streamliners, the front suspension was a four-link system based on drawings sent to Arfons by Craig Breedlove.

Green Monster 27 was driven as a motorcycle for only one day. Arfons ran on Sunday, July 24, 1989 – fifteen days after his nephew Craig was killed while challenging the water speed record with a J–35 jet hydroplane.

Concerned that the canard wings might lift the back end of the vehicle by putting too much downforce on the nose, Arfons drove it without the canard wings installed.

Still adjusting to driving a motorcycle instead of a car, Arfons kept the skids extended on each of his three trial runs. On his third run, after accelerating for about a mile or so on the basic engine, Arfons hit the afterburner.

When the engine torqued over the right side skid dug in enough to yaw the vehicle off to the right. The sideways airflow over the air intake scoop abruptly generated over 1000 pounds of lift– enough to pull the vehicle's front end straight up.

Arfons later estimated he was traveling 350 to 400 mph when this happened. While still in mid-air the vehicle rotated at least once, 360 degrees around its longitudinal axis.

The vehicle, including its Kevlar/epoxy body, survived the crash with no serious damage. As Arfons discovered the next year, even if the motorcycle version had not had serious stability problems, he still would have had trouble because the afterburner had a combustion instability that made it screech like a banshee.

Arfons did not return until late October 1990. Green Monster 27 was now technically a four-wheel car. Arfons had taken his two forged wheels and installed them on the front axle.

After consulting with Alcoa engineers, who told him he would not need a second pair of forged wheels as long as he kept their diameter small enough, Arfons machined from billets a pair of wheels for the rear only seventeen inches in diameter. (The new rear wheels were very similar to the front wheels Bruce Crower ran that year on a little 1150 horsepower Chevy-powered streamliner Crower built to go 440 mph.)

The rear wheels were mounted outboard on a rigidly mounted axle braced by diagonal struts. Mindful of his 1966 crash, the rear wheel bearings were lubricated by a total loss oil system that cut in at speeds above 350.

To avoid a repeat of his 1989 crash, Arfons cut away the curved top portion of the air intake scoop and kept the canard wings installed at all times. He also enlarged the vertical stabilizer. Unaware of the combustion instability, Arfons had not removed the wheel well from the tail pipe.

Required by track officials to keep his first trial run below 200 mph, Arfons discovered a severe shimmy while averaging 175 through the mile. He parked the car for the day while he and his crew considered their options overnight.

The next day they raised the air pressure in the front suspension struts by a couple of hundred pounds. On the next trial run Arfons averaged 338 through the mile, briefly firing the afterburner as he approached the mile.

The car handled well, requiring minimal steering input from Arfons to stay on course. It was on his next trial run that Arfons discovered the combustion instability.

While approaching the mile, Arfons hit the afterburner, stayed in it, got out of it when he felt the screech, then went in and out of burner hoping the screech would go away. It wouldn't. Arfons averaged only about 305 mph through the mile. He parked the car to consider his options for 1991.

An option proposed by Arfons' son, Tim, was to eliminate the afterburner altogether and replace it with water injection as the method for augmenting thrust.

However, the small size of Green Monster 27 did not make this an easy option to implement. Later, after consulting with veteran J–85 jet racer Wayne Knuth, Arfons rebuilt the tail pipe and afterburner into a configuration similar to what Knuth used on his jet dragsters.

When Arfons returned one more time in 1991 it was to once again run at the Bonneville Nationals. Reliable power was not a problem. Unfortunately, Arfons discovered that if he launched on the basic engine, then hit the afterburner at speed the car would veer off to the right and not come back.

If he launched on afterburner, then got out of burner, the car would veer off to the left and not come back. The culprit turned out to be the rear suspension.

Not sure that the combustion screech was the only source of vibration, Arfons had also installed elastometric shock mounts to give the rear axle a little movement. When they got the car back to the shop they discovered the shock mounts were compressing a lot more than they had anticipated.

This additional compression allowed the vehicle to lean like a motorcycle. Which way it leaned depended on which way the engine torqued over, which in turn depended on whether the engine was going into or coming out of afterburner.

Arfons briefly considered again rigidly mounting the rear axle and adding an additional ten feet on to the front of the car. Although both moves were probably steps in the right direction, there still lay before him the potential problems in the 350 mph required beyond the speeds Green Monster 27 had already run.

He reluctantly concluded that with the limited amount of time and money he had to work with, the odds were weighted too heavily against him.

It is worth noting that Sir Malcolm Campbell was sixty-two, about the same age as Arfons when Green Monster 27 first saw action, he too pursued a project (the first turbo-jet hydroplane) that, although unsuccessful, was ultimately met with great success by those who followed.

Epilogue
Duel in the Desert

It was billed as 'duel in the desert'. Two jet cars sharing the vast prehistoric expanse known as Black Rock Desert in Nevada.

Shades of 1964–65 when two American hot rodders, Craig Breedlove of California and Ohioan Art Arfons, took turns shattering the record at Bonneville Salt Flats in Utah. When they began their blistering duel, the land speed record stood at 407 mph. When they finished, Breedlove reigned supreme at 600.601 mph.

He was the first to average 400, 500 and 600 miles an hour. And despite the twilight of his years (Craig Breedlove enjoyed his sixtieth birthday on March 23, 1997), one more notch belonged on his six-gun, so to speak. Breedlove not only wanted to become the first man in history to average 700 miles an hour, but the first to officially exceed the speed of sound on land. This time he would take dead aim with a 48,000 horsepower Spirit of America – Sonic Arrow.

While the same Art Arfons still wanted 'one more hurrah', his Green Monster No. 27 had serious speed limitations. If all systems were go, it could 'only' hit 650 miles an hour. Maybe good enough for his fourth land speed record, but miles short of supersonic capability. But Arfons, now seventy-one, could only watch helplessly.

Breedlove would be challenged by Thrust SSC, the baddest contender of all time. Fifty-four feet in length... seven tons in weight... packing a potential 106,000 horsepower punch.

In 1983, Richard Noble of England fulfilled his nine-year 'impossible' dream by driving his own Thrust 2 to a new land speed record of 633.4 mph at the same Black Rock Desert. But now in his early fifties, Noble realized he couldn't put the total package together *and* drive the car himself, so he turned over the wheel to British RAF pilot, Andy Green.

The pre-1997 hype clearly favored Craig Breedlove.

A year earlier, at opposite ends of the globe, the two jet cars made their debuts. Noble's beast limped its way to a 'top' speed of 330 across a Jordanian desert. Breedlove's bullet generated unbelievable speed, reaching 677 mph on its seventh run. Unfortunately, it was a ninety degree giant loop.

Despite the runaway ride, Spirit of America – Sonic Arrow seemed a shoo-in when the two cars would share the Black Rock playa, starting in September of 1997.

In pre-Black Rock speed runs, Thrust SSC clocked a very hopeful 540 in Jordan. The team was definitely heading in the right direction.

Despite money problems, both Noble and Breedlove kept their date with history.

Breedlove oozed assurance. "I'm confident we'll get the record. I'm very confident about that. I have a six-run scheduled to get up to record speed. Ideally, it would be six days. That would be the ideal scenario.

"We'll bring it [up to speed] by increments. After the 675 run [October 1996], it has to buoy your confidence. Now we have to keep the damn thing down [on the ground] and run when it's still."

Once Breedlove hit 700, he would study the data, send the car through the sound barrier by remote control, then drive the car.

Noble had no such plan. "We're going to be here until the desert floods, the car can't go any faster, or we break it" [Mach 1].

On September 6, Breedlove made a run of 227. "It was very, very good, very solid. It's all working well. That's encouraging. That's a big hurdle to get over to get the first run in."

The following day, Andy Green took a leisurely 148 mph stroll across Black Rock.

"It's very easy to criticize this car," said Noble. It's a huge car. It has two engines. What has happened is we had the courage to make a big quantum leap. The question is whether we are right. History will say."

On September 8, Spirit of America became a battle casualty when it ingested a foreign object which badly damaged its J-79 engine during a 328 mph sortie. The car had to return to California for a new power plant, repairs which would take about a week.

"The plan was to make a 300, 400 and 500 run," said a disappointed Breedlove. "It either occurred on the run or shutdown. We may find out when we tear it down. It could have been a cartridge or rock. We walked that course [fifteen miles], picking things up by hand. That's why we do it."

Thrust SSC was now front and center.

The spotlight would become brighter and brighter with each run.

* September 10: Green recorded runs of 428 and 517 mph.

Noble raved, "We have a car that's very, very stable, very fast. We have a reliable car and a lot more performance. Andy finds the car is easier to drive, more predictable on this desert than it was in Jordan.

* September 12: Green reached 624, following an earlier run of 550.

"We're all very pleased," said Andy Green. "The first one we took it nice and gentle. The second run taken in and out of [after]burner at 580 and 610. We proved the point: we can do almost any [run] profile and the car will behave itself."

* September 16: Buoyed by the influx of much-needed capital, Breedlove made test runs of 259 and 343, his first since engine damage.

"It seems to be working well. I think the car is running better than last year. It's not any different than going to Indy in the number one car, crashing it, taking the number two car and hoping you don't crash it. The car last year got to up to 675 with minimum afterburner. The potential is there."

Thrust SSC remained idle.

* September 20: After gusting winds prevented any runs for several days, Thrust SSC clocked 553.39 mph when the car's computer system shut off the engine.

"When you build the world's most complex car," explained Green, "you expect things like this. The good news is the abort system acted exactly as we expected."

Breedlove made a short burst of 313 to test the car's downforce. He went 381 the previous day.

* September 22: Laid-back could best describe Andy Green. Nothing seems to get him excited, not even a blistering ride of 687.941 mph.

"It was a gentle, country ride. There's a lot left. That car's still not trying. It's cruising."

"It was an impressive run," conceded Breedlove. "Their car seems quite stable and seems to work very well."

Richard Noble told reporters, "You saw a bit of history. This was the fastest officially timed run of all time. We're deep in the transonic range now. In these projects there's always something lurking. There are a lot of gremlins still lurking around."

* September 23: A land speed record must be set by making two runs in opposite directions within a sixty minute time span. Thus back-to-back bursts of 693.507 and 719.137 mph went into the *unofficial* category. Dual chutes on the seven ton car failed to deploy after the first run. Green overshot the end of the thirteen mile course by some 1.4 miles. By the time the team repacked the chutes and turned the car around, the clock had ticked past the sixty minute deadline. Noble and Green were philosophical.

"I think it gives you an idea of the enormous potential of this car," said Noble. "We think there's a good thirty, forty percent of power left. What you have seen today is very, very remarkable. Nobody has done this before." (Cracking the 700 mph barrier, that is.)

Green said, "It's a thrill for the whole team. We've designed, operated the safest car. Now, we have the fastest. We didn't get the record. We're aiming to make it the fastest car, to reach Mach 1." He referred to the chute failure as "...no big deal. The brakes are still operating."

* September 25: Morning rain delayed any runs for almost three hours. But it would be a glorious day for Richard Noble... for Andy Green... for Great Britain. Thrust SSC blasted across the Black Rock Desert at an official 700.661, then backed it up with an even quicker 728.008. Average speed: 714.114 mph.

Thus, the second longest reign in land speed history ended at thirteen years and eleven months. Noble expressed no sadness at having his record broken by his protégé. It was a necessary step towards going supersonic.

"I've been working six years to get rid of it" [the record], said Noble. "We have a long way to go yet, but this was an important first step, a fantastic first step.

"We have to go to Mach 1, of course. I hope we can do it while we're here this autumn. I hope the weather, the money will let us do it."

Green said of the run, "We came here to go supersonic. So we're only about two-thirds of the way there. I can actually start feeling the shock waves on the car. I'm getting more used to the feel. It [the car] is very fast, very smooth. The car is very stable.

"I'm not nervous. I drive Thrust at about 1 G. A Tornado [the fighter plane he flies] can reach 8 G and even a fairground ride can reach something like 4 G.

"The thing that really hits you going at these sorts of speeds is the sound. When you reach 630, you start to get the shock waves. I experience two – one above my head and one underneath me – which are very loud. That's actually the thing you notice most of all."

Breedlove was gracious in defeat. "It was a good run. I can only congratulate Andy. He deserves the credit, the limelight right now. In my life I've been in the right place three times. It's a wonderful milestone [to reach 700]."

Would Craig Breedlove pack it in?

"It's a tougher record to get now than it was an hour or two ago. I think we have the best team in America to do it. It's now a higher mountain to climb."

* September 27: Mechanical problems continued to plague Craig Breedlove. A slight vibration in the front end of the car limited him to a 330 run. Just twenty-four hours earlier, Breedlove had clocked a respectable 531.

Thrust SSC was idle, with no runs scheduled.

"I don't know how long it'll take to reach Mach 1," said Green. "Hopefully, we can do it in the next couple of weeks."

* September 30: Wind gusts of thirty-five miles an hour delayed any speed runs for both teams.

"We have to push on with the speed now," said Noble. "We have to build the Mach number. That's the crucial thing."

Originally, Breedlove's jet car was a five-wheeler, but after the front-end vibrations, the center front wheel was removed, making it a four-wheeler. Team operations manager, Bill Breedlove (a distant cousin), said, "Without the center wheel, it makes for easier access to clean the other two wheels. We believe it should be fine now."

The reason for the change was to keep dirt from forming around the front wheels. The accumulation of dirt had caused the vibration.

* October 1: Time seemed to be running out for Richard Noble.

"I figure eight days [of money are left]. If I'm clever with it... if we don't get any unbudgeted expenses maybe we can stay eight, nine, ten days. We're on restricted time, restricted money."

Shell Oil, Breedlove's prime sponsor, gave Breedlove reassurance. "If I continue to operate on a cost-effective basis they'll continue to fund the team. I may be here until November. We're not going to give up. We're going to push on. We just have to make some progress."

* October 6: Thrust SSC reached Mach 0.95, averaging 721 mph on two runs, but not within the required sixty minute time frame. A photograph taken by air showed the dust raised by the shock waves, spreading out 150 feet either side of the twelve foot wide car.

* October 7: Andy Green inched the British jet closer to Mach 1 with a single run estimated at 750 (Mach 0.98). Videotape of the run reportedly showed shock waves over the top of the car. It was the sixtieth total run. That included earlier test runs on a British airfield and on the Jordanian desert in 1996–97.

* October 13: British pride translated into more funding for Noble and his team. And almost fifty years to the day that man achieved supersonic flight – October 14, 1947, with U.S. Air Force Captain Chuck Yeager in the rocket-powered Bell X-1 – Thrust SSC not only broke the sound barrier, but did so twice. Noble called it "so near, and yet so far" as the turn-around time for the crucial second run was a mere fifty seconds too late for an official land speed record.

Green actually made three runs, the first at 749.647, or Mach 0.997. His thunderous 764.168 sortie (Mach 1.007) and 760.125 run (Mach 1.003) were just a Monday stroll for Andy Green. "It was very smooth. It's more like driving a fighter plane." Green said he could see the shock waves forming over the car. "It was quite amazing. It looked like a heat haze running over the top of the car in a very smooth line."

Richard Noble was both elated – at the first official supersonic performance – and disappointed, because the team missed the land speed record "by just fifty lousy seconds".

He knew that would come in just a matter of days. In the meantime, he would savor the taste of Mach 1. "It's a great, great moment. We've achieved the first supersonic run in history. It's an enormous technical achievement. It's a team achievement most of all and one that all of us can be enormously proud of."

When Green set a new speed record of 714.1 mph, congratulations came from Queen Elizabeth II. Prime Minister Tony Blair added his congratulations to Richard Noble, praising the team for its "sensational achievement".

* October 15: At 9:09.21 a.m. (Nevada time), Andy Green began his journey into the record books. Using a 6.5 mile distance to enter the measured mile, Green pushed Thrust SSC to a run that shattered windows miles away. Two cracks of thunder. The power and force of a sonic boom.

First run: 759.33 mph. The speed of sound, which varies according to weather and altitude, was calculated at 748.11 miles an hour. The run translated at Mach 1.05. The work, however, was half done.

"You've just seen a supersonic run," said Noble, "but we've got to be back within the hour. This is where the tension starts."

Only once in six weeks at Black Rock had the British team been able to beat the sixty minute turn-around deadline.

With six minutes to spare, Thrust SSC rumbled across the desert and through the measured mile at 766.609 mph, hitting a peak speed of 771.402. Average speed for the two runs: 763.035 mph. Or Mach 1.20.

Richard Noble hugged his wife, Sally. The team lifted both Noble and Andy Green onto their shoulders. Green looked at Noble.

"Well done, Richard. Can I stop now?"

Richard Noble replied: "Hooray, we bloody did it." Then he added, "It's been a magic morning. We've just achieved what we set out to do all those years ago.

"Undoubtedly, this is the greatest day of my life. It's a hell of an achievement. I feel like going to sleep."

Tony Blair telephoned Noble and told him, "I am totally in awe of your achievement."

Green admitted he was a little jittery between runs. "I got tense at the other end while waiting to re-arm parachutes, but I took a deep breath and just relaxed."

Believe it or not, the speeds were slower than expected. Thrust designer, Ron Ayers, expected the car to reach 800 miles an hour.

The car's rate of acceleration dipped sharply as Thrust SSC approached Mach 1.0. Ayers said it seemed as if the car faced a second barrier after going supersonic. "It's like it is running into a brick wall."

Craig Breedlove watched the two runs from a hilltop. "It was a beautiful run. You could see the shock waves."

It was far from a concession speech... On the contrary.

Quietly, and without fanfare, Breedlove had finally cracked into the 600 mile an hour speed zone. And with the annual snows holding off into November, his relentless pursuit for a sixth land speed record continued.

And with his amazing success rate, his tenacity and a fresh injection of cold, hard cash, Breedlove was assured a return to Black Rock in 1998.

He could well become the first driver to shatter the 800 mile an hour barrier.

But then again, who remembers the second man to break the four minute mile? Who was the second man to walk on the moon?

As Thrust SSC operations manager, Adam Northcote-Wight so aptly put it: "You can make a record any day, but you can only make history once."

(This epilogue was added to the second edition of *Man Against the Salt*, 1997.)